Racing & Foot

CW00743147

JUMPS RACING

GUIDE 2011-2012

Statistics • Results
Previews • Training centre reports

Raceform

Contributors: Neil Clark, Nick Deacon, Steffan Edwards, Cathal Gahan, Sarah Hall, Dylan Hill, Mark Howard, Tony Jakobson, Kel Mansfield, Steve Mellish, Mark Nelson, Dave Nevison, Ben Osborne, Nick Watts, Richard Williams

Feedback!

If you have any comments or criticism about this book, or suggestions for future editions, please tell us.

Write: Nick Watts, 2011-12 Jumps Annual,
Racing & Football Outlook,
Floor 23, 1 Canada Square,
London E14 5AP.

email rfo@rfoutlook.co.uk or **Fax** 0207 510 6457

Designed and edited by Nick Watts and Dylan Hill

Published in 2011 by Outlook Press
Raceform Limited, Compton, Newbury, Berkshire RG20 6NL

A catalogue record for this book is available from the British Library.

ISBN 978-1-906820-74-9

Printed and bound by CPI Group (UK) Ltd, Croydon, CR0 4YY

racing & football outlook

Contents

Introduction		4
Trainer profiles	Lawney Hill	6
	James Ewart	14
	Graham McPherson	21
British 15 to follow		28
Irish 15 to follow		32

2011-2012 Preview

Ante-post tips	36
Jerry M (Ireland)	50
Downsman (Berkshire)	53
Hastings (West Country)	57
Borderer (North)	61
Southerner (South)	65
John Bull (Midlands)	69
Aborigine (Newmarket)	73
Hunter chasers	76
Dave Nevison	78
Morning Mole	80
Time Test	84

2010-2011 Review

News diary	89
Big-race review	101
Novice review	116
Big-race and novice index	126

Statistics, Races and Racecourses

Trainer statistics	129
Trainer and jockey tables	150
Fixture list	155
Big-race dates	157
Big-race records	158
Track-by-track guide	177
Record and standard times	222

Final furlong

Top point recruits with Cathal Gahan	232
Competition	235
Horse index	238

Outlook

Editor's introduction

THE start of the new jumps season arrives at a difficult time for racing and the winter game in particular. There's been so much arguing about the fixture list for 2012, caused by dwindling horse numbers and prize-money, that we were not even able to carry the calendar for next year – its release was finally due in November though given the number of warring factions it would be no surprise if New Year's Eve came around before trainers knew their options for the following day.

Jumps racing has also faced some very harsh public scrutiny following the deaths of Ornais and Dooneys Gate in the Grand National, and there has to be a fear that much more bad press could see the sport have to seriously consider its future.

The reason for both crises essentially boils down to the same thing – the sharp decline of public interest in racing.

And that makes it hard to understand for those of us who love the sport because last season once again proved absolutely thrilling in what has been a golden era for jumps racing.

The sight of Denman and Kauto Star going head to head at the front of the Gold Cup three fences from home was an astonishing spectacle, even if neither was ultimately able to hold off the young challenger Long Run.

THREE KINGS: (from left) Long Run, Denman and Kauto Star in the Gold Cup

BIG BUCK'S: another astonishing talent in the jumping ranks

That victory had the look of a changing of the guard with Long Run seemingly set to dominate for years to come, but maybe that impression comes as a result of how much the likes of Kauto Star and Denman have spoilt us.

Until Best Mate came along no horse had won more than one Gold Cup for 30 years, so in reality it would be no surprise to see the likes of Captain Chris, Diamond Harry, Jessie's Dream or Quito De La Roque firmly in the mix come Cheltenham in March.

The hurdling front sees one established superstar in Big Buck's and a thrilling new champion in Hurricane Fly hoping to become a festival hero yet again.

With many more stars doubtless ready to emerge over the coming months, it's clear that those who stick with the jumping game are going to be in for a treat once again.

As ever there are young talents coming through in the training ranks as well and we have been fortunate enough to speak to two of the best this autumn in Lawney Hill and James Ewart, as well as the fascinating tale of lawyer-cum-trainer Graeme McPherson, while our regional experts have been do-ing the rounds finding out all that has been happening at the yards in their area.

Leading judges Richard Williams and Nick Watts have digested all the gossip to come up with their 15 top prospects for the campaign from either side of the Irish Sea, while you will also get the views of our ante-post expert Steffan Edwards, *RFO* columnists Steve Mellish and Dave Nevison and time guru Mark Nelson.

Dylan Hill assesses the form of the top races of last season, and you will notice a new feature at the back of the book as Cathal Gahan runs the rule over the new recruits from point-to-point likely to make waves under rules.

Then there's the usual reams and reams of statistics to stay armed with throughout the campaign, broken down into the top-ten trainers and course by course, with ten-year trends for all the top races and all the latest record and standard times thrown into the mix as well.

Make sure you keep up to date with the latest news and views in the *RFO* every week and with this annual you should have all the ingredients for a profitable season.

Profiles for punters
Lawney Hill

LAWNEY HILL: now a recognised presence in the National Hunt arena

Profile by Sarah Hall

DEEP in the picturesque Oxfordshire countryside lies Woodway Farm, the home of trainer Lawney Hill. Before embarking on her training career, Hill rode 47 winners as an amateur jockey, including five under rules. I wondered whether her race riding background has benefited her in the training sphere?

"I think it is a huge advantage," she says. "When I discuss with jockeys about the running and riding of a race, they know that I have had previous experience, although only a small amount, but they give you respect for that."

Hill has held a training licence since 2005 and in those six years the figures speak for themselves with winners increasing year on year – six, then 18, followed by 26.

At the time of going to print, Hill has sent out 14 winners so she is well on the way to maintaining her progressive record.

Looking to the impending season, Hill comments that: "We try not to make targets, as you tend to get disappointed if you don't reach them, and because our number of winners has increased each season then there is a lot more pressure. It also becomes difficult in November time when we have to compete with the top yards."

In the 2010-2011 season Hill trained four doubles, quite a feat, and one that thrust her training skills into the limelight.

"It was wonderful, as people really take notice of you, the yard makes the headlines and we have been fortunate enough to do it a few times now and it makes a big difference."

Another training exploit that has put Hill on the map is her knack with new recruits. On numerous occasions the shrewd trainer has produced winners who have failed to score for previous trainers and most notably first time out.

So what happens at Woodway Stables to transform the runners?

"I think what we try and do is rejuvenate them. It is very different here to a lot of places," she explains. "Instead of going straight up and down the gallops, we ride them around the grass gallops and across the fields. We will do a lot of slow cantering rather than galloping flat out. I think that it helps a great deal."

There also seems to be a great deal of emphasis on schooling, a tactic that has worked wonders with horses that need to rebuild their confidence. Hill states that she will school her horses around two times a week and enlists the talent of jockeys to pop them over a variety of jumps too.

Which jockeys can Hill rely on this season? "We like to get the top boys when we can," she says. "Like AP McCoy, and David Bass and Harry Skelton are great lads. They listen to you, are really keen, and will certainly go far." Skelton and Bass do well for

AIDAN COLEMAN: gets plenty of rides for the Hill team where possible

Hill, with both jockeys returning a healthy profit from their rides in the last five seasons.

It is also proves lucrative to keep an eye out when McCoy is in the saddle as in the last five seasons the champion jockey holds a remarkable 50 per cent strike rate for the Oxfordshire handler.

"We also use Aidan Coleman a great deal too," she adds. "Although he is more difficult to book in the winter time as he rides for Venetia Williams who has a large string of horses."

When Coleman is booked for rides he is also one to note as he holds a 37 per cent strike-rate, with an impressive £44.12 profit to £1 level-stakes.

With the yard on an upward curve it comes as no great surprise that jockeys want to ride her horses. "We get a lot of jockey's calling us up now to ride out over the summer which is great."

Not only does Woodway Farm have the facilities to invigorate the horses, Hill's strategic placing of her horses has paid dividends with 13 racecourses returning a healthy profit last year. Be sure to keep an eye out for her runners at Worcester as, last year the yard had a 20 per cent strike-rate and an incredible £90.50 profit to £1 level-stakes.

FONT: gave Lawney Hill a trip out to Royal Ascot last summer

It is also worth taking note when the Oxfordshire handler takes her string on the long journey to Sedgefield as in 2010 the stable were 3-3 at the track and returned a £6.64 to £1 level-stakes.

With success achieved at so many courses I wonder whether it is hard for Hill to pick a track where she would relish a winner the most?

"I would obviously love a winner at the Cheltenham Festival, as there is such a buzz there and it is the mecca of National Hunt racing," she says. Although Hill has yet to saddle a winner at the March meeting, the yard has tasted some success at Prestbury courtesy of Mid Div And Creep, a pointer trained by her husband Alan. The bay mare finished second at odds of 100-1 in the Foxhunters behind Zemsky.

"It was amazing," she recalls. "And the funniest thing was that a racecourse representative approached us after the race and invited us all for a drink and just as we got to hospitality she turned around and said, I am so sorry but I thought you were with the winning horse as you made so much noise!"

Mid Div And Creep followed up her great run in the Foxhunters with a win in a hunter chase at Cheltenham in May. "It was incredible, as she won by 34 lengths," Hill recounts.

The 11-year-old remains a horse to follow this term as Hill intends to run the relentless galloper under rules and run in some staying chases. Gina Andrews will probably retain the ride as she knows her well.

Font, who was previously in training with Paul Nicholls, is yet another example of Hill's unique way with new recruits.

The son of Sadler's Wells won on his debut for the yard in a hurdle race at Fontwell and also ran in the Queen Alexandra Stakes at Royal Ascot.

He'd not run on the Flat since October 2007 and faced a stiff task, but put up a creditable display to finish sixth. Hill describes him as "a horse who has taken us to places we had only dreamed of."

With Hill adamant that her current run of success won't just be a flash in the pan, she is a trainer to keep on-side, not just for this season but many more to follow. With that in mind, I ask what race would she most like to win?

"I would love to win the Gold Cup, as it is a hugely recognised race in the racing world and would really show that you are up there with the best," she says. "But the non-racing public would remember a winner of Grand National, so either of those will do!"

With her sights set firmly on her goals, the view at the top of the hill certainly looks bright.

The horses

Aghill 7-y-o gelding
Denel – Hannah's Pet (Fidel)

He has been a cracking horse since he came to us from the Rose Dobbin yard. He stays well so we took him to Sedgefield for a long distance hurdle in June where he won very easily. He will be campaigned in similar events this season and will try chasing again in time as he jumps a fence really well. The Midlands National could be a possible target.

Amirico 6-y-o gelding
Lord America – Maori's Delight (Idiots Delight)

He was in training with Venetia Williams last term and I am hoping that he will be another one to benefit from a change of scenery – it may just perk him up a bit. He won a maiden hurdle over 2m4f on heavy ground last November and I think he is a horse who has a bright future and will definitely jump a fence in time.

Aurorian 5-y-o gelding
Fantastic Light – Aurelia (Rainbow Quest)

He was previously in training with Richard Hannon where he ran well in staying Flat handicaps. He looks like he needs decent ground and is one that I am looking forward to running over hurdles this season. He will be out in October.

Betavix 8-y-o gelding
Cloudings – Lay It Off (Strong Gale)

An ex-pointer who lost his way a bit but we knew that he had some ability. I think that the change in stable and routine has worked well for him as he won cosily on his first outing for us at Worcester in a 2m4f hurdle race. I was very pleased for his owner as his win cemented what he always thought of him. We will put him in 2m4f-3m races and I think we will have a lot of fun with him.

Chapolimoss 7-y-o gelding
Trempolino – Chamoss (Tip Moss)

He is a horse who had always threatened

AGHILL: won at Sedgefield during the summer and appreciates a good trip

to win and we were thrilled when he finally broke his duck at Worcester in August. He travelled and jumped well throughout and the winning margin was 9l. He schools fantastically at home, is very impressive and does everything very easily. He will be aimed at long distance chases this term on decent ground. A nice prospect.

Divine Folly 6-y-o gelding
Kotashaan – Jennys Grove (Strong Gale)

A lovely horse who was very green when he first came to us but has improved on each run. He won a bumper at Taunton in Janu-

ary and we were very pleased with him. David Bass has ridden him in all his races and he likes him a lot. We then decided to have a tilt at the Grade 2 Bumper at Newbury won by Ericht. We knew it was a slight step up in class, but he ran really well and finished fourth. He is one who needs a bit of cut in the ground.

Font 8-y-o gelding
Sadler's Wells – River Saint (Irish River)

He was previously in training with Paul Nicholls and is another one who relished a change of scenery as he won for us on his

FRONTIER DANCER: lost his confidence over fences but has lots of ability

first outing at Fontwell in May. He then ran at Royal Ascot where Richard Kingscote gave him a cracking ride and he finished sixth in the Queen Alexandra. We were thrilled with his performance.

Frontier Dancer 7-y-o gelding
New Frontier – All The Gear (Nashamaa)

He is owned by Jump For Fun and some of the syndicate are involved with Our Friends In The North – the owners of Imperial Commander. He has slightly lost his confidence though, so we will do lots of intensive schooling with him and maybe drop him in class to get him back to his best. I am looking forward to his arrival and think he could be a decent sort.

Genuine Pearl 9-y-o gelding
Desert King – Pearl Kite (Silver Hawk)

A dual Irish bumper winner who won a 3m hurdle race at Worcester in June, where he pulled clear of the field in good fashion. He will be campaigned in staying hurdles this season and he goes well on good to soft ground, he wouldn t want extremes. He is lightly raced for his age and I think he could do well.

Haarth Sovereign 7-y-o gelding
Alhaarth – Summer Queen (Robellino)

It has taken a long time to get him going. He won a hurdle race for us at Huntingdon, but consequently went up the weights and found life a bit hard after that. However, he got his head back in front at Towcester in April after which I gave him a break. He then came back at Newton Abbot in September and ran well to finish third behind Illysantachristina. I would like to win another hurdle and then go chasing with him, as he jumps a fence well and he would get 2m4f.

King Ozzy 7-y-o gelding
King Charlemagne – Kingpin Delight (Emarati)

His owner is very enthusiastic and he also sponsor the yard. He was previously in training with Martin Keighley and the gelding is another one who did well first time out for us by winning a hurdle race over 2m1f at

LADY IN RED: Lawney pictured at her yard near Watlington in Oxfordshire

Bangor. The trip, I think, was perhaps a little too short for him, so he was stepped up to 2m4f110yds at Southwell where he finished third behind Red Not Blue. He was 9lb higher that day though and the race wasn't quite run to suit him. Last time out he was third again behind Sweet World, but we were happy with him. We will have a lot of fun with him this winter running in both hurdle and chases as he is very adaptable.

Mid Div And Creep 11-y-o mare
Sovereign Water – Knightsbridge Red (Montelimar)

She has been a revelation. She is only tiny and the idea was to run her in ladies point-to-points where she won twice very convincingly. So, after that, we decided to go to Cheltenham for the Foxhunter's and we thought we were tilting at windmills so were thrilled when she finished second. She then went back to the evening meeting and won a hunter chase by 34l. She is now joining

MINELLA THEATRE (white cap): ran in some good races for Henrietta Knight

my yard and we will have a go at some long distance chases.

Minella Theatre 8-y-o gelding
King's Theatre – Ring Of Water
(Northern Baby)

He was previously with Henrietta Knight and slightly lost his way towards the end of last season but I am hoping that a change of scenery will spark a revival. He will head to Wincanton at the end of October for the Badger Ales Trophy.

My Matilda 8-y-o mare
Silver Patriarch – Upton Lass
(Crash Course)

A sweet little horse that has needed lots of schooling due to her nervous nature. She was brought down at Uttoxeter last year and consequently lost her confidence a bit. She was given a positive ride by Tom Scudamore at Fontwell in May 2010 to win by a length and a half. She is a game mare who stays well and is a chaser in the making.

Ravethebrave 7-y-o gelding
Rashar – Mrs Blobby (Rontino)

I bought him at Doncaster Sales out of Alan

King's yard. He is a horse who will need intensive schooling to get his confidence back and, eventually when it has returned, he is a horse who we could really have a lot of fun with. He has won a hurdle race and chase in the past and has run at some top racecourses including Cheltenham and Newbury. However, it may be a case of starting him off somewhere low key and take it from there.

Safe Investment 7-y-o gelding
Gone West – Fully Invested (Irish River)

He came to us from Ben Pollock's yard and since joining us he was won two races over hurdles. He was well handicapped and having struggled over fences last season the return to hurdles suited him. He has been a little star so far and I am hoping that can continue this season. He seems pretty versatile regarding ground although he wouldn't want it too fast. He will jump a fence in time.

Shammy Buskins 9-y-o gelding
Shambo – Quistaquay (El Conquistador)

He is quite a quirky character and had run in quite a few point-to-points before running under rules. He has won a hurdle and four handicap chases for us and he definitely needs 3m plus. He is a talented sort but has been reluctant to line up recently. He usually runs on late in his races and has been placed on numerous occasions.

Smart Freddy 5-y-o gelding
Groom Dancer – Smart Topsy (Oats)

He is a lovely sort whose owner bred him and he was broken in here as a two-year-old. He showed some promise in bumpers and has progressed well, finishing second behind the Nicky Henderson-trained Problema Tic at Southwell in January. Since that run he finished fifth at Ascot behind Sonofvic but hated the going as it was like a bog and very soft, so we then gave him a bit of break which certainly seems to have done him the world of good as he has notched up two back-to-back wins at Southwell and Stratford over 2m on good ground. He will now be aimed at 2m4f races on good ground and will appreciate a stiffer track. He's a classy horse who could head to Cheltenham and will jump a fence in time.

Super Villan 6-y-o gelding
*Alflora – Country House
(Town And Country)*

He has come from Mark Bradstock's and I am looking forward to him this season as, although yet to break his duck, he is very consistent and has been placed on his last

five starts. He is a big type with a lot of promise and certainly looks to be a nice horse in the making. I want to win another hurdle with him before he goes chasing.

Turtlethomas 5-y-o gelding
*Turtle Island – Makingyourmindup
(Good Thyne)*

He is a massive horse so it has taken a while for him to fill his frame. On his first outing in a bumper at Huntingdon, he hated the going as it was very soft and sticky. As he had won a point-to-point we knew that he could jump and stay so he was sent out again in March for a hurdle when the going was better and it made a real difference as he hacked up – the winning margin was 18l. His future lies over fences but I would like him to win another hurdle before he does chasing.

Universal Soldier 6-y-o gelding
*Winged Love – Waterland Gale
(Fourstars Allstar)*

I am very excited to have Universal Soldier back after a stint at Nicky Henderson's yard. It has taken a while for him to mature as he is a very big horse with a long, raking stride. He hacked up at Chepstow in a 3m handicap hurdle race in January, his latest start, and he will be out again in October. He could well be an RSA Chase horse and I think he could be really decent.

RAVETHEBRAVE: winning at Kempton but could return somewhere low-key

Profiles for punters
James Ewart

YOUNG GUN: James Ewart is climbing the training ladder fast at just 33

Profile by Dylan Hill

SEVERAL seasons ago I had the pleasure of hosting a dinner with Mick Fitzgerald joined by a couple of competition winners (luckily they didn't complain that the prize of Fitzgerald's company was cancelled out by having to put up with mine at the same time).

It proved to be a valuable experience in many ways because this pair were mad-keen punters and had cottoned on to a winning formula that has paid handsome dividends ever since.

Their system was to look for young trainers whose skills were still underrated by the betting market, and in the preceding months they had found one man to make the formula pay more than any other – James Ewart.

From his first winner, Kimbambo at Kelso in January 2005, to a breakthrough campaign in 2006-07 when he sent out seven winners, Ewart's horses returned a level-stakes profit of more than £65 to £1 level stakes.

The following campaign was a disappointment, but there's been marked progress ever since and last season took the upward curve to a new high with a career-best 16 winners, returning a £21.14 profit. Only once in the last five seasons has Ewart's strike-rate dipped below a highly creditable 13 per cent.

The 33-year-old Ewart was only 26 when he took out a licence in 2004, but he had already received a tremendous grounding in the game.

His father, Neil Ewart, bred and trained point-to-pointers, and Ewart was a regular competitor on the pointing circuit from the age of 16.

Pursuing his dream of holding his own licence, he undertook work experience with the likes of Nicky Henderson and Jonjo O'Neill before continuing to learn his trade under Ferdy Murphy.

During that time Ewart began spending his summers in France, paving the way for a spell as assitant trainer and amateur jockey to Guillaume Macaire, though the French expedition came about more as a result of boredom than inspired planning.

"Ferdy used to empty his yard of horses and staff during the summer so I was at a loose end, but his daughter was married to Guy Petit, a French bloodstock agent, so he suggested I could spend some time with him," recalls Ewart.

"I had been with Guy for a couple of weeks when he told me he had horses in training with Macaire, so we drove down and I ended up staying for a month before returning to Ferdy."

Ewart certainly made a big impression on Macaire during that month because the 19-time French champion trainer flew him out regularly during the winter to ride in amateur races before making their arrangement a permanent thing.

"I was second on my first ride for him and won on my second, so we soon had a good

GUILLAUME MACAIRE: a huge influence on Ewart's style of training

rapport," he says. "I was physically fitter and more motivated than most of the French amateurs and I used to get on some top-class horses."

Ewart was the champion amateur in 2000 and won three times at France's top jumps track Auteuil (from just five rides), and many assumed he would turn professional, but the itch to train horses was always stronger.

"I wanted to take the plunge while I was still young enough to do it," he says. "It takes ten years to establish yourself as a trainer so it's a young man's game. In a way being naive was a good thing, though, because I might not have done it had I known how hard it is!"

The opportunity came thanks to his parents' farm near Dumfries in the Scottish borders, close to Len Lungo's old yard. "I took a corner of the farm to utilise, turning farm buildings into stables."

Ewart has steadily built up the facilities over the years, helped by boldly taking out a big loan from a generous bank manager, and

SA SUFFIT: back in training and could be aimed at the Hennessy Gold Cup

now has a top-class set of facilities including a five and a half furlong sand gallop with wing fences and full railings, and a grass gallop with hurdles and traditional chase fences.

It's a similar operation to that of Macaire, whom Ewart admits has been a big influence in terms of training and schooling his horses, though he hasn't entirely based his style on the Frenchman.

"For care and attention to horses it would be Nicky Henderson," he says. "I think you cherry-pick your favourite aspects of different trainers and make your own mixture."

Ewart also feels his location gives him plenty of advantages despite not ruling out a possible move south one day.

"Lucinda Russell is the only other trainer in Scotland still growing so there's a void which we hope to fill. There are fewer horses and the quality is lower, so races are easier to win.

"The negative is that northern horses are often badly handicapped when they come south. There's a definite north/south divide in handicapping which is difficult to remedy."

One horse Ewart hopes will be well enough handicapped for a major southern assignment is stable star Sa Suffit, who may well be a leading hope for the Hennessy Gold Cup as he returns from a minor injury suffered on his only start last season.

He also has an exciting team of novice chasers, headed by the hugely exciting Vosges, who he believes could prove to be the best in the north before tackling bigger prizes.

The horses

Aikman 7-y-o gelding
Rudimentary – Omas Lady
(Be My Native)

Jumping proved a real problem for him at the start of last season as he came down on his hurdling debut at Musselburgh and then made a bad mistake at the last when second next time. However, he got better as the season progressed and showed some really good form, beating the Tolworth winner Minella Class at Huntingdon and finishing seventh, beaten just 11 lengths, in the Neptune Hurdle at Cheltenham. He also ran a decent race when we stepped him up to 3m at Aintree and he finished sixth in the Sefton. He goes novice chasing, and even though he doesn't look a natural we're hoping he will again improve with time.

Allow Me 6-y-o gelding
Daylami – Time Honoured (Sadler's Wells)

He showed real promise a couple of seasons ago before missing last season with a small injury. He showed real consistency and wasn't out of the first four in five attempts, twice finishing second in bumpers before taking a close third on his hurdling debut at Newcastle. He's really tough and will start off in novice hurdles at 2m4f, and he would prefer a flat, galloping track. He's definitely one to follow.

Best Lover 9-y-o gelding
Great Palm – Droid (Belgio)

He's extremely fragile and has run only once in the last two seasons, but he made a big impressin that day when landing a novice chase at Hexham on his first run over fences. He had a small operation on a tendon after that and now his legs look better than ever. We will still be very careful with him, only running him on soft or heavy ground, but hopefully we will get four or five runs into him. He has the speed to win over 2m but will probably be stepped up in trip. He starts off in handicap chases on a mark of 125 and should be very exciting.

Bishops Heir 6-y-o gelding
Turbo Speed – Linns Heir
(Leading Counsel)

He ran only once last season when pulled up at Carlisle, but he is a very good horse as he showed when winning twice and finishing fifth in a Grade 2 novice hurdle at Kelso during the previous campaign. He has the physique to do really well in novice chases and will start over fences from 2m to 2m4f. He needs soft or heavy ground.

Captain Americo 9-y-o gelding
Lord Americo – Excitable Lady (Buckskin)

He did well last season, winning over hurdles at Kelso and then doing much better in his second season as a novice chaser as he won at Newcastle and finished third behind Wayward Prince in a Grade 2 race at Wetherby, beaten only 11 lengths. We then took him to Cheltenham, but he was pulled up in the 4m National Hunt Chase. I still think he's better than that and the unfamiliar jockey might not have helped because he wants strong riding. He will again mix hurdling and chasing, but we will start off over fences as he is rated 8lb lower on 127 and he should have a good chance of exploiting that mark. He needs a proper test of stamina and will hopefully pick up a good staying pot somewhere.

Classic Cut 7-y-o gelding
Classic Cliche – Leading Line
(Leading Man)

We had high hopes for him in staying handicap chases last season but the campaign was scuppered by a really unlucky incident in the Northumberland National in November. He looked like he was going to beat the winner, Belon Gale, when that horse made a mistake and lifted the kick bar of the fence into the air, bringing our horse down. It's down in the form book as a fall but really it was a freak accident. He was injured in the fall but is ready to run again and should enjoy some of the extreme conditions in the north in top staying handicaps.

QUICUYO: puts in a typically bold leap as he wins at Ayr in January

Conceptual Art 4-y-o gelding
Haafhd – Hasty Words (Polish Patriot)

He had three starts on the Flat for Michael Bell in 2010, finishing third twice and fourth once in maidens from 7f to 1m. We've got him to go novice hurdling and he will start off over 2m. I don't think he will be top-class but he's still a decent prospect.

Plus Jamais 4-y-o gelding
Caballo Raptor – Branceilles (Satin Wood)

A half-brother to Sa Suffit, he seems to have a great deal of ability. We have been very patient with him and he should be ready to run in a bumper in November. He will want plenty of cut in the ground and a galloping track.

Premier Grand Cru 5-y-o gelding
Kaldounevees – Last Harvest (Kahyasi)

He won on his hurdling debut in France in 2009 and did well for us when he got some good ground in the late spring and early summer. I believe the better surface is the key to him so he won't be out until he gets

those conditions, when he will be going novice chasing.

Quicuyo 8-y-o gelding
Acatengo – Quila (Unfuwain)

All of his last four wins have come at Ayr and he was again successful there last January when hacking up in a 2m handicap chase. His form tailed off after that, but we have given him a wind operation which hopefully will get him back on track. We will send him to Ayr as often as possible and mix hurdling and chasing if necessary, but he is better over fences because of his fantastic jumping.

Sa Suffit 8-y-o gelding
Dolpour – Branceilles (Satin Wood)

He's been the stable star ever since I acquired him from France and he won on his British debut at Catterick in January 2009. The following season he won three times over fences and was rated 152 at his peak, though he's just slipped to 149 now. Last season was a real frustration, though, as he was off the track until February because of the bad weather and then got struck into when fourth on his return at Carlisle, which meant he couldn't run again as he picked up an infection. He's only eight, though, and I feel there is still time for him to win a major handicap chase. He is likely to return in the Charlie Hall Chase, and the Hennessy Gold Cup could be his big aim as he will have a lot in his favour there. The only negative would be that he is a poor traveller, but we would have to find a way around that. He is definitely a soft-ground specialist and prefers a flat, galloping track.

Signalman 7-y-o gelding
Silver Patriarch – Kairine (Kahyasi)

He was a decent novice hurdler in 2008/09, but he has glass legs which means he has hardly run since. He made it to the track twice last season, both times in novice chases at Hexham in March, and was second on each occasion, beaten less than three lengths. I would hope that he is able to win a novice chase, but he will only run on ground that has some cut in it.

Swallow 5-y-o gelding
Lavirco – Pocahontas (Nikos)

He's run three times in bumpers over the last couple of seasons, doing best when fifth at Carlisle on his debut. He seems much better than that at home, though, and he is also a gorgeous-looking horse with a lovely pedigree. He just needs to develop mentally as he has been tense whenever he goes to the racecourse. He will now run in novice hurdles, starting over 2m, and he has the potential to do well as he is an exceptional jumper. He will probably be better on a flat track and a sounder surface.

Thorlak 4-y-o gelding
Caballo Raptor – Temara (Rex Magna)

One for the future, he is a half-brother to the Champion Chase winner Azertyuiop and Bipbap, who was also a champion in France. He hasn't run yet but shaped well in a racecourse gallop with Premier Grand Cru after the Scottish National meeting in April. He will be ready for a bumper in November and could be very good.

SIGNALMAN (left): showed good form as a novice hurdler three seasons ago

Ueueteotl 3-y-o gelding
Tikkanen – Azturk (Pocahontas)

He's an exciting home-bred who is precocious and has worked well at home. I've already earmarked a juvenile bumper at Carlisle for him at the end of October and I have high hopes.

Vosges 4-y-o gelding
Turgeon – Vanilla Sky (Kaldounevees)

He ran in four three-year-old hurdles in France before joining us last season and went on to do very well, gaining his second win in the Scottish Triumph Hurdle at Musselburgh. He disappointed twice after that, but he had had a long season and I think he wants a sounder surface. Despite his age he will go straight novice chasing and would be the pick of my horses in that sphere. He already jumps incredibly well in schooling and has the scope of a chaser, and he could improve dramatically over fences.

Zaru 5-y-o gelding
Laveron – Zianini (Dom Pasquini)

He was still a big baby last season so he did well to finish in the first four in four of his five races. He had heart problems as a youngster and the treatment he had may still have affected him. His last run was his debut over hurdles at Kelso and he was again keen, which didn't help him to jump well, but he stayed on well to finish fourth, beaten only 11 lengths, which was very pleasing. Better ground and flat, galloping tracks will help.

Unnamed 4-y-o gelding
Milan – Strong Wishes (Strong Gale)

We call him 'Porsche' at home because he looks exceptional. He's a half-brother to last season's good novice chaser William's Wishes. I would hope he's good enough to win a bumper this season and whatever he does he will be even better when he goes over an obstacle because he jumps very well.

VOSGES (left): did well over hurdles and could come into his own chasing

Profiles for punters

Graeme McPherson

TOP TEAM: Graeme McPherson (right) with Mick Finn and Fairview Sue

Profile by Neil Clark

AMERICAN architect Daniel H. Burnham once said: "Make no little plans; they have no magic to stir men's blood. Make big plans, aim high in hope and work." Graeme McPherson, QC, has clearly taken Burnham's advice to heart.

Having reached the top in one extremely competitive profession – the law, in which he became the youngest barrister in 2008 to take silk – the immensely likeable and enthusiastic 40-year-old is now determined to reach the heights in another demanding field: training racehorses.

McPherson's rise in the training ranks has been meteoric. It's only two years since he first took out his licence in October 2009 and in that time he's already trained 14 winners from his base at Martins Hill in the lovely Cotswold countryside near to Stow-on-the-Wold.

"In our first winter we had around seven or eight horses and half of them won," he recalls. "Then last year we had 15 and nine of them won."

McPherson's interest in racing began in Dorset when he attended point-to-points with his family. "My father loved racing. We used to go a lot to point-to-points at places like Badbury Rings and Larkhill, and to Wincanton and Salisbury."

After university and law school, McPherson qualified as a barrister in 1993 and then became involved in racing as an owner with Northamptonshire-based trainer John Upson.

"I owned Blunham Hill, who won five chases, and another horse, The River Joker, who was probably the slowest horse who ever raced! I also rode out for John and

he was full of encouragement. We had a lot in common as we were both people who had come into racing from other fields."

McPherson also rode in point-to-points – "really badly" by his own admission – with one winner at Thorpe Lodge in Lincolnshire.

With his wife Seanin, who hails from Northern Ireland, McPherson moved to rural Gloucestershire in 2004 to train pointers.

"We had a couple of horses and six boxes. In 2005 I had a bad fall, and decided to give up riding, but it was a blessing in disguise because when we put someone else on our horses, we discovered that they went much better. We took out a permit in 2007 and in the 2008/09 season we trained a hunter chase winner at Cheltenham, Rien A Perdre. People were asking us if we'd train for them so in 2009 we took out a full licence."

McPherson's first winner as a public trainer came in February 2010, when Fairview Sue readily landed a bumper at Southwell by 7l. Since then it's been a case of onwards

THE DAY JOB: McPherson (centre) with Luca Cumani and Darryll Holland

and upwards.

Asked for the secret of his success, he says: "First and foremost I have got a first-class team. Mick Finn, who heads the team, has been in racing all his life, he is just a supreme horseman in terms of knowing what a horse needs and what a horse wants. I think we work well as a team.

"Jodie Mogford is another key figure. He's local and he's been with us from the start. He's in every day and having an experienced jockey riding our horses and going racing with them and knowing them is a tremendous positive for a small yard starting off. My wife Seanin doesn't ride out any more as she broke her leg a couple of times and has had three children, but she's passionate about the horses and loves her racing".

McPherson believes the excellent facilities at his yard and the relaxed atmosphere also helps the horses in his care.

"We've got a 5f uphill all-weather gallop, a 3f canter circle, a grass schooling field, an all-weather school lane and a 60x25 outdoor school. And we've got 200 acres where horses can graze and be hacked out. We're in a lovely part of the countryside and I think the horses really enjoy it here."

I've visited many yards and certainly the atmosphere at Martins Hill is one of the most relaxed I've experienced. And it's not hard to understand how horses, who perhaps have become a little overlooked in much larger yards, thrive on the individual attention given to them in such a tranquil setting. I ask McPherson what he is enjoying most about his new career.

"The business and the owning side because I know I can leave the horses in good hands with Mick. I also enjoy the placing – it doesn't matter how fit you get the horse if there's one better than you in the race, whereas any horse can win in the right race. A win's a win and I'm yet to have an owner complain they've won a bad race!"

McPherson's legal background may also have been an advantage in the analytical side of training. "It probably does it no harm. It gets you used to doing the paper exercises and working things through."

McPherson specialises in commercial and sports law. "It's all litigation, when people and companies have fallen out with one another. Within the sporting field it'll be contractual dispute and disciplinary work. Racing is the single biggest sport I do – I worked on the Howard Johnson case and did the Kieren Fallon Derby injunction – but I also work in other sports such as football, rugby and cricket. When Portsmouth went under I was involved quite a lot, and have also been involved in disputes between players and agents. I'm passionate about sport and am a big Southampton supporter. I'm delighted with how they've done this year.

"I think that having two different jobs is refreshing and a lovely way to balance things. They are both very different exercises and there are times when you might be getting bogged down a bit on the training and come back to it completely fresh when everything is clearer. You'll be doing something else and you suddenly think, 'that's the race to go for'. You could end up spending 18 hours a day on the horses and lose perspective."

McPherson loves Cheltenham, but he would prefer to win the Grand National than a festival winner.

"Ever since I was a kid the National has always been the race for me and having a National runner is something that would be fantastic. I don't think we've got anything in the yard now that would be that quality within the next couple of years, but we have got a couple of youngsters who have come in this year having won their Irish point-to-points and are big, strapping, chasing types so they might be National sorts in about four years.

"That said, I wouldn't say no to a festival winner either. We had our first festival runner, Harry Hunt, in the Fred Winter in March and the thrill was so great that I didn't sleep for about three nights. Having had one festival runner, we're hungry for more."

Asked where he would like the yard to be in two or three years, McPherson says: "We're 37 boxes now. I wouldn't want to get any bigger than 40. What I really want to do is to increase the quality year after year and end up with a yard of 40 nice horses."

Seeing the way he has achieved success in two different professions, it would be a brave man to bet against McPherson realising his next ambition.

The horses

Chorizo 10-y-o gelding
Kahyasi – Bayariyka (Slip Anchor)

He was a decent point-to-pointer, winning seven in one season three years ago. He lost his way for Richard Guest – he's fallen from 124 to 105 in the handicap – so we'll send him pointing and put him back under rules when he's enjoying life again. Hopefully there's a bit more to come from him.

Cocacobana 6-y-o gelding
Snurge – Dun Dun (Saddlers' Hall)

He had one run for Rebecca Curtis when mid-division at Bangor but the owners are local to here and wanted to move him closer to home. He was second for us first time out at Hereford behind Mono Man, who went on to win an Ascot bumper under a penalty. He was placed in a couple of novice hurdles but just fell short at that level, and he should do well now that he's going handicapping. He's rated 100 and he's a big, strong horse and so he should be able to carry top weight in a 0-100 handicap. He hasn't quite got the pace for 2m so 2m4f will be the trip for him.

Constant Cupid 7-y-o gelding
Winged Love – Eva Ross (Furry Glen)

We've had him since we started pointing. I would never had him as a soft-ground horse, but he went to Hereford in January in the mud and won by 10l – it could have been 20! At Chepstow a month later we thought it would be soft enough for him, but it wasn't. We'll see him at his best when it's hock-deep. He'll start the season hurdling but after that he'll go chasing as he jumps a fence well.

Dancing Emily 5-y-o mare
Anshan – Goodthyne Lady (Good Thyne)

She absolutely hacked up at Taunton first time out in March and was placed at Ffos Las even though she didn't like the race being run at a crawl. She's a big, scopey mare who will definitely jump a hurdle and probably a fence as well. She'll be running over 2m4f over hurdles and is very exciting.

Fairview Sue 7-y-o mare
Alflora – Tall Story (Arzanni)

She was quite slow coming into herself, but the owner has been very patient. She was third at 125-1 on her first run at Hereford and then won an all-weather bumper at Southwell by 8l hard held. I got it all wrong with her last year. We tried to wait for the right ground, but it was still too soft when we took her to Fakenham and it took her a while to get over it. Two and a quarter miles on good ground should be just right for her and I think she's got the potential to be a really nice mare.

Gypsy George 10-y-o gelding
Sovereign Water – Query Line (High Line)

His owners, Nailsworth Estate, sponsor the yard. They had Rien A Perdre when he won at Cheltenham and what they'd like above anything is to have a Cheltenham Foxhunters runner. We aimed him at the race last year but he broke his pelvis at Wetherby in February. He's had a long summer break and he'll be aimed at the Foxhunters again. He's a soft-ground horse.

Harry Hunt 4-y-o gelding
Bertolini – Qasirah (Machiavellian)

He was moderate on the Flat in Ireland, but Tom Malone bought him for us and he was beaten a head first time out at Hereford. He then won very cosily at Bangor and he wasn't disgraced in the Fred Winter at Cheltenham either. He'll start off over hurdles again, but he will probably go chasing as he's got the size and the scope.

Himayna 7-y-o mare
Generous – Himaya (Mouktar)

She was with Tim Vaughan for the first half of this year and has improved 7lb from moving here. I'm not going to claim that we've got her any fitter, but she's one who has benefited from the change of scenery. She has been desperately unlucky, losing by less than 3l three times. If she can improve her jumping – that's the one area that lets her down –

GYPSY GEORGE: has the Cheltenham Foxhunters as his aim this season

she'll be really good.

Miss Brownes Fancy 3-y-o filly
Encosta De Lago – Be Dignified
(Be My Guest)

She was with David Wachman on the Flat over in Ireland and was moderate in relation to the quality of his yard. However, she's got size and scope about her and I think she will be really nice for juvenile hurdling with the fillies' allowance.

Porta Vogie 9-y-o gelding
Supreme Leader – Decent Preacher
(Decent Fellow)

He's a steady chaser, but he'll make one mistake in every race. If it's a bad one it stops him, if not he goes on runs his race. He's won at Huntingdon and he loves 2m4f/2m6f on a flat track and decent ground.

Presented 4-y-o gelding
Presenting – Rustic Court (Quayside)

He's not a typical Presenting. He finished second in his first point-to-point behind a really nice horse and won his maiden as a

four-year-old next time out. He's a sharp, light horse and he's definitely got the speed to be decent in bumpers, though he needs to settle down. We know he jumps and stays well and I think eventually he'll be a really nice 3m novice hurdler.

Quel Bruere 7-y-o gelding
Sassanian – Housseliere (April Night)

He had a dreadful wind problem when we got him and since we had his wind done he's shown good form in patches, winning by 25l at Hereford on his first run over fences. He's still a really quirky horse – his form in his last five runs last season was 'F2P2P' and you just don't know which horse is going to turn up. On his day he's a nice horse and a lovely one to have in the yard.

Quizwork 7-y-o gelding
Network – Galene De Saisy (Montorselli)

My favourite horse in the yard – I absolutely love him. He was placed in couple of Newbury novice hurdles but was big and backward and we'll see him to better effect this season. We've also had his wind done since he made a noise at Bangor. He'll start over

RORY BOY (orange cap): on his way to winning at Warwick in November 2009

hurdles but will then go chasing and I think fences will be the making of him.

Rory Boy 6-y-o gelding
Aldebaran – Purr Pleasure
(El Gran Senor)

He was a really nice horse for Nigel Twiston-Davies and won a four-year-old chase at Warwick really well, but he became sour and his mark plummeted from 135 to 115. It's fingers crossed that a change of scenery and perhaps a less stiff gallop can sweeten him up again. Even if he only improves 10lb, he has a lot of potential.

Society Shares 6-y-o gelding
Moscow Society – Presenting Shares
(Presenting)

He was very nice in Ireland, running well in two point-to-points and a Punchestown bumper. He didn't show us anything like the same form so we had him scanned and he'd got a slight tendon injury. He was fired and since then he's had a good year off. Everything he's been doing here is showing us he's got no problems so hopefully we'll see the horse who ran so well in Ireland. He'll want 2m4f or 2m6f and decent ground over hurdles and I think he's got a bit of ability.

Tickatack 6-y-o gelding
Tikkanen – The Flyingcannister
(Little Bighorn)

He's a lovely horse. He's unusually bred in that's he's by an American-bred horse called Tikkanen, who is not a natural jumps sire, but he did well in point-to-points in Ireland – he was second on his second run and then won his maiden very impressively. We bought him at the Cheltenham Sales in April and we really like him. We'll probably give him one run in a bumper just for experience as it will be his first run on a rules track and I wouldn't be at all surprised if we don't go straight novice chasing with him. He jumps a fence beautifully.

Traditional Bob 6-y-o gelding
Saddlers' Hall – Portia's Delight (The Parson)

He's a half-brother to Beat The Boys and I really like him. Fifteen months ago he was second in a good bumper at Stratford. Last year we thought that it would be his season but we took him to Wincanton to run in a bumper and he got brought down on the bend and really got kicked about quite badly. Physically he got over it quickly, but next time out at Fontwell he simply wouldn't go past other horses. We had a fairly quiet season with him as a result, but he's had a really long summer and he's come back like a bull. We'll go hurdling with him first time out.

Verde Goodwood 5-y-o mare
Lomitas – Dissolve (Sharrood)

She came from the sales in August. She had been running well enough for Paul Webber, but I think the change of scenery might just perk her up a little bit. She's rated 100 and is perfectly capable winning off that.

Vision Of Lights 6-y-o gelding
Fantastic Light – Kadassa (Shardari)

The most cruelly named horse in the yard as he's only got one eye! He ought to be a flat horse on his breeding but he's just kept on growing. First time out last year he ran really well in a bumper at Bangor, finishing third when very green, but he didn't really go on from there. He's had a good summer, and will go straight novice hurdling. Because he's only got sight in one eye his depth of perception is an issue, but we'll school and school him and the penny will drop even if it might take a bit longer with him. He'll love stepping up from 2m to 2m4f.

Willies Yard 6-y-o gelding
Mr Combustible – Proper Primitive (Primitive Rising)

He finished second in a maiden point-to-

point in Ireland in June and came to us in the August sales. He will want good ground, so he'll come back in the spring. I can see him being a nice spring chaser.

Wychwoods Mist 4-y-o filly
Umistim – Blackchurch Lass (Taum Go Leor)

She didn't seem too special before her first run but then won at Southwell at 50-1. It didn't look a bad bumper on paper, but she beat the second by 8l and the third by 15l and three winners have come out from behind her since. We look at her now and think she's quite a special little filly. The plan with her is to run her in an EBF qualifier, and all being well get her ready for the EBF final at Sandown or the Aintree mares' bumper.

Young Jim 5-y-o gelding
Winged Love – Sitoco (Eagle Eyed)

I really like him and he may prove to be a very good buy. He won his Irish point-to-point this year and had a good summer out. Though he'll be competitive in bumpers, I don't think he'll be quick enough to win one and his future is certainly in races over 3m – hurdles to start with and then fences.

Unnamed 5-y-o gelding
Midnight Legend – Miss Millbrook (Meadowbrook)

He's big and backward, so I'm not sure if he will be ready to run in a bumper this year, but he is going to be some horse in time. Three and a half miles ended up being the distance for his sister, Wychwoods Legend, who was very useful.

Unnamed 4-y-o gelding
Great Palm – Woodside (Terimon)

He's a very nice horse with a real future. He's already one of the biggest in the yard even though he's only four. There's no rush with him as we own him so there's no pressure to get him to the track. He will probably get a bumper run this year just for experience. I think patience with him will pay off and he'll be a really nice chaser in two or three years time.

Richard Williams' 15 Best of British

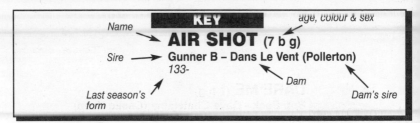

KEY

Name → **AIR SHOT** (7 b g)

Sire → **Gunner B – Dans Le Vent (Pollerton)**
133-

Last season's form

age, colour & sex

Dam

Dam's sire

AL FEROF (6 gr g)
Dom Alco - Maralta (Altayan)
F3111-

There's no better place for finding future top-class winners than the Supreme Novices' Hurdle at the Cheltenham Festival. Al Ferof won the race this year beating Spirit Son by two lengths. Previously he had won a Newbury novice by 15 lengths and a Taunton novice by 20 lengths. His owner John Hales is not interested in staying hurdlers and so Al Ferof will go chasing now. The Arkle Trophy is a possibility but he has so much stamina that the RSA Chase is an option too.

Paul Nicholls, Ditcheat

BYGONES IN BRID (5 b g)
Old Vic - St Carol (Orchestra)
120-

Had three runs in bumpers, winning at Musselburgh before coming second in a Grade 2 at Newbury. He took his chance in the Cheltenham bumper but ran no sort of race, reportedly pulling muscles. He's recovered now and is set to go novice hurdling in the colours of Spurs mananger Harry Redknapp.

Alan King, Wroughton

CAPTAIN CHRIS (7 b g)
King's Theatre - Function Dream (Strong Gale)
222211-1

Was a horse to follow last season and we make no apologies for including him again in these lists because he is a top-class chaser with winning form at Kempton and Cheltenham. After a string of seconds, he won three on the bounce including the Arkle Trophy over 2m. He could lay down a challenge to Long Run in the King George.

Philip Hobbs, Withycombe

CRISTAL BONUS (5 b g)
Della Francesca - Cristal Bonus (Loup Solitaire)
16257-

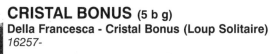

An ex-French horse who joined Evan Williams last November, running twice for him, Cristal Bonus has now moved to Paul Nicholls at Ditcheat. Williams thought so highly of this five-year-old that he ran him in the International Hurdle and Cleeve Hurdle, both at Cheltenham. That was asking a lot of one so inexperienced and he could only manage midfield each time. He is the property of Robin Geffen, who joint-owned St Leger winner Arctic Cosmos.

Paul Nicholls, Ditcheat

DARE ME (7 b g)
Bob Back - Gaye Chatelaine (Castle Keep)
11-

He was a good bumper horse two season ago, finishing second behind Megastar at Aintree on Grand National day. We only saw Dare Me twice last season, first when demolishing a field of novice hurdlers at Exeter in October and then when following up there in November, both times over 2m1f. He was being aimed at the Supreme Novices' before he knocked a leg. He's completely recovered now and is ready to go novice chasing over distances longer than 2m. Good ground suits best.

Philip Hobbs, Minehead

HELL'S BAY (9 b g)
Supreme Leader - Queen's Flagship (Accordion)
6R15221-

Was in the form of his life last season when sent novice chasing and, if he can build on that level, he should be worth following. He won a 3m3f event at Newton Abbot in August and four runs later beat Medermit in a 2m5f novice chase at Cheltenham on New Year's Day. Colin Tizzard wanted to run him in the Jewson at the Festival but a slight leg injury put an end to his season. He's versatile as regards ground and trip and, even though he's nine years old, he does not have too many miles on the clock. Goes well at Cheltenham.

Colin Tizzard, Sherborne

KAUTO STONE (5 ch g)
With The Flow - Kauto Relka (Port Etienne)
1261173-

Here's a name and a pedigree to conjure with. This half-brother to Kauto Star won the same Grade 1 race in Auteuil that Long Run did. French form doesn't get much better than that and if ever a horse screamed 'promising' it is this one. He hasn't raced in Britain yet and could be anything. This will be a new experience for him as he's never raced anywhere but Auteuil. However, his close relative proved so versatile that it's not expected to be a problem.

Paul Nicholls, Ditcheat

MICHEL LE BON (8 b g)
Villez - Rosacotte (Rose Laurel)
3/131/1/-

It seems ages since Michel Le Bon demolished a small field of novice chasers at Newbury coming home 60 lengths clear. This happened at the Hennessy meeting in late November 2009 and, because of injury, he hasn't been out since. Paul Nicholls has never lost faith in him and hopes to run him in the Hennessy itself. That may seem ambitious but there's nobody better at getting a horse ready for that great race than Nicholls. Were he to win the Hennessy, he could go right to the very top.

Paul Nicholls, Ditcheat

PEDDLERS CROSS (6 b g)
Oscar - Patscilla (Squill)
1127-

Peddlers Cross's unbeaten record came to an end in the Champion Hurdle when he was narrowly beaten by Hurricane Fly. It was one of the hottest Champions for years and Oscar Whisky, who was five lengths back in third, went on to win at Aintree. Peddlers Cross was also in that Aintree race but finished a well-beaten seventh, with his brave Cheltenham effort having taken its toll. He is set to go novice chasing this season with the Arkle a distinct possibility.

Donald McCain, Cholmondeley

REMEMBER NOW (5 ch g)
Anabaa Blue - Bleu Ciel Et Blanc (Pistolet Bleu)
672110-

He may not be as good as his half-brother Binocular but he can still make an impact at a high level. He had two wins in handicaps before being sent off 3-1 favourite for the Swinton Hurdle in which he finished plum last, a desperate effort and clearly not his true form. Expect to see the JP McManus colours carried to victory in a valuable handicap hurdle or two this season.

Nicky Henderson, Lambourn

SAINT ARE (5 b g)
Network - Forteana (Video Rock)
5317F31-0

Joined Tim Vaughan at the end of 2010 and the French import showed he was a decent novice hurdler with some close efforts. He won the one that mattered, though, the Grade 1 Sefton Novices' Hurdle at Aintree in April. That race was over 3m1f and this season he will be aimed at long-distance novice chases. He is versatile as regards the ground and appears to go best on flat tracks. Expect to see him at Newbury and, of course, Aintree.

Tim Vaughan, Aberthin

SALUT FLO (6 b g)
Saint Des Saints - Royale Marie (Garde Royale)
10528112/-

Due to injury, Salut Flo hasn't been seen since coming second at Haydock in April 2010. He will return in the autumn a year older and, in all probability, a great deal stronger. He raced twice since arriving from France, the first time winning a 2m3f handicap chase by 12 lengths at Doncaster on good ground. A winner over hurdles and fences in France, he's versatile both ground-wise and distance-wise, and he could make into a terrific handicap chaser.

David Pipe, Nicholashayne

SPIRIT SON (5 b g)
Poliglote - Kirzinnia (Zino)
11121-

A French import who came second to Al Ferof in the always informative Supreme Novices' Hurdle at Cheltenham. He then went on to win the Grade 2 novice hurdle over 2m4f at Aintree. He may have met something special at the festival and there was over three lengths back to the third, stablemate Sprinter Sacre and another length to Cue Card. At Aintree he beat Cue Card by 13 lengths suggesting he is improving rapidly. Spirit Son will stick to hurdling this season, a discipline at which he is sure to prove top class.

Nicky Henderson, Lambourn

SPRINTER SACRE (5 b/br g)
Network - Fatima III (Bayolidaan)
2113-

Came third in the Supreme Novices' Hurdle at Cheltenham and is arguably the most interesting of the first three home in a race that invariably throws up stars of the future. He was still something of a baby when he went to Cheltenham despite having two novice hurdle wins under his belt, one at Ffos Las, the other at Ascot. Sprinter Sacre looked like a festival winner as he turned for home but he hung fire when he met the hill and ran on for third. He has the stamp of a chaser and the Arkle has been pencilled in.

Nicky Henderson, Lambourn

WISHFULL THINKING (8 ch g)
Alflora - Pousssetiere Deux (Garde Royale)
F12121-1-

With the likes of Captain Chris in the yard, Philip Hobbs is not short of top-quality chasers and in Wishfull Thinking he has another right out of the top drawer. Last season he won one Grade 3 and two Grade 2 novice chases and begun this season by lifting a handicap chase at Punchestown in May. He handles a variety of tracks (wins at Aintree and Cheltenham) and distances of between 2m and 2m5f. Hobbs is mulling a crack at the Paddy Power Handicap Chase as well as the Tingle Creek. This is a horse with options.

Philip Hobbs, Minehead

Nick Watts' 15 Irish Horses to Follow

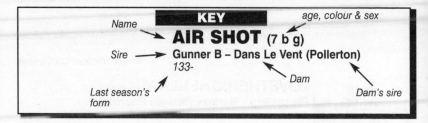

KEY

Name → **AIR SHOT** (7 b g) ← *age, colour & sex*

Sire → **Gunner B – Dans Le Vent (Pollerton)**
133-

Last season's form ↗   *Dam* ↙   *Dam's sire* ↖

ARVIKA LIGEONNIERE (6 bg)
Arvico - Daraka (Akarad)
41241/-

He had to miss last season due to a minor niggle, so we never got to saw this impressive physical specimen running over fences. Hopefully he can steer clear of injury and show us what we all missed. The season before he was a very good novice hurdler who competed over a range of trips, winning over 2m and 2m4f and finishing fourth in the Albert Bartlett behind Berties Dream. He looks best over shorter, though, and could be an Arkle type.

Willie Mullins, Co Carlow

CHICAGO GREY (8 gr g)
Luso - Carrigeen Acer (Lord America)
313211F2518-

A good and progressive novice who ran 11 times in a busy campaign. Not quite up to tackling the best over 3m, his astute trainer gave him the target of the four-miler at the Cheltenham Festival, and he duly obliged, beating Beshabar comfortably. The form of that race as franked when Beshabar went on to win the Scottish National. Now that his stamina has been proven, talk of the Grand National is in the air and he is a strong candidate.

Gordon Elliott, Trim

FIRST LIEUTENANT (6 ch g)
Presenting - Fourstargale (Fourstars Allstar)
41311-3-

Considering he is a chaser in the making, he did pretty well over hurdles last season, winning two Grade 1s, including the Neptune Investments at the Cheltenham Festival. He may have been a shade fortunate there, as he looked beaten until Oscars Well made a hash of the last, but it still bodes well for his real occupation – chasing. He's sure to stay 3m in time, but he may be one for the shorter Jewson this season as he's not short of toe.

Mouse Morris, Fethard

HIDDEN CYCLONE (6 b g)
Stowaway - Hurricane Debbie (Shahanndeh)
113111-

Very well campaigned last season to win five of his six starts – on the other he was barely disgraced when only narrowly beaten by First Lieutenant and Zaidpour in a Grade 1 at Leopardstown's Christmas meeting. He didn't always show hurdles the greatest of respect, but that can happen with horses who are made for chasing and it would be surprising if he didn't jump fences a lot better. Staying is his game and he could end up as an RSA Chase candidate.

Shark Hanlon, Co Carlow

LOVETHEHIGHERLAW (5 ch g)
Presenting - Markiza (Broken Hearted)
12-1-

He didn't go for the Cheltenham Festival bumper last season, with his trainer preferring to keep him fresh for Punchestown. It proved an inspired decision too, as he just got the better of a thrilling duel with the hitherto unbeaten Waaheb by a short head. He is already as low as 12-1 for the Supreme Novices, and that's not surprising, as if he takes to hurdling he should go to the very top. He's won a point-to-point over 2m4f, so he stays well, but he's not short of speed and he may be kept to the the minimum trip for the time being.

Willie Mullins, Co Carlow

MORNING ROYALTY (4 b g)
King's Theatre - Portryan Native (Be My Native)
-2

A half-brother to the stable's very good mare Morning Supreme. He's only had the one start, making his debut at the Punchestown Festival in May, where he was a 5l second behind King Vuvuzela. It was a comfortable defeat, but he impressed with the way he travelled and he could be a good prospect for novice hurdles this season. His relative was very headstrong and used to like front-running, so it's interesing that he was held up before being brought through later in the race. That should have taught him something.

Willie Mullins, Co Carlow

QUITO DE LA ROQUE (7 b g)
Saint Des Saints - Moody Cloud (Cyborg)
12111-1

What a fantastic novice season he had – only being beaten once in six starts, and that by the RSA Chase winner Bostons Angel. We knew of his prowess in soft and heavy ground, but what impressed about him was his versatility later in the season, winning a Grade 1 at Aintree on good ground. After that he won again at Punchestown on good to yielding, so he can go on anything and he may develop into a Gold Cup outsider. He should at least make hay in Graded contests through the Irish winter.

Colm Murphy, Co Wexford

REALT DUBH (7 b g)
Beneficial - Suez Canal (Exit To Nowhere)
1F12113-12-

Couldn't have done much more in his novice campaign, winning thrice in Grade 1 company, twice beating Cheltenham scorer Noble Prince in the process. On his final start of the campaign he locked horns with Arkle hero Captain Chris and looked like beating him until succumbing after the last. He should improve again this season, and looks a strong Ryanair candidate, with 2m may be a touch on the short side for him these days. Never runs a bad race and a thoroughly likeable type.

Noel Meade, Co Meath

RISING TIME (5 b m)
Old Vic - Dawn's Double (King's Ride)
-1

Her trainer is in need of a good young horse coming through the ranks and this mare could be the one. She's distantly related to the great Dawn Run, and although she was an unconsidered 16-1 shot for her debut at Fairyhouse last April she won in the style of a useful horse. She travelled well, and threaded her way through horses to lead approaching the furlong pole. She kept on well from there to win by a length and a quarter and will be one to note when sent hurdling.

Paul Nolan, Co Wexford

SAMAIN (5 b g)
Black Sam Bellamy - Selva (Darshaan)
111-

Although Mullins failed to win the Cheltenham bumper this season, it's probably because he left his best two prospects, Lovethehigherlaw and Samain, at home. This one was unbeaten in all four starts, and was particularly impressive on his final two starts at Naas and the Curragh. It will be fascinating to see what route his trainer takes, and whether he is kept to 2m or tried over further. It will also be fascinating to see how he is campaigned with Lovethehigherlaw and who emerges the best. Therefore put them both in your list!

Willie Mullins, Co Carlow

SIR DES CHAMPS (5 b/br g)
Robin Des Champs - Liste En Tete (Video Rock)
1/11-

Very lightly raced, and therefore it's still hard to ascertain just how good he might be. He was a well-supported 9-2 favourite for the Martin Pipe Conditionals' Hurdle at the Cheltenham Festival, but looked very unlikely to justify that support halfway through the race. However, he made tremendous late headway to join issue at the last, and he was very strong up the hill. He might go chasing this season, but if he doesn't he probably still has more to offer over hurdles.

Willie Mullins, Co Carlow

SON AMIX (5 gr g)
Fragrant Mix - Immage (Bad Conduct)
22422-9292

He's unlikely to reach the top over fences, but could be very interesting in a good handicap off a light weight. It was just those conditions that brought out the best in him over hurdles last season, as he finished runner-up to Buena Vista in the Pertemps Final at Cheltenham. More recently, he made his chasing debut at Listowel in horrible conditions. He couldn't get to Toomdeely, but wasn't given a hard time of it and he jumped well for the most part. Definitely one to note.

Thomas Cooper, Co Kerry

STEPS TO FREEDOM (5 b g)
Statue Of Liberty - Dhakhirah (Sadler's Wells)
1F1-01

It's unusual for one of Gordon Elliott's to be transferred here, but that's what happened to this horse after he'd won the Aintree bumper. Harrington has been running him on the Flat this season, and he's put in some impressive displays, including when not beaten far in a Listed event at Galway in August. Good ground definitely suits him best, as he has a lot of speed, so he's not one to watch when the going gets heavy in the winter. However, give him some spring ground and then you'll see what he's made of.

Jessica Harrington, Co Kildare

WAAHEB (4 b g)
Elsuive Quality - Nafisah (Lahib)
111-2

Seriously impressive in his first three starts in bumpers, so much so that JP McManus saw fit to buy him from one of Weld's long-serving patrons, Dr Ronan Lambe. There wasn't an instant return on his investment for McManus, as he lost out to Lovethehigherlaw at Punchestown, but it was still a very good effort and one that bodes well for his career over hurdles this season. He appears to go well on most types of ground, so he's versatile in that regard, and he's likely to be best suited by 2m.

Dermot Weld, Co Kildare

WEAPON'S AMNESTY (8 ch g)
Presenting - Victoria Theatre (Old Vic)
3F1221/

The forgotten horse somewhat in Irish racing, but think back to what he did to Long Run in the RSA Chase a couple of season's ago and you'll soon remember him. Just for the record, he had Nicky Henderson's Gold Cup winner over 7l away in third when he won at the 2010 festival. His trainer reports him ready for the new season following an injury-induced absence in 2010-2011, and while it might take him a while to get going he's young enough to still be a serious player in March.

Charles Byrnes, Co Limerick

Outlook

Ante-Post Preview with Steffan Edwards

King George/Gold Cup

LAST season it was a case of out with the old and in with the new as **Long Run** deposed grand old stagers Kauto Star and Denman as the best staying chaser around.

His success in the King George was perhaps less of a surprise than his Gold Cup win as he had shown a liking for Kempton the previous year, whereas he had come up short in both previous visits to Cheltenham. In the end, though, it was simply a case of youth winning out as he ran out an emphatic winner of the blue riband.

While Long Run is clearly the one to beat this time around, he's priced accordingly and I'm prepared to take a couple of shots at him with young, unexposed rivals who have the potential to step up massively this season.

He was only winning off a mark of 133 in a Class 3 handicap at Sandown, but when **MON PARRAIN** made a winning debut in this country in March he looked something special. His jumping was impeccable and he bolted up by 22l from a solid yardstick, earning an RPR of 162 without being asked a serious question.

The fact that he had missed work prior to that demolition job and his trainer Paul Nicholls had expected him to need the outing made the performance stand out even more, and it was no surprise to see him sent off a well-backed favourite to follow up in the Topham at Aintree.

Racing off a 16lb higher mark over the big fences, he was electric the whole way round, barely touching a twig, and was still swinging away jumping the last. It was therefore both surprising and disappointing to then see him caught by course specialist Always Waining on the run to the elbow. He was rallying again close home, but those who had backed him down to 1.01 in running must have been wondering how on earth he had lost. Nicholls was equally puzzled.

It couldn't have been lack of stamina as he'd won over 3f further at Sandown, and it may have been a case of weakness in a young horse. It's worth remembering that 12 months earlier Long Run, at the same age, was finishing tired in the RSA Chase and his stamina for 3m at that track was being questioned, but as a six-year-old he strongly saw out the Gold Cup distance over another 2f.

Just from a ratings standpoint, and given his age, Mon Parrain is already well on the way to challenging for top honours this season. For his Feltham and RSA runs Long Run was given RPRs of 167 and 160 respectively, while Mon Parrain was given marks of 162 and 161 for his two efforts last season.

Admittedly Mon Parrain didn't achieve the same level of form as Long Run when trained in France, but it's quite possible that was due to the testing ground he was asked to race on over there. Good spring ground clearly suits him much better, and there's no knowing how far he can progress for a full season under the care of the champion trainer.

Just like Long Run last season, it looks like Mon Parrain will kick off his campaign in the Paddy Power Gold Cup. Long Run was sent off favourite when effectively running off a mark of 153 and finished third in the race, while Mon Parrain will be asked to run off 152 and also looks sure to head the market (the sponsors opened up betting with him as 6-1 favourite).

Success or even honourable defeat at Cheltenham in November will bring the King George into the picture, and his slick jumping will be a valuable asset around Kempton. Nicholls has Master Minded earmarked for the race at the moment, but he's not shied away from running more than one in the big races in the past and the horses represent different owners as well, so that's of no great

concern. The 25-1 available with some bookmakers looks fair, although bigger should continue to be available on the leading exchanges, at least until the Paddy Power in November.

It follows that if he were to be successful, or simply run well in defeat at Kempton, then the Gold Cup would come into consideration. While he's not short of speed, his Sandown win showed us that he shouldn't have a problem with 3m-plus, and his pedigree is also encouraging on that front.

His sire's best progeny have raced over various distances and include Betfred Gold Cup winner Bounce Back, Triumph Hurdle runner-up Franchoek and Game Spirit winner Don't Be Shy, but he's out of a Kadalko mare and her three highest-rated progeny are the stayers Notre Pere, Pride Of Dulcote and Ladalko, so there's plenty

LONG RUN (left): deposed Kauto Star last season but now faces new challengers

MON PARRAIN: *full of potential*

of encouragement to be found there that he's bred to get the a trip.

The 33-1 for the Gold Cup, which is generally available, also looks worth taking, for providing that things go even reasonably to plan in the first half of the season, he could easily find himself the stable's leading contender for the race after Christmas.

Given his age he has more scope than most for improvement, and he's already starting from quite a high base.

Master Minded has spent the vast majority of his life running over distances around 2m but he showed improved form for the step up to 2m4f at Aintree in April. He now finds himself second-favourite for both the King George and Gold Cup, though, and while the trip at Kempton might be within reach – and even that is far from certain – the Gold Cup distance is likely to be a bridge too far. He certainly makes no appeal at the prices.

Kauto Stone is another exciting prospect to have joined the Nicholls yard. Last year he won the Grade 1 four-year-old chase at Auteuil that Long Run took in 2009 prior to coming over here. He also has a verdict over Mon Parrain, having beaten him 14l back in May 2010, but that was on testing ground and Mon Parrain has since improved for a sound surface.

It will be interesting to see whether Kauto

King George

Kempton, 26 December 2011

	Bet365	Coral	Hills	Lads	P Power	S James	Tote	VC
Long Run	Evs	Evs	6-4	5-4	11-10	11-10	Evs	Evs
Master Minded	5	5	4	9-2	6	5	9-2	9-2
Captain Chris	8	8	7	8	9	7	7	8
Riverside Theatre	10	10	-	10	6	10	10	10
Wishfull Thinking	10	10	10	10	12	12	14	10
Kauto Star	8	-	-	-	-	16	-	16
Noble Prince	16	-	-	-	-	14	16	16
Diamond Harry	16	-	-	-	-	20	20	20
Mon Parrain	25	-	-	-	25	25	-	25
Jessies Dream	25	20	-	-	-	25	-	20
Time For Rupert	20	-	-	-	-	20	25	20
Bostons Angel	20	-	-	-	-	25	16	16
Nacarat	25	20	-	-	-	20	16	20
Quito De La Roque	20	20	-	-	-	25	25	20

each-way 1/4 odds, 1-2-3
Others on request, prices correct at time of going to press

CAPTAIN CHRIS: should find Kempton right up his street for the King George

Stone adapts to the fences over here as well as Mon Parrain has, as he's not the biggest, but if he does he could easily develop into a contender for the big prizes.

I'm not sure that last season's staying novices were up to much. **Bostons Angel** edged out **Jessies Dream** in a bunch finish to the RSA Chase, but the best of them was surely **Time For Rupert**, who broke a blood vessel in the race so had a valid, though concerning, excuse for his disappointing effort, and **Quito De La Roque**, who skipped Cheltenham but won at Aintree and Punchestown. Time For Rupert looks the

likeliest of that lot to make the jump to the top level, but for the time being I'm happy to be against them all.

CAPTAIN CHRIS has the right sort of profile for the King George. Stamina saw him through in the Arkle and he promises to be very much suited by a step up to 3m this term. Given that he's shown a tendency to jump out to his right in the past and is three from three over obstacles at Kempton, the race couldn't be taking place at a more suitable track.

Testing ground would be against him, but it's rarely been softer than good to soft there on Boxing Day in recent years and it's hard not to see him running a big race.

Last year's Hennessy one-two **Diamond Harry** and **Burton Port**, together with 2010 RSA Chase winner **Weapon's Amnesty**, are all due back from injury this term.

There are obvious concerns with backing horses returning from season-ending injuries at this stage, but it's hard not to be excited at the return of Weapon's Amnesty in particular as he was an impressive winner of an RSA that has worked out tremendously well – Burton Port and Long Run chased him home that day. If he shows he's back to his best, he'll be a threat to all in the Gold Cup as he reserves his best for Cheltenham.

He's not as good right-handed so won't be lining up at Kempton.

Paul Nicholls has been positive about **Michel Le Bon** during the close season, but the gelding hasn't been seen out since easily taking a four-runner novice event on his chasing debut almost two years ago. He's got a long way to go to become a Gold Cup candidate, and to a lesser extent the same goes for his stablemate **Aiteen Thirtythree**, who is a galloping sort probably best suited to a flat track which means it's easy to see why he has the Hennessy Gold Cup as his big early-season target.

What A Friend ran a cracker in last year's Gold Cup to be beaten a nose for third, but

RUBI LIGHT (right): ran a fine race in the Ryanair and should improve

it's hard to imagine him going three places better.

Incredibly there's talk that **Sizing Europe** will once again be asked to try to stretch out to 3m, and possibly beyond, this season. Seemingly his owners are not happy enough to have a top-class two-miler and are desperate for a Gold Cup horse, but all the evidence to date suggests he's nowhere near good enough to compete with the best over 3m-plus.

Despite nominating the Gold Cup as **Somersby**'s aim for 2011 following a fine second in the Arkle the previous year, Henrietta Knight didn't run the gelding beyond 2m4f all season. The Gold Cup is again the stated objective, but whether he ends up there is anyone's guess, and there will doubtless be plenty of indecision along the way.

Among the other horses set to be stepped up in trip is **Poquelin**, who has been found out at Grade 1 level on more than one occasion and hasn't been obviously crying out for further.

I don't see **Noble Prince** wanting to go 3m, while the horse he beat in the Jewson, **Wishfull Thinking**, who is also a possible for the King George, looks Philip Hobbs's second string to me behind Captain Chris.

Quel Esprit and **Mikael D'Haguenet** both have serious jumping issues to overcome, **Grands Crus** will be a novice giving him

other options, while **Pandorama** needs a bog to contend in the top races.

Riverside Theatre ran well but was put in his place by Long Run in last year's King George and then missed Cheltenham due to a hairline fracture to his pelvis. He would have been a leading player in the Ryanair and that race will surely be the aim again.

RUBI LIGHT is an interesting horse. Progressive in testing ground in Ireland last season, Robbie Hennessy's gelding handed out a 10l thrashing to Roberto Goldback in the Red Mills Chase prior to travelling over to Cheltenham and surprised many with an even better display in the Ryanair.

There was concern that the ground would be too fast for him but he proved the doubters wrong with a fine third behind Albertas Run, keeping on having been headed in the manner of a horse who will benefit from a greater test of stamina as he gets older.

He's a proper galloping type and, as a six-year-old who has the scope to improve again this season, he's definitely one who could become a Gold Cup horse, especially as the staying division in Ireland looks relatively weak at the moment and offers an opportunity to climb the rankings quicker.

His unlucky fall at the last on his reappearance, when in the process of handing out a beating to Sizing Europe, confirmed that impression.

Gold Cup

Cheltenham, 17 March 2012

	Bet365	Coral	Hills	Lads	P Power	S James	Tote	VC
Long Run	9-4	9-4	**5-2**	**5-2**	2	9-4	**5-2**	9-4
Time For Rupert	14	12	**16**	14	**16**	14	14	14
Captain Chris	14	14	14	**16**	**16**	14	**16**	**16**
Master Minded	14	14	14	**16**	**16**	14	-	-
Weapon's Amnesty	16	16	**20**	16	16	16	16	14
Wishfull Thinking	16	16	14	16	-	14	-	**20**
Diamond Harry	14	**20**	16	**20**	16	16	16	**20**
Burton Port	**20**	-	**20**	**20**	16	**20**	-	16
Riverside Theatre	20	-	16	-	16	20	-	**25**
Denman	16	**20**	14	20	-	**25**	20	**25**
Quito De La Roque	16	20	**25**	**25**	16	20	20	16
Bostons Angel	**25**	**25**	**25**	**25**	**25**	**25**	-	16
Mon Parrain	25	**33**	25	-	-	**33**	25	**33**
Rubi Light	-	-	-	-	-	**50**	-	-

each-way 1/4 odds, 1-2-3
Others on request, prices correct at time of going to press

PAUL NICHOLLS: regrets not running Master Minded in the Ryanair

Ryanair Chase

BEING doubtful about **MASTER MINDED**'s ability to stretch to 3m and beyond makes him an even better bet to my mind for the Ryanair and I see no problem in backing him now even though he's already the favourite.

The dual Champion Chase winner looked back to his awesome best when stepped up to 2m4f at Aintree on his final start last season and clearly the slower pace of races over that sort of distance suits him better these days. Furthermore, Paul Nicholls has shown that he can keep getting his top horses to come back for more.

The Champion Chase is now a no-no and stepping up to the Gold Cup distance would be quite a stretch, irrespective of what happens in the King George, for which the Melling Chase has been no sort of guide in the past. In contrast, the Ryanair, in which Nicholls wishes he had run him last year, looks the ideal target.

Master Minded is one of only a few horses who regularly posts RPRs in the mid-170s, something that would make him almost impossible to beat in this race, and his record of 12 from 17 since coming from France, with genuine excuses for a number of those rare defeats, underlines his class.

Ryanair Chase

Cheltenham, 16 March 2012

	Bet365	Coral	Hills	Lads	P Power	S James	Tote	VC
Master Minded	5	-	-	-	-	6	-	5
Noble Prince	6	-	-	-	-	7	-	6
Riverside Theatre	8	-	-	-	-	7	-	8
Albertas Run	10	-	-	-	-	10	-	8
Poquelin	10	-	-	-	-	8	-	10
Wishfull Thinking	12	-	-	-	-	12	-	8
Kalahari King	12	-	-	-	-	12	-	10
Sizing Europe	14	-	-	-	-	12	-	14
Realt Dubh	-	-	-	-	-	16	-	16
Great Endeavour	20	-	-	-	-	20	-	20
Punchestowns	20	-	-	-	-	20	-	20
Royal Charm	20	-	-	-	-	16	-	20
Somersby	16	-	-	-	-	20	-	20
Tranquil Sea	25	-	-	-	-	20	-	20

each-way 1/4 odds, 1-2-3
Others on request, prices correct at time of going to press

PEDDLERS CROSS (left): a top-class hurdler and a worthy Arkle favourite

Arkle Trophy/RSA Chase

THE Arkle isn't a particularly good ante-post race because it tends to be won by the best hurdler in the race and those are the ones who dominate the market from an early stage.

That's certainly the case this year with last season's Champion Hurdle runner-up **Peddlers Cross** heading the market, and he is a worthy favourite. He was beaten by a truly outstanding horse in March, and let's not forget he is a former point-to-point winner and bred to make a chaser. That said, there's little margin in the prices at the moment.

Close up behind him in the betting are three of the first four from the Supreme Novices' Hurdle – **Al Ferof**, **Sprinter Sacre** and **Cue Card** – along with 2010 Supreme winner **Menorah**.

At a push I'd say Al Ferof is the one who is slightly underrated as he beat Sprinter Sacre and Cue Card handily enough last March and was also second to Cue Card in the Champion Bumper in 2010. He clearly relishes the hill at Cheltenham.

It's 8-1 the field for what looks at this stage like an open-looking RSA Chase, but the one horse that stands out for me is **FIRST LIEUTENANT**, who got up in the final stride to win the Neptune at last season's festival.

He had won a Grade 1 hurdle at Leopardstown over Christmas in heavy ground but, being a son of Presenting, a quicker surface was always likely to suit him better, and that, coupled with a longer trip, saw him improve and stay on just that bit too strongly for his rivals at Cheltenham.

Clearly having that tip-top course form is a huge plus and, as he's always been a chaser in the making, it's this season that

FIRST LIEUTENANT (right): preparing to power up the Cheltenham hill

he'll show what he's really capable of.

A former point-to-point winner who has already made a successful chasing debut in unsuitably soft ground at Tipperary, he is seen by his trainer Mouse Morris as a future Gold Cup horse, and Morris is well capable of judging such a horse having sent out War Of Attrition to take the race in 2006.

Arkle Trophy

Cheltenham, 14 March 2012

	Bet365	Coral	Hills	Lads	P Power	S James	Tote	VC
Peddlers Cross	**7**	6	**7**	6	6	6	-	6
Sprinter Sacre	9	**10**	**10**	8	**10**	8	-	**10**
Al Ferof	10	10	**12**	**12**	**12**	10	-	8
Menorah	-	12	12	10	-	10	-	**14**
Solwhit	-	14	-	-	-	16	-	16
Thousand Stars	16	16	-	-	-	16	-	16
First Lieutenant	-	-	-	-	12	20	-	12
Sam Winner	12	**20**	**20**	-	-	16	-	12
Poungach	-	**20**	**20**	-	-	16	-	14
Cue Card	14	**20**	**20**	20	-	**20**	-	16
Sanctuaire	-	25	-	16	-	16	-	16
Salden Licht	16	20	-	20	-	**25**	-	20
Arvika Ligeonniere	20	20	-	-	-	**25**	-	20
Get Me Out Of Here	25	-	-	-	-	**25**	-	16

each-way 1/4 odds, 1-2-3
Others on request, prices correct at time of going to press

War Of Attrition, who is also by Presenting, ran second in the shorter Supreme Novices' Hurdle as a hurdler before taking in the Arkle as a six-year-old (finished seventh) in his novice chasing season.

While in theory it's possible that First Lieutenant could go the Arkle route, I can't see him having the pace to win it and the fact he went for the 2m5f race as a hurdler, and needed every yard of the trip, suggests that the 3m race will suit him better.

The RSA Chase has had a bit of a reputation in the past for being a hard race that takes its toll on young horses, but the exploits of the likes of Long Run, Albertas Run and Denman in recent years show that it's not necessarily a race that breaks horses. Indeed, having had Weapon's Amnesty win the race in 2010 and Magnanimity go close last year, the owners clearly don't have any negative feelings towards the race. Given he's a dual Grade 1-winning hurdler I believe it's even less likely that he would be considered for the Grade 2 Jewson over 2m4f.

He will be a seven-year-old in March, which is ideal for the RSA (ten of the last 12 winners were that age), he's a previous festival winner, he loves good ground, and his style of racing and pedigree all point to him doing better both over fences at 3m, so there's plenty to like about his chances.

WEAPON'S AMNESTY: won the RSA for the same owners

RSA Chase

Cheltenham, 15 March 2012

	Bet365	Coral	Hills	Lads	P Power	S James	Tote	VC
Grands Crus	**8**	7	**8**	**8**	**8**	7	-	**8**
Bobs Worth	**10**	8	**10**	8	**10**	8	-	8
First Lieutenant	10	10	**12**	8	**12**	10	-	8
Peddlers Cross	**12**	-	-	-	**12**	12	-	10
Sam Winner	12	-	-	-	12	**16**	-	14
Rebel Rebellion	16	-	-	-	-	**20**	-	-
Silviniaco Conti	16	**20**	**20**	**20**	**20**	16	-	14
Sir Des Champs	**20**	**20**	**20**	-	16	**20**	-	**20**
Mossley	16	14	**25**	20	20	20	-	14
Chablais	-	-	**25**	20	-	**25**	-	-
Hidden Cyclone	**25**	**25**	**25**	16	16	20	-	**25**
Back In Focus	**25**	**25**	**25**	-	**25**	**25**	-	**25**
Champion Court	20	20	**33**	-	20	20	-	20
Sonofvic	**33**	**33**	-	-	-	20	-	**33**

each-way 1/4 odds, 1-2-3
Others on request, prices correct at time of going to press

Champion Chase

THERE'S a vulnerable look to the head of the Champion Chase market this year. Defending champion **Sizing Europe** will be a ten-year-old come March and there's again talk of him being stepped up in distance this year, while **Big Zeb** will be 11 this time around.

Finian's Rainbow is no spring chicken either, despite this upcoming season being his first out of novice company. He didn't get home in the Neptune as a hurdler and failed to hold off Captain Chris in the Arkle having travelled strongly throughout – he's all speed and might just be more effective on a flat track.

Captain Chris and **Wishfull Thinking** are apparently being aimed at the King George, but both will be deserving of respect if dropped to 2m afterwards for the Champion

Chase. The superb record of Arkle winners in the following year's Champion Chase is a big positive in Captain Chris's favour.

We already know that **Master Minded** is going to be running over 2m4f-plus this season, while **Noble Prince**, **Mon Parrain** and **Flat Out** are others we can expect to be doing their racing beyond 2m.

Realt Dubh doesn't look quite quick enough to win a Grade 1 over 2m on good ground, and a lot of the rest of those listed in the ante-post market are has-beens and never-will-bes.

The exception could be **GHIZAO**, who was let down by his jumping at Cheltenham and Aintree last term. He would have probably beaten Finian's Rainbow at Aintree but for a blunder two out, while in the Arkle a bad mistake at the top of the hill ended his chance.

GHIZAO: still seen as a top prospect over 2m by the champion trainer

PAST IT? Last year's one-two Sizing Europe (right) and Big Zeb are getting on

Clearly some work needs to be done, but his form from earlier in the campaign when defeating Captain Chris twice, including at Newbury when giving him 10lb, reads well. Nicholls has said that he sees the Haldon Gold Cup and Tingle Creek as early-season targets, so he clearly still rates him

a top 2m prospect, and he looks a big price at 25-1 for the Champion Chase.

Incidentally, don't be surprised if one of the top novices takes his chance in this race rather than the Arkle, as right now the novice event looks like being the more classy and competitive of the two.

Champion Chase

Cheltenham, 15 March 2012

	Bet365	Coral	Hills	Lads	P Power	S James	Tote	VC
Sizing Europe	9-2	4	4	4	4	4	5	5
Big Zeb	11-2	6	6	6	6	8	13-2	5
Finians Rainbow	8	8	8	10	8	8	8	8
Captain Chris	8	8	10	8	12	9	9	8
Noble Prince	-	14	-	-	-	14	-	12
Master Minded	10	10	10	-	8	16	10	16
Realt Dubh	16	16	20	16	-	20	16	16
Medermit	16	14	14	-	-	25	-	16
Ghizao	14	25	20	-	14	20	20	16
Captain Cee Bee	12	20	16	20	-	33	25	20
Crack Away Jack	-	-	-	25	-	33	-	33
Golden Silver	16	-	20	-	-	40	33	25
Tataniano	-	-	40	-	-	40	-	25
Woolcombe Folly	25	-	25	-	-	50	-	33

each-way 1/4 odds, 1-2-3
Others on request, prices correct at time of going to press

Champion Hurdle/World Hurdle

FOR me the fruitless enterprise of trying to get **Big Buck's** beaten in the World Hurdle is over. Barring an injury he'll win again, and he's rightly already odds-on to do so.

I also think **Hurricane Fly** is going to be very difficult to depose in the Champion Hurdle. He beat a really good horse in Peddlers Cross last year, and he dotted up at Punchestown afterwards. He seems to be improving, which is scary for the opposition as his record already stands at 11 wins from 13 starts over timber, including nine Grade 1 wins.

He's unbackable at 7-4 ante-post, but he's going to take a lot of beating assuming he enjoys a trouble-free build-up as he looks different gravy at the moment.

Perhaps **Oscar Whisky** has the best chance of reversing form with Hurricane Fly as he's still relatively inexperienced and open to improvement, but I wouldn't back him to do so and there's a chance he might step up in trip anyway.

It's hard to see another horse who raced in last year's Champion troubling Willie Mullins' stable star, while time has shown that **Binocular** didn't beat a great deal in the previous year's renewal and Triumph Hurdle horses tend to struggle the following season, so that puts me off **Zarkandar** and **Grandouet**.

The two novices who look most likely to make the leap to the big time are **Oscars Well** and **Spirit Son**.

Oscars Well tanked along in the Neptune, looking for all the world as though he'd rather be going 2m at a stronger pace rather than dawdling along over 2m5f, and he was still in with every chance when crashing out at the final flight. Now proven on good ground as well as the mud he was competing in back in Ireland, he could well be suited by the demands of a Champion Hurdle.

That said, Spirit Son's form reads the better of the two. Having finished second in the Supreme, he bolted up at Aintree and, having had only five career starts, it will be a surprise if we have already seen the best of him.

His trainer Nicky Henderson holds him in the highest regard, expects plenty of improvement and considers him Champion Hurdle material, and with Binocular and Oscar Whisky in the yard he's well placed to judge. As far as I can see he's the only possible play against the favourite at the moment.

Champion Hurdle

Cheltenham, 14 March 2012

	Bet365	Coral	Hills	Lads	P Power	S James	Tote	VC
Hurricane Fly	13-8	7-4	13-8	7-4	7-4	13-8	7-4	6-4
Spirit Son	10	8	10	10	10	10	10	8
Zarkandar	10	12	10	10	12	12	12	10
Peddlers Cross	10	8	7	-	10	12	10	10
Binocular	14	12	12	10	12	12	10	14
Oscar Whisky	14	16	16	14	16	16	14	14
Oscars Well	20	20	16	16	16	20	20	16
Grandouet	20	16	20	20	20	20	16	16
Al Ferof	14	10	-	-	25	25	10	14
Menorah	14	20	16	-	25	25	16	16
Sprinter Sacre	20	-	-	-	25	33	20	20
Topolski	33	25	-	33	25	25	-	33
Thousand Stars	25	-	33	-	-	25	14	33
Unaccompanied	33	-	33	-	25	33	-	33

each-way 1/4 odds, 1-2-3
Others on request, prices correct at time of going to press

SPIRIT SON: looks the only threat to Hurricane Fly at this stage

Recommended Bets

King George
2pts Mon Parrain 25-1
(generally)
1pt Captain Chris 9-1
(Paddy Power)

Champion Hurdle
1pt e-w Spirit Son 10-1
(generally)

Champion Chase
1pt Ghizao 25-1
(Coral)

RSA Chase
1pt First Lieutenant 12-1
(Hills, Paddy Power)

Ryanair Chase
2pts Master Minded 6-1
(Stan James)

Gold Cup
2pts Mon Parrain 33-1
(generally)
1pt Rubi Light 50-1
(Stan James)

World Hurdle

Cheltenham, 16 March 2012

	Bet365	Coral	Hills	Lads	P Power	S James	Tote	VC
Big Buck's	4-6	4-6	**4-5**	**4-5**	**4-5**	8-11	**4-5**	4-6
Grands Crus	8	-	11-2	10	9	8	7	7
Oscar Whisky	7	6	10	6	10	7	8	8
Thousand Stars	7	10	10	8	8	8	8	10
Oscars Well	14	-	-	-	-	14	-	14
Mourad	14	12	14	14	12	14	14	14
Peddlers Cross	16	-	-	-	-	16	-	16
Bobs Worth	10	-	10	12	12	20	10	10
Back In Focus	25	-	20	-	-	25	-	20
Champion Court	25	-	20	-	-	25	-	25
Solwhit	16	-	16	-	-	33	25	25
Cue Card	-	-	-	-	20	33	-	-
First Lieutenant	33	-	-	-	-	33	25	20
Cross Kennon	33	33	-	-	-	33	-	33

each-way 1/4 odds, 1-2-3
Others on request, prices correct at time of going to press

Ireland by Jerry M

T WAS a good Ol Cheltenham Festival for the Irish, with the pinnacle of course being the Champion Hurdle, brought back to the Emerald Isle after a four-year break by **Hurricane Fly**.

The seven-year-old proved invincible throughout the season, winning all five of his races and rarely looking like being beaten. He will be hard to dislodge again this season.

Another horse to run well on the first day of the festival, without quite winning, was *NOEL MEADE*'s **Realt Dubh**, who finished third in the Arkle behind Captain Chris.

He had a quite outstanding novice season, winning three times at Grade 1 level and only narrowly losing out to his nemesis Captain Chris in the big 2m novice chase at the Punchestown Festival.

That came over a bare 2m, and judged on that and his Arkle effort, where he stayed on without ever looking like winning, it looks as though longer trips will suit this season.

The obvious race for him would be the Ryanair Chase over 2m5f, and as there seems no good reason why he shouldn't improve again as a second-season chaser, he could well be involved. Quotes of around 16-1 for that race currently look big.

In terms of strength in depth, Meade's team was a little bit down on where it has been in previous years, but that's not something you could level at *JESSICA HARRINGTON*, who continues to go from strength to strength.

REALT DUBH: a stellar novice chasing campaign bodes well for this season

DISASTER: Oscars Well (second left) sprawls at the final hurdle, ruining his chance

She got on the scoresheet at Cheltenham courtesy of Bostons Angel, and was unlucky not to have a brace with **Oscars Well**.

He was going as well as anything in the Neptune Investements before sprawling on landing having jumped the last.

That handed victory to Mouse Morris' First Lieutenant, with Oscars Well trailing home in sixth.

Prior to his Cheltenham near miss, the six-year-old had looked extremely impressive when routing Grade 1 winners Zaidpour and Shot From The Hip by a wide margin.

It looks like he will stay over hurdles for the time being, and while he does have Hurricane Fly to contend with in that discipline, races like the Hatton's Grace at Fairyhouse could be made for him.

COLM MURPHY trained one of the success stories of last season in **Quito De La Roque**, who proved to be more than just a mudlark.

His ability to handle deep conditions will always help him during the winter, but his wins in the spring at Aintree and Punchestown proved that he has definite class to go with his staying ability.

His only defeat of the season came at the hands of Bostons Angel at Leopardstown's Christmas meeting, where he got going a fraction too late and was beaten three-quarters of a length.

Things will inevitably be tougher for him this season as he is out of novice company, and rated 159, meaning he will have to take on the big boys.

However, races such as the Lexus Chase and the Hennessy Gold Cup in February fall well within his compass and he should be competitive in those.

Kempes won the Hennessy last season, but he's not the most consistent of horses and there's room for a top Irish stayer to come through, particularly as Joncol had a disappointing campaign.

WILLIE MULLINS had a good Cheltenham, and he has a prime candidate for the opening race of the 2012 festival in **Lovethehigherlaw**, who is already 12-1 in a place for the

TWO GOOD HORSES: Lovethehigherlaw (left) pips Waaheb at Punchestown

Supreme Novices.

He didn't go for the Champion Bumper last season, with Mullins electing to keep him fresh for Punchestown, and it worked a treat.

In what was one of the race of the festival, he got the better of a protracted duel with Waaheb, with a short head the winning margin.

This season he will go novice hurdling, and although he ought to stay further than 2m, it would be no surprise to see him kept to the minimum trip, as he is related on the dam's side to Champion hurdlers Morley Street and Granville Again.

He could go right to the top, and if he wins his first couple of novices this side of Christmas don't expect that 12-1 to last.

One of Mullins' more unexpected triumphs at Cheltenham was **Sir Des Champs**, who came from a mile back to win the Martin Pipe Conditionals Hurdle under Emmet Mullins.

To say it was an unlikely success does not really do it justice, as he well behind running down the hill. Turning in though, he picked up really strongly and always looked

like getting there once jumping the last.

He's only raced three times over hurdles, so whether he goes chasing just yet is open to question.

However, whichever discipline he tackles this season, keep him on your side.

The same goes for **Arvika Ligeonniere**, who looks an Arkle prospect if all goes well with him.

He was well touted for the race early last season, but he picked up a slight niggle and Mullins decided to give him the season off.

Apparently it was nothing too serious, and Mullins' ample patience could now be rewarded.

Invincible Irish

Lovethehigherlaw
Oscars Well
Realt Dubh

Berkshire by Downsman

NICKY HENDERSON may not have been able to wrest the trainers title from Paul Nicholls' grasp in April, but there were plenty of other objectives realised, including, of course, his first ever Cheltenham Gold Cup.

There was many an eyebrow raised when the six-year-old **Long Run** was well and truly turned over in the Paddy Power Gold Cup on his reappearance.

There were excuses aplenty afterwards, including trip, jockey and his jumping to name but three.

However, there were just some suspicions around that time that a number of the team were not performing as connections would wish, and with the benefit of hindsight, this horse may have been one of them.

It was not really until around December that the Henderson team really hit their straps and by this time Nicholls had opened up a handy advantage at the top of the table.

The early Arctic blast then intervened, frustrating the Seven Barrows supporters still further, but Long Run's impressive win against an admittedly below par Kauto Star in the revamped King George in January not only signalled he would be a major player at Cheltenham come March but that the the stable were back operating at near full capacity.

Despite talk of a trip to France after his brilliant win at Cheltenham, Long Run was retired for the season and enjoyed a break at his owner Robert Waley-Cohen's home in the Cotswolds.

He returned in late July looking big and well, and it would appear likely that the Betfair Chase at Haydock will be his warm-up for a King George repeat bid.

While everything went well with Long Run, little went right for **Binocular**, Henderson's 2010 Champion Hurdle winner.

His woes have been well documented, and his overall form leaves him a few pounds light of the brilliant Hurricane Fly, the reigning title holder. However, on his day he is still a very good horse.

Long Run looks the one to beat in the Gold Cup once again, but Henderson has one or two who might give him a serious challenge, either at Prestbury or in the King George.

Riverside Theatre, who did not stop improving last season and finished second in the Kempton showpiece, is back in good order after having had to miss the festival, while the return of **Burton Port** is also eagerly anticipated.

A smart staying novice two seasons ago, he ran a blinder under a big weight in the Hennessy Gold Cup, but returned home with leg problems. His jumping was some way below what it had been during his first season – he may have been feeling the leg injury – but if he comes back as good as ever, a big race must come his way.

Arguably the smartest of a vintage clutch of novice chasers last season was **Finian's Rainbow** and he ended the season on a high with his game win at Aintree, which was no more than he deserved after his second in the Arkle at Cheltenham.

Some at Seven Barrows believe he may prove better over a distance of ground as he gets older, but 2m seems the preferred option for his second season with the Queen Mother as the target. He will have to improve somewhat to challenge the very best however.

Henderson seems well looked after in the second-season chaser department with **Quantitativeeasing**, **Mr Gardner**, **Master Of The Hall** and the game Punchestown Festival winner **Shakalakaboomboom** all sure to pay their way in upper-tier handicaps.

Spirit Son's first season over hurdles followed a similar path to Finian's Rainbow's over fences in that he just missed out at Cheltenham but won at Aintree.

Just run out of it on the run-in by Al Ferof in the Supreme Novices, he turned in a most impressive display at Aintree and

MINELLA CLASS: last season's Tolworth winner is likely to go chasing

connections will certainly have one eye on the Champion Hurdle when he launches into his second season.

He possesses impressive speed and, with few miles on the clock, has a healthy dose of improvement in him.

Strength in the novice hurdling division is a given for Henderson followers as a rule and 2010-11 was no exception

Indeed, the stable were split between **Sprinter Sacre** and Spirit Son in the Supreme at Cheltenham, and Sprinter Sacre, the less battle-hardened of the two also ran a terrific race to finish third after looking the likely winner at the last.

He pulled too hard for his own good in that race, but will have grown up a lot as a result.

He has also undergone surgery to aid his wind, and if he can run that well with an infirmity, albeit slight, he looks a most exciting prospect for fences.

Others likely to take up the chasing option for the first time include the imposing Tolworth Hurdle winner **Minella Class**.

Great things were predicted for this Irish bumper winner last autumn and he did not

let his trainer down. Predictably, the same applies for fences, a job for which he is tailor-made.

There is a wealth of potential novice chase talent in **Master Fiddle**, **Gibb River**, **Prince Of Pirates**, **Owen Glendower** (a good ground horse) and the EBF Final winner **Skint** to name but a few.

But the one to look forward to most has to be the Albert Bartlett winner **Bobs Worth**. He did not stop improving all season and, after much debate within Seven Barrows and amongst the owners, he swerved the Neptune Investments at Cheltenham in favour of the longer race and won it in great style.

Bred by his jockey Barry Geraghty, he is ultra tough with stamina and a turn of foot, and, provided he jumps he must take high rank among the staying novice chasers.

Binocular apart, **Oscar Whisky** was the top hurdler in the yard and he did really well to end a profitable campaign with a third in the Champion Hurdle and a win in the Aintree Hurdle on Grand National day.

Chasing may be his game one day, but it could be that he will tackle Big Buck's and company in staying hurdles this season.

Grandouet was another to come to the fore at the Punchestown Festival after a game effort in the Triumph and a heavy fall at Aintree when he was brought down travelling well. He looks open to plenty of improvement and it will be interesting to see what will be his best trip.

Henderson makes hay in the races restricted to mares and one to follow here is **Whoops A Daisy**, who carries the colours of the Let's Live Racing Syndicate. She could be in action fairly early in the autumn with a Listed event at Wetherby a possible target.

The same partnership will be active with **Arctic Actress** in mares only novice hurdles, but my pick for stardom in this department is **Darlan**, a lovely son Milan. Heavily backed on his debut in the spring, he always looked the winner under Andrew Tinkler and strode clear to win by a very wide margin.

Ericht showed plenty of ability and landed an impressive win at Huntingdon. He failed to cut much ice in the Festival Bumper, but is much better than that performance might suggest.

Mono Man is another favourite of mine, and was unbeaten after two outings.

Hit The Headlines, **Lets Get Serious** are two more bumper winners to conjure with, but just preferred on my list is **Fourth Estate**, another impressive winner, this time at Ayr's Scottish Grand National meeting.

ALAN KING was in something of a rebuild mode after a relatively low-key, by his own high standards, season in 2009-10, and it was good to see him have a Cheltenham Festival winner with Bensalem.

Unforunately Bensalem is out for the season, but **Medermit**, his star novice chaser, is very much back for his second term over fences. Although there were a few teething problems during his rookie campaign, he won his Grade 1 at Sandown and he was placed at both the Cheltenham and Aintree Festivals.

King is keen to tackle his old adversary Captain Chris in the Haldon Gold Cup at Exeter in November and then take the conditions-race route with the Peterborough Chase a possible target. It will be interesting to see if he gets 3m if tried at some future date.

West End Rocker, King's smart staying chaser, will be hunting big races again with the Becher Chase at Aintree a major autumn objective.

Expect more from **Stoney's Treasure** as well. Very much a talking horse in the first half of last season, he got his act together in the late winter, and looks open to plenty of improvement.

Torphichen, a winner of three races over fences for Eddie O'Grady last season, has been bought by Million In Mind for 2m handicaps, and there will be plenty of interest when the giant **Araldur** returns to fences after a consistent season over timber last term.

Mille Chief was a star hurdler at Barbury

MILLE CHIEF: stays hurdling for now

Castle last season, and he is likely to remain over the smaller obstacles, as will two smart juveniles, **Kumbeshwar** and **Dhaafer**.

King should be particularly strong in the novices chase department, with another classy hurdler from last term **Walkon**, leading the pack.

Salden Licht, a smart performer on the Flat and in handicap hurdles, is another to get excited about, as is **Habbie Simpson**, a very consistent staying novice hurdler last season.

Iolith, **Invictus**, **Trenchant** and **Jetnova**, who won three of his six starts over hurdles last season and beat the smart Skint at Plumpton, should do well over middle and staying distances.

Pride In Battle won two novices hurdles at Newbury during his first season and he could be seen over fences, but not before King tries to exploit his handicap mark over timber. A similar plan could be put on the agenda for the four year old **Smad Place**.

Of the novice hurdlers, pride of place must go to **Montbazon**. It is a fairly safe bet that this son of Alberto Giacometti will be on many a list to follow following his exploits in bumpers last term. He won the valuable DBS bumper at Doncaster and was then second in the big Aintree bumper. He has done well and might run in one more bumper before going hurdling.

Valdez might do the same, but **Medinas** will go straight novice hurdling as will Bygones In Brid another good bumper horse last term.

King, like Henderson, does well in mares' events, and both **Tante Sissi** and **Golden Firebird** should win their share of races restricted to the fairer sex. The latter may try for a listed bumper first however.

Volcan Surprise and **Titeuf De Tierce** are two new names to conjure with from France for hurdles, while **Quotica De Poyans** and **Hold On Julio** will graduate from the Irish point to point arena and will go handicap chasing. Another winning pointer **Gods My Judge** should be noted for bumpers.

OLIVER SHERWOOD has a clutch of promising youngsters at Rhonehurst and **Fair Bramble** is one sure to make his mark in novice hurdles according to his trainer.

A three-parts brother to the very useful

Wogan, he finished third on his only outing last season in a bumper, and has thrived during the summer.

Knockalongi represented Sherwood in the Festival Bumper, but it all proved too much for him on the day.

However, he had won well on his previous start at Doncaster and his trainer describes him as a really nice sort.

Majorica King finished second on his debut to the classy Ericht at Huntingdon and then tackled a couple a good class events.

He should win his maiden hurdle, while **Milgen Bay** should land an overdue first success, whether it be over hurdles or fences. He was a model of consistency last season over the smaller obstacles, but should do better once chasing.

Sherwood's near neighbour *CHARLIE MANN* endured something of a nightmare start to the season after losing five or six of his very best horses towards the end of the 2009-10 campaign.

However, things picked up in the spring and he manged to win a big prize with **Fine Parchment** at Newbury in March. Mann believes he has another big one in him this term.

The Whitcoombe trainer firmly believes in investing and he has a couple promising ex-Irish pointers in the four-year-old **Shocking Times** and the year older **Low Gale**. Both may tackle hurdles this season.

Marengo Bay showed plenty of ability in a light season last term and he could develop into a good novice chaser, a remark which also applies to **Sum Laff**, a winner at Fontwell last season.

Airmen's Friend and **Head-Hunted** are two more names to conjure with over hurdles, and a note must be made of the German import **Next Hight**. He ran in the 2010 German Derby and was placed at Group 2 level on the Flat.

Berkshire's best

Darlan
Salden Licht
Spirit Son

The West by Hastings

L AST season *PAUL NICHOLLS* was crowned champion jumps trainer for the sixth year in a row, amassing over £2.4 million total prize-money in Britain alone. Established stars Big Buck's, Master Minded, Kauto Star and Denman will once again go for glory at the highest level, but it's the considerable new blood being injected into the all-conquering Manor Farm Stables that will be key in Nicholls' bid to make it a magnificent seven.

Pick of the hurdlers is **Zarkandar**, who stepped up on some useful Flat form in France when belying a lack of hurdling experience to make a winning British debut in the Grade 2 Adonis at Kempton.

Next time out he hurdled and travelled with greater fluency when finishing clear in the Triumph Hurdle at Cheltenham, and he showed no ill effects from those heroics when

signing off with another Grade 1 win at Aintree. He's since had a breathing operation and, with top-flight experience under his belt, it's frightening to think what's in store for this second season. He could well be the one to dethrone the current champion hurdler Hurricane Fly come March.

Al Ferof is also a must for any ten to follow list. Having chased home Cue Card in the Champion Bumper at Cheltenham, big things were expected of him as a hurdler last winter and, despite a shaky start, he lived up to expectations. He barely left second gear when enjoying confidence-building wins over timber at Taunton and Newbury, and proved himself on the bigger stage when outgunning Spirit Son in the Supreme on a return to Prestbury Park in March. The lightly raced six-year-old is being aimed at the Arkle Trophy and has the world at his feet.

ZARKANDAR: could be the one to dethrone Hurricane Fly at Cheltenham

What A Friend could emerge from the shadow of Nicholls' other chasing stars this winter. Part-owned by Sir Alex Ferguson, he first shaped as a potential champion when netting back-to-back Grade 1 chases two seasons ago. The highlight of a light campaign last winter was a fast-finishing fourth in the Gold Cup at Cheltenham. When last seen he wasn't given a hard time by Daryl Jacob once all chance had gone in the Grand National at Aintree, an effort best overlooked. At just eight years of age, he still has plenty to offer the jumping game.

There's a big handicap chase to be won with **Rebel Du Maquis**, who was very useful as a hurdler and last season raised the bar to win three as a novice chaser. He left the handicapper red-faced when routing the opposition at Stratford in May and acquitted himself well enough when ninth of 22 off a career-high rating in an ambitious tilt at the Galway Plate in July. He remains a decent prospect for the winter ahead.

Nicholls' **Silviniaco Conti** was hailed as a potential superstar after streaking clear of Captain Chris, who has subsequently taken all before him over fences, in the Grade 2 Persian War at Chepstow. He then treated subsequent winner Karabak with similar contempt in the same grade at Ascot.

Although the bubble was somewhat deflated after finishing only third in the International at Cheltenham and fourth in the Kingwell at Wincanton, he remains a contender for the top. He could well come into his own once upped in trip and, with chasing a viable option this season, plans remain fluid.

Another smart hurdler expected to make a big impact as a chaser in the coming months is **Sanctuaire**. The French import quickly climbed the rank as a novice hurdler, peaking with an impressive display in the 2010 Fred Winter. In April he showed the benefit of a wind operation when bouncing back with a game win off 144 in the Scottish Champion Hurdle. He can refuse to settle but possesses the talent to go far over birch.

Leading owner Graham Wylie has strengthened the squad with the likes of **Quwetwo**, who claimed the scalp of Zaynar when notching a third win as a hurdler at Kelso in February. He's built like a chaser and it shouldn't be long before he's making waves over the larger obstacles.

Wylie's **Grandioso** can thrive as a hurdler for Nicholls. He posted an impressive 5l win on his debut for Howard Johnson at Musselburgh in February. Next time out he still held every chance with 2f to go only to fade into a creditable ninth of 20 in a Grade 2

QUWETWO: a newcomer to the Ditcheat team from Howard Johnson's yard

GREAT ENDEAVOUR (right): went close in the December Gold Cup last year

bumper at Aintree's Grand National meeting. He's out of a sister to a winning hurdler and should make a seamless transition to timber.

French import **Kauto Stone** has joined his illustrious half-brother Kauto Star at Ditcheat and rates an exceptional prospect. He picked up a Grade 2 as a hurdler in France but it's his subsequent exploits over fences that mark him out. Last November he allowed jockey Christophe Pieux the luxury of easing down when running away with France's top four-year-old chase at Auteuil.

Exciting recruit **Dualla Lord** barely broke sweat when racking up a sequence of wins as a hugely progressive pointer. He put in a typically fluent round when finishing in splendid isolation to make it four wins from as many starts for Richard Barber in a mixed Open at Cotley in April. Expect similar fireworks under rules for Nicholls.

Final Gift is another to join the master of Ditcheat after impressing between the flags in Ireland. He stepped up on a promising debut second to forge clear in a geldings' maiden at Dromahane in April for trainer John Costello. He's in very capable hands on this eagerly awaited switch to rules.

DAVID PIPE can enjoy another fruitful campaign from **Grands Crus**, who made huge strides as a hurdler last winter. He showed an awesome cruising speed before leaving his rivals for dead when completing a hat-trick in the Cleeve Hurdle at Cheltenham. More recently there was no disgrace in chasing home the mighty Big Buck's at both Cheltenham and Aintree. Last autumn he coped well with 'fixed brush' hurdles at Haydock and the plan is to go chasing in November.

Classy chaser **Great Endeavour** can pick up a few big handicap prizes this winter. He burst on to the scene with a courageous win in the Plate at the 2010 Cheltenham Festival and was in the process of running a blinder off a career-high mark of 148 there in March only to crash out at the second-last fence.

Pipe can also expect big things from the five-year-old **Dynaste**, who dug deep to make all off a mark of 130 over hurdles at Taunton in December. There's time on his side and he should reach greater heights once switched to fences. The talented grey is definitely one to follow closely.

The same goes for a slightly darker horse in **Swing Bowler**, who made short work of brushing aside a small turnout for a Wincanton bumper in May.

PHILIP HOBBS suffered a blow with the news that his Champion Bumper winner Cheltenian is likely to miss the season.

However, novice chasers **Captain Chris**

DESTROYER DEPLOYED: staying on for second behind Cheltenian

and **Wishfull Thinking** served up many highlights for the Withycombe trainer last winter and both can continue to play starring roles. Captain Chris shrugged off the smart Finian's Rainbow in the Arkle at Cheltenham and proved it was no fluke by following up in the Grade 1 Ryanair Chase at Punchestown. Wishfull Thinking jumped like a buck when leaving the likes of Medermit standing at Aintree and was last seen making a mockery of a rating as high as 159 at Punchestown.

Shrewd Welshman *TIM VAUGHAN* can build upon the solid platform of a tremendous summer campaign, with Grade 1 winners **Spirit Of Adjisa** and **Saint Are** leading the charge.

Spirit Of Adjisa added courage to his notable list of qualities when plundering a big prize at Punchestown in May. He remains relatively lightly raced in this sphere and, providing the subsequent wind operation has the desired effect, he can continue to put Vaughan on the map.

As a hurdler, Saint Are's crowning glory came when surging clear of Cantlow and Sparky May in the 3m110yds Sefton Hurdle at Aintree in April. He's taken to fences like a dream in schooling sessions at his home in the Vale of Glamorgan and a fruitful novice chase campaign beckons.

Vaughan can also plunder big races with **Destroyer Deployed**, who looked the part when winning bumpers at Towcester and Fontwell in February. However, it wasn't until he was really tested that the sparks flew, finishing a cracking second to Cheltenian at Cheltenham. He can prove very hard to beat as a novice hurdler.

JONJO O'NEILL also has an unmissable hurdler in **Ballyclough**, who left behind some well-touted rivals when scoring on his only bumper sighting at Haydock in March. The brother to classy jumper Crocodile Rock could rack up plenty of wins as a novice.

Siberian Tiger could prove a real money-spinner for Evan Williams. He was a high-class performer on the Flat and as a hurdler, and over the summer he showed versatility when tasting success as a novice chaser at Haydock and Ffos Las. He should continue to do well over fences.

Best of the West

Al Ferof
Saint Are
Zarkandar

The North
by Borderer

The northern jumping scene was dealt a severe blow in August with the BHA banning Howard Johnson for four years. The hugely successful County Durham-based trainer, who was responsible for seven Cheltenham Festival winners, immediately announced his retirement.

Chief patron Graham Wylie has split his string between the yards of Paul Nicholls and Willie Mullins while sending several others to the sales, leaving a significant void in our region.

DONALD MCCAIN, however, continues to go from strength to strength and he enjoyed his greatest moment at Aintree in April when sending out **Ballabriggs** to win the Grand National under a terrific ride from Jason Maguire.

The ten-year-old won the world's greatest race off a mark of 150 and he will once again be targeted at the race next spring.

A race like the Betfair Chase at Haydock in November is a possible starting point for the Trevor Hemmings-owned gelding.

The Arkle Trophy promises to be a fantastic affair in March, provided the likes of Menorah, Solwhit and Sprinter Sacre line up. The one they will all have to beat, though, is **Peddlers Cross**.

Rated 170 over timber, the former Irish pointer won the Fighting Fifth Hurdle at Newbury before finishing an excellent second in the Champion Hurdle behind the mighty Hurricane Fly.

Only beaten a length and a quarter, he was over the top by the time he went to Aintree. He's likely to make his chasing debut at Bangor and is a most exciting prospect.

Peddlers Cross is not the only novice chaser to follow from the Cheshire-based operation. **Tornado Bob** was a dual winner over hurdles last term and was unlucky not to make it three at Ascot.

Previously trained in Ireland, he will go straight over the larger obstacles and threatens to improve again when tackling 3m for the first time.

While Ballabriggs will undoubtedly be the stable's number one contender for the National again, don't be surprised if the lightly raced **Glenwood Knight** emerges as a contender.

His form figures are hardly inspiring over fences, but he is a very talented performer who won at Uttoxeter in decisive fashion and certainly wasn't done with when crashing out behind Aiteen Thirtythree at Newbury last time. The eight-year-old could be well treated off his mark of 135.

Another emerging force among the northern ranks is *LUCINDA RUSSELL*. The Kinross-based trainer had her best ever season last winter with 41 winners.

BALLABRIGGS: back to Aintree again

WHO'D HAVE THOUGHT IT? Poker De Sivola, in fourth place, wins the Bet365

Stable star **Silver By Nature** flew the flag once again, winning the Haydock Grand National Trial for a second successive year.

The grey found the conditions too lively in the National itself and will be steered clear of Merseyside next spring.

He will, however, continue to be a force in the leading staying handicaps provided there is soft or heavy in the going description.

Russell has two interesting prospects for novice chases, namely **Blenheim Brook** and **Bold Sir Brian**.

The former won three times over hurdles and reached a rating of 137. Being an ex-Irish pointer, he promises to be even better once sent chasing and has won over trips ranging from 2m to 3m.

The latter won the Grade 2 novice hurdle at Kelso in March beating the likes of Desert Cry. Although well beaten at Aintree next time, he has very little mileage on the

clock and his whole career has been geared towards fences. It is time for him to start showing what he is capable of.

Rarely does a Cheltenham Festival go by without *FERDY MURPHY* appearing on the roll of honour.

The West Witton trainer was at it again in March with **Divers** providing him with his eighth Festival success.

A two and three-quarter length winner of the Centenary Novice Chase off a mark of 132, he starts his second season over fences off a 7lb higher rating.

Not surprisingly, his first main target is the Paddy Power Gold Cup in November over the same course and distance. Expect him to take in the Colin Parker Memorial Chase at Carlisle towards the end of October en route. Murphy did the same with L'Antartique in 2007.

Poker De Sivola provided the Irishman with more big race success during the spring when taking the Bet365 Gold Cup under Timmy Murphy.

A former Festival winner himself, the eight-year-old is rated 141 and his whole season will be geared towards the Grand National.

Kalahari King ran another magnificent race in the Ryanair Chase when only finding Albertas Run a length too good.

Pulled up at Aintree next time, he appears to be at his best over 2m4f on decent ground, but could be tried over further this term. Indeed, it will be interesting to see if he is given an entry in the King George.

Langholm-based *JAMES EWART* continues to make an impression and his seasonal tallies in recent seasons have been 12, 14 and 16.

The former assistant to Guillaume Macaire looks particularly strong in the novice chase department this term.

Vosges was twice a winner at Musselburgh including the Scottish Triumph Hurdle and is a fine jumper. Despite only being a four-year-old, he goes over fences and could take advantage of his age allowance.

Former pointer **Aikman** also developed into a decent novice hurdler, earning an official rating of 135.

The Rudimentary gelding enjoyed his finest hour to date in the Sidney Banks Memorial Novice Hurdle at Huntingdon when lowering the colours of Grade 1 winner Minella Class.

A creditable sixth and seventh at Cheltenham and Aintree respectively, he ought to win plenty of races in the north before venturing south later in the campaign.

Premier Grand Cru is another potential chaser for this season having won over hurdles at Aintree during the spring.

AIKMAN: good novice last season who lowered the colours of Minella Class

BENNY BE GOOD (left): a good prospect for the Keith Reveley team

A winner over timber at Pau in France before arriving in the Borders, he has the make and shape of a chaser and was rated 113 over hurdles. There is every chance we still haven't seen the best of him.

KEITH REVELEY will be delighted to have stable star **Tazbar** back in training.

The nine-year-old, who is rated 154 over fences, missed the whole of last term due to a leg problem.

Successful in three of his four starts, his only defeat since sent chasing came at the hands of Long Run in the Grade 1 Feltham Novice Chase in December 2009 before he went on to beat Neil Mulholland's Midnight Chase by 14l next time at Huntingdon. A high-class performer, let's hope he can return to something like his best.

Stablemate **Benny Be Good** won three times last winter and developed into an above average novice chaser, collecting all three victories at Sedgefield.

It won't be easy off his mark of 143 but he looks capable of winning a good pot this season. If he stays 3m, he could be ideal for something like the Skybet Chase at Doncaster towards the end of January.

Kings Grey is another Reveley runner to keep close tabs on this season. The grey never quite lived up to expectations over hurdles being placed on three occasions.

However, the Huntingdon bumper winner has always been viewed as a chaser in the making and is fully expected to recoup those losses with interest over fences.

Northern rocks

Divers
Peddlers Cross
Vosges

The South by Southerner

SUCCESSFULLY laying a horse out to win on a particular day takes a great deal of planning and, when the horse in question is a moderate handicap chaser, it also takes a great deal of skill.

NICK GIFFORD not only achieved this feat but he did it in the glare of worldwide publicity when **Royal Wedding** landed the 2m6f Grabbie's Alcoholic Ginger Beer Handicap Chase at Fontwell in April on the day that Prince William and Kate Middleton tied the knot in Westminster Abbey.

Royal Wedding can only be described as a fun horse for the gaff tracks but he got the job done on the day that mattered and his place in history is secure.

Tullamore Dew was Gifford's top chaser last season. The nine-year-old won a brace of novice chases at Plumpton and signed off his campaign with a good third in the 2m4f110yds Centenary Novices Handicap Chase at the Cheltenham Festival in March.

Gifford will be looking for an opportunity to take Tullamore Dew back to Prestbury Park this winter as the gelding also finished second to Spirit River in the 2010 Coral Cup on his only other visit to the Cotswold track.

Dee Ee Williams is probably the most talented horse at Findon, but the giant gelding is a law unto himself these days and frequently refuses to show his best ability.

That said, he usually goes well fresh and likes good ground, so first time out on decent going could be the time to chance supporting him.

Alderluck is another of Gifford's inmates who is difficult to predict but the chestnut is more than capable on his day. He won a 3m2f novice chase at Plumpton on heavy going in February and should find a staying handicap chase or two in the months to come.

Neil Harvey is far more consistent than Dee Ee Williams or Alderluck but he doesn't take much racing and has only made it to

the racecourse seven times since making his debut in 2008. However, his record reads three wins, three seconds and a third.

The eight-year-old won a 2m5f novices chance at Folkestone in March on his final start last season and, although you will probably need to be patient, Neil Harvey is worth watching out for this term.

Nomecheki is a similar type. The French-bred is not easy to keep sound but has plenty of ability, as five wins from twelve career starts confirms.

Ballybach only managed two appearances last term but his half a length second under top weight in a 2m3f110yds novices handicap hurdle at Ascot in October and his

TULLAMORE DEW: likes Cheltenham

TOCCA FERRO: denied by injury at Newbury last season but will be back soon

ready victory in a 2m maiden chase at Folkestone on his fencing bow in January suggest he will be well worth keeping an eye when returning to action.

The strongly-built **General Kutuzov** is another second-season chaser who should pay his way. The seven-year-old opened his account over fences in a 2m4f110yds beginners' chase at Lingfield in February and the following month finished a creditable second under a big weight in a 2m6f110yds novices handicap chase at Newbury.

Useful hurdler **Pascha Bere**, who began his chasing career with a win at Plumpton in February and chased home smart fencing recruits Starluck and Hidden Keel on his next two starts, shouldn't be hard to place.

Oscar Papa and **On Trend** are a couple of young novice chasers to note.

The first-named is a Plumpton bumper winner who finished second in three of his five starts over hurdles last season, while the latter is an Irish point-to-point winner who won first time out over hurdles at Lingfield in November and made the frame in three further appearances under rules.

Oscar Papa's half-brother **Specialagent Alfie** hinted at ability when ninth in a stronger than average Fontwell bumper in April and the five-year-old is the proverbial dark horse who could be anything.

Gifford has been busy buying promising young horses in Ireland and France during the summer and, while it's early days to make any forecasts about the new blood, it will be very interesting to see how an as yet unnamed three-year-old gelding by Catcher In The Rye gets on, as he is a close relative of Bradbury Star who was a star chaser for Nick's father Josh when he held the licence at The Downs Stables.

Hampshire-based *EMMA LAVELLE* is another trainer with a wedding on her mind. In her case, her own as she is due to walk down the aisle with former jockey and long-time partner Barry Fenton next May.

The couple have been in training for the big day for long enough having been together for over 12 years and, on breeding, there's a good chance the union will be a success as Lavelle's parents have been married for over 50 years!

Lavelle was very hopeful of celebrating another big day with **Tocca Ferro** in the Totesport Trophy at Newbury in February.

The handsome grey was favourite for the race after a commanding victory over the course and distance in the Gerry Fielden Hurdle in November, but he suffered a small tear in a tendon a few days before the race and was forced on to the sidelines for rest of the season.

Understandably, Tocca Ferro will be trained for the same race again which will be called the Betfred Trophy this season.

Easter Meteor is still a maiden over hurdles but showed more than enough last term to suggest he can put that right this season, although, he will only really come into his own when he tackles fences.

The gelding is a full-brother to former stable-companion Easter Legend who won the valuable mares' novice chase final at

Newbury in March and is now at stud.

The time to back Lavelle's **Zarrafakt** is first time out. The Rudimentary gelding has been successful three years running on his seasonal bow in November.

Daymar Bay showed plenty of promise in two bumpers last winters, winning on his debut on Lingfield's Polytrack in November and finding only Shuil Royale too good for him at Wincanton on good to soft turf in February. The five-year-old should pay his way over hurdles this season.

The Heron Island gelding **Black Noddy** finished an encouraging third in a Uttoxeter bumper on his only start to date last November and he too should make up into nice novice hurdler this winter.

Camas Bridge is yet another promising young horse Lavelle should do well with in the months to come. Second to the promising subsequent novice hurdle winner Trustan Times in an Irish point-to-point last October, the five-year-old was fourth in a Fontwell

ZARRAFAKT: the time to get him is first time out as he goes well fresh

MEGASTAR: a useful hurdler last season who will now go chasing

bumper on his rules debut in February.

GARY MOORE has plenty of ammunition for the new campaign headed by **Sire De Grugy**.

The striking-looking chestnut produced a good performance when running away with the 2m Grade 2 WilliamHill.com Dovecot Novices Hurdle at Kempton in February.

He was unable to follow up in the John Smith's Top Novices Hurdle at the Grand National meeting but ran a stormer at Aintree to finish third on ground much quicker than ideal.

Sire De Grugy could easily win more races over hurdles but he's built to jump fences and should make a top-class novice.

Megastar is another who should do well over fences for Moore this winter.

The six-year-old was a smart bumper horse and, although he didn't quite live up to expectations over hurdles, he ran plenty of very good races over hurdles and has the size and scope to make a chaser.

Moore has a fine record in the big handicap hurdles and it wouldn't be a huge surprise if he saddles Sunley Peace and Swift Lord to pick up decent prizes over timber this term.

Swift Lord was a faller when sent off favourite for a point-to-point won by Peddlers Cross at Liscaroll a couple of years ago on his sole outing between the flags. He won a Downpatrick bumper a few months later.

Moore has taken his time with the Spectrum gelding and he was making just his fourth appearance over hurdles when cruising home 28l clear of subsequent scorer Dashing Doc in a 2m1f novice hurdle at Hereford in March this year.

Sunley Peace won a maiden hurdle at Wincanton in March and was having only his fifth start over jumps when landing a well contested handicap hurdle at Sandown the following month on the final day of last season.

Southern stars

Sire De Grugy
Tocca Ferro
Tullamore Dew

Midlands by John Bull

Back in the 2008/09 *RFO Jumps Guide* we predicted that trainer *CHARLIE LONGSDON* would be someone that we'd all be hearing a lot more about in the months and years ahead, and so it has proved.

Last season the upwardly mobile North Oxfordshire handler saddled 44 winners, an increase of 27 on the season before.

This year Longsdon looks booked for further success as the quality of his horses in his care continues to improve.

Grandads Horse won a bumper at Newton Abbot in August 2010 and wasn't seen again before lining up in a 2m1f novice hurdle on his first run for Longsdon at Stratford the following April.

Although beaten less than 2l by Falcon Island, the pair finished 7l clear of the field in a race whose form has worked out really well.

On his next start, a 2m5f maiden at Southwell a month later, the son of Bollin Eric justified market support to open his account over timber.

Then, on his seasonal reappearance in an extended 2m4f novice hurdle at Uttoxeter in September, the five-year-old justified some hefty bets when recording an impressive 3l success over Forever Waining, with the first two finishing 15l clear of the pack.

On the evidence of what we've seen thus far, Grandads Horse should have no trouble in making his presence felt in higher grade handicap hurdles and, beyond that, Longsdon believes he can make into a good 3m chaser when he's eventually sent over fences next year.

GRANDADS HORSE (left): has done really well for Charlie Longsdon

Hildisvini is another exciting prospect. The five-year-old won a bumper in fine style at Warwick in January and then made a winning debut over timber at Sandown a month later.

He followed up under a penalty at Lingfield in March, when he wasn't stopping at the end of the 2m4f race.

This winter Longsdon informs that he will send the Milan gelding down the Pertemps Final route and we can expect him to make his presence felt in good handicap hurdles on soft ground at distances from 2m4f and 3m.

Hidden Keel looked the real deal in novice chases last year, winning three of his last four starts. He ended the campaign with a 21l romp at Exeter, which saw his official rating go up to 149.

The first target for the Kirkwall gelding this winter will be the Colin Parker Memorial Intermediate Chase at Carlisle on October 30, in which Weird Al and Little Josh memorably dead-heated last year.

"We'll find out then whether he'll be good enough to take on the big boys," Longsdon said.

Paintball, who ran respectably in the Fred Winter at the Cheltenham Festival, provided Longsdon with his first winner at Cheltenham when he won a 0-140 handicap hurdle at Prestbury Park in April.

"He'll have a run on the Flat at Nottingham and then run at either Aintree or Ascot in late October," Longsdon informed.

"He'll be racing against decent horses, but I'm hopeful that there is still further improvement to come."

Longsdon also nominates **Hazy Tom** and **Qhilimar** as horses to follow. While the racing public's attention was focused on the Grand National on April 11 this year, Hazy Tom, a five-year-old son of Heron Island was landing a bumper in impressive fashion on his racecourse debut at Bangor.

Longsdon then brought him back at Worcester in September and he was even more impressive, thrashing dual bumper winner Thespis Of Icaria by 9l.

On the strength of his two displays thus far, he's definitely one to keep on the right side of in the months ahead, particularly when he goes hurdling.

Qhilimar, a seven year old Ragmar gelding

HIDDEN KEEL (right): might be good enough to take on the big boys

won on his first start for Longsdon when he got up by a short-head in an extended 3m chase at Sandown off a mark of 122 in February.

He refused six from home in the Midlands National at Uttoxeter on his next outing, but Longsdon believes the best is yet to come.

"Hopefully he'll be able to improve further up to the 135-140 mark. He has got plenty of ability."

Given the French-bred's liking for Newbury, where he's finished first and fourth in two appearances, watch out for him in staying chases at the Berkshire track on testing ground.

It'll be exactly 30 years ago next spring since one of Midlands jump racing's greatest moments when the 48-year-old Northamptonshire farmer and Jockey Club member Dick Saunders became the oldest man in history to win the Grand National, piloting Grittar to a memorable success.

Saunders, one of the most popular men in racing, sadly passed away in 2002 but his daughter, the trainer *CAROLINE BAILEY*, has kept the family tradition going and is hopeful of further success this winter.

Bailey nominates **Morning Moment** and **Three Chords** as two of her inmates to follow in the months ahead.

The former landed an impressive 6l success in a 2m5f handicap chase at Uttoxeter in July – his first run after more than a year off.

"He's nine but he's a great big horse and has only had four races," Bailey says.

"There should be more to come and hopefully he'll be progressive."

Staying chases will be the gelding's forte, with his trainer aiming him at the staying chases at Warwick which Bailey's veteran chaser Arnold Layne has done so well in.

Three Chords, a seven-year-old Winged Love gelding, won two chases last season around the 3m mark and Bailey believes that he can improve further.

"We're quite excited by him and hopefully he'll be able to go from what he achieved last year."

The biggest disappointment for our region at last year's Cheltenham Festival was the lacklustre showing of *PAUL WEBBER*'s **Time For Rupert** in the RSA Chase.

The gelding won two novice chases at Prestbury Park in impressive style in the autumn but could only finish fifth when sent off 7-4 favourite for the one that really mattered.

It transpired afterwards that the son of Flemensfirth broke a blood vessel in the race, which was the result of a lung infection.

Furthermore, the quick ground would not have been in the horse's favour either, as nearly all his best performances have come with some cut in the ground, so all things considered it's best if we put a line under the run.

Webber reports his stable star to be fully recovered now and he'll start the campaign off with a run in the Charlie Hall Chase at Wetherby in late October.

An impressive performance then and races such as the Hennessy, the King

TIME FOR RUPERT: a Gold Cup type

George and of course the Gold Cup could be on the cards.

If he does get to the Gold Cup safe and sound, and there's some juice in the ground, his excellent record at Prestbury Park would make him a serious each-way alternative to the likely red-hot favourite Long Run.

The RSA Chase was not all doom and gloom for the Midlands as **Wayward Prince**, trained by Birmingham handler *IAN WILLIAMS* ran a blinder to finish a staying-on third, only a length behind the Irish-trained winner Bostons Angel.

The Alflora gelding was probably still feeling the after-effects of that effort when he could only finish fourth when sent off 7-4 favourite for the Grade 2 Mildmay Novices Chase at Aintree three weeks later.

The seven-year-old clearly has tremendous stamina reserves, and looks tailor-made for the Hennessy, and beyond that could shape into a live contender for the Welsh or Scottish Nationals.

RENEE ROBESON didn't have much luck with her stable star **Ogee** last season, who never got his favoured ground conditions when it mattered.

In fact, almost every time he was declared to run it seems the heavens opened, as occurred at Newbury in March when the chestnut wasn't suited by the rain-softened ground in an extended 3m2f handicap chase in which he was sent off favourite.

The upshot of a winless campaign is that the eight-year-old, owned by Robeson's brother Sir Evelyn de Rothschild, is now a very nicely handicapped horse, and when he does get his optimum conditions – around 3m on good ground on a left-handed track – don't hesitate to back him.

Because of the greater likelihood of better ground, spring always seems the time when we see Ogee at his best, and if he gets his conditions, then William Hill Handicap Chase at the Cheltenham Festival a race in which he finished an excellent close-up third in 2009, and the 3m1f handicap chase at Aintree on Grand National Day look obvious targets.

Robeson's **Omaruru** entered *John Bull*'s notebook when he finished a staying-on second at odds of 25-1, behind an odds-on Alan King hotpot in a juvenile hurdle at

Warwick in November.

After three more decent efforts, he finally got his head in front at Newbury in early March when he landed an extended juvenile hurdle from dual winner Two Kisses.

The horse had a bad bout of colic in September, but provided he makes a full recovery, he can be a force to be reckoned with in staying handicap hurdles as the further he'll go, the better he'll go.

RICHARD NEWLAND, one of our featured trainers in last year's Jumps Guide, has done really well since first taking out a licence in 2006, and the Worcestershire handler nominates **Act of Kalanisi** and **Connectivity** as two of his horses to follow in the months ahead.

"Both are coming back from slight injuries picked up in their last races, but they've had a good summer and are exciting horses on the up.

"Act Of Kalanisi broke a little bone in his pastern when he won a handicap hurdle at Ascot in February. He'll reappear in either the Elite Hurdle at Wincanton on Badger Beer day on November 5 or in the Greatwood Hurdle at Cheltenham a week later.

"He won over an extended 2m3f at Ascot, but I'm keen to drop him back to 2m. I think 2m on a stiff track could suit him best. If all went well in his first run, then the Ladbroke at Ascot before Christmas would be the target. I'm hopeful he'll be able to win another handicap."

Of Connectivity, Newland says: "He won his last two races, at Towcester and Uttoxeter, very impressively and has risen from a mark of 115 to one of 140.

"He tweaked a ligament but is fine now. He'll go straight to the 3m fixed brush handicap hurdle at Haydock on November 19 which was won last year by Grand Crus."

Midlands magic

Grandads Horse
Morning Moment
Wayward Prince

Newmarket
by Aborigine

NEWMARKET'S leading jumps trainer *LUCY WADHAM* is looking to **El Dancer** to be the jewel in her crown this season and believes he is capable of challenging for top novice chasing honours.

The seven-year-old quickly proved his worth over hurdles and in 2009 rounded his campaign off with a tremendous win in a Grade 2 novice hurdle at Aintree during the Grand National meeting.

Sadly for all concerned he injured himself slightly just after the start of the following season and it was decided to let him have a spell on the sidelines.

The way he has been shaping on the gallops indicates that he has retained his sparkle, and it should be pointed out that he has already run in novice chase company.

This imposing individual seems sure to make his mark at the highest level and his trainer's enthusiasm about him is infectious.

Wadham will also be considering fences for her smart hurdler **Alarazi** in due course though he is likely to start off over hurdles.

The seven-year-old gave Wadham a tremendous triumph at Sandown, when he came storming up the hill to beat Via Galilei in the Imperial Cup.

In retrospect, the temptation of a tilt at the £75,000 bonus offered if he won the County Hurdle a week later at the Cheltenham Festival should have been resisted. He ran a lacklustre race, finishing only 15th behind Final Approach.

His final outing was a solid fourth in a Grade 2 novice hurdle at Aintree during the Grand National meeting. He should have a great future over fences.

Stable companion **Baby Shine** was also in action at the Grand National meeting and is a mare with a touch of class.

A point-to-point winner in Ireland before she joined Wadham, she scored in a Southwell bumper at the first time of asking before following up at Huntingdon in February.

Though she did not win again, her third to Swincombe Flame at Sandown and her fourth to Tempest River in Listed bumpers at Sandown and Aintree were fine efforts.

Her schooling sessions on the Links indicate she is proficient in that aspect of the game, and she is expected to run up a winning sequence before the turn of the year.

Like a large number of the Wadham horses, **Wiesentraum** was bought in Germany. He was a big backward individual and in the circumstances did well to finish second to Another Dimension on his second outing at Huntingdon in March.

Once again at Newbury he showed up prominently until fading in the straight to be fifth to Mizen Station.

Looking at him on the heath he is now much more the finished article, and once his attentions are turned to hurdling we will be hearing a great deal more of him.

ALARAZI: won the Imperial Cup

The Black Baron has had his training problems, but the form he's been showing in his work on the heath indicates he will have little difficulty in making up for lost time.

NEIL KING has quickly established himself at HQ, easily filling the additional boxes that he built at his St Gatien yard last year.

King is delighted with one of his newcomers **Quanah Parker**, who won two races on soft ground at Ayr for Richard Whittaker. This half-brother to the Cheltenham Festival winner Silk Affair will stick to hurdling this season but he has the size and scope to be a top-notch chaser in time.

Another recent acquisition **Ontheslate** was bought at the Ascot Sales and King tells me he will take the bumper route before going hurdling.

While **Ballyvoneen** is another member of the team expected to contribute to his keep.

The good news from the former winning point-to-point rider King is that **Russian Flag**, who he regularly uses as his hack on the heath, is back on song. As King points out he loves the stiff finish at Sandown, where he has run most of his best races.

King does well with dual-purpose horses and **Fashionable Girl** has underlined her trainer's talents. She has paid her way on the all-weather and the plan is to send her hurdling this season as she looks the sort to do well at the winter game.

King also pointed out **I've Been Framed** as a horse to follow. The seven-year-old gelding made my gallops notebook several times last year and did connections proud by winning handicap hurdles over 2m4f, at Huntingdon and Fakenham.

He is a likeable individual and strikes me as the type to establish himself as a top handicap chaser, as he has been schooling satisfactorily up on the Links training grounds.

JAMES EUSTACE has enjoyed considerable success with the few jumpers he has had, and his stronger team at the Park Lodge stables just off the High Street this season is headed by the potentially smart novice hurdler **Iron Condor**.

Last season the four-year-old Tobougg gelding was given one run over hurdles in decent company at Sandown. He was far from disgraced either, finishing sixth to Kumbeshwar in February, when a mistake at the first rather dented his confidence.

He had been good enough to win on the all-weather at Kempton back in September last year, and after a summer break he came back to run a couple of encouraging races on the Flat, particularly when winning over 1m3f110yds at Yarmouth.

His schooling sessions up on the Links have been encouraging and he should be able to land his novice hurdles before becoming a useful handicapper.

Wily Fox was also good enough to win on the Flat having scored under Jack Mitchell in a Lingfield maiden in February.

Though he has not won since then, he has run some good races and his trainer reckons he will shine under rules.

Baan was Group-placed on the Flat when with Mark Johnston, and though he is getting on in years, ran well enough last season for Eustace with his best hurdling effort being an 8l second to Sinbad The Sailor at Ludlow. There are definitely races in him.

Stable companion **Go Set Go** will also feature novice hurdling and looks set to make his mark at the winter game. Placed in two of his three starts in bumpers, his best effort came on his final run at Kempton, where he was right up with the leaders in a competitive race turning for home.

He faded in the closing stages to be third behind Be My Present, but has strengthened appreciably during the summer and will probably have his final permitted bumper run before being aimed at novice hurdles.

NOEL QUINLAN has tasted Cheltenham Festival success with **Silk Affair** and though there is nothing of her quality in his current jumping team, the previous winner **Joan D'arc** could prove a winter warmer for the hard working Irishman.

Last season she won three of her five races, and though she's gone up in the weights, confirmed she had retained her ability, when winning on the Flat at Yarmouth.

MARK TOMPKINS tasted top hurdling success with his Bula Hurdle winners Halkopous and Staunch Friend back in the 1990s and he could again find himself in the spotlight at Cheltenham with the underrated **Akula**.

There was a lot to like about his form last year when he followed up a maiden Ludlow win with some smart efforts in good company.

Firstly, he was third to Sam Winner at Cheltenham returning to the course to finish fourth to Local Hero in the Triumph Hurdle itself.

He was dropped back into handicap company for the Fred Winter Novices Hurdle at the Festival meeting but was feeling the effects of a busy first hurdling season, and finished only 15th to What A Charm.

Looking at him on the heath, it is clear he had done well over the summer, and his shrewd trainer will use his handicap mark to good effect, planning to sharpen him up with a run on the Flat.

JOHN BERRY keeps a hurdler on two on the move every year and the versatile **Kadouchski**, usually manages to score.

This was the case last year when he landed a conditional jockeys handicap hurdle at Sandown. Although he is high enough in the weights, he is progressive and always a serious factor if there is give in the ground.

Hot off the Heath
Akula
El Dancer
Wily Fox

Hunter chasers
by Neil Clark

HUNTER chases are regarded by some as a good opportunity to head to the bar for some liquid refreshment, but they are usually a very good betting medium and can provide some thrilling excitement, as last year's Cheltenham Foxhunter's proved.

The red-hot favourite and 2010 winner Baby Run was 2l clear and looking good for a repeat win when blundering two from home and unshipping 16-year-old rider Willie Twiston-Davies, handing the race to 33-1 shot Zemsky, with 100-1 rag Mid Div and Creep, ridden by the excellent ladies' champion point-to-point Gina Andrews, finishing second ahead of 25-1 shot Oscar Delta.

Although the surprise Northern Irish winner was the fourth winner to go off at odds of 20-1 or bigger in the last six years, the key advice given in last year's annual of ruling out any runner aged more than ten once again proved sound.

Baby Run made amends for his mishap when landing the Aintree Fox Hunters' a month later and finished off the campaign with a third in the Bet365 Gold Cup at Sandown. Nigel Twiston-Davies' admirable front-runner will be 12 next year, and while he'll still be a formidable opponent, the stats suggest that the value will lie in opposing him at the big festivals with younger rivals.

The horse to follow could be the seven-year-old **My Flora**, winner of the John Corbet Cup at Stratford in late May, a race which is usually an excellent place to look for stars of the future.

Sheila Crow's Alflora mare went into the race on the back of a very impressive win

ZEMSKY: picked up the pieces after Baby Run departed at Cheltenham

in a hunter chase at Bangor when, despite being eased down at the finish by stable jockey and champion men's point-to-point rider Richard Burton, she still recorded a 20l success. In the John Corbet Cup it was a similar story as she surged clear of the field two from home to record a 9l victory. If she can stay sound, then she looks to have every chance of emulating Cappa Bleu, Crow's 2009 Cheltenham Foxhunters' winner.

It would also be wrong to dismiss **Zemsky** as a lucky horse who won't win at the top level again. He was already running a blinder when Baby Run departed, and the form of the race was boosted when Mid Div and Creep went on to land the four-miler at Cheltenham's hunter chase meeting in May. He could improve at the age of eight.

There's no better form guide for picking winners at Stratford's prestigious hunter chase meeting in late May than the previous year's results and so it proved again this year.

The winner of the Ladies' Hunter Chase was **Lady Myfanwy**, who had won the event in 2009 and finished second behind Cannon Bridge in the 2010 renewal. The Sir Harry Lewis mare is still only ten and given her great record at the meeting she will still be the one they all have to beat if lining up next year.

The Champion Hunters' Chase, formerly known as the Horse and Hound Cup, went to another horse with a great record at the meeting as 2009 winner Southwestern came in at 12-1, but he will be 13 next year and it may be worth siding with one of this year's younger placed horses.

The Rebecca Curtis-trained **Heron's Well** was upsides the winner at the last but went right on the flat and lost two places on the run-in to finish fourth. With another year's experience under his belt, the eight-year-old could be ready to step up to the plate in 2012.

Another to keep on the right side is Edward Haynes' **Surenaga**. The son of Arctic Lord won last year's Lady Dudley Cup and stayed on strongly under an excellent ride from his trainer to land the extended 3m Royal Artillery Gold Cup Chase at Sandown in February at 14-1.

The nine-year-old was still very much in contention when crashing out three from home in the Champion Hunters' Chase at Stratford but showed there were no ill effects

SALSIFY: Punchestown winner

from that fall when finishing the campaign with an excellent third in the Summer National at Uttoxeter. The horse will be aimed at the Cheltenham Foxhunters and looks sure to bag more victories in the months ahead.

Last year we nominated **On The Fringe** as an Irish hunter chase to follow and having easily landed a heavy-ground hunter chase at Leopardstown in February under Nina Carberry, Enda Bolger's Exit To Nowhere gelding was sent off the 3-1 favourite at Cheltenham. He never really managed to get in the race, but even so he only lost second place on the run-in and, at the age of six, he clearly shouldn't be written off just yet.

Salsify won the Champion Hunter Chase at the Punchestown Festival in May, a race won by On The Fringe in 2010 and Baby Run in 2009. Aged only six, Rodger Sweeney's gelding rates a really exciting prospect and it will be fascinating to see how he gets on if aimed at top hunter chases in Britain.

Willie Mullins's **Boxer Georg** ran Baby Run to less than a length in the Aintree Fox Hunters' and, apart from a mistake at the Canal Turn and another two from home, he took to the unique National fences really well. We can expect his astute trainer to line him up for a repeat run next April and he could take all the beating.

Dave Nevison
Read Dave's diary every week in the RFO

Long Run could reign over us for some time to come

THE old guard got turned over in last season's Gold Cup and it is really difficult to see Nicky Henderson's fantastic young chaser **Long Run** not being top or close to the top of the tree for some time to come.

Denman and Kauto Star were both admirable again last season, but with talk of retirement surrounding both of them as we approach the new season it is hard to see them coming back.

Henderson would seem to be a fitting place to start, and despite the influx of several of the Graham Wylie horses to Paul Nicholls the Lambourn veteran must surely be thinking he will have a chance at being the champion trainer this season.

Spirit Son finished second in the Supreme Novices' Hurdle last season after mopping up in the West Country.

He went on to win the 2m4f novice hurdle at the Grand National meeting and after that Barry Geraghty said he felt Cheltenham came a year too soon for him. He will be much stronger this season and I cannot imagine he won't be campaigned to win a Champion Hurdle this season.

He might not be good enough to beat Hurricane Fly, but he will be winning races along the way and hopefully he will be a strong and confident horse for the festival this time around.

Sprinter Sacre was third in the Supreme and he is being switched to novice chases this season with the Arkle as the obvious target.

Captain Conan is a French import who cost a lot of money so unsurprisingly has ended up in the Michael Buckley colours and I am told he will be a serious novice hurdler this season.

Simonsig is an Irish bumper winner who was bought privately and he is being talked about as one to look out for when it appears over hurdles, possibly in the novice at the Hennessy meeting.

While on the subject of Henderson, his former pupil assistant Tom Symonds has now branched out on his own and is a rookie who can be expected to go well.

Tweedledrum is a filly that Symonds hopes can make the grade from the Flat. She will go in mares' novice hurdles and her Flat speed should enable her to win against jumpers.

I was seriously impressed by the Alan King yard when I was invited along by a mate to his owners' open day in mid-August. I had never been to Barbury Castle before, but the horses looked in absolutely in fantastic shape and it was revealed that King had recently changed his feed supplier and was very pleased with the results.

Salden Licht was not quite top-class as a hurdler but is set to go novice chasing this season and looks set to make an impact.

He will be targeted at the Arkle and the fact that he stays well enough to get 2m4f comfortably means he falls into the same category as My Way De Solzen, who won the race for King in 2006 having excelled over

ZARKANDAR: the only possible danger to Hurricane Fly this season

further. If he jumps as well as that horse did he could seriously make the grade.

Charlie Longsdon came of age as a trainer last season and his horses never seemed to hit any sort of flat spot. He has carried it on in the early part of this term.

Hazy Tom was backed off the boards in a bumper on his debut in September and absolutely won as he liked.

I think this one is a class act and could go for the bumper at the Paddy Power meeting before either switching to hurdles or going for the festival bumper.

If I were to give a tip for the trainer to follow then there is no doubt it would be Longsdon.

As for hurdlers, it pained me a great deal to see **Hurricane Fly** win the Champion Hurdle last season after my ante-post bet on him the previous season failed to materialise.

He was a Group 2 horse on the Flat and possesses such a turn of foot that not many jumpers can live with him. He will be favourite next year and in my view will win.

It seems impossible that **Quevega** won't win the mares' hurdle for the umpteenth time as well.

The only horse that I think could be a danger to Hurricane Fly is **Zarkandar**, who was seriously impressive at both Kempton and Cheltenham last year before struggling at Liverpool.

He won over 1m7f on the Flat and needs more than 2m at a track like Aintree, but at Cheltenham he will be tough to beat.

Two jockeys who are definitely going to make the grade this season are Jeremiah McGrath, who I mentioned in my *RFO* column after his terrific spare winning ride in the mares final at newbury.

Henderson will be his main supplier along with Alan Swinbank for whom the young jockey has a very good strike-rate.

He has had a quiet summer with the intention of preserving his claim a bit longer, and needs to ride just one more to lose his 7lb claim. He is seriously strong young jockey and skilful judging by the Newbury ride.

Kielan Woods has hit gold, being teamed up with Longsdon, and although he doesn't get on all the stars, the stable is growing fast enough for him to get on plenty of horses most 7lb claimers could only dream about.

So far as I can see he has only been an asset to the horses he has ridden and Woods is certainly well worth his claim and one to be with.

Outlook

Morning Mole by Steve Mellish

New order set to rule for a good while yet

LAST season will be remembered as one when the pecking order changed. At the start of the winter Binocular was generally considered the best 2m hurdler around, while Kauto Star, Imperial Commander and Denman were the dominant 3m chasers.

A year later things look very different. Binocular won two of his five starts but was less than convincing, often showing signs of temperament, and his official rating dropped by 7lb.

Imperial Commander rather scrambled home for his only win of the season and his mark fell by 15lb.

Age finally seemed to be catching up with the great Kauto Star, who didn't have to be at his best to take a weak Grade 1 at Down Royal and his rating fell by a whopping 20lb.

Indeed, despite failing to win a race, Denman actually fared best in terms of the figures, with his mark still as high as 177 after terrific placed efforts in the Hennessy Gold Cup and the Cheltenham Gold Cup.

In both those main championship divisions we have a new order with Hurricane Fly and Long Run establishing themselves as the clear best.

Hurricane Fly boasts an astonishing record since joining Willie Mullins from France, winning nine of his ten starts, all in Grade 1 company. His last two victories at Cheltenham and Punchestown leave no doubt at all that he's the best around.

Frighteningly for the opposition, he's also just six and could be open to further improvement.

Long Run also came from France and had quite a reputation when he joined Nicky Henderson. He did fine in his first season in Britain, but, like many French imports before him, he really found his form in his second campaign. Ridden by owner's son Sam Waley-Cohen, he took chasing's two most significant races, the King George and the Gold Cup, by 12 lengths and seven lengths respectively. He's proven on flat tracks and undulating ones, and he's seemingly put any jumping problems behind him. Only injury or an inexplicable loss of form can stop him dominating the three-mile division for a few seasons yet.

Hurricane Fly and Long Run may be new heads of their respective disciplines, but one horse who still rules the roost is Big Buck's. Quite simply, he's the best staying hurdler we've seen in years, being unbeaten since switched to hurdles in this country and yet to be extended. The very promising Grands Crus was expected to test him in the championship races, but he went the same way as all his previous rivals when they met at Cheltenham and Aintree.

With Hurricane Fly, Long Run and Big Buck's to look forward to, how can 2011/12 be anything other than a terrific season? And over the next two pages you will find five horses who can hopefully make it a profitable one to boot.

Al Ferof 6yo gelding
3112/F3111- (Paul Nicholls)

No prizes for originality here, but I can't think of a more exciting prospect for this winter.

In his first season under rules, this former point-to-pointer ran in bumpers, winning two of his four starts and proving himself one of the best around when chasing home Cue Card at the Cheltenham Festival.

Last season his attentions were turned to hurdles and things didn't go immediately to plan as he fell on his first start and was then only third in the Challow Hurdle. Things got better from then on, though, as he took his final three races culminating in victory in the Supreme at Cheltenham. Spirit Son, Sprinter Sacre and Cue Card, the three who chased him home at Cheltenham, are all useful novices and that race looks very hot.

Smart hurdler though he clearly is, it's chasing he was bought for and it was soon announced that he'd go novice chasing this winter. He's fluent over hurdles and has experience in points, so he has everything you want to take him to the top. He could take all the beating in the Arkle.

Our Island 6yo gelding
117- (Tim Vaughan)

This gelding joined Tim Vaughan after taking an Irish point. Sent over hurdles, he took two of his three starts, meeting his only defeat when seventh in the Albert Bartlett. The ground would have been a bit lively for this dour stayer and he's the type who will always do best when the mud is flying.

Whether he goes chasing – he's from the family of Gunther McBride – or remains over hurdles this season, he's one to have on your side when stamina is the main requirement.

AL FEROF: has everything you want to take him to the top over fences

TAIL OF THE BANK: jumping the last in third at Newbury before staying on

Poungach 5yo gelding
131- (Paul Nicholls)

With just three runs under his belt, a bumper and two hurdles, the best is yet to be seen of Poungach.

His best effort came on his final start when he routed 13 opponents by upwards of eight lengths. He travelled beautifully throughout and could be named the winner turning for home. Rated 137 following that win, he has the potential to be a fair bit better as he gains experience.

Tail Of The Bank 8yo gelding
56F11/0F132- (Laura Young)

Despite winning two of his five starts over hurdles and finishing with a rating of 124, it was always as a chaser that he was really going to thrive.

Switched to fences in January, he had just four runs but is already rated 12lb higher than he was over timber. His best effort came

on his final start in a valuable handicap at Newbury. Stepped up to 2m4f, he made the winner, Fine Parchment, pull out all the stops.

The way he finished the race and a glance at his breeding – he's from the family of an Irish National winner and the smart staying chaser Ten Of Spades – suggests he'll need at least that trip to be seen at his best. He's got a good handicap chase in him this winter.

Tullamore Dew 9yo gelding
2572/912123- (Nick Gifford)

A pretty useful hurdler, this nine-year-old is already just as good over fences after just five starts. He won twice but his best effort came at the Cheltenham Festival when he finished third to Divers in the Centenary Novices' Handicap Chase.

The way he kept on having got a little outpaced turning for home suggests 3m could suit him ideally and he could be very interesting if tried at Ascot or somewhere similar as he showed a tendency to jump slightly to his right at Cheltenham.

Time Test with Mark Nelson

Long Run leads the way as king Kauto says farewell

There's something very different about the chase ratings in this year's annual. Every year since the 2006/07 season the top spot has belonged to one chaser, but last term the inevitable occurred.

Time finally caught up with the mighty **Kauto Star**, and although his best effort came when third in the Gold Cup, the figure of 76 he recorded wasn't sufficient to make it into the top ten of last season's efforts on the stopwatch.

This beckons the dawn of a new era in the staying chase division, in which Gold Cup hero **Long Run** leads the way.

I had been critical of earlier efforts by Nicky Henderson's progressive chaser in his first season in Britain, but only on the basis that his speed figures were poor.

That all changed last year as he finally came of age. Despite being beaten on his seasonal return, it was a clear signal of intent. His third in the Paddy Power Gold Cup was a significant improvement on what he had previously achieved and, despite having only two subsequent starts, he won them both and the figures continued to improve.

His King George success was much more like it, and any thoughts that he may not be able to reproduce a similar number at Cheltenham were shot to pieces when his Gold Cup success came alongside a lifetime-best on the clock.

If we are critical, his best figure is still 8lb below what Kauto Star managed at the top of his game but he'll only be seven at this season's festival, so there's the likelihood of better to come.

It was surprising that connections let **Pandorama** take his chance in the Gold Cup as his very best figures came on ground with plenty of give.

Under the right conditions Noel Meade's chaser could give any rival a run for his money, and he remains an exciting prospect for the season ahead.

Currently rated just 1lb below Long Run, targets this term will surely be ground dependent, so the likelihood of a rematch at the Festival is slim, unless we have a particularly wet spring.

The 2010 Gold Cup Winner **Imperial Commander** had a curtailed season due to injury he picked up after making a successful start to the campaign in the Betfair Chase.

A bid for back-to-back victories at Cheltenham went astray after he clouted the fourth-last and he eventually pulled-up lame and was reported to have bled.

Connections avoided Aintree to give him time and it's likely we'll see him again at Haydock for a repeat in the Betfair Chase.

His best number from the season before last puts him 3lb above Long Run's current figure, so he remains a serious player if he gets his career back on track this term.

The two-mile division is very tight with **Sizing Europe** just coming out on top thanks to his Queen Mother success at the Festival.

His ability to stay further than 2m is a big advantage in the championship races and it's worth noting he's only been beaten once in four starts at Cheltenham.

He was too strong at the finish for **Big Zeb** at Prestbury Park, but roles were reversed when the pair met again at Punchestown. The latter is extremely consistent and his ability to handle most types of ground will stand him in good stead again this term.

Conditions were probably too quick for **Golden Silver** both at Cheltenham and Punchestown, and he's better judged on his defeat of Big Zeb in the Tied Cottage Chase. He can make his mark again this winter when conditions should be more favourable.

Former 2m champion, **Master Minded** had a poor time against the clock last season until scooting up at Aintree in the Melling Chase over 2m4f.

Some juice in the ground looks the key to his ability and although he may no longer have the pace to mix it with the best over the minimum trip, he'll be a very intriguing runner over farther this term, with the King George at Kempton a possible target.

Many eyes will be on Kauto Star's half-brother who is due to start his British career for Paul Nicholls. **Kauto Stone** won the top four-year-old steeplechase in France, following in the footsteps of Long Run who took the same race the year before. We'll let the stopwatch determine how good he is as the season unfolds.

The new wave of novice chasers is always something to look forward to and Nicholls is also responsible for **Silviniaco Conti** who clocked a top-class figure over timber last season. Although his numbers diminished in subsequent starts, he remains a bright prospect for fences this term.

I'm also looking forward to the return of **Pere Blanc** whose figures were nicely on an upward curve over hurdles last season. There should be more to come if he takes to birch as anticipated this year.

Tazbar is an interesting second-season chaser, due to return from an injury which occurred immediately after I flagged him up in last year's annual.

His only defeat over birch came at the hands of Long Run and he seems particu-

SILVINIACO CONTI: novice chaser who clocked a great time over hurdles

BINOCULAR: disappointed last season but showed his class at Kempton

larly suited by a test of stamina on a flat circuit. If retaining all his ability, he may yet develop into a serious Grand National prospect.

After highlighting **Hurricane Fly** as the potential number one hurdler in last year's annual, the Willie Mullins-trained gelding duly won all five starts, including the Champion Hurdle at Cheltenham, plus the Leopardstown and Punchestown equivalents.

His Leopardstown success was the best effort on my timepiece and he has the potential to improve on his current figure if anything can provide him with a sterner test this season.

Nothing really came close last term, so while he doesn't have the best hurdle figure, it would be churlish to knock him, as he simply didn't need to run any faster in order to beat what was put in front of him.

Binocular missed Cheltenham, but had previously clocked a number in the Christmas Hurdle suggesting he retained all of his ability, so it was disappointing he didn't put up more of a fight at Punchestown.

The 2010 Champion Hurdle winner looks to have his quirks and it will be interesting to see which way he goes as the new season develops. His Christmas Hurdle figure will have dropped away by the time the 2012 festival comes around, so he'll need a big effort at some stage this term to get back in the mix.

It's difficult to see where the challenge to Hurricane Fly will come from, as **Peddlers Cross** was only second best at Cheltenham without any obvious excuses. He's a fair way adrift of the champion on my figures, so needs to continue progressing.

Former novices **Spirit Son** and **Al Ferof** may step up to the plate, although the latter may be destined for the bigger obstacles this year and may prove to be an Arkle contender for the Nicholls yard.

The pair filled the first two places in the Supreme Novices Hurdle at last year's Festival and Spirit Son then went on to destroy a decent field at Aintree.

With just four outings under his belt, Spirit Son has plenty of potential to improve and by following the ratings each week in the *RFO* we should soon be able to establish whether he's likely to prove a threat to Hurricane Fly.

Big Buck's dominated the staying division and extended his unbeaten run to 12 when easily accounting for Grands Crus in the Liverpool Hurdle on his final start of last season.

Despite his long run of success, his achievements on the clock last year didn't match those on the track, though. There's no doubt his Aintree success was the best from a time perspective, but it was 11lb adrift of his best figure from the season before.

Perhaps the quality of opposition wasn't enough to stretch him, but the possibility of sterner tests await with **Thousand Stars** likely to take on the challenge this season, following his Grade 1 success over 3m1f in Auteuil over the summer.

There are also options for **Oscar Whisky** who was a creditable third in the 2011 Champion Hurdle.

He posted an improved time when stepped up to 2m4f at Aintree, finishing ahead of Thousand Stars, and it would be no surprise to see him have a crack at 3m.

It would certainly breathe some life into a very uncompetitive division and I fancy the pair could give Big Buck's something to think about if they take up the mantle.

Last season's top chasers

	Horse	Speed rating	Distance in furlongs	Going	Track	Date achieved
1	Long Run	87	26	Gd	Cheltenham	Mar 18
1	Sizing Europe	87	16	Gd	Cheltenham	Mar 16
3	Pandorama	86	24	Hy	Leopardstown	Dec 28
3	Riverside Theatre	86	21	Sf	Ascot	Feb 19
5	Golden Silver	84	16	Sf	Punchestown	Jan 30
6	Imperial Commander	83	24	Gs	Haydock	Nov 20
6	Poquelin	83	21	Gs	Cheltenham	Dec 11
8	Big Zeb	82	16	Sf	Punchestown	Jan 30
8	Denman	82	26	Gs	Newbury	Nov 27
10	Master Minded	81	20	Gd	Aintree	Apr 8

Last season's top hurdlers

	Horse	Speed rating	Distance in furlongs	Going	Track	Date achieved
1	Binocular	83	16	Gs	Kempton	Jan 15
2	Celestial Halo	80	16	Gs	Wincanton	Feb 19
2	Silviniaco Conti	80	19	Gs	Ascot	Nov 20
4	Hurricane Fly	79	16	Sf	Leopardstown	Jan 23
5	Overturn	78	16	Gd	Ayr	Apr 16
6	Karabak	76	20	Gs	Cheltenham	Dec 11
6	Mille Chief	76	16	Gs	Wincanton	Feb 19
8	Menorah	75	16	Gs	Cheltenham	Nov 14
9	Al Ferof	74	16	Gd	Cheltenham	Mar 15
9	Starluck	74	16	Gs	Kempton	Jan 15

SPEED WITHOUT THE FALSE STARTS!

My top-rated runners are printed in *Racing & Football Outlook* for Tuesday to Friday races every week, but if you want my complete ratings, you have to subscribe to my Time Test Masterlist. For details, call Raceform on 01635 898781.

Top-notch speed ratings at a very reasonable rate!

2010-2011 Review

Outlook

News Diary

by Richard Williams

September

1 A gamble is landed at Hereford on the filly Am I Blue in the 2m4f handicap hurdle. Her trainer Delyth Thomas knows nothing about it but the crowd are none too impressed and emit a caustic jeer of disbelief. Chalked up at 15-2 on course and available at 25-1 in the morning, Am I Blue is backed down to an SP of 5-1 and comes home 19 lengths clear under Richard Johnson. Johnson had replaced 5lb conditional jockey Dean Coleman just before racing. Earlier, Coleman had telephoned the course and spoken to the declarations clerk, with the news that he had been to the dentist and was feeling unwell. The filly had been tailed off at Worcester 15 days earlier and beaten out of sight the time before at Newton Abbot. Thomas, who is better known as a trainer of arabs, says: "I went down to the bookmakers to have £5 each-way, even though I don't bet, but I was expecting 50-1. When I saw 5-1 I went to the Tote. I've no idea where the money has come from. It's nothing to do with me. She's my only horse to race under rules and I've got her

right after her problems. She has had problems with her spine and also with ulcers."

6 Coral cut Tony McCoy from 5-2 to 15-8 for the BBC's Sports Personality of the Year after Andy Murray is knocked out of the US Open. No jockey has ever won the award although Frankie Dettori came third in 1996.

9 It's Park Hill Stakes day at Doncaster and Harry Findlay, a leading owner under both codes but best known for his part-ownership of Denman, is on the premises. He bumps into BHA chief executive Nic Coward near the parade ring and gives him a piece of his mind, loudly calling for his resignation. Findlay had been warned off for six months by the BHA disciplinary committee for laying his own horse Gullible Gordon, a punishment later reduced to a fine of £4,500 on appeal. Not bitter then.

15/16 Barry Geraghty has two days to remember at the week-long Listowel festival, riding Alfa Beat to victory in the Guinness Kerry National on the Wednesday and breaking his nose in a fall two races later.

On Thursday he spends the morning having his nose reset and in the afternoon picks up the feature race, the Guinness Handicap Hurdle, on St Devote.

19 Despite Ireland being in dire economic straights, crowd figures at the Listowel festival are up on five of the seven days compared to the previous year. The highlight was ladies' day on Friday when 27,131 showed up.

October

4 Seven horses from Nigel Twiston-Davies's stable test out the repositioned penultimate fence on Cheltenham's Old Course and the riders include Paddy Brennan and Carl Llewellyn. Back in May, the fence was moved around the corner into the straight because statistics showed that horses were seven times more likely to fall at that fence than any other. Having negotiated the final three fences once, the jockeys decide to do so again but the first horse hits the penultimate fence hard and falls, bringing

ALFA BEAT: wins the 2010 Kerry National. He did the same the following year

down two others. Horses and riders are un-hurt. Despite this accident, clerk of the course Simon Claisse says: "Paddy Brennan said the new second-last couldn't be in a better place."

7 Following Betfair's AGM, a price range for its shares is agreed at between £11 and £14. Betfair is selling just over ten per cent of its shares to financial institutions and if the shares can be floated at £14, Betfair would be valued at nearly £1.5 billion which would admit it to FTSE (the UK's 100 highest capitalised companies). The flotation is set to net founders Andrew Black and Edward Wray a combined windfall of between £261 and £333 million. Black and Wray, who started the business in 2000, have a stake of 22.5 per cent and are among a group of 14 major investors holding 75 per cent of the company. No new shares are being issued.

10 The name of Josef Vana will forever be linked to the Velka Pardubica, the Czech Republic's extraordinary 4m2f steeplechase run over enormouse fences and through ploughed fields. Vana is just as extraordinary as the race. At the age of 57 he wins the stamina-sapping contest for the seventh time as a jockey and the eighth time as a trainer. He appears to stop riding close home on Tiumen but survives a photo finish to beat Amant Gris by a nose. The British interest is the Charlie Mann-trained Mr Big, who comes home last of the 12 finishers. Mann himself rode the winner of the race in 1995

21 Despite an economy crawling along at a snail's pace, William Hill announce that they expect operating profits for 2010 to be at the top end of forecasts. They have had a run of favourable football results and an increase in gross win from machines. This contributes to group net revenue rising 22 per cent in the 13 weeks to September 28. Hills have 2,350 shops and their chief executive, the sometimes outspoken Ralph Topping says: "We've seen positive performance from our growing online business too."

22 Betfair shares trade for the first day on the London stock market and a company that BHA chairman Paul Roy co-founded and chairs is revealed as a major backer. The

company in question is New Smith, but Roy stresses that there is no conflict of interest between his chairmanship of the BHA and his position as head of the fund management company. "I have a number of fund managers who have a large element of discretion as to what they buy and sell and how they invest in their portfolios. My interest are all declared. It is not a conflict." Betfair's flotation gets off to a flying start, the shares climbing steadily throughout the day from an initial £13, rising 19 per cent to £15.50.

23 The chairman of Gala Coral Group, Neil Goulden, is critical of Paul Roy saying: "It's amazing and truly hypocritical to criticise the exchanges' unfair tax and levy advantages on the one hand and then seek to profit from that with the other." Trainer Mark Tompkins chimes in: "I find it unbelievable that the leader in racing can be associated with this investment." However Paul Dixon, president of the Racehorse Owners' Association, defends Roy: "This is Paul's company and not Paul individually who has done this."

25 Betfair shares maintain their price of £15.50 as the row over BHA chairman Paul Roy continues. Roy says that he would continue to press racing's case for Betfair to make a bigger contribution to the sport even if that affected the betting exchange's profits to the detriment of New Smith, the company which purchased millions of pounds worth of shares in the betting exchange.

28 Paddy Mullins, training great and head of an extensive racing family, dies peacefully aged 91. A trainer for over 50 years under both codes, he was best known for his handling of Dawn Run, the mare who completed a Champion Hurdle (1984) and Gold Cup (1986) double. His son Willie dominates the Irish training ranks while his other sons Tony and Tom are also well established, as is his daughter Sandra. His other son George has a horse transport business. Meanwhile, following pressure from Aintree's chief executive Julian Thick, the BBC agrees to cover three races from Aintree on November 21, one of which is the famous Becher Chase. The fixture was previously included in the cutback in meetings that had reduced the BBC's racing output to 13 days for 2010.

November

3 The Horsemen's Group. an umbrella organisation which represents owners, jockeys, trainers, breeders and stable staff, plans to reveal details of its minimum prize-money tariff. Once the policy is implemented, members will be urged to boycott races that fail to meet the criteria. The move comes as a response to the continuing fall in levy income, and the tariff will include a list of proposed minimum levels of prize-money for each class of race, both Flat and jumps.

6 Ruby Walsh sustains a double fracture in his right leg in a fall at Down Royal. His day is going swimmingly up to that point, with a double on Kauto Star and The Nightingale. But Corrick Bridge's fall in the handicap chase puts a dampener on things. Walsh is taken to Royal Victoria Hospital in Belfast and is told he will be out of action for months. Kauto Star's win in the JNwine.com Champion Chase restores any respect he might have lost for falling in the Cheltenham Gold Cup. In beating race-fit rivals Sizing Europe and China Rock by four lengths, the ten-year-old shows that he is anything but over the hill, and should be a major player in the big races coming up.

12/13/14 For some people, Cheltenham's Open meeting marks the start of the jumps season proper, although officially it begins on May 1. The bookmakers take a hammering on the Friday with Dave's Dream (3-1) and Aegean Dawn (6-4) bringing up a double for Nicky Henderson. Cue Card (8-13) and Time For Rupert (7-2) are other short-priced winners. On Saturday, punters are kiboshed as Little Josh (20-1) lands the Paddy Power Gold Cup Chase from Dancing Tornado and the 2-1 favourite Long Run. The winner is trained by Nigel Twiston-Davies and ridden by his son Sam who turned 18 less than a month previously. The proud father says: "For a boy aged 18 to kick a horse into every fence like that takes some balls. It was an absolutely superb front-running effort." He also insists that Paddy Brennan remains his No. 1 jockey. The day is marred by Christian Williams breaking both arms when coming down on Beshabar in the 3m novice chase. The fall happens at the resited second-last fence. On the third day of the Open meeting Menorah wins the Greatwood Hurdle, showing that he has retained all his ability since winning the Supreme Novices' the previous season. Paul Nicholls has a double with Arkle prospect Ghizao in the open-

LITTLE JOSH: out in front in the Paddy Power Gold Cup with Long Run trailing

PEDDLERS CROSS: beats Starluck (left) and Binocular (right) at Newbury

er and Rock On Ruby in the bumper. David Pipe gets on the scoresheet with the grey Grands Crus in the 2m5f handicap hurdle.

17 Tony McCoy touches even money for BBC's Sports Personality of the Year as Racing For Change and sections of parliament put their weight behind him. Laurence Robertson, Conservative MP for Tewkesbury, whose constituency includes Cheltenham, and Mansfield's Labour MP Alan Meadle, set the ball rolling by posting an early-day motion supporting the champion. Part of the motion reads: "This house believes that...this accolade is long due to him."

21 Peter Monteith dies at his home in Rosewell, Midlothian at the age of 61. The death astonished his fellow professionals, many of whom had been with him earlier in the day at Kelso where he had saddled a second and a third. He was a qualified chartered surveyor who turned to training in 1982. He sent out more than 400 winners including Moment Of Truth who he also owned and whose 17 victories included the Northumberland Gold Cup Novices' Chase at Newcastle. He gained a rare victory for Scotland at the Cheltenham Festival when Dizzy, owned by his father Bill, won the County hurdle in 1994. Two huge banners, partly funded by Racing For Change, are erected on a site used by Exeter racecourse adjacent to the A38 to bring McCoy's claim to the attention of passing motorists.

26 Shares in Betfair come off their high of £15.50 to trade at £14 following sell notes from several analysts. These point to the increasing threat of regulation around the globe. The recent loss of of an appeal in Australia's federal court over the payment for raceday data to New South Wales appears to have raised the alarm among City pointy heads.

27 Newbury's Hennessy meeting is enriched by the addition of the Fighting Fifth Hurdle which migrates south from Newcastle because of an icy blast hitting the north of England. Newbury strips back its covers to reveal good to soft going and proceeds to stage an eight-race card, beginning at 11.55 and ending with a race at 3.40. The Fifth is won by Peddlers Cross who sees off Starluck and Binocular. The Hennessy Gold Cup falls to the Nick Williams-trained Diamond Harrry who beats Burton Point and Denman, the last-named bidding for an unprecented third win in the race. It's the biggest win in the career of 27-year-old jockey Daryl Jacob and it's also a high-water mark for Williams who is both trainer and accountant. "It's all down to my wife Jane," he says. "She does all the training and I just pick the races."

December

6 Jump racing is in the grip of a freeze-out and the only action is on the all-weather. There's further reason not to be cheerful when Nigel Twiston-Davies announces that Imperial Commander won't have recovered from injury in time for the King George on Boxing Day. This prompts bookmakers to shorten Kauto Star, seeking his fifth consecutive Kempton big-race win, to even money for the event. Meanwhile, the covers are down at Cheltenham.

8 Tony McCoy is given the Sportsman of the Year trophy, an award decided by 700-plus sports journalists. AP says: "I think of people like Lester Piggott and Frankie Dettori as proper racing stars so for me to win the award is flattering." He is the first jockey to land it in its 62-year history.

10/11 Cheltenham strips off its blankets to reveal good to soft going for its two-day meeting, the only race lost being the cross-country chase on Friday. On Saturday there's an eight-race card beginning at 11.40, meaning an early start for racegoers with any distance to travel. And those of them who backed the Paul Nicholls runners leave with their pockets bulging. The Ditcheat master wins half of the races, including the prestigious and renamed Vote AP Gold Cup Handicap Chase with Poquelin at 16-1. The reason for the long price is partly due to the presence of stablemate Robinson Collonges in the field who is ridden by Noel Fehily. Poquelin is ridden by Ian Popham and the horse becomes the race's first dual winner since its inauguration in 1963 when it was sponsored by Massey Ferguson. In 2010 Poquelin was sent off at 7-2. Nicholls also wins the rerouted-from-Sandown Tingle Creek Chase with Master Minded (10-11), the 2m handicap chase with Woolcombe Folly (4-1) and the JCB Triumph Hurdle Trial with Sam Winner (4-7). Possibly the day's highlight is Menorah's relatively simple win in the 2m1f International Hurdle after which he he is quoted at 4-1 for the Champion Hurdle. Philip Hobbs, his trainer, completed an International/Champion double with Roost-

er Booster in the 2002-03 season.

14 Nic Coward, the BHA's chief executive, says that he will resign from the post in the spring, citing a job offer as general secretary to the Premier League. The 44-year-old, who drew a salary of £286,000 in 2009, has been in office the best part of four years and had been in a constant struggle to raise levy from the bookmakers to bolster the sport. His most recent attempt to fix the levy resulted in a referral to the secretary of state for Culture, Olympics, Media and Sport. Perhaps he is tiring of all the in-fighting. If he isn't, the racing public certainly is. Meanwhile, in unrelated news, Betfair shares take a dive on the markets. They fall by 16 per cent to £9.90 following the first set of financial results since flotation. Chief executive David Yu reveals half-year betting revenue growth up more than 11 per cent and says he is "pretty pleased".

17 Over in 'austerity Ireland', Horse Racing Ireland reveals a five per cent reduction in prize-money for 2011. These cuts are the result of a decline in government contributions to the sport. William Hill says it will close 20 of its shops in the country. Hills's shops in Northern Ireland are not affected.

19 Tony McCoy wins BBC's Sports Personality of the Year award which gives a huge boost to the sport. He is the first jockey to win it. The 15-times champion jockey's qualities of consistency, strength, will-to-win and longevity are finally recognised by the public at large. Racing For Change is a key player in the bid to get the public behind McCoy who, during the campaign, admitted to being embarrassed at being the focus of attention. However, he issued this warning to his colleagues: "Everyone will be expecting me not to be as hungry as I once was, so I'm going to work even harder to prove them wrong." Meanwhile, with a week to go before the King George, Kempton's turf track is under covers. Unfortunately the covers themselves are under four inches of snow. Level-headed clerk of the course Barney Clifford reflects: "It's just a question of whether the expected thaw arrives in time. The snow has assisted in insulating the ground. We have had temperatures as low as -8C."

23 Britain is covered in snow and Chepstow has no choice but to call off the December.

January

4 Celtic Bookmakers, owned by former Irish government minister Ivan Yates, goes into receivership prompting Irish bookmakers' leader Sharon Byrne to describe the collapse as a sign of things to come. The chain has 49 shops and a spokesman attributes the demise of the company to a 50 per cent decline in turnover. Concerning the fate of the 237 employees, Yates says: "We'll try to save over a hundred and I'll be doing all in my power to assist this transfer." He stresses that all winning bets with Celtic would be honoured and that, over the past year, he had been searching for an investor or another bookmaker to buy into the chain.

7 Nigel Twiston-Davies accuses the BHA of not wanting the best horses in the William Hill King George VI Chase after racing's ruling body declined his request to allow Gold Cup winner Imperial Commander to participate in the race eight days hence. Having scratched the horse from the original entries because of an injury picked up when winning the Betfair Chase, the trainer had initially said that the rearranged race would come too soon for Imperial Commander. He says: "The way the horse is blossoming, we suddenly thought 'let's have a go'. Surely it's sensible to put it back to the six-day stage. If that happened you make a supplementary entry. But the BHA seem determined not to have the best horses in the race." BHA spokesman Paul Struthers replies: "We left it at the 48-hour declarations because it was called off after the declarations and the race is being held at the same course, albeit three weeks later. If we hadn't kept it at the declaration stage everyone who had had a bet ante-post would have had those bets voided. Whatever we do there is always going to be someone who isn't happy."

27 meeting which features the Welsh National. It hopes to reschedule on 8 January.

26 The King George falls victim to the Arctic conditions and is rescheduled for January 15.

9 The rescheduled Coral Welsh National (televised by BBC) is won by Synchronised and Tony McCoy which means the champion has won all four of the Nationals that really matter, the Grand National and the Scottish and Irish versions.

10 Howard Johnson is charged with a series of offences by the BHA, the most serious of which is racing Striking Article eight times after he had undergone a palmar neurectomy (denerving operation). The offences carry potentially lengthy bans if proved. The operation is the surgical removal or severing of all, or part of, the palmar digital nerves which causes the horse to lose sensation in the back of the foot. A guilty finding of wilful cruelty could result in a ten-year ban. He is also being charged with administering anabolic steroids to three of his horses and of 'failing to conduct his business of training racehorses with reasonable care and skill'. The discovery that Laurabolin, an anabolic steroid, had been given to Whisky Magic, Mintaka Pass and Montoya's Son came as a result of an intelligence-led visit by drug testers to Johnson's yard 12 months previously. Johnson's main patron, Graham Wylie, says: "I feel sorry for Howard because he works so hard and always puts the horses first."

11 The Horsemen's Group makes recommendations on minimum prize-money levels and warns racecourses which do not comply that they could have their races boycotted. The Group, which represents owners, trainers, jockeys and stable staff, refuses to accept that courses do not have the money to fund races up to standard tariff. However Racecourse Association chairman Ian Barlow has already written to 4,000 owners, and all trainers, to tell them that racecourses do not have the money.

15 A historic fifth consecutive King George VI Chase eludes Kauto Star who can only finish a distant third to Long Run and Riverside Theatre, both trained by Nicky Henderson. The winner is ridden by amateur Sam Waley-Cohen, son of Long Run's owner Robert. Few big races are won by amateurs and Waley-Cohen joins a select band that includes Marcus Armytage (Grand National), Colin Magnier (Champion Hurdle) and Jim Wilson (Cheltenham Gold Cup). A certain Hackedorf tweets: "Wonderful for Sam Waley-Cohen after all the abuse he's had from armchair jockeys. Could see early on he had got the horse jumping well. Great result to get the 1-2 for Seven Barrows." Totesport slash Long Run (9-2 from 20s) into second favourite for the Cheltenham Gold Cup. Imperial Commander's jolly.

19 There's good news for the racing industry in that figures show that a day at the races is increasingly popular. Attendance figures rise for the second year running, 5,769,381 people going through the gates in 2010, a rise of 0.9 per cent despite the bad weather that decimated the fixture list in December, and the fact that there were 35 fewer meetings in 2010 as compared to the year before. Not only that, but a record number of viewers tuned in for the King George VI Chase.

30 Peter Cundell, trainer of top-class jumpers Bachelor's Hall and Celtic Ryde, is at Kempton to saddle his last runner. This brings to an end an era which has lasted 100 years, given that he took over from his father Ken who in turn took over from his second cousin Frank. The Cundell base is at Compton in Berkshire and was the setting for the television programme Trainer. Cundell comments that his own children have "too much sense to get involved in racing". Compton, of course, was the former home of the *Racing & Football Outlook*.

February

9 Despite a 35 per cent cut in Levy Board prize-money allocations, Jockey Club Racecourses is able to add £2.2 million to prizes for 2011. The JCR is the most powerful racecourse owner in Britain with Cheltenham, Aintree, Newmarket and Epsom in its portfolio.

12 Newbury's Totesport Trophy meeting is abandoned after only one race because two horses die from electric shocks in the paddock before that race. As darkness falls, engineers from the Southern Electricity Board discover a cable that runs underneath the grass at the spot where the horses fell. Colin Pritchard, a groom leading up Marching Song, says: "I pulled my horse on to the grass to get the jockey legged up, then he started freaking out." He adds that he felt a tingling sensation in his arm. Jonjo O'Neill attributes the death of his Fenix Two to the horse stepping off the rubber path and on to the grass. "They looked like they were electrocuted. That might be totally crazy but that's what it looked like." Two other horses are also affected but survive. The incident makes headlines across both the news and sports media.

13 Electrocution is confirmed as the cause of death of two horses at Newbury the day before. Newbury hopes to run the abandoned on February 18.

CARNAGE: Newbury gets abandoned

15 Cyril Stein, the driving force behind Ladbrokes from 1956 to 1993, dies aged 82. He was one of the first to realise the potential of betting shops and he also led the Ladbrokes £645 million takeover of Hilton Hotels.

16 Jeremy Hunt determines the levy for 2011-12 and it's not good news for racing. There had been hopes for £130m-£150m but instead the levy raised from the layers will be between £73m and £80m. The minister's decision was delivered three and a half months after the racing industry and the bookmakers failed to reach an agreement, resulting in a referral to the culture secretary. Hunt restated his annoyance at having to intervene and urged the two sides to develop a "less adversarial relationship".

22 The vet James Main is struck off the official vets' register for his part in the Moonlit Path affair which saw Nicky Henderson fined and disqualified from making entries for his horses for three months. He had admitted injecting the mare, who was owned by the Queen, with tranexamic acid, a banned blood-clotting agent, on the morning of her racecourse debut at Huntingdon in 2009. And he had admitted knowing that he was in breach of the rules.

March

4 With 11 days to go to the Cheltenham Festival, Coral are the first high street chain to go non-runner no bet on all races at the meeting. Ladbrokes have offered the same concession on the four championship races since December. Paddy Power offer to refund all losing bets if Cue Card wins the opening race, the Supreme Novices' Hurdle. Cue Card has a racecourse spin at Wincanton the day before and Colin Tizzard says: "I couldn't be happier".

7 It looks as if Paddy Power will have the money to refund bets on the Supreme if Cue Card wins. Their latest set of financial results is highly impressive, 2010 profits rising 55 per cent to E104.2 million and turnover rising 39 per cent. What is interesting about the figures is that almost three-quarters of their profits were generated online.

8 Steve Whiteley is the biggest winner in Tote Jackpot history when he nets £1.45 million from a bet of £2. It is the 61-year-old's first crack at the Jackpot having learnt of the bet's existence when travelling to Exeter racecourse by bus. He takes advantage of a promotional offer from the racecourse and says: "I got the free bus up here when a mate told me there was a million quid in the Jackpot from Ffos Las. I didn't know what to do. |I wrote two down in each race first but when my mate said that was £32, I said that was more than I could afford so I chose one in each race." When asked about his plans for the future he replies: "I'm a heating engineer – well I was."

13 A blow for punters on the 13th, and unluckiest, day of the month as Binocular is withdrawn from the Champion Hurdle, owing to the possibility of a positive drugs test if he ran. The previous year's winner of the big race had been 3-1 favourite with Stan James to retain his crown. He is ruled out on BHA advice when medication, that was used to clear an allergy, failed to clear his system. The disturbing thing about this is that the BHA and trainer Nicky Henderson were alive to the possibility of this happening several days before the announcement.

15 It's Champion Hurdle day at the Cheltenham Festival and the Willie Mullins-trained Hurricane Fly wins the big one under Ruby Walsh who has only recently recovered from a broken leg. It looks a classy renewal and quite possibly Binocular wouldn't have been involved. Ireland are responsible for two other winners, Sizing Australia in the cross-country and Quevega in the mares' race. The latter, also trained by Mullins and ridden by Walsh, is the Irish banker of the meeting and wins by ten lengths. It's the mares third victory in the race.

16 Those who bet on Ireland to have a low-scoring Festival are out of pocket big-time in an incredible day for the island termed Hibernia by the Romans. Ireland lands six of the seven races on day two of the Festival, with the bumper the only race to escape its clutches. You could say that St Patrick's Day came early for the visitors and, ironically, it was the race that they had dominated in recent history that scuppered the clean sweep. With Hibernia leading Albion nine races to five at the end of the second day, it looks a formality that Ireland's previous record of ten winners at the meeting will be smashed. The first four places in the Champion Chase are filled by Irish runners, the one leading them home being Sizing Europe.

17 Big Buck's follows in the footsteps of Quevega when he lands his race, the World Hurdle, for the third time. And it's another winner for Ruby Walsh who says: "Dropping your whip on a horse as idle as Big Buck's is hardly ideal. It was a schoolboy error but he gets you out of trouble." Only one winner for Ireland, Noble Prince in the Jewson Novices' Chase.

18 Gold Cup day at the Festival is all about the six-year-old Long Run and his amateur jockey Sam Waley-Cohen. They come home seven lengths clear of the 'old guard' represented by Denman and Kauto Star, both former Gold Cup winners. Long Run breaks the track record and becomes the first six-year-old to win since Mill House in 1963. It's

a first Gold Cup for Nicky Henderson after over 30 years of training. And it's the first win for an amateur rider since Jim Wilson brought home Little Owl 30 years earlier. The Irish knock in three more winners, Final Approach, Sir Des Champs and Zemsky giving them 13 for the meeting.

27 The Irish jump jockey's championship looks wide open. Paul Townend is at 6-4, Davy Russell 7-4 and Paul Carberry 2-1 with Boylesports. Townend, though, has a broken collar bone and could be out until April 24. There are 21 Irish racing days left and he is set to miss nine of them.

31 Paddy Brennan quits as stable jockey to Nigel Twiston-Davies after four, and pretty successful years. The 29-year-old and the trainer insist that there has been absolutely no falling out but Brennan's position had looked a tad untenable with Twiston-Davies giving so many of the stable's rides to his up-and-coming son Sam. In addtion, his other son Willie shapes like a rising star. Brennan is to keep the ride on Imperial Commander. He says: "I would like to thank Nigel and all the staff at the yard for their support over the years. I hope that Nigel will continue to have a big call on me when I'm riding as a freelance."

PADDY BRENNAN (left): now freelance after splitting from Nigel Twiston-Davies

KEEPING IT IN THE FAMILY: Donald McCain with Ballabriggs and 'Ginger'

April

9 There's always a fairytale on Grand National day and this time it's supplied by Ballabriggs. He is trained by Donald McCain son of the living legend and slightly bonkers Ginger who trained four Grand National winners, including Red Rum three times. Ginger says of his surprisingly sane son: "He's made a cracking job of it. He's done it by the book. If ever I meet his father, I'll congratulate him." There are two fatalities during the race resulting in Becher's Brook being bypassed second time round.

23 Tony McCoy is champion jockey in Britain for the 16th consecutive year. It's an astonishing record but what is nearly as astonishing is that Richard Johnson has been runner-up to him 13 times. McCoy closes the day, and the season, on 218 winners, 67 ahead of Johnson. There's no good news for the English jockey because McCoy insists he is going for the title again: "The goal is always the same. As mush as I've enjoyed the races I've won, they are all in the past. It's all about the future now." Paul Nicholls is champion trainer. Nicky Henderson is a close second thanks to his Gold Cup victor Long Run.

24 It's the first day of the jumps season in Britain but in Ireland the struggle continues for the jockeys' jumps title. Davy Russell moves to within five of Paul Townend with a double at Fairyhouse.

Summer

9 May Paul Townend holds off a spirited challenge from Davy Russell to be crowned leading Irish jockey with 80 winners, four ahead of his rival. Willie Mullins is top trainer with €2,412,247 almost twice as much as his nearest pursuer Noel Meade.

12 August Howard Johnson is banned from racing for four years following a BHA inquiry into charges relating to horse welfare and administering prohibited substances. The County Durham trainer receives three of his years for authorising a denerving operation on a horse called Striking Article and then running him eight times. The palmar neurectomy caused the horse to lose feelings in the back of his foot. The verdict reads: "Johnson has shown a reckless disregard for the rules so as to jeopardise the future welfare of a gelding in training." The 58-year-old Johnson announces his retirement and his principal patron Graham Wylie later says that he will transfer his horses to Paul Nicholls and Willie Mullins.

15 August The Grand National fences at Aintree are to be altered once again in the interests of safety and the changes should be in place by the autumn in time for the Becher Chase. The landing side of Becher's Brook will be reprofiled to reduce the drop by between four and five inches. Levelling work will also be undertaken on the landing side of the first fence (fence 17 on the second circuit) to reduce the drop and

level the landing. The fourth fence will be reduced in height. *Off The Bit*, the *Racing & Football Outlook*'s columnist thinks that the BHA might be looking in the wrong direction. He writes: "Why not start by reducing the field size? Forty runners on any racetrack, over any fences, can be a recipe for mayhem." Nigel Twiston-Davies says that the race is in danger of becoming a glorified handicap hurdle.

26 August Betfair's share price hits £6.02.

19 September Ginger McCain, the trainer of Red Rum, dies aged 80. He became a national institution through his association with Red Rum who won the Grand National three times, in 1973, 1974 and 1977. And to prove he was much more than a one-horse trainer, he also saddled Amberleigh House to win the great race in 2004. The one-time taxi driver took out a permit in 1953 and 16 years later had a full licence, training from a small stable behind a used car salesroom close to the beaches of Southport, where he used to exercise his horses. McCain was a forthright character, never afraid to speak his mind, especially when it came to defending the traditions of Aintree. His son Donald, who took over from his father in 2006, says: "I learned so much from him about Grand National horses and training but the biggest thing he taught me was that if you are good straight and honest you'll never come to much harm."

RED RUM: Ginger McCain's National hero soars over the old-style Bechers

Outlook

Big-race review
by Dylan Hill
November 2010 to May 2011

1 JNwine.com Champion Chase (Grade 1) (3m)
Down Royal (IRE) November 6 (Soft)
1 **Kauto Star** 10-11-10   R Walsh
2 **Sizing Europe** 8-11-10   A E Lynch
3 **China Rock** 7-11-10   Barry Geraghty
4/7F, 5/1, 5/1. 4l, nk. 7 ran. 6m 22.20s
(Paul Nicholls).

A solid return for **Kauto Star**, though he wasn't seriously pushed with chief rival **Sizing Europe** ridden too conservatively to determine whether he really stayed 3m. Kauto Star was produced to lead three out and held on comfortably as Sizing Europe, at his best when making the running over 2m, could never land a serious blow, just holding off the progressive **China Rock** for second.

2 Paddy Power Gold Cup Handicap Chase (Grade 3) (2m4f110yds)
Cheltenham November 13 (Good To Soft)
1 **Little Josh** 8-10-8   S Twiston-Davies
2 **Dancing Tornado** 9-10-4   A P Heskin (5)
3 **Long Run** 5-11-6   Mr S Waley-Cohen (5)
20/1, 20/1, 2/1F. 2¾l, 2l. 18 ran. 5m 12.26s
(Nigel Twiston-Davies).

A modest renewal with **Long Run** well below the form he showed later in the season, enabling **Little Josh** to pull off a 20-1 surprise. Little Josh made the running and was always in command, kicking clear off the home turn as **Dancing Tornado** was the only horse to challenge from the rear and Long Run looked one-paced in third, presumably wanting further to bring his engine into play. **Poquelin**, **Great Endeavour** and **Sunnyhillboy** filled the next three places before going on to lead the way in the Vote AP Gold Cup at the track the following month, though the latter pair were badly in need of this outing and the fact that the fourth, **Mad**

Max, was beaten 8l further that day suggests this was the weaker contest, with Little Josh possibly set to struggle when upped in class.

3 Greatwood Handicap Hurdle (Grade 3) (2m110yds)
Cheltenham November 14 (Good To Soft)
1 **Menorah** 5-11-12   Richard Johnson
2 **Bothy** 4-10-2   Danny Cook (3)
3 **Manyriverstocross** 5-10-13   W Hutchinson
6/1, 16/1, 11/2F. nk, 5l. 17 ran. 4m 2.34s
(Philip Hobbs).

A typically strong contest with several using the race as a stepping stone to tougher tasks, in particular the gutsy **Menorah**. Given a fairly lenient initial mark of 151 having won what proved to be a strong Supreme Novices' Hurdle, Menorah fought hard to see off a very well-handicapped rival in **Bothy**, who was able to finish second in the Totesport Trophy and Coral Cup off higher marks, while **Manyriverstocross** ran his usual good race at a strongly-run 2m and **Any Given Day** coped admirably given he would come into his own over further.

4 Dobbins & Madigans at Punchestown Hurdle (Grade 1) (2m)
Punchestown (IRE) November 14 (Soft To Heavy)
1 **Solwhit** 6-11-10   D N Russell
2 **Voler La Vedette** 6-11-5   P Townend
3 **Donnas Palm** 6-11-10   D J Condon
11/10F, 5/2, 3/1. 2½l, 1½l. 4 ran. 4m 4.40s
(C Byrnes).

Solwhit took his Grade 1 tally to six as he raced to a comfortable comeback win over the mare **Voler La Vedette**, underlining the fact that he was a much stronger rival for Hurricane Fly than many would subsequently give him credit for. Solwhit was always prominent and kicked for home early to prevent a challenge from Voler La Vedette, who stayed on past the front-running **Donnas Palm** to grab second with the former Champion Hurdle winner **Sublimity** a distant fourth to mark his decline.

5 Betfair Chase (registered as the Lancashire Chase) (Grade 1) (3m)
Haydock November 20 (Good To Soft)
1 **Imperial Commander** 9-11-7   P Brennan
2 **Tidal Bay** 9-11-7   Brian Hughes
3 **Planet Of Sound** 8-11-7 Richard Johnson
10/11F, 16/1, 17/2. 1¼l, 8l. 7 ran. 6m 11.20s
(Nigel Twiston-Davies).

A successful return for Gold Cup hero **Imperial Commander**, who put a clutch of second-tier staying chasers firmly in their place with a comfortable victory, though slight question-marks remain about the full merit of his performance after **Tidal Bay**, having all but dropped himself out earlier, finished powerfully to whittle down his winning margin. Imperial Commander had long put the race to bed by then, however, as he took up the running just after halfway and stayed on too strongly for **Planet Of Sound**, who was his main rival for most of the contest. **Nacarat** struggled to see out the trip in the conditions but still finished ahead of the disappointing **What A Friend**.

6 Coral Hurdle (registered as the Ascot Hurdle) (Grade 2) (2m3f110yds)
Ascot November 20 (Good To Soft)
1 **Silviniaco Conti** 4-11-4   Noel Fehily
2 **Karabak** 7-11-0   Wayne Hutchinson
3 **Restless Harry** 6-11-4   Henry Oliver
100/30, 3/1, 9/1. 7l, 1½l. 8 ran. 4m 34.94s
(Paul Nicholls).

The emergence of a potential new star as **Silviniaco Conti** routed a strong field on his first run outside novice company. Taking over at the third-last, Silviniaco Conti soon eased clear, giving 4lb and a seven-length beating to a useful yardstick in **Karabak**, and despite being outpaced when dropped down to 2m subsequently, he clearly remains a top-class prospect over further. **Restless Harry** was outpaced before staying on well again in third ahead of the out-of-sorts **Zaynar**.

7 Hennessy Gold Cup Handicap Chase (Grade 3) (3m2f110yds)
Newbury November 27 (Good To Soft)
1 **Diamond Harry** 7-10-0   Daryl Jacob
2 **Burton Port** 6-10-1   Barry Geraghty
3 **Denman** 10-11-12   Sam Thomas
6/1, 15/2, 4/1F. 1¼l, 14l. 18 ran. 6m 27.81s
(Nick Williams).

Denman's bid for a third Hennessy win under top weight ended in honourable failure as he got left behind by a handicap blot in **Diamond Harry**, who was always cantering all over the favourite before comfortably seeing off the dour stayer **Burton Port**. Jumping much better than during a slightly sketchy novice season, Diamond Harry kicked clear with Denman in the straight and took charge from the second-last, appearing to win with plenty in hand, though he would have been tested far more had Burton Port not made a bad mistake five out, and with both horses subsequently ruled out for the season the form is still to be tested. Denman proved he had lost little of his ability by holding off **The Tother One** and **Niche Market** for third, while **Weird Al** and **Pandorama** were both major disappointments.

8 stanjames.com Fighting Fifth Hurdle (Grade 1) (2m110yds)
Newbury November 27 (Good To Soft)
1 **Peddlers Cross** 5-11-7   Jason Maguire
2 **Starluck** 5-11-7   Timmy Murphy
3 **Binocular** 6-11-7   A P McCoy
9/4, 7/1, 5/6F. 1¼l, 6l. 5 ran. 4m 0.00s
(Donald McCain).

Switched from Newcastle because of snow, this was an intriguing clash between **Binocular**, the top 2m hurdler in Britain at the time, and the horse many would see as his successor by the end of the season in **Peddlers Cross**, but it didn't produce a fair reflection of their ability even though the young pretender won in hugely impressive fashion. Binocular, looking some way short of peak fitness, was well beaten on his reappearance for the second successive season as he was even left behind by **Starluck** in the closing stages, but Peddlers Cross, who had won at Cheltenham and Aintree over 2m4f, did brilliantly to drop down in trip and see off that solid yardstick even in a slowly-run race, taking over a modest pace three out and outsprinting Starluck from the last.

9 Keith Prowse Hospitality Tingle Creek Chase (Grade 1) (2m110yds)
Cheltenham December 11 (Good To Soft)
1 **Master Minded** 7-11-7   Noel Fehily
2 **Petit Robin** 7-11-7   Barry Geraghty
3 **Somersby** 6-11-7   Hadden Frost
10/11F, 6/1, 13/2. 8l, ½l. 9 ran. 4m 1.20s
(Paul Nicholls).

Back on track with a winning return at Ascot after his disastrous 2009/10 campaign, **Master Minded** continued his comeback with his first Grade 1 win in more than 18 months in another

MENORAH (left): quickens clear of Cue Card in what proved a moderate race

race held in unfamiliar surroundings after Sandown's abandonment. Master Minded jumped as boldly as ever and powered clear on the run-in, but he still didn't prove he was back to his very best at the trip as **Petit Robin** got closer than he had on all six previous runs at the top level and **Somersby** understandably failed to run to his best having reared over on the paddock walkway before the race, also making a notable mid-race blunder.

10 stanjames.com International Hurdle (Grade 2) (2m1f)

Cheltenham December 11 (Good To Soft)
1 **Menorah** 5-11-4   Richard Johnson
2 **Cue Card** 4-11-4   Joe Tizzard
3 **Silviniaco Conti** 4-11-8   Noel Fehily
7/4F, 15/8, 5/2. 4½l, ½l. 9 ran. 4m 3.50s
(Philip Hobbs).

An unusual renewal with a clutch of up-and-coming hurdlers having the race to themselves, and **Menorah** did far more than **Cue Card** and **Silviniaco Conti** to advance his championship credentials. Menorah probably didn't even have to run to his Greatwood form as the novice Cue Card failed to find as much as expected off the bridle and Silviniaco Conti proved a sitting duck between the last two on this drop down in trip, leaving Menorah to quicken impressively clear up the hill in what proved a moderate race.

11 Vote A. P. Gold Cup Handicap Chase (Grade 3) (2m5f)

Cheltenham December 11 (Good To Soft)
1 **Poquelin** 7-11-12   Ian Popham (5)
2 **Great Endeavour** 6-10-5   Timmy Murphy
3 **Sunnyhillboy** 7-10-2 Richie McLernon (3)
16/1, 13/2, 9/1. 1l, 6l. 16 ran. 5m 10.26s
(Paul Nicholls).

A second successive win in the race for **Poquelin**, defying a 12lb higher mark, though the 5lb claim of talented rider Ian Popham played a big part as he still came up just short at Grade 1 level after. Popham had Poquelin beautifully poised to strike turning for home and was always just holding **Great Endeavour** in a driving finish, while **Sunnyhillboy** ran a cracker to just pip **Calgary Bay** for third having been left behind by several early mistakes. It was 11l back to **Little Josh**, who still ran creditably off a 9lb higher mark until hitting the second-last, with **Mad Max** next.

12 Bar One Racing Hatton's Grace Hurdle (Grade 1) (2m4f)

Fairyhouse (IRE) December 15 (Soft)
1 **Hurricane Fly** 6-11-10   P Townend
2 **Solwhit** 6-11-10   D N Russell
3 **Voler La Vedette** 6-11-5   A E Lynch
11/4, EvensF, 8/1. 1½l, 1¾l. 11 ran. 5m 6.40s
(W P Mullins).

PANDORAMA (second right): still on the bridle approaching the final fence

A terrific clash between the top two Irish hurdlers as **Hurricane Fly**, the only horse to beat **Solwhit** in his previous seven races in Ireland, got the better of his old rival even over a longer trip. The more stamina-laden Solwhit was the first to strike for home in the straight, but he still couldn't shake off Hurricane Fly as he asserted close home and won going away with **Voler La Vedette** again close behind in third and **Mourad** doing well to challenge in fourth over an inadequate trip.

13 John Durkan Memorial Punchestown Chase (Grade 1) (2m4f)
Fairyhouse (IRE) December 15 (Soft)
1 **Tranquil Sea** 8-11-10   A J McNamara
2 **J'y Vole** 7-11-5   D J Condon
3 **Roberto Goldback** 8-11-10   R M Power
5/2, 4/1, 13/2. ¾l, ¾l. 8 ran. 5m 12.50s
(E J O'Grady).

Successive reschedulings, eventually seeing the race switched from Punchestown, killed off British interest in the race and cleared the way for **Tranquil Sea** to make his Grade 1 breakthrough. Always prominent, he proved too strong for a string of challengers as **J'y Vole** ran on for second ahead of **Roberto Goldback**, **Glencove Marina** and disappointing favourite **Cooldine**, and though just 3¹/₂l covered that quintet Roberto Goldback and Glencove Marina would both run well at the top level again to frank the form to a degree.

14 Lexus Chase (Grade 1) (3m)
Leopardstown (IRE) December 28 (Heavy)
1 **Pandorama** 7-11-10   P Carberry
2 **Money Trix** 10-11-10   D N Russell
3 **Joncol** 7-11-10   A P Cawley
7/2J, 7/1, 5/1. 6l. ¾l. 12 ran. 6m 30.00s
(Noel Meade).

A clearcut victory for **Pandorama**, who showed himself to be the best of an admittedly modest bunch of Irish staying chasers. Disappointing subsequently in the Gold Cup, Pandorama had his favoured soft ground on this occasion and was able to produce a telling burst of speed from the last, drawing clear of **Money Trix** and **Joncol**. **Kempes** was still going well when unseating his rider two out, though the fact that the fourth, **Glencove Marina**, was beaten around 5l further than he was later in the Hennessy suggests Kempes wouldn't have been able to match Pandorama anyway.

15 A.P. Wins Sports Personality Long Walk Hurdle (Grade 1) (3m110yds)
Newbury December 29 (Good To Soft)
1 **Big Buck's** 7-11-7   A P McCoy
2 **Lough Derg** 10-11-7   Tom Scudamore
3 **Restless Harry** 6-11-7   Henry Oliver
2/13F, 40/1, 12/1. 6l, hd. 6 ran.
(Paul Nicholls).

Big Buck's made it a perfect ten since being

switched to hurdles nearly two years previously. Having scared off all worthwhile opposition just like when making a winning reappearance at the same track in November, Big Buck's eased clear of the game **Lough Derg**, who just held off **Restless Harry** for second with the leading trio 20l clear of **Kayf Aramis** in fourth.

16 Paddy Power Dial-A-Bet Chase (Grade 1) (2m1f)
Leopardstown (IRE) December 29 (Heavy)

1 **Big Zeb** 9-11-12		Barry Geraghty
2 **Golden Silver** 8-11-12		P Townend
3 **Scotsirish** 9-11-12		D J Condon

EvensF, 15/8, 22/1. 1¾l, 1l. 4 ran. 4m 24.90s (C A Murphy).

A terrific clash between three of the first four in the subsequent Champion Chase and **Big Zeb** showed that he was still a major force with a battling victory. Big Zeb was all out to hold off **Golden Silver** and **Scotsirish**, but he had been three lengths clear after the last and, having reportedly missed a key piece of work to account for his tired finish, he would prove much the best horse in the race, even though Golden Silver managed to turn the tables next time at Punchestown when Big Zeb was left in front much too early. **Captain Cee Bee** hated the heavy ground.

17 paddypower.com iPhone App Festival Hurdle (Grade 1) (2m)
Leopardstown (IRE) December 29 (Heavy)

1 **Hurricane Fly** 6-11-10		P Townend
2 **Solwhit** 6-11-10		D N Russell
3 **Luska Lad** 6-11-10	Andrew J McNamara

8/11F, 6/4, 20/1. 2l, shd. 5 ran. 4m 10.80s (W P Mullins).

Another tremendous performance from **Hurricane Fly**, who proved even more superior to the reopposing **Solwhit** over a slowly-run 2m as he won easily with a stunning turn of foot. Hurricane Fly led on the bridle at the last before drawing clear as Solwhit was left to fight off **Luska Lad**, who was flattered by his proximity having dictated the modest gallop, whereas **Thousand Stars** could never land a blow from the rear in fourth.

18 Cheltenham & Three Counties Club Hurdle (2m4f110yds)
Cheltenham January 1 (Good To Soft)

1 **Oscar Whisky** 6-11-4		Barry Geraghty
2 **Any Given Day** 6-11-8		Jason Maguire
3 **Celestial Halo** 7-11-8		Harry Skelton

3/1, 7/2, 9/2. 7l, 6l. 7 ran. 5m 0.50s (Nicky Henderson).

A very similar race to a Grade 2 won at the track the previous month by **Karabak**, but **Oscar Whisky** proved far too good for those who had figured in that contest with a hugely impressive performance. Oscar Whisky led on the bit before the last and had far too much speed for the progressive **Any Given Day**, even being eased before the finish to point the way to a crack at the Champion Hurdle. Any Given Day was in turn clear of **Celestial Halo** and Karabak, who had no chance conceding 8lb to the winner.

19 Coral Welsh National Handicap Chase (Grade 3) (3m5f110yds)
Chepstow January 8 (Soft)

1 **Synchronised** 8-11-6		A P McCoy
2 **Giles Cross** 9-10-2		Harry Skelton
3 **I'moncloudnine** 8-10-3	Dougie Costello

5/1, 12/1, 16/1. 2¾l, 9l. 18 ran. 7m 53.70s (Jonjo O'Neill).

Mudlark **Synchronised** landed his second big handicap in successive seasons as he followed up victory in the Midlands National despite a seemingly harsh rise in the weights. Synchronised's stamina wasn't even fully tested in a race run at only a fair gallop, and he showed real class to ease past **Giles Cross** between the last two and storm to victory, hinting at plenty more to come on soft ground. The first two pulled 9l clear of **I'moncloudnine** and **Ballyfitz**, who would both go on to post similar strong finishes in other good staying chases, with an even bigger gap back to favourite **Maktu** and **Silver By Nature**, whose yard had been most held up by the bad weather.

20 williamhill.com Christmas Hurdle (Grade 1) (2m)
Kempton January 15 (Good To Soft)

1 **Binocular** 7-11-7		A P McCoy
2 **Overturn** 7-11-7		Jason Maguire
3 **Starluck** 6-11-7		Timmy Murphy

13/8F, 7/1, 3/1. 3¾l, 2¼l. 6 ran. 3m 53.60s (Nicky Henderson).

Binocular showed something like his true colours for the only time all season as he won a fairly soft renewal. **Overturn** turned the race into a strong test of stamina for the trip and seemed to run much better than he did under more restraint in the Champion Hurdle, but Binocular was still able to lay up comfortably and quickened decisively clear in the straight. That said, **Starluck** wasn't suited by the run of the race in third and, while **Khyber Kim** was well beaten in fourth, subsequent races showed that he had lost his zip, questioning just how much Binocular achieved in victory.

21 William Hill King George VI Chase (Grade 1) (3m)
Kempton January 15 (Good To Soft)
1 **Long Run** 6-11-10   Mr S Waley-Cohen
2 **Riverside Theatre** 7-11-10   B Geraghty
3 **Kauto Star** 11-11-10   A P McCoy
9/2, 10/1, 4/7F. 12l, 7l. 9 ran. 6m 3.04s
(Nicky Henderson).

Kauto Star passed the baton on to another potential great as **Long Run** stormed to a comfortable win with the four-time champion only third. Long Run was always travelling much better than the favourite and eased clear in the straight, though the fact that Kauto Star was still beaten just 19l in a race which saw everything conspire against him – he was found to have bled and be suffering from a small infection, while he also clouted the second-last when still likely to finish second – suggests Long Run didn't have to run to the form he showed at Cheltenham in the Gold Cup. **Riverside Theatre** stayed on strongly into second on his first attempt at the trip, while **Nacarat**, who again didn't stay in fourth, was the only other horse to run close to form with **Planet Of Sound**'s breathing problems resurfacing and **Forpady-deplasterer** and **Albertas Run** both pulled up.

22 Victor Chandler Chase (registered as the Clarence House Chase) (Grade 1) (2m1f)
Ascot January 22 (Good To Soft)
1 **Master Minded** 8-11-7   A P McCoy
2 **Somersby** 7-11-7   Hadden Frost
3 **Mad Max** 9-11-7   David Bass
4/7F, 8/1, 8/1. shd, 20l. 9 ran. 4m 4.90s
(Paul Nicholls).

A real thriller as **Master Minded** was all out to hold off the fast-finishing **Somersby** to show that he was still just about the top two-miler in Britain, though as the Champion Chase would prove that wasn't really saying much. Master Minded led five out and soon looked in command, but he lacked his old acceleration to shake off Somersby, who hit top gear from the second-last and only just failed to get up. The pair were 20l clear of **Mad Max**, who had his limitations well exposed, while **Petit Robin** was going well when he fell five out, suffering a season-ending injury in the process.

23 BHP Insurances Irish Champion Hurdle (Grade 1) (2m)
Leopardstown (IRE) January 23 (Soft)
1 **Hurricane Fly** 7-11-10   P Townend
2 **Solwhit** 7-11-10   D N Russell
3 **Thousand Stars** 7-11-10   Ms K Walsh

4/9F, 3/1, 14/1. 3½l, 2l. 5 ran. 3m 52.10s
(W P Mullins).

Hurricane Fly made it a hat-trick of Grade 1 wins in little over two months as he mastered **Solwhit** yet again. Given a test at championship speed by the presence of **Thousand Stars** as a pacemaker, Hurricane Fly jumped better than ever and showed his trademark burst of speed at the last to win well, while Solwhit ran a sound race in second and Thousand Stars also pointed to his fine spring form by staying on well once headed between the last two. **Voler La Vedette** was 9l back in fourth.

24 Argento Chase (registered as the Cotswold Chase) (Grade 2) (3m1f 110yds)
Cheltenham January 29 (Good To Soft)
1 **Neptune Collonges** 10-11-0   A P McCoy
2 **Tidal Bay** 10-11-0   Brian Hughes
3 **Punchestowns** 8-11-5   Barry Geraghty
11/2, 5/2, 11/10F. 1¼l, 30l. 5 ran. 6m 48.78s
(Paul Nicholls).

Traditionally one of the best Gold Cup trials, this had little impact on the top of the staying division as veterans **Neptune Collonges** and **Tidal Bay** dominated while young hope **Punchestowns** was hugely disappointing. Otherwise below-par on his return from an 18-month lay-off, Neptune Collonges still proved good enough to make all the running as Tidal Bay proved at his most frustrating, again staying on all too late in a race that should have been there for the taking at his best. Punchestowns jumped badly before fading into third, leaving him with much to prove over fences.

25 Rewards4Racing Cleeve Hurdle (Grade 2) (3m)
Cheltenham January 29 (Good To Soft)
1 **Grands Crus** 6-11-4   Tom Scudamore
2 **Knockara Beau** 8-11-0   Jan Faltejsek
3 **Restless Harry** 7-11-4   Henry Oliver
2/1F, 33/1, 7/1. 10l, hd. 14 ran. 6m 3.60s
(David Pipe).

A chance for the young stayers to establish their own pecking order, with several exciting handicap graduates trying a step up in class, and **Grands Crus** was the one to take a giant leap forward with a tremendous win. Racing keenly under restraint, Grands Crus still had enough in his locker to bound clear once asked to quicken two out and won without coming off the bridle, and with runner-up **Knockara Beau** landing a handicap next time before finishing fourth in the hugely competitive Pertemps Final off 156, this confirmed the winner as by far the closest stayer to Big Buck's. Knockara Beau just held off the game **Restless Harry** for second with **Bensalem**, who just ran out of steam on his reappearance, and **Organisateur** the main disappointments.

26 Hennessy Gold Cup (Grade 1) (3m) Leopardstown (IRE) February 12 (Heavy)

1 **Kempes** 8-11-10		D J Casey
2 **Glencove Marina** 9-11-10		R M Power
3 **Joncol** 8-11-10		A P Cawley

5/1, 25/1, 13/8F. 4½l, 4½l. 9 ran. 6m 26.70s (W P Mullins).

A tragic contest as **Glencove Marina** died of a heart attack after his gallant effort in second and **Money Trix** suffered a fatal injury, but looking to the future **Kempes** emerged as another promising young staying chaser. Kempes quickened up well to make amends for his late mishap in the Lexus, though this looked a slightly weaker race with Glencove Marina able to run into second ahead of the disappointing **Joncol**, who ran a flat race in third, and Kempes has questions to answer after pulling up twice subsequently.

27 totesport Trophy Handicap Hurdle (Grade 3) (2m110yds)
Newbury February 18 (Soft)

1 **Recession Proof** 5-10-8	Dougie Costello
2 **Bothy** 5-10-10	Danny Cook (3)
3 **Notus De La Tour** 5-11-1	Tom Scudamore

12/1, 8/1, 10/1. shd, 1¼l. 15 ran. 3m 52.96s (John Quinn).

A fiercely competitive race in which the first six were separated by less than 3l, helped by the fact that no horse would prove much better than their original handicap mark. The unexposed **Recession Proof**, who would just come up short against the best novices later, led the way on only his fourth run over timber, travelling well in such a big field and just seeing off the unlucky **Bothy**, who paid the price for a 9lb rise following his similar near miss in the Greatwood. **Notus De La Tour** and **The Betchworth Kid** filled the places ahead of **Soldatino**.

28 Betfair Ascot Chase (Grade 1) (2m5f 110yds)
Ascot February 19 (Soft)

1 **Riverside Theatre** 7-11-7	Barry Geraghty
2 **Gauvain** 9-11-7	Daryl Jacob
3 **Deep Purple** 10-11-7	Paul Moloney

11/10F, 14/1, 10/1. 10l, 11l. 7 ran. 5m 23.31s (Nicky Henderson).

Easy pickings for **Riverside Theatre** once **Pride**

Of Dulcote had suffered a fatal fall as he easily landed a race which failed to attract any of the major players from Cheltenham or Aintree at this trip. Soft ground negated the affect of dropping down in distance after his King George second and he proved far too strong for his rivals, with **Gauvain**, running a cracker after being found out at the top level over 2m, the only horse to keep him in sight. Peterborough Chase winner **Tartak** was the best of the specialists at the trip but jumped poorly in fifth.

29 totesport.com Grand National Trial Handicap Chase (Grade 3) (3m4f)
Haydock February 19 (Heavy)

1 **Silver By Nature** 9-11-12	Peter Buchanan
2 **Ballyfitz** 11-10-10	David England
3 **Le Beau Bai** 8-11-0	Jake Greenall (7)

10/1, 14/1, 15/2. 15l, 6l. 14 ran. 7m 42.30s (Lucinda Russell).

Given a chance by the handicapper having been dropped 7lb after a disappointing run in the Welsh National, **Silver By Nature** took full advantage by storming to a second successive 15l win in this race to again show himself to

SILVER BY NATURE: a top-class chaser when the mud is flying

be a top-class chaser in gruelling conditions. Only four out of the 14 runners managed to get round, yet Silver By Nature defied his big weight by easing clear from the fourth-last and stayed on strongly from the rock-solid **Ballyfitz**, who jumped better than ever in second to provide a solid backbone to the form. **Carruthers** found the trip beyond him in fourth.

30 Bathwick Tyres Kingwell Hurdle (Grade 2) (2m)

Wincanton February 19 (Good To Soft)
1	**Mille Chief** 5-11-2	Robert Thornton
2	**Celestial Halo** 7-11-6	Harry Skelton
3	**Ronaldo Des Mottes** 6-11-2	T Murphy

15/8, 8/1, 12/1. nse, 18l. 5 ran. 3m 43.20s (Alan King).

Champion Hurdle dark horse **Mille Chief** just enjoyed a successful warm-up but was pushed far too close to really justify his festival aspirations and wouldn't recover in time for his spring efforts at Cheltenham and Ayr. Having burst into the picture with a stunning handicap win at Sandown on his previous start, Mille Chief hinted that could be the limit of his ability as he struggled to exploit a 4lb concession from **Celestial Halo**, while **Silviniaco Conti** was a below-par fourth.

31 Racing Post Handicap Chase (Grade 3) (3m)

Kempton February 26 (Good To Soft)
1	**Quinz** 7-11-0	Richard Johnson
2	**Mount Oscar** 12-10-10	Aidan Coleman
3	**Nacarat** 10-11-12	Paddy Brennan

8/1, 50/1, 5/1. 1¼l, 18l. 16 ran. 6m 12.00s (Philip Hobbs).

Another disappointing renewal of a race possibly losing its lustre due to its proximity to Cheltenham, with only two horses involved in the finish including a 12-year-old veteran at 50/1, though **Quinz** still did well to win as a novice. Quinz looked to have been collared at the last as **Mount Oscar**, recovering from a bad blunder four out, produced a strong challenge, but he pulled out more to win going away. The first two pulled well clear of **Nacarat**, who had won on good ground in 2009 but again saw his stamina ebbing away in the straight in softer conditions, and with little depth to the race there was a 13l gap to the rest.

32 Stewart Family Spinal Research Handicap Chase (Grade 3) (3m 110yds)

Cheltenham March 15 (Good)
1	**Bensalem** 8-11-2	Robert Thornton
2	**Carole's Legacy** 7-11-5	Barry Geraghty
3	**Reve De Sivola** 6-10-13	Daryl Jacob

5/1, 9/1, 9/1. ½l, 11l. 19 ran. 6m 10.00s (Alan King).

Victory 12 months late for **Bensalem**, who had looked a likely winner in 2010 when falling two out and landed a well-hatched plan to make amends. Left on the same mark, Bensalem had

QUINZ (left): manages the feat of winning the Racing Post Chase as a novice

been deliberately campaigned over hurdles to protect that rating and saw the race map out perfectly as he was held up off a furious gallop and crept gently into contention before just proving strong enough in a thrilling finish. **Carole's Legacy** made him pull out all the stops, though, as the pair pulled clear of the novice **Reve De Sivola**, who was very well weighted on his hurdles form but typically made too many mistakes, while **Great Endeavour**, despite badly missing the break, had still only just been headed when falling two out.

33 Stan James Champion Hurdle Challenge Trophy (Grade 1) (2m110yds)
Cheltenham March 15 (Good)

1 **Hurricane Fly** 7-11-10   R Walsh
2 **Peddlers Cross** 6-11-10   Jason Maguire
3 **Oscar Whisky** 6-11-10   Barry Geraghty
11/4F, 9/2, 7/1. 1¼l, 5l. 11 ran. 3m 53.71s
(W P Mullins).

Kept out of the festival by injury for the previous two years, **Hurricane Fly** finally dispelled the doubts about his ability as he got the better of **Peddlers Cross** in a terrific duel. The early gallop was surprisingly modest, but Hurricane Fly and Peddlers Cross pulled clear in the straight and Hurricane Fly, having travelled well throughout, just had the better change of gear at the last before holding on bravely up the hill. The quality of the race was hard to weigh up with all but one of the runners – the bitterly disappointing **Khyber Kim** – never having run in it before following Binocular's late defection, but **Oscar Whisky** and **Thousand Stars**, having both run fine races behind, went on to finish a clear first and second at Aintree next time, suggesting the first two are brilliant hurdlers even though Peddlers Cross disappointed there. **Menorah** had his limitations exposed at this level, while **Clerk's Choice** got much closer to him in sixth than at Cheltenham in December as he confirmed that he is a progressive youngster on good ground. **Overturn** and **Dunguib** were next, while **Mille Chief** ran no sort of race.

34 David Nicholson Mares' Hurdle (Grade 2) (2m4f)
Cheltenham March 15 (Good)

1 **Quevega** 7-11-5   R Walsh
2 **Sparky May** 6-11-5   Keiran Burke
3 **Ocean Transit** 6-11-0   David Bass
5/6F, 4/1, 50/1. 10l, 1l. 14 ran. 4m 48.08s
(W P Mullins).

A third successive win in the race for festival queen **Quevega** and this proved the easiest of the lot as she barely came off the bridle to annihilate the opposition. Novice **Sparky May** looked the only possible rival on the form book, and as she compromised her chance by pulling badly in the early stages, eventually tanking down the hill and simply giving Quevega a handy lead to the last, the champion was left with a straightforward chance for the hat-trick.

35 sportingbet.com Queen Mother Champion Chase (Grade 1) (2m)
Cheltenham March 16 (Good)

1 **Sizing Europe** 9-11-10   A E Lynch
2 **Big Zeb** 10-11-10   Barry Geraghty
3 **Captain Cee Bee** 10-11-10   A P McCoy
10/1, 3/1, 14/1. 5l, 4l. 11 ran. 3m 54.92s
(Henry De Bromhead).

Back at his favourite course and distance after an unsuccessful attempt at becoming a staying chaser, **Sizing Europe** proved he is a real star over 2m with a stunning performance, leading a remarkable clean sweep of the first four places for the Irish. Jumping well in front, Sizing Europe seemed to take a breather coming down the hill as the field bunched but then quickened away again in the straight more strongly than he ever had before to see off the defending champion **Big Zeb**, who seemed to run close to his best in second and probably wouldn't have won even on subsequent Punchestown form. **Captain Cee Bee** also ran on well to take third ahead of **Golden Silver**, who confirmed he could run to his best at Cheltenham after flopping twice previously, while **Somersby** was the best of the British runners in fifth ahead of **French Opera**. **Master Minded** was well beaten even before a blunder two out relegated him to eighth and, for all the misleading focus on a summer breathing operation reviving him, he again lacked the speed to be competitive on this slightly quicker going.

36 Coral Cup Handicap Hurdle (Grade 3) (2m5f)
Cheltenham March 16 (Good)

1 **Carlito Brigante** 5-11-0   D N Russell
2 **Bothy** 5-10-10   Danny Cook (3)
3 **Orsippus** 5-10-8   D J Condon
16/1, 12/1, 33/1. 6l, ½l. 22 ran. 5m 9.30s
(Gordon Elliott).

A demolition job from **Carlito Brigante**, who had been quietly campaigned after finishing fourth in the 2010 Triumph Hurdle and proved much better than his official mark of 140. Carlito Brigante was always cruising and had easily taken the measure of smart novice **For Non Stop** when that one fell at the last, allowing him to cruise home and earn a step up to Grade

1 company when his stamina just failed him at Aintree and Punchestown. **Bothy**, perhaps benefiting from a step up in trip, proved his love of big-field handicaps with another fine effort to hold off former festival winner **Orsippus** for second, and the form was given a significant boost when the fourth, **Battle Group**, went on to win at Aintree the following month. There was another decent gap after that one with highly-weighted pair **Solix** and **Walkon** both running fine races.

37 Ryanair Chase (registered as the Festival Trophy) (Grade 1) (2m5f)

Cheltenham March 17 (Good)

1 **Albertas Run** 10-11-10   A P McCoy
2 **Kalahari King** 10-11-10   Graham Lee
3 **Rubi Light** 6-11-10   A E Lynch
6/1, 7/1, 16/1. 1l, 2l. 11 ran. 5m 7.30s (Jonjo O'Neill).

A second successive win in the race for middle-distance king **Albertas Run**, who bounced back to form yet again on his favoured good ground to land a modest renewal. The form pick at his best with Riverside Theatre ruled out through injury and likely contenders Master Minded and Somersby opting for the Champion Chase, Albertas Run was able to stay in the front rank despite making several mistakes and hung on up the hill as **Kalahari King**, whose progress from the rear had also been checked by a couple of errors, just got going too late. Irish raider **Rubi Light** ran a cracker in third as that trio pulled clear of the disappointing **Poquelin** and **Voy Por Ustedes**, who showed up well on his reappearance, while **J'y Vole**, reported to have had an interrupted preparation, found less than expected in sixth with **Tartak** and **Gauvain** also below-par.

38 Ladbrokes World Hurdle (Grade 1) (3m)

Cheltenham March 17 (Good)

1 **Big Buck's** 8-11-10   R Walsh
2 **Grands Crus** 6-11-10   Tom Scudamore
3 **Mourad** 6-11-10   P Townend
10/11F, 7/2, 8/1. 1¾l, 2¾l. 13 ran. 5m 50.80s (Paul Nicholls).

The most eagerly-awaited battle of the festival saw **Big Buck's** complete a memorable hat-trick as he proved utterly dominant once again despite being handed a much different task to those faced in previous renewals. An extremely modest gallop turned the race into a sprint in the straight, but Big Buck's was always beautifully poised just off the pace, quickening into the lead between the last two, and was well

on top at the line despite hanging left after his rider has dropped his whip. The rest were hugely flattered to finish so close, with just 9l covering the next eight, though **Grands Crus** built on the big impression made in the Cleeve Hurdle by coming through for a clear second ahead of Irish raider **Mourad**, and **Rigour Back Bob** ran an eye-catching race from the rear in fifth. **Zaynar** was the big disappointment of the contest.

39 Vincent O'Brien County Handicap Hurdle (Grade 3) (2m1f)

Cheltenham March 18 (Good)

1 **Final Approach** 5-10-12   R Walsh
2 **Get Me Out Of Here** 7-11-7   A P McCoy
3 **Nearby** 7-11-8   Chris Davies (7)
10/1, 7/1, 66/1, 33/1. nse, 1½l. 26 ran. 3m 54.77s (W P Mullins).

Wisely pulled out of the rescheduled Totesport Trophy when prize-money dropped in order to protect what was felt to be a terrific handicap market for a more valuable prize, **Final Approach** justified connections' bold stance as he got up on the line to deny **Get Me Out Of Here**. Final Approach took an age to get going, being pushed along three out and still no better than midfield after the second-last, but he flew up the hill to thwart Get Me Out Of Here, who was revitalised after an operation to aid his breathing and ran a stormer given he was again reported to have choked on the run-in. The overall form didn't look special, though, as little over 5l covered the first ten, with notable efforts from **Nearby** in third and top-weight **Salden Licht** in fifth.

40 totesport Cheltenham Gold Cup Chase (Grade 1) (3m2f110yds)

Cheltenham March 18 (Good)

1 **Long Run** 6-11-10   Mr S Waley-Cohen
2 **Denman** 11-11-10   Sam Thomas
3 **Kauto Star** 11-11-10   R Walsh
7/2F, 8/1, 5/1. 7l, 4l. 13 ran. 6m 29.70s (Nicky Henderson).

One of the most memorable races of all time as legendary champions **Denman** and **Kauto Star** served it up to the opposition, but ultimately neither could prevent **Long Run** confirming his new status as the best staying chaser around. Kauto Star put his Kempton disappointment behind him, travelling and jumping superbly, but he just didn't have the legs of old from the second-last, hanging on to an honourable third, while Denman did brilliantly to last even longer, particularly on ground so quick that the course record was broken, though that also

FINAL APPROACH (nearside): set to mow down his rivals up the famous hill

makes it debatable whether he quite ran to his Hennessy form. Nonetheless Long Run proved much the best of the younger generation as he was the only horse able to lay up with the old guard despite a few minor mistakes before being driven clear between the last two for a clearcut victory. **What A Friend** ran a cracker to finish a short-head behind Kauto Star, pulling 8l clear of **Midnight Chase**, who marked his arrival as a high-class chaser stepping out of handicap company, with **Tidal Bay** finishing typically fast behind him. **Pandorama** found the ground too quick but was still best of the Irish in seventh as **Kempes** and **China Rock** were pulled up, as was **Imperial Commander**, who dropped out quickly from the fourth-last and was found to be lame as well as breaking a blood vessel.

41 Johnny Henderson Grand Annual Challenge Cup Handicap Chase **(Grade 3) (2m110yds)**
Cheltenham March 18 (Good)
1 **Oiseau De Nuit** 9-11-6   S Clements (7)
2 **Askthemaster** 11-10-11   P T Enright (3)
3 **Leo's Lucky Star** 9-11-0   Danny Cook (3)
40/1, 50/1, 20/1. 3¼l, 2¼l. 23 ran. 3m 52.80s
(Colin Tizzard).

A skinner for the bookmakers with the first three all priced at least 20-1, but there was no fluke about **Oiseau De Nuit**'s victory as he bounced back to form in terrific fashion. The formerly progressive chaser resumed his upward curve

back on his favoured good ground as he took command at the second-last and stayed on strongly, and he would have followed up off a 9lb higher mark at Aintree next time but for a catastrophic early blunder meaning he could do no better than second. Irish veteran **Askthemaster** chased him home ahead of **Leo's Lucky Star**, who pulled 6l clear of **De Boitron** in fourth and was comfortably the best of those held up as very few horses ever landed a blow.

42 BGC Partners Liverpool Hurdle **(Grade 1) (3m110yds)**
Aintree April 7 (Good To Soft)
1 **Big Buck's** 8-11-7   R Walsh
2 **Grands Crus** 6-11-7   Tom Scudamore
3 **Won In The Dark** 7-11-7   A E Lynch
4/6F, 3/1, 66/1. 5l, 7l. 11 ran. 6m 10.20s
(Paul Nicholls).

An even more stunning performance from **Big Buck's**, who wasn't even forced off the bridle as he toyed with **Grands Crus** and won with remarkable ease. Grands Crus was ridden differently to Cheltenham, taking on Big Buck's as early as the third-last when he jumped into the lead, but with the pace already much stronger that simply played into the hands of Big Buck's even more and he proved massively superior once again. **Carlito Brigante** was the only other horse to challenge the big two before his stamina folded two out, eventually finishing fourth as **Won In The Dark** stayed on well on his first attempt at the trip, while **Knockara Beau**

MASTER MINDED: in total command as he clears the last in the Melling Chase

was a distant fifth ahead of **Khyber Kim**.

43 totesport Bowl Chase (Grade 1) (3m1f)

Aintree April 7 (Good To Soft)
1 **Nacarat** 10-11-7   Paddy Brennan
2 **Carole's Legacy** 7-11-0   A P McCoy
3 **Follow The Plan** 8-11-7   T J Doyle
7/2, 4/1, 40/1. 6l, 3¾l. 6 ran. 6m 31.70s
(Tom George).

With **Denman** paying the price for his Gold Cup exertions, **Nacarat** was left with a relatively straightforward task in seeing off some fairly modest rivals for the grade, though he did the job brilliantly with a spectacular round of jumping. Back on his favoured ground for the first time since winning the Charlie Hall Chase on his seasonal debut (the going was barely worse than good and officially changed to good for the next day), Nacarat was never seriously challenged as he found a tremendous rhythm and galloped on strongly to see off **Carole's Legacy** and **Follow The Plan**. Denman finished fifth, easing home once his chance had gone, and **Punchestowns** finished lame in sixth.

44 John Smith's Melling Chase (Grade 1) (2m4f)

Aintree April 8 (Good)
1 **Master Minded** 8-11-10   R Walsh
2 **Albertas Run** 10-11-10   A P McCoy
3 **Somersby** 7-11-10   Robert Thornton
11/2, 11/4F, 5/1. 9l, ½l. 10 ran. 4m 57.50s
(Paul Nicholls).

A step up in trip opened a potentially exciting new chapter in **Master Minded**'s career as he produced arguably his best performance in more than two years with a stunning victory. Held up to get the trip, Master Minded was always cruising and found plenty when let down between the last two, proving it was the 2m trip as much as good ground that had held him back at Cheltenham as he quickened clear of Ryanair winner **Albertas Run**, seemingly with plenty more up his sleeve. Albertas Run again made several mistakes in the back straight and couldn't get away with them against a much stronger rival than he had faced at the festival, while **Somersby**, who had been expected to appreciate the step up in trip more, still lacked the necessary speed in third. **Tartak** bounced back to form in fourth from **French Opera**, who was beaten the same distance as he had been in the Champion Chase, while **Mad Max** ran his best race of the season in sixth.

45 John Smith's Aintree Hurdle (Grade 1) (2m4f)
Aintree April 9 (Good)
1 **Oscar Whisky** 6-11-7   Barry Geraghty
2 **Thousand Stars** 7-11-7   Ms K Walsh
3 **Salden Licht** 7-11-7   Robert Thornton
6/1, 16/1, 25/1. nk, 10l. 8 ran. 4m 45.30s
(Nicky Henderson).

Big guns **Peddlers Cross** and **Binocular** were both bitterly disappointing, but this still produced a tremendous race as **Oscar Whisky** and **Thousand Stars** followed up fine runs in the Champion Hurdle by fighting out the finish. Once again it was Oscar Whisky who just had the edge, leading five out and committing for home at the third-last before just holding the more patiently-ridden Irish raider as the pair pulled well clear of **Salden Licht**. Binocular was left behind from two out in fourth, the step up in trip possibly counting against him, and Peddlers Cross had nothing left in the tank after a fine season as he finished seventh.

46 John Smith's Grand National Handicap Chase (Grade 3) (4m4f)
Aintree April 9 (Good)
1 **Ballabriggs** 10-11-0   Jason Maguire
2 **Oscar Time** 10-10-9   Mr S Waley-Cohen
3 **Don't Push It** 11-11-10   A P McCoy
14/1, 14/1, 9/1. 2¼l, 12l. 40 ran. 9m 1.20s
(Donald McCain).

Held back to just one run over fences since establishing his Aintree credentials with victory in the Kim Muir in 2010, **Ballabriggs** rewarded connections' patience as he produced a similar bold-jumping performance from the front to enable trainer Donald McCain to follow in his family's legendary National tradition. Ballabriggs was pushed all the way by a horse campaigned in identical fashion in **Oscar Time**, aimed at the race since his Irish National second, but he found most on the run-in having made much of the running, forcing a pace fast enough to expose all of the dubious stayers in the field. That said, with few of the principals getting home even on good ground and veteran **State Of Play** able to plug on into fourth and finish closer than he had in his two previous cracks at the race, this may not have been a vintage renewal and the first two may struggle to do as well in the race off higher

marks as top-weight **Don't Push It** managed in following up his 2010 win with a gallant third. **Niche Market** and **Big Fella Thanks** faded from the last having shown up well for a long way, while the hard-luck stories were favourite **The Midnight Club**, who was staying on when stopped in his tracks by a faller three out and did well to recover to sixth, and **Killyglen**, who looked a huge threat when falling four out.

47 Isle of Skye Blended Whisky Scottish Champion Handicap Hurdle (Grade 2) (2m)
Ayr April 16 (Good)
1 **Sanctuaire** 5-10-8   R Walsh
2 **Bygones Of Brid** 8-10-8   Graham Lee
3 **Overturn** 7-11-10   Jason Maguire
9/2J, 14/1, 13/2. 1¾l, 1½l. 9 ran. 3m 38.10s
(Paul Nicholls).

Given a long break and a breathing operation after three lacklustre runs during the winter, one-time leading juvenile **Sanctuaire** bounced back to form as he eased to an impressive win. Settling much better than when he blotted his copybook at Sandown the following week, Sanctuaire cruised into the lead on the bridle at the last and edged clear of **Bygones Of Brid**, who ran close to Champion Hurdle form with top-weight **Overturn** to show that Sanctuaire still has a long way to go to be regarded in the highest class.

48 Coral Scottish Grand National Handicap Chase (Grade 3) (4m110yds)
Ayr April 16 (Good)
1 **Beshabar** 9-10-4   Richard Johnson
2 **Merigo** 10-10-0   Timmy Murphy
3 **Always Right** 9-10-0   James Reveley
15/2, 20/1, 15/2. ¾l, nk. 28 ran. 8m 2.50s
(Tim Vaughan).

A strange renewal with 22 of the 30 runners racing from out of the handicap thanks to the presence of **Neptune Collonges** at the top of the weights, helping classy novice **Beshabar**, one of those able to race off his correct mark, to claim victory. Always in the front rank, Beshabar jumped superbly and pulled out more in the straight to just hold off the challenge of the 2010 winner **Merigo**, who was 12lb wrong after a disappointing season and ran a better race in defeat than 12 months before, while **Always Right** also went close from 3lb out of the handicap. The trio pulled 30l clear of veteran **Lothian Falcon** in fourth, while Beshabar's Cheltenham conqueror **Chicago Grey** was among the disappointments along with another novice, **The Minack**, and **Blazing Bailey**.

49 bet365 Gold Cup Handicap Chase (Grade 3) (3m5f110yds)
Sandown April 23 (Good To Firm)
1 **Poker De Sivola** 8-10-12   Timmy Murphy
2 **Faasel** 10-10-12   C O'Farrell (5)
3 **Baby Run** 11-10-12   Sam Twiston-Davies
11/1, 14/1, 6/1F. 2¼l, 1¼l. 18 ran. 7m 16.30s
(Ferdy Murphy).

An extremely modest renewal of Britain's end-of-season highlight, with only two horses rated above 140 and a couple of veterans filling the places, but **Poker De Sivola** landed a remarkable win in the manner of one with plenty in hand. The 2010 National Hunt Chase winner was ridden with hugely exaggerated waiting tactics, even being detached in last with a circuit to run, and it didn't help that a fairly modest gallop meant there were several still in contention at the death with 6l covering the first five, but he still managed to pick them up with a tremendous late rattle, coming from sixth three out to get up on the flat. **Faasel** plugged on for second, while **Baby Run**, the best hunter chaser in training, ran as well as could be expected in third given how hunters have struggled to make a mark in top handicaps.

50 bet365.com Celebration Chase (Grade 2) (2m)
Sandown April 23 (Good To Firm)
1 **French Opera** 8-11-2   A P McCoy
2 **Chaninbar** 8-11-2   Sam Twiston-Davies
3 **Cornas** 9-11-2   Leighton Aspell
2/1, 33/1, 15/2. 2l, 1¾l. 6 ran. 3m 48.90s
(Nicky Henderson).

A much deserved win for **French Opera**, who had run creditably at Cheltenham and Aintree and took advantage of having his sights lowered to a more realistic level. Under an aggressive ride, French Opera didn't seem as comfortable racing right-handed but still proved good enough to see off a trio of smart handicappers, led by the moody **Chaninbar**, who finally showed his true colours by holding off **Cornas** and **Oiseau De Nuit** for second having refused to race on each of his previous three starts. **Tataniano**, conceding 4lb all round, also ran a decent race in fifth, beaten less than 5l, while suggesting he's flattered by his Grade 1 win as a novice in 2010.

51 Ladbrokes Irish Grand National Handicap Chase (Grade A) (3m5f)
Fairyhouse (IRE) April 25 (Good)
1 **Organisedconfusion** 6-9-13   N Carberry
2 **Western Charmer** 9-10-6   A E Lynch
3 **Sunnyhillboy** 8-10-6   Richie McLernon
12/1, 16/1, 6/1F. 5l, 1l. 25 ran. 7m 35.10s
(A L T Moore).

Organisedconfusion became the youngest winner for 26 years in a race already dominated by youngsters as he burst on to the staying scene in terrific fashion. Crucially racing off a feather weight, Organisedconfusion needed to prove his stamina but seemed to improve hugely for the step up in trip as he pulled clear of the second-season novice **Western Charmer** from the second-last. Favourite **Sunnyhillboy** ran well in third, keeping on strongly having met interference four out, and there were decent gaps back to the rest, with standing dish **A New Story**, who had run as well as ever even at the age of 13 when third defending his cross-country title at Cheltenham, beaten further in fifth than when placed in the two previous renewals to suggest the form could be very strong. **Quantitativeeasing** travelled best of all but seemed to run out of stamina in the closing stages.

52 Boylesports.com Champion Chase (Grade 1) (2m)
Punchestown (IRE) May 3 (Good To Yielding)
1 **Big Zeb** 10-11-12   Barry Geraghty
2 **Sizing Europe** 9-11-12   Timmy Murphy
3 **Captain Cee Bee** 10-11-12   A P McCoy
9/4, 11/8F, 5/1. ¾l, 9l. 6 ran. 4m 11.70s
(C A Murphy).

Big Zeb turned around Cheltenham form with **Sizing Europe** in an absolute thriller between the season's two outstanding 2m chasers. Ridden closer to Sizing Europe than at the festival, Big Zeb even took over in front at the second-last and always had the edge thereafter, though Sizing Europe also stuck on superbly and only just paid the price for being unable to stretch the winner as much on this slightly easier track. **Captain Cee Bee** had also looked much more of a threat in the closing stages before making a couple of costly late mistakes as he settled for third, well clear of the below-par **Golden Silver** and **J'y Vole**.

53 Punchestown Guinness Gold Cup (Grade 1) (3m1f)
Punchestown (IRE) May 4 (Good)
1 **Follow The Plan** 8-11-10   T J Doyle
2 **Vic Venturi** 11-11-10   Barry Geraghty
3 **Rare Bob** 9-11-10   P Carberry
20/1, 40/1, 20/1. 11l, 4½l. 8 ran. 6m 28.60s
(Oliver McKiernan).

A shock result as **Follow The Plan**, well exposed as just below top-class, proved good enough to land a strange contest in which all

FOLLOW THE PLAN (right): avoids the carnage to claim a surprise victory

of the leading contenders fluffed their lines. Third behind **Nacarat** at Aintree on his most recent start, Follow The Plan barely needed to improve on that running to beat fellow outsiders **Vic Venturi** and **Rare Bob** and would have still been second had the unfortunate **Roberto Goldback** not unseated his rider at the last. **Kauto Star** ran no sort of race and was pulled up, as was **Kempes**, while **Tranquil Sea**, sixth in the race in 2010, possibly saw his stamina exposed in a more strongly-run race, unseating when tailed off four out, and Nacarat failed to settle and dropped into fourth.

54 Ladbrokes.com World Series Hurdle (Grade 1) (3m)

Punchestown (IRE) May 5 (Good)
1 **Quevega** 7-11-5   R Walsh
2 **Mourad** 6-11-10   Ms K Walsh
3 **Carlito Brigante** 5-11-10   D N Russell
8/11F, 11/2, 16/1. 1¼l, 5½l. 10 ran. 5m 45.60s
(W P Mullins).

Out on her own among the mares, **Quevega** showed that she also remained Ireland's top staying hurdler as she saw off stablemate **Mourad** in a terrific battle. Having travelled supremely well, Quevega struck for home first in the straight but was then forced to pull out all the stops as Mourad pushed her close, confirming the progress he had made during the season. The pair pulled away from **Carlito**

Brigante, who was close up at the last but just seemed to run out of steam as he was nearly caught for third by **Voler La Vedette**, while **Luska Lad** and **Won In The Dark** also did well to finish within 10l of Quevega.

55 Rabobank Champion Hurdle (Grade 1) (2m)

Punchestown (IRE) May 6 (Good)
1 **Hurricane Fly** 7-11-12   R Walsh
2 **Thousand Stars** 7-11-12   Ms K Walsh
3 **Binocular** 7-11-12   A P McCoy
1/2F, 9/1, 5/1. 5l, 4l. 6 ran. 3m 49.60s
(W P Mullins).

Hurricane Fly completed a brilliant unbeaten season as he finished in front of **Thousand Stars** for the fourth time with British raiders **Binocular** and **Menorah** behind. Hurricane Fly was more impressive than ever, cruising through to lead on the bridle at the last before producing his usual electric turn of foot, and Thousand Stars also seemed to run a career-best in second as he got closer to the winner than at Cheltenham even though a strongly-run race saw Menorah beaten further than he had been that day. An enterprising decision to make the running with Binocular was scuppered by his refusal to jump straight, seeing him lose the lead to Menorah before staying on back past that horse, who again had his limitations exposed at the top level.

Outlook

Top novices
by Dylan Hill

1 Independent Newspaper Novices' Chase (registered as the November Novices' Chase) (Grade 2) (2m)
Cheltenham November 14 (Good To Soft)
1 **Ghizao** 6-11-2   Timmy Murphy
2 **Captain Chris** 6-11-2   Richard Johnson
3 **Loosen My Load** 6-11-8   A E Lynch
13/2, 5/2F, 7/2. 10l, nk. 5 ran. 4m 2.38s
(Paul Nicholls).

A red-hot novice chase with three smart previous winners joined by subsequent Arkle hero **Captain Chris** on his chasing debut, but all four had no answer to an outstanding display from the outsider **Ghizao**, who quickened clear two out to win easily and would follow up by giving 10lb and a six-length beating to the runner-up again at Newbury next time. Though Captain Chris would steadily leave that form behind over fences, Ghizao did enough to show that he was a high-class novice and it may just be that small fields suit him best given his lack of size and jumping errors in the Arkle.

2 DRS Contracts Novices' Chase (3m1f110yds)
Cheltenham December 11 (Good To Soft)
1 **Time For Rupert** 6-11-9   Will Kennedy
2 **Chicago Grey** 7-11-9   P Carberry
3 **Quinz** 6-11-9   Richard Johnson
10/11F, 9/2, 6/1. 8l, 9l. 8 ran. 6m 29.40s
(Paul Webber).

Time For Rupert, hugely impressive on his chasing debut at Cheltenham, strengthened his burgeoning reputation with another outstanding victory. Time For Rupert jumped superbly and took command in the closing stages, forging clear of the subsequent National Hunt Chase winner **Chicago Grey** up the hill, with **Quinz**, who had already won a handicap chase at Ascot and went on to land the Racing Post Chase, boosting the form further in third.

Not right later in the season, Time For Rupert showed he belongs in the top bracket of staying chasers with this performance.

3 Bar One Racing Drinmore Novice Chase (Grade 1) (2m4f)
Fairyhouse (IRE) December 15 (Soft)
1 **Jessies Dream** 7-11-10   Timmy Murphy
2 **Realt Dubh** 6-11-10   P Carberry
3 **Head Of The Posse** 7-11-10   D J Casey
7/2, 9/2, 8/1. 5l, hd. 9 ran. 5m 5.90s
(Gordon Elliott).

A tremendously strong contest as the second and fourth, **Realt Dubh** and **Bostons Angel**, went on to win five Grade 1 races between them by the end of the season yet weren't good enough to get close to **Jessies Dream** and **Mikael D'Haguenet**, who were neck and neck when the latter fell at the last. Jessies Dream stayed on strongly and looked good enough to follow up in the RSA but for Bostons Angel's superior stamina, which adds to the impression that Mikael D'Haguenet, who had jumped superbly prior to his unfortunate tumble, remains a top-class prospect despite failing to jump as well subsequently with his confidence perhaps affected.

4 sportingbet Supports Heros Charity Challow Novices' Hurdle (Grade 1) (2m5f)
Newbury December 29 (Good To Soft)
1 **Backspin** 5-11-7   A P McCoy
2 **Court In Motion** 5-11-7   Sam Thomas
3 **Al Ferof** 5-11-7   Harry Skelton
5/1, 5/1, 5/2. 8l, 1¾l. 8 ran. 5m 21.22s
(Jonjo O'Neill).

A hugely impressive win from **Backspin**, who only needed to be pushed out to triumph in decisive fashion but tragically died in his box after just one more run. It's hard to know where Backspin would have ranked, for although he disappointed on that occasion this race worked out well with the smart **Court In Motion** finishing ahead of the subsequent Supreme winner **Al Ferof** in second while hardened handicap graduate **For Non Stop** was next.

5 **Tigmi Travel Dipper Novices' Chase (Grade 2) (2m5f)**

Cheltenham January 1 (Good To Soft)
1 **Hell's Bay** 9-11-4   Joe Tizzard
2 **Medermit** 7-11-4   Robert Thornton
3 **Reve De Sivola** 6-11-7   Daryl Jacob
16/1, 9/2, 4/1. ¾l, 22l. 13 ran. 5m 21.60s (Colin Tizzard).

Well beaten by Time For Rupert and Finian's Rainbow on his two previous starts, **Hell's Bay** dented several similar reputations when landing a surprise win. With market leaders **Mr Thriller** and **Reve De Sivola** jumping badly and **Master Of The Hall**, not for the last time, coming up short at this level, Hell's Bay was challenged only by **Medermit**, who was cruising close behind two out but lacked a change of gear and was always being held. Hell's Bay was subsequently ruled out of Cheltenham and Aintree though injury, though Medermit's failures there suggest he would probably have struggled to follow up this victory anyway.

6 **32Red Novices' Hurdle (registered as the Tolworth Hurdle) (Grade 1) (2m110yds)**

Sandown January 8 (Heavy)
1 **Minella Class** 6-11-7   Barry Geraghty
2 **Megastar** 6-11-7   Jamie Moore
3 **Toubab** 5-11-7   Sam Thomas
6/4F, 9/2, 2/1. 7l, 3½l. 5 ran. 4m 13.80s (Nicky Henderson).

An extremely moderate renewal, particularly with none of the runners appearing to appreciate the heavy ground, but **Minella Class** coped best to run out a comfortable winner. Minella Class produced a decisive burst after the third-last to leave his rivals toiling and was always holding **Megastar**, who would just turn the tables on better ground at Cheltenham, while **Toubab** plugged on at one pace in third.

7 **Coral Future Champions Finale Juvenile Hurdle (Grade 1) (2m110yds)**

Chepstow January 8 (Soft)
1 **Marsh Warbler** 4-11-0   Fearghal Davis
2 **Houblon Des Obeaux** 4-11-0   A Coleman
3 **Smad Place** 4-11-0   Wayne Hutchinson
8/1, 20/1, 9/4. 2¾l, ¾l. 8 ran. 4m 9.50s (Brian Ellison).

One of the strongest renewals in many years

MINELLA CLASS: ploughs through the mud to land a weak Tolworth Hurdle

on paper, but it didn't quite work out that way as **Marsh Warbler** made the most of a shrewd tactical move to pull off a surprise win. Marsh Warbler was ridden close to a modest gallop and struck for home early, staying on well to see off **Houblon Des Obeaux**. In contrast the two best horses in the field, **Smad Place** and most notably **Sam Winner**, would have appreciated a stiffer test even on the soft ground, with Sam Winner, despite setting the juvenile standard with two early-season wins at Cheltenham, soon looking in need of much further.

8 **Frank Ward Solicitors Arkle Novice Chase (Grade 1) (2m1f)**

Leopardstown (IRE) January 23 (Soft)

1 **Realt Dubh** 7-11-12		P Carberry
2 **Noble Prince** 7-11-12		Barry Geraghty
3 **Mr Cracker** 6-11-12		D N Russell

5/2F, 3/1, 7/1. shd, 10l. 6 ran. 4m 14.80s (Noel Meade).

A Grade 1 double for **Realt Dubh**, who still didn't entirely convince as he was helped by the late fall of a big rival for the second time and was all out to hold off **Noble Prince**. Left clear at the last when **Saludos** came down at Leopardstown over Christmas, Realt Dubh didn't appear to be going as well as **Flat Out** when that one fell in front two out, and he may well prove to be the best two-miler in the field having missed the rest of the season through injury. However, Realt Dubh fought hard to beat Noble Prince, who would prove better over further and briefly looked like outstaying the winner, while **Mr Cracker** was left behind in third and Saludos broke a blood vessel in fifth.

9 **Neptune Investment Management Novices' Hurdle (registered as the Classic Novices' Hurdle) (Grade 2) (2m4f110yds)**

Cheltenham January 29 (Good To Soft)

1 **Bobs Worth** 6-11-12	Barry Geraghty
2 **Rock On Ruby** 6-11-12	Harry Skelton
3 **Habbie Simpson** 6-11-9	Robert Thornton

7/2, 6/1, 9/1. 2¼l, 9l. 10 ran. 5m 24.85s (Nicky Henderson).

An excellent race which came within a short-head of producing two festival winners as **Bobs Worth** saw off **Rock On Ruby**. Bobs Worth didn't look to be travelling as well as Rock On Ruby or favourite **Backspin** down the hill, but he picked up well from the second-last and outstayed the runner-up on the run-in, pointing to a step up to 3m in March, while Rock On Ruby, a horse with the speed to have easily beaten Megastar over 2m previously, also did

well to pull 9l clear of Habbie Simpson in third. Something seemed to be amiss with the ill-fated Backspin, who hung badly right when headed, while **Champion Court**, a Grade 2 winner over course and distance, was also below-par.

10 **totepool Challengers Novices' Chase (registered as the Scilly Isles Novices' Chase) (Grade 1) (2m4f110yds)**

Sandown February 5 (Good)

1 **Medermit** 7-11-4		Robert Thornton
2 **Captain Chris** 7-11-4		Richard Johnson
3 **Mr Gardner** 8-11-4		Felix De Giles

5/2F, 4/1, 7/1. ½l, 7l. 9 ran. 5m 9.20s (Alan King).

A very competitive contest won in good style by **Medermit**, whose outstanding jumping meant he had the race pretty much put to bed long before **Captain Chris** ate into his lead on the run-in. However, with the runner-up only getting to grips with fences at Cheltenham and comprehensively reversing the form, Medermit proved to be flattered by this win, which may well remain the high point of his chasing career at Grade 1 level. Captain Chris was 7l clear of **Mr Gardner** and **Rock Noir**, while **Reve De Sivola** was again not fluent behind.

11 **Dr. P.J. Moriarty Novice Chase (Grade 1) (2m5f)**

Leopardstown (IRE) February 12 (Heavy)

1 **Bostons Angel** 7-11-10		R M Power
2 **Magnanimity** 7-11-10		D N Russell
3 **Mikael D'Haguenet** 7-11-10		P Townend

8/1, 6/1, 11/10F. hd, 5½l. 6 ran. 5m 36.30s (Mrs John Harrington).

Bostons Angel matched Realt Dubh in winning a second Grade 1 contest since the Drinmore as he fought off **Magnanimity** in a desperate finish with the Willie Mullins big guns of **Mikael D'Haguenet** and **Quel Esprit** both turned over. Having outstayed his rivals over 3m at Christmas, Bostons Angel again saw very testing conditions bring his stamina into play as he came out on top, seeing out his race far better than Mikael D'Haguenet, who wouldn't have won even without being badly hampered two out by the faller Quel Esprit, another who looked beaten at the time.

12 **Deloitte Novice Hurdle (Grade 1) (2m2f)**

Leopardstown (IRE) February 12 (Heavy)

1 **Oscars Well** 6-11-10		R M Power
2 **Zaidpour** 5-11-9		P Townend
3 **Shot From The Hip** 7-11-10	A J McNamara

7/1, EvensF, 6/1. 5½l, 3½l. 10 ran. 4m 28.40s (Mrs John Harrington).

By far the strongest novice hurdle run in Ireland all season, this saw **Oscars Well** win the battle of the Grade 1 winners against the more highly-touted **Zaidpour** in hugely impressive fashion. Oscars Well travelled supremely well and quickly settled the issue with a decisive burst of speed between the last two, easily beating Zaidpour, who had looked a star when winning what proved to be a very sub-standard Royal Bond and ran his best race in sticking on gamely for second. **Shot From The Hip** would prove much better than this at Punchestown as he just saw off **Hidden Universe** for third.

13 thebettingsite.com Adonis Juvenile Hurdle (Grade 2) (2m)
Kempton February 26 (Good To Soft)
1 **Zarkandar** 4-10-12   Daryl Jacob
2 **Molotof** 4-10-12   Barry Geraghty
3 **Kumbeshwar** 4-11-2   Robert Thornton
8/1, 3/1, 4/1. 2¼l, 15l. 9 ran. 3m 56.50s
(Paul Nicholls).

A race that has fast become the key juvenile trial for Cheltenham and that was the case again even though five of the first six had never run over hurdles in Britain. French recruits **Zarkandar** and **Molotof** led the way, the subsequent Triumph Hurdle hero just proving strongest from the second-last, and with another prominent festival finisher, the more experienced **Kumbeshwar**, left 15l behind in third, this was clearly a massive run from Molotof as well.

14 Stan James Supreme Novices' Hurdle (Grade 1) (2m110yds)
Cheltenham March 15 (Good)
1 **Al Ferof** 6-11-7   R Walsh
2 **Spirit Son** 5-11-7   Barry Geraghty
3 **Sprinter Sacre** 5-11-7   A P McCoy
10/1, 5/1, 11/1. 2l, 3¼l. 15 ran. 3m 52.10s
(Paul Nicholls).

A terrific contest with five of the first six in the market pulling well clear, and **Al Ferof** and **Spirit Son** stayed on far better than strong-travelling duo **Sprinter Sacre** and **Cue Card**. The latter pair looked to have the race between them turning for home, but it paid to be held up off a very strong gallop and Al Ferof, despite appearing outpaced down the hill, came through best of all with a wonderful late burst. Spirit Son also ran a cracker, even leading briefly at the last, and strongly franked the form at Aintree, though he was possibly helped by the step up to 2m4f, something that may also prove to be true of Al Ferof. Cue Card had been a red-hot favourite on the back of a fine second to Champion Hurdle contender Menorah, but

AL FEROF (left): has Spirit Son in his sights at the last in the Supreme

that form didn't work out and he found disappointingly little, being beaten to third by Sprinter Sacre, while **Recession Proof** was another to finish well in a fine fifth. There was a 7l gap back to **Rathlin**, who just proved best of the Irish from **Zaidpour** after that one made a bad blunder three out, while **Hidden Universe** ran a shocker at the festival for the second time.

15 Irish Independent Arkle Challenge Trophy Chase (Grade 1) (2m)
Cheltenham March 15 (Good)
1 **Captain Chris** 7-11-7   Richard Johnson
2 **Finian's Rainbow** 8-11-7   Barry Geraghty
3 **Realt Dubh** 7-11-7   P Carberry
6/1, 7/2, 17/2. 2¾l, 6l. 10 ran. 3m 51.68s
(Philip Hobbs).

This looked a weak renewal, with just one of the first five in the market having been rated above 142 over hurdles and a combination of injuries and the new 2m4f Grade 2 chase taking away much of the strength in depth, and so it proved with very few ever getting into contention behind **Captain Chris**. Having taken four runs to get off the mark over fences in a three-runner affair at Kempton, Captain Chris was never going particularly well but at least impressed with his jumping and hit top gear in the straight, staying on strongly to see off **Finian's Rainbow**, who had travelled by far the best throughout but was just outgunned. The pair pulled 6l clear of sole Irish raider **Realt Dubh** and **Medermit**, both of whom would have liked further, while **Ghizao** was well beaten in fifth after making a succession of mistakes.

16 Centenary Novices' Handicap Chase (Listed Race) (2m4f110yds)

Cheltenham March 15 (Good)

1 **Divers** 7-11-4   Graham Lee
2 **Quantitativeeasing** 6-11-11   A P McCoy
3 **Tullamore Dew** 9-11-11   Liam Treadwell
10/1, 7/1, 13/2. 2¾l, 2l. 20 ran. 5m 7.50s
(Ferdy Murphy)

Reduced to a 0-140 handicap for the first time, this obviously lacked the quality of previous renewals but still contained a stack of well-handicapped young chasers, most notably **Divers**. The race wasn't run to suit Divers as he was held up off a modest gallop and found it hard to find a way through with more than half the field in contention three out, but he quickened smartly to lead after the last and won going away. **Quantitativeeasing** strictly emerged as the best horse at the weights in second over **Tullamore Dew**, while **Vino Griego** was fourth ahead of the favourite **Definity**.

17 141st Year of the National Hunt Challenge Cup (Amateur Riders' Novices' Chase) (4m)

Cheltenham March 16 (Good)

1 **Chicago Grey** 8-11-6 Mr Derek O'Connor
2 **Beshabar** 9-11-6   Mr Tom David
3 **Be There In Five** 7-11-6   Mr S W-Cohen
5/1F, 9/1, 20/1. 4½l, 8l. 16 ran. 8m 20.70s
(Gordon Elliott).

This race has become an increasingly crucial guide to the top long-distance chases and **Beshabar**'s Scottish National win maintained its fine run, even suggesting this was probably the strongest ever running. A cut above his rivals on his smart 3m form, **Chicago Grey** was officially rated at least 20lb higher than each of the last six previous winners, in turn leaving Beshabar on a lofty mark at Ayr, and the pair made their class count here as Chicago Grey crept quietly into contention and quickened clear whole Beshabar stuck on well having been prominent throughout. The pair drew away from **Be There In Five** and **Alfa Beat**, who were in turn well clear of **Some Target**.

CHICAGO GREY (nearside): won a classy running of the National Hunt Chase

18 **Neptune Investment Management Novices' Hurdle (registered as the Baring Bingham Novices' Hurdle) (Grade 1) (2m5f)**
Cheltenham March 16 (Good)
1 **First Lieutenant** 6-11-7   D N Russell
2 **Rock On Ruby** 6-11-7   Daryl Jacob
3 **So Young** 5-11-7   R Walsh
7/1, 13/2, 2/1F. shd, 4½l. 12 ran. 5m 10.50s (M F Morris).

A dramatic finish saw **Oscars Well** arguably throw away victory with a terrible mistake at the last before **First Lieutenant** got up on the line to deny **Rock On Ruby**. Oscars Well had quickened into a narrow lead when he blundered away his chance, eventually finishing fourth, but the Irish still prevailed as First Lieutenant, who had just won a very slowly-run Grade 1 over 2m at Leopardstown, left that form behind stepping up in trip, staying on strongly up the hill. Rock On Ruby had been nominally left as the main British contender after Bobs Worth's surprise defection to the Albert Bartlett and Backspin's tragic death to perhaps cast doubt over the form, particularly after the first three were all well beaten subsequently, but he still ran a good race in second, while **So Young**, a heavily-backed favourite on the strength of two very easy wins at a lower level, would also have finished closer but for a mistake at the last. **Megastar** was beaten less than 9l in fifth, just pipping **Minella Class**.

19 **RSA Chase (Grade 1) (3m110yds)**
Cheltenham March 16 (Good)
1 **Bostons Angel** 7-11-4   R M Power
2 **Jessies Dream** 8-11-4   Timmy Murphy
3 **Wayward Prince** 7-11-4   A P McCoy
16/1, 10/1, 15/2. nk, ¾l. 12 ran. 6m 16.55s (Mrs John Harrington).

A bitterly disappointing performance from **Time For Rupert** left this race at the mercy of the Irish raiders, who filled three of the first four places, though with little over a length covering them to suggest there may not have been a star among them. Yet again, however, **Bostons Angel** showed that his battling qualities should never be underestimated as he outstayed his Drinmore conqueror **Jessies Dream**, who had looked the likely winner when jumping to the front two out, while fellow grinders **Wayward Prince** and **Magnanimity** also saw out the trip well to suggest they may have big futures over further. Time For Rupert was never going well but stayed on for an unlikely fifth, a remarkably brave effort given he

was found to have broken a blood vessel, while **Master Of The Hall** was next with **Aiteen Thirtythree** and **Wymott**, two other fancied horses, pulled up. **Quel Esprit** and **Mikael D'Haguenet** both fell when still going well.

20 **Fred Winter Juvenile Handicap Hurdle (Grade 3) (2m110yds)**
Cheltenham March 16 (Good)
1 **What A Charm** 4-10-6   P Townend
2 **Kumbeshwar** 4-11-10   Charlie Huxley (3)
3 **Dhaafer** 4-10-10   Robert Thornton
9/1, 33/1, 16/1. nk, 4½l. 23 ran. 3m 58.50s (A L T Moore).

What A Charm, good enough on the Flat to win the Leopardstown November Handicap in 2010, landed a major plot as he cruelly touched off top-weight **Kumbeshwar** having run three modest races over hurdles from a mark at least 6lb too low to have got a run in each of the previous three renewals. What A Charm was always going well off the pace and battled past Kumbeshwar, who was clearly the best horse in the race as he would prove at Aintree, while favourite **Plan A**, another giving away stacks of weight to the winner, also ran a good race in fourth.

21 **Weatherbys Champion Bumper (Standard Open National Hunt Flat Race) (Grade 1) (2m110yds)**
Cheltenham March 16 (Good)
1 **Cheltenian** 5-11-5   Richard Johnson
2 **Destroyer Deployed** 5-11-5   A Coleman
3 **Aupcharlie** 5-11-5   Mr J P McKeown
14/1, 66/1, 33/1. 5l, 4½l. 24 ran. 3m 51.85s (Philip Hobbs).

Remarkably the second successive Champion Bumper dominated by British runners as they filled eight of the first ten places with **Cheltenian** leading the way, being ridden clear of the more one-paced **Deployer Destroyed** after both had been kept close to the pace throughout. **Go All The Way** and **Cinders And Ashes** were other domestic runners to shape with plenty of promise, more so than the slightly disappointing favourite Ericht in sixth. **Aupcharlie** was the only Irish runner to get competitive in third, though the best of the Irish seemed to stay at home with Steps To Freedom winning at Aintree and Lovethehigherlaw touching off Waaheb at Punchestown.

22 **Jewson Novices' Chase (registered as the Golden Miller Novices' Chase) (Grade 2) (2m4f)**
Cheltenham March 17 (Good)
1 **Noble Prince** 7-11-4   A P McCoy

2 **Wishfull Thinking** 8-11-4   R Johnson
3 **Loosen My Load** 7-11-4   A E Lynch
4/1, 7/2F, 11/2. 4l, 5l. 11 ran. 4m 49.82s
(Paul Nolan).

The inaugural running of this race more than lived up to its Grade 2 status – though possibly at the expense of the two Grade 1 novice chases – with five horses who would have been near the front of the market in either of those contests, and three of them fought out the finish with **Noble Prince** coming out on top. Much improved for a step up to 2m4f, Noble Prince even looked outpaced at the top of the hill but stormed home from the last to win going away and, considering he seemed to have the Powers Gold Cup in the bag when falling next time, he could even be top-class if **Wishfull Thinking** was in the same form he showed later at Aintree and Punchestown. Wishfull Thinking made a bad mistake at the last this time but was still beaten at the time, while **Loosen My Load** was a terrific third with smart mare **Blazing Tempo** splitting **Radium** and **Mr Thriller** behind. **Mr Gardner** and **Robinson Collonges** were the two major disappointments.

23 JCB Triumph Hurdle (Grade 1) (2m1f)
Cheltenham March 18 (Good)
1 **Zarkandar** 4-11-0   Daryl Jacob
2 **Unaccompanied** 4-10-7   P Townend
3 **Grandouet** 4-11-0   Barry Geraghty
13/2, 11/2, 13/2. 2¼l, 2¾l. 23 ran. 3m 54.20s
(Paul Nicholls).

The lack of an obvious juvenile star led to a bumper field of 23 going to post, but the cream still rose to the top with the four market leaders dominating and **Zarkandar** produced a brilliant performance. Always going well, he cut through the field on the home turn to lead at the last and stayed on strongly up the hill to hold off the Irish filly **Unaccompanied**, who stuck on well in second. **Grandouet** and **Sam Winner** ran hugely contrasting races, with Grandouet travelling powerfully but failing to get up the hill, whereas Sam Winner got well behind before finishing best of all. The 200-1 maiden **Sir Pitt** was next, but there's little doubt about the strength of the form as the next five were all relatively well fancied with **Sailors Warn**, second to Unaccompanied in a Grade 2 at Leopardstown, proving the depth of the Irish challenge by finishing ahead of **Third Intention** and **Local Hero**, who had been first and second in the opposite order in a Grade 2 at the track previously, while **Smad Place** ran well but just found conditions too quick. **Houblon Des Obeaux** and hard-pulling filly **A Media Luz** were the big disappointments.

24 Albert Bartlett Novices' Hurdle (registered as the Spa Novices' Hurdle) (Grade 1) (3m)
Cheltenham March 18 (Good)
1 **Bobs Worth** 6-11-7   Barry Geraghty
2 **Mossley** 5-11-7   A P McCoy
3 **Court In Motion** 6-11-7   Jack Doyle
15/8F, 12/1, 9/1. 2¼l, 6l. 18 ran. 5m 42.20s
(Nicky Henderson).

Bobs Worth landed a major gamble as he proved his stamina in comprehensive fashion to see off smart stablemate **Mossley**. Not even a mistake at the third-last could halt Bobs Worth's progress as he made smooth headway to lead between the last two and quickened up impressively on the run-in, though Mossley, the only confirmed three-miler to figure in the finish in a race which saw many run off their feet, ran a cracker in the circumstances to push him all the way. The pair pulled clear of the non-staying **Court In Motion**, who had won a Grade 2 over 2m4f but ran out of legs over 3m on heavy ground on his previous start and again failed to get home despite travelling very strongly to the final flight, while **Champion Court** was also left behind in the straight in fourth. **Kilcrea Kim** was fifth, beaten nearly 15l, to advertise the strength of the form given he was officially rated 142 after winning a strong Grade 3 handicap at Sandown on his previous start, with Bobs Worth surely good enough to have also landed the Neptune.

BOBS WORTH: top staying hurdler

25 Matalan Anniversary 4-Y-O Juvenile Hurdle (Grade 1) (2m110yds)
Aintree April 7 (Good To Soft)
1 **Zarkandar** 4-11-0   R Walsh
2 **Kumbeshwar** 4-11-0   Robert Thornton
3 **Houblon Des Obeaux** 4-11-0   A Coleman
4/6F, 11/1, 28/1. 1¼l, 29l. 9 ran. 4m 2.80s
(Paul Nicholls).

Zarkandar completed a Cheltenham/Aintree double but had luck on his side and was still forced to work extremely hard to land the odds. Zarkandar was clearly nowhere near the same level of form as at Cheltenham, but he still knuckled down well and fought off **Kumbeshwar** in a driving finish, with the runner-up building on his fine effort in the Fred Winter. **Grandouet** and the front-running **Palawi** were the only two others seriously involved before both were taken out by the latter's fall when he was probably fading, though Grandouet was travelling best of all at the time and would surely have won judged on his subsequent Punchestown triumph, while there was a 29l gap back to **Houblon Des Obeaux** in third.

26 totepool Manifesto Novices' Chase (Grade 2) (2m4f)
Aintree April 7 (Good To Soft)
1 **Wishfull Thinking** 8-11-4   R Johnson
2 **Medermit** 7-11-4   Robert Thornton
3 **Royal Charm** 6-11-4   R Walsh
9/4, 15/8F, 100/30. 10l, 23l. 7 ran. 5m 4.10s
(Philip Hobbs).

An outstanding performance from **Wishfull Thinking**, who set a searching pace and maintained the gallop brilliantly to thrash favourite **Medermit** by even further than Captain Chris had managed in the Arkle. Medermit was back racing over a more suitable trip but still could never get close to Wishfull Thinking, who jumped magnificently and had the field well strung out, setting up his productive end of the campaign with a win in a valuable handicap to follow at Punchestown. **Royal Charm**, unbeaten in his two previous chases, was a further 23l adrift in third ahead of **Tharawaat**.

27 John Smith's Top Novices' Hurdle (Grade 2) (2m110yds)
Aintree April 8 (Good)
1 **Topolski** 5-11-4   Daryl Jacob
2 **Oilily** 8-10-11   A D Leigh
3 **Sire De Grugy** 5-11-4   Jamie Moore
11/2, 14/1, 9/2F. ¾l, 6l. 13 ran. 3m 59.70s
(David Arbuthnot).

Little strength in depth with no top-eight finishers from the Cheltenham Festival, but this race often provides far more of a speed test than the festival anyway and classy Flat recruit **Topolski** proved well suited as he maintained his unbeaten record over hurdles. Having crept slowly into contention, Topolski found a smart turn of foot to see off the strong challenge of Irish raider **Oilily**, and they were 6l clear of **Sire De Grugy**, who had won a soft Grade 2 at Kempton on his previous start. It was another 7l back to Imperial Cup winner **Alarazi** to provide a solid look to the form.

28 John Smith's Mildmay Novices' Chase (Grade 2) (3m1f)
Aintree April 8 (Good)
1 **Quito De La Roque** 7-11-4   D N Russell
2 **Sarando** 6-11-4   Will Kennedy
3 **Golan Way** 7-11-4   Leighton Aspell
6/1, 50/1, 8/1. nk, 2¾l. 8 ran. 6m 20.20s
(C A Murphy).

The Irish staying novices just about proved to have the edge over their British counterparts again as **Quito De La Roque**, beaten only by RSA winner Bostons Angel in four previous runs over fences, scrambled home from 50-1 shot **Sarando** in a race which saw most of his main rivals fail to give their running. Needing to prove his effectiveness on good ground, Quito De La Roque did that by travelling supremely well throughout and would have won more easily but for knuckling on landing after the second-last, recovering well to outbattle Sarando. **Golan Way** was a tremendous third given he ruined his chance with several blunders, still battling back past the disappointing **Wayward Prince** and **Radium**, while **Robinson Collonges** and **The Giant Bolster** failed to complete for the second successive races and **Master Of The Hall** also fell when well beaten.

29 John Smith's Sefton Novices' Hurdle (Grade 1) (3m110yds)
Aintree April 8 (Good)
1 **Saint Are** 5-11-4   Richard Johnson
2 **Cantlow** 6-11-4   Dominic Elsworth
3 **Sparky May** 6-10-11   Keiran Burke
33/1, 28/1, 4/1F. 4l, 2¼l. 19 ran. 6m 9.60s
(Tim Vaughan).

Typically for this race, a war of attrition went against those with hard runs at Cheltenham behind them and **Saint Are** was able to land a soft victory from **Cantlow**. Sent to the front before the fourth-last in a race run at a modest gallop, Saint Are shook off the challenge of the favourite **Sparky May**, who pulled just as she had when second to Quevega in the mares' race at Cheltenham and failed to get home over the longer trip, and was always holding Cantlow. Sparky May was the only horse priced less than 25-1 to make the first six as **Court In Motion** fell when nicely poised two out, **Mossley** was pulled up, **For Non Stop** broke a blood vessel and **Back In Focus**, a Grade 2 winner on heavy ground at Haydock, failed to act on a quicker surface.

30 John Smith's Mersey Novices' Hurdle (Grade 2) (2m4f)

Aintree April 9 (Good)

1 **Spirit Son** 5-11-4   Barry Geraghty
2 **Cue Card** 5-11-4   Joe Tizzard
3 **Rock On Ruby** 6-11-4   Daryl Jacob
3/1, 5/2F, 9/2. 13l, 8l. 9 ran. 4m 52.20s
(Nicky Henderson).

A cracking contest with **Spirit Son** and **Cue Card** stepping up in trip to take on **Rock On Ruby**, and Spirit Son proved much the best of them as he stormed to a hugely impressive triumph. Always going well, Spirit Son hit the front three out and simply powered further and further clear, relishing the extra distance as he extended his Supreme Hurdle superiority over Cue Card from 4l to 13l. Cue Card didn't seem to do much wrong either, running slightly in snatches but coming through to hold every chance before staying on at one pace, and he pulled well clear of Rock On Ruby, who may have been slightly below-par as he just held off **Drill Sergeant** for third. **Sam Winner** was another expected to relish the step up to 2m4f and ensured the race was a true test from the front, but he disappointingly faded into sixth.

31 John Smith's Maghull Novices' Chase (Grade 1) (2m)

Aintree April 9 (Good)

1 **Finian's Rainbow** 8-11-4   Barry Geraghty
2 **Ghizao** 7-11-4   R Walsh
3 **Dan Breen** 6-11-4   Jason Maguire
10/11F, 3/1, 8/1. 2l, 22l. 7 ran. 3m 54.60s
(Nicky Henderson).

Finian's Rainbow gained compensation for his gallant effort at Cheltenham, but it took a couple of late blunders from a rejuvenated **Ghizao** to help him scramble to victory. Finian's Rainbow made all the running but looked sure to be collared by Ghizao, who stayed on strongly despite losing his momentum at each of the final two fences. The pair pulled well clear of **Dan Breen** and **Starluck**, who failed to convince with his jumping, while **Gilbarry** was run off his feet in fifth before benefiting from a step up in trip and drop in class to win a soft Grade 2 at Ayr the following week.

32 Powers Gold Cup (Grade 1) (2m4f) Fairyhouse (IRE) April 24 (Good)

1 **Realt Dubh** 7-11-10   P Carberry
2 **Loosen My Load** 7-11-10   A E Lynch
3 **Mr Cracker** 6-11-10   D N Russell
9/2, 4/1, 12/1. 11l, 5½l. 7 ran. 4m 58.50s
(Noel Meade).

Another remarkable victory for **Realt Dubh**, who was yet again given an enormous helping hand by the fall of his main rival just as **Noble Prince** looked set to build on the big impression he had left at Cheltenham. Realt Dubh clearly deserves credit for his jumping under pressure, standing up to land a third Grade 1 victory, but he wasn't travelling as well as the stronger stayer Noble Prince when that one fell two out having just moved into the lead. Realt Dubh was left to see off **Loosen My Load**, who was hampered by Noble Prince but still saw off **Mr Cracker** for second, while **Mikael D'Haguenet** never got into contention from the rear.

33 Evening Herald Champion Novice Hurdle (Grade 1) (2m)

Punchestown (IRE) May 3 (Good To Yielding)

1 **Shot From The Hip** 7-11-12   A P McCoy
2 **Hidden Universe** 5-11-12 Mr R McNamara
3 **Far Away So Close** 6-11-12   M N Doran
11/2, 11/4F, 6/1. 9l, 4l. 7 ran. 3m 49.70s
(E J O'Grady).

A hugely impressive performance from **Shot From The Hip**, who had little to beat in a moderate Grade 1 but could hardly have done the job in more commanding fashion as he stormed clear in the straight and finished much further in front of **Hidden Universe** than he had previously at Leopardstown. Hidden Universe held on to second from **Far Away So Close**, while **Rathlin** and **Oilily** were well below-par.

34 Growise Champion Novice Chase (Grade 1) (3m1f)

Punchestown (IRE) May 3 (Good To Yielding)

1 **Quito De La Roque** 7-11-10   D N Russell
2 **Western Charmer** 9-11-10   P Carberry
3 **Head Of The Posse** 8-11-10   D J Casey
7/2, 14/1, 11/1. 14l, 1l. 8 ran. 6m 29.20s
(C A Murphy).

Quito De La Roque was presented with a fairly straightforward opportunity once favourite **Quel Esprit** had failed to complete yet again and he duly completed a big spring double. Though Quito De La Roque was hard at work from an early stage, he powered clear of a modest bunch of rivals for the grade, with **Western Charmer** perhaps needing more of a stamina test after finishing second in the Irish

SHOT FROM THE HIP: on his way to a hugely impressive win at Punchestown

National and **Head Of The Posse** let down by his jumping. Quel Esprit had earlier been cruelly brought down by a loose horse, while **Mr Thriller**, still a novice this season, was going well when falling four out.

35 Ryanair Novice Chase (Grade 1) (2m)
Punchestown (IRE) May 5 (Good)
1 **Captain Chris** 7-11-12   Richard Johnson
2 **Realt Dubh** 7-11-12   P Carberry
3 **Saludos** 7-11-12   R M Power
4/6F, 3/1, 8/1. 1¼l, 16l. 5 ran. 4m 10.10s
(Philip Hobbs).

A disappointing contest with only three serious contenders and the form dubious, but **Captain Chris** still impressed with his battling qualities as he landed a workmanlike victory. **Saludos**, always likely to need softer ground, could never get Captain Chris off the bridle in front and the Arkle winner knuckled down well when strongly pressed by **Realt Dubh** in the straight, with the first two both arguably better over further.

36 Cathal Ryan Memorial Champion Novice Hurdle (Grade 1) (2m4f)
Punchestown (IRE) May 6 (Good)
1 **Spirit Of Adjisa** 7-11-10 Richard Johnson
2 **Prima Vista** 6-11-10   P Carberry
3 **First Lieutenant** 6-11-10   D N Russell
16/1, 8/1, 13/8. shd, 2½l. 6 ran. 4m 53.70s
(Tim Vaughan).

Having won only at Bangor and Market Rasen in his second season as a novice hurdler, **Spirit Of Adjisa** took a huge rise in class in his stride as he set a well-judged pace and kept enough in the tank to repel **Prima Vista** in a thrilling finish. **First Lieutenant** was just below his best in third with favourite **So Young** even more disappointing in sixth, but even so Prima Vista had appeared to have more up his sleeve when beating Supreme sixth Rathlin in a Grade 2 at Fairyhouse on his previous start and the form may still be decent.

37 AES Champion 4YO Hurdle (Grade 1) (2m)
Punchestown (IRE) May 7 (Good)
1 **Grandouet** 4-11-0   Barry Geraghty
2 **Kumbeshwar** 4-11-0   Robert Thornton
3 **Twinlight** 4-11-0   R Walsh
5/2, 6/1, 8/1. 9l, ½l. 7 ran. 3m 47.40s
(Nicky Henderson).

Grandouet made amends for his Aintree mishap as he stormed to a convincing win over **Kumbeshwar** with Triumph runner-up **Unaccompanied** a disappointing fourth. Though it's impossible to say whether Grandouet would have beaten an on-song Unaccompanied, he saw out the race much better than he had at Cheltenham, easing clear of the consistent Kumbeshwar, who held off highly-rated Grade 3 winner **Twinlight** for second.

Big-race index

All horses placed or commented on in our big-race review section, with race numbers

A New Story 51
Albertas Run 21, 37, 44
Always Right 48
Any Given Day 0, 10
Askthemaster 41
Baby Run 49
Ballabvriggs 46
Ballyfitz 29
Battle Group...........................36
Bensalem 25, 32
Beshabar................................48
Big Buck's 15, 38, 42
Big Fella Thanks 46
Big Zeb 16, 35, 52
Binocular...........8, 20, 45, 55
Blazing Bailey 48
Bothy.........................3, 27, 36
Burton Port..............................7
Bygones Of Brid 47
Calgary Bay 11
Captain Cee Bee 16, 35, 52
Carlito Brigante.........36, 42, 54
Carole's Legacy 32, 43
Carruthers...............................29
Celestial Halo..................18, 30
Chaninbar 50
Chicago Grey...........................48
China Rock 1, 40
Cooldine..................................13
Cornas.....................................50
Cue Card..................................10
Dancing Tornado 2
De Boitron...............................41
Deep Purple............................28
Denman 7, 40, 43
Diamond Harry...........................7
Don't Push It............................46
Donnas Palm.............................4
Dunguib 33
Faasel......................................49
Final Approach........................39
Follow The Plan 43, 53
For Non Stop 36
Forpadydeplasterer.................21
French Opera.............35, 44, 50
Gauvain..............................28, 37
Get Me Out Of Here................39
Giles Cross..............................19

Glencove Marina..........13, 14, 26
Golden Silver 16, 35, 52
Grands Crus 25, 38, 42
Great Endeavour 2, 11, 32
Hurricane Fly 12, 17, 23, 33, 55
I'moncloudnine.........................19
Imperial Commander...............5, 40
J'y Vole....................13, 37, 52
Joncol 14, 26
Kalahari King...........................37
Karabak................................6, 18
Kauto Star 1, 21, 40, 53
Kayf Aramis 15
Kempes................14, 26, 40, 53
Khyber Kim 20, 33, 42
Killyglen...................................46
Knockara Beau 25, 42
Le Beau Bai..............................29
Leo's Lucky Star.......................41
Little Josh............................2, 11
Long Run 2, 21, 40
Lothian Falcon.........................48
Lough Derg...............................15
Luska Lad 17, 54
Mad Max 2, 11, 22, 44
Maktu.......................................19
Manyriverstocross.....................3
Master Minded........9, 22, 35, 44
Menorah................3, 10, 33, 55
Merigo......................................48
Midnight Chase........................40
Mille Chief 30, 33
Money Trix.........................14, 26
Mount Oscar 31
Mourad.....................12, 38, 54
Nacarat 5, 21, 31, 43, 53
Nearby.....................................39
Neptune Collonges..............24, 48
Niche Market.......................7, 46
Notus De La Tour 27
Ocean Transit..........................34
Oiseau De Nuit...................41, 50
Organisateur...........................25
Organisedconfusion 51
Orsippus..................................36
Oscar Time..............................46
Oscar Whisky.............18, 33, 45
Overturn 20, 33, 47

Pandorama 7, 14, 40
Peddlers Cross 8, 33, 45
Petit Robin................................9, 22
Planet Of Sound 5, 21
Poker De Sivola 49
Poquelin.........................2, 11, 37
Pride Of Dulcote 28
Punchestowns 24, 43
Quantitativeeasing 51
Quevega...............................34, 54
Quinz...31
Rare Bob.....................................53
Recession Proof...........................27
Restless Harry..................6, 15, 25
Reve De Sivola............................32
Rigour Back Bob..........................38
Riverside Theatre....................21, 28
Roberto Goldback 13, 53
Ronaldo Des Mottes 30
Rubi Light....................................37
Salden Licht...........................39, 45
Sanctuaire...................................47
Scotsirish....................................16
Silver By Nature.....................19, 29
Silviniaco Conti 6, 10, 30
Sizing Europe 1, 35, 52
Soldatino.....................................27

Solix..36
Solwhit 4, 12, 17, 23
Somersby...............9, 22, 35, 44
Sparky May..................................34
Starluck..................................8, 20
State Of Play................................46
Sublimity 4
Sunnyhillboy 2, 11, 51
Synchronised................................19
Tartak.........................28, 37, 44
Tataniano.....................................50
The Betchworth Kid 27
The Midnight Club 46
The Minack 48
The Tother One 7
Thousand Stars 17, 23, 33, 45, 55
Tidal Bay 5, 24, 40
Tranquil Sea 13, 53
Vic Venturi..................................53
Voler La Vedette.............4, 12, 23, 54
Voy Por Ustedes 37
Walkon 36
Weird Al 7
Western Charmer..........................51
What A Friend 5, 40
Won In The Dark..................42, 54
Zaynar 6, 38

Novice index

All horses placed or commented on in our novice review section, with race numbers

A Media Luz 23
Aiteen Thirtythree.......................19
Al Ferof.....................................4, 14
Alarazi...27
Alfa Beat......................................17
Aupcharlie...................................21
Back In Focus 29
Backspin..................................4, 9
Be There In Five..........................17
Beshabar.....................................17
Blazing Tempo 22
Bobs Worth 9, 24
Bostons Angel 3, 11, 19
Cantlow.......................................29
Captain Chris.............1, 10, 15, 35
Champion Court 9, 24
Cheltenian...................................21
Chicago Grey..........................2, 17
Cinders And Ashes......................21
Court In Motion.............4, 24, 29

Cue Card.................................14, 30
Dan Breen....................................31
Definity 16
Destroyer Deployed......................21
Dhaafer.......................................20
Divers 16
Drill Sergeant 30
Far Away So Close 33
Finian's Rainbow....................15, 31
First Lieutenant 18, 36
Flat Out 8
For Non Stop 4, 29
Ghizao.....................................1, 15, 31
Gilbarry.......................................31
Go All The Way 21
Golan Way....................................28
Grandouet....................23, 25, 37
Habbie Simpson 9
Head Of The Posse 3, 34
Hell's Bay 5

Hidden Universe 12, 14, 33
Houblon Des Obeaux 7, 23, 25
Jessies Dream 3, 19
Kilcrea Kim 24
Kumbeshwar 13, 20, 25, 37
Local Hero 23
Loosen My Load 1, 22, 32
Magnanimity 11, 19
Marsh Warbler 7
Master Of The Hall 5, 19, 28
Medermit 5, 10, 15, 26
Megastar 6, 18
Mikael D'Haguenet 3, 11, 19, 32
Minella Class 6, 18
Molotof 13
Mossley 24, 29
Mr Cracker 8, 32
Mr Gardner 10, 22
Mr Thriller 5, 22, 34
Noble Prince 8, 22, 32
Oilily 27, 33
Oscars Well 12, 18
Palawi 25
Plan A 20
Prima Vista 36
Quantitativeeasing 16
Quel Esprit 11, 19, 34
Quinz 2
Quito De La Roque 28, 34
Radium 22, 28
Rathlin 14, 33
Realt Dubh 3, 8, 15, 32, 35
Recession Proof 14
Reve De Sivola 5, 10
Robinson Collonges 22, 28
Rock Noir 10
Rock On Ruby 9, 18, 30
Royal Charm 26
Sailors Warn 23
Saint Are 29
Saludos 8, 35
Sam Winner 7, 23, 30
Sarando 28
Shot From The Hip 12, 33
Sir Pitt 23
Sire De Grugy 27
Smad Place 7, 23
So Young 18, 36
Some Target 17
Sparky May 29
Spirit Of Adjisa 36
Spirit Son 14, 30

REALT DUBH: triple Grade 1 winner

Sprinter Sacre 14
Starluck 31
Tharawaat 26
The Giant Bolster 28
Third Intention 23
Time For Rupert 2, 19
Topolski 27
Toubab 6
Tullamore Dew 16
Twinlight 37
Unaccompanied 23, 37
Vino Griego 16
Wayward Prince 19, 28
Western Charmer 34
What A Charm 20
Wishfull Thinking 22, 26
Wymott 19
Zaidpour 12, 14
Zarkandar 13, 23, 25

Trainer Statistics

By race type

	Hurdles				Chases			
	W	R	%	£1 stake	W	R	%	£1 stake
Handicap	19	133	14	+0.06	9	78	12	-31.42
Novice	49	155	32	+7.31	26	82	32	-14.64
Maiden	8	42	19	-11.78	0	0	-	+0.00

By jockey

	Hurdles				Chases				Bumpers			
	W	R	%	£1 stake	W	R	%	£1 stake	W	R	%	£1 stake
Barry Geraghty	30	111	27	-11.86	21	73	29	-19.81	7	24	29	-6.64
A P McCoy	30	71	42	+10.13	7	26	27	-6.43	10	21	48	+15.67
Andrew Tinkler	8	68	12	-18.50	8	42	19	-16.56	4	20	20	-8.17
David Bass	8	51	16	-0.64	2	11	18	+2.00	4	14	29	-0.50
Felix De Giles	3	10	30	-5.92	3	11	27	+1.25	1	3	33	-0.25
Jeremiah McGrath	3	9	33	+11.70	0	1	-	-1.00	0	2	-	-2.00
Mr S Waley-Cohen	0	0	-	+0.00	2	4	50	+6.00	0	0	-	+0.00
Richard Killoran	2	22	9	-8.13	0	0	-	+0.00	0	2	-	-2.00
D J Casey	0	1	-	-1.00	0	0	-	+0.00	0	0	-	+0.00
Jake Loader	0	0	-	+0.00	0	0	-	+0.00	0	1	-	-1.00

By month

	Hurdles				Chases				Bumpers			
	W	R	%	£1 stake	W	R	%	£1 stake	W	R	%	£1 stake
May 2010	5	21	24	+14.85	1	7	14	-3.50	4	8	50	+4.25
June	3	13	23	+0.41	1	2	50	+4.00	1	2	50	-0.33
July	1	5	20	-3.67	1	2	50	-0.09	0	0	-	+0.00
August	1	3	33	+3.00	0	1	-	-1.00	0	0	-	+0.00
September	2	7	29	+5.00	0	0	-	+0.00	0	0	-	+0.00
October	3	17	18	-10.97	2	11	18	-5.00	2	5	40	+4.00
November	10	39	26	-10.42	7	26	27	-2.76	1	11	9	-9.17
December	6	26	23	+0.85	1	14	7	-12.09	2	8	25	+5.75
January 2011	17	56	30	-7.50	15	34	44	+10.65	4	9	44	-1.49
February	12	54	22	-33.15	10	26	38	+1.57	3	11	27	-2.07
March	12	69	17	-7.64	3	27	11	-13.25	4	20	20	-6.13
April	10	34	29	+20.67	2	25	8	-20.09	4	13	31	-2.33

By horse

	Wins-Runs	%	£1 level stakes	Win prize	Total prize
Long Run	2-3	67	+7.00	£387,668.00	£403,733.00
Oscar Whisky	3-4	75	+8.29	£131,135.00	£170,762.00
Riverside Theatre	2-3	67	+1.60	£100,315.00	£138,817.00
Finian's Rainbow	4-5	80	+0.86	£84,720.20	£112,527.20
Carole's Legacy	1-5	20	-2.38	£17,103.00	£82,222.50
Bobs Worth	4-4	100	+8.82	£80,126.50	£80,126.50
Binocular	2-4	50	-0.28	£51,879.10	£70,030.10
Spirit Son	3-4	75	+3.06	£41,795.45	£63,185.45
French Opera	2-5	40	+2.50	£45,608.00	£54,568.50
Eradicate	1-6	17	+11.00	£42,757.50	£45,749.50
Mossley	3-6	50	+1.28	£18,705.65	£40,765.65
Burton Port	0-1	-	-1.00	£0.00	£37,432.50
Skint	2-5	40	+9.75	£33,058.50	£35,815.05
Punchestowns	1-4	25	-2.33	£13,912.00	£30,321.00
Master Of The Hall	3-6	50	+1.11	£26,150.40	£28,562.40

NICKY HENDERSON

All runners

	Wins	Runs	%	Win prize	Total prize	£1 Stake
Hurdle	84	348	24	£698,020.07	£963,671.05	-29.22
Chase	43	176	24	£838,877.01	£1,178,192.71	-42.56
Bumper	26	88	30	£54,779.11	£68,601.24	-5.89
TOTAL	153	612	25	£1,591,676.19	£2,210,465.00	-77.66

By course – last four seasons

	Hurdles				Chases				Bumpers			
	W	R	%	£1 stake	W	R	%	£1 stake	W	R	%	£1 stake
Aintree	7	50	14	-3.13	5	35	14	+1.91	2	13	15	+18.00
Ascot	22	80	28	+12.02	9	26	35	-6.46	4	10	40	-0.67
Ayr	4	16	25	+8.50	2	16	13	-10.00	2	2	100	+2.88
Bangor-On-Dee	7	21	33	+1.51	1	8	13	-3.67	2	11	18	-3.75
Cheltenham	27	161	17	+33.91	5	97	5	-75.83	4	21	19	-3.13
Chepstow	2	10	20	-1.00	0	4	-	-4.00	1	5	20	-1.00
Doncaster	6	33	18	-11.83	2	14	14	+1.00	2	8	25	+2.83
Exeter	2	9	22	-4.56	3	7	43	+2.50	1	4	25	-0.25
Fakenham	5	16	31	+1.04	6	12	50	+3.24	3	7	43	-0.24
Ffos Las	7	19	37	+15.37	4	10	40	-2.45	2	6	33	-0.88
Folkestone	2	4	50	+2.83	3	9	33	-4.17	0	1	-	-1.00
Fontwell	1	12	8	-10.00	3	7	43	-0.55	4	13	31	-0.75
Haydock	2	34	6	-15.89	0	4	-	-4.00	2	6	33	-2.23
Hereford	7	25	28	-2.00	1	2	50	-0.33	3	6	50	+1.08
Huntingdon	20	54	37	+3.37	7	22	32	+0.25	7	18	39	-5.35
Kelso	0	2	-	-2.00	1	2	50	-0.27	0	0	-	+0.00
Kempton	23	100	23	-18.85	21	61	34	+20.31	7	18	39	-1.04
Kempton (A.W)	0	0	-	+0.00	0	0	-	+0.00	2	5	40	+8.75
Leicester	2	5	40	-0.09	7	14	50	+11.48	0	0	-	+0.00
Lingfield	1	7	14	-4.90	2	2	100	+0.90	0	0	-	+0.00
Lingfield (A.W)	0	0	-	+0.00	0	0	-	+0.00	0	2	-	-2.00
Ludlow	19	50	38	+24.59	4	13	31	-3.30	8	20	40	-0.69
Market Rasen	4	18	22	-8.68	2	5	40	-1.44	2	3	67	+1.85
Musselburgh	3	7	43	+2.98	0	2	-	-2.00	1	2	50	-0.50
Newbury	27	127	21	+1.74	15	68	22	-20.57	9	26	35	-3.88
Newcastle	1	2	50	-0.50	0	1	-	-1.00	0	0	-	+0.00
Newton Abbot	7	20	35	+1.76	0	1	-	-1.00	0	4	-	-4.00
Perth	1	7	14	-4.63	1	7	14	-2.00	1	2	50	+0.00
Plumpton	2	17	12	-11.88	2	8	25	-2.63	0	2	-	-2.00
Sandown	18	79	23	-2.79	7	27	26	-2.39	0	10	-	-10.00
Southwell	4	14	29	+0.85	1	5	20	-3.00	0	5	-	-5.00
Southwell (A.W)	0	0	-	+0.00	0	0	-	+0.00	3	6	50	-0.31
Stratford	8	25	32	+3.77	0	11	-	-11.00	1	4	25	-2.00
Taunton	4	22	18	-9.85	2	5	40	+1.50	1	6	17	-4.39
Towcester	6	20	30	+9.41	3	6	50	+1.75	3	13	23	+1.94
Uttoxeter	7	25	28	+9.49	1	4	25	-2.09	3	9	33	+2.23
Warwick	4	13	31	+1.11	4	11	36	-4.56	2	7	29	+1.25
Wetherby	3	9	33	-2.02	0	4	-	-4.00	0	0	-	+0.00
Wincanton	6	38	16	-18.89	2	12	17	-4.33	0	4	-	-4.00
Worcester	5	21	24	-1.92	1	2	50	+4.00	2	5	40	-0.71

By race type

	Hurdles				Chases			
	W	R	%	£1 stake	W	R	%	£1 stake
Handicap	10	100	10	-53.92	14	110	13	-34.82
Novice	35	125	28	-11.23	21	74	28	-13.73
Maiden	10	38	26	+36.14	0	0	-	+0.00

By jockey

	Hurdles				Chases				Bumpers			
	W	R	%	£1 stake	W	R	%	£1 stake	W	R	%	£1 stake
R Walsh	16	51	31	+3.28	6	39	15	-16.50	1	5	20	-3.47
Harry Skelton	15	62	24	+22.42	4	25	16	-8.88	2	9	22	-4.31
Ryan Mahon	8	33	24	-5.94	9	41	22	-14.43	1	10	10	-4.50
Noel Fehily	6	20	30	-0.85	9	20	45	+3.29	2	6	33	+1.50
Nick Scholfield	5	24	21	-5.04	10	37	27	-5.15	0	5	-	-5.00
Ian Popham	7	39	18	-14.42	4	17	24	+9.68	1	4	25	-1.25
A P McCoy	3	10	30	-5.65	6	17	35	+8.63	0	0	-	+0.00
Daryl Jacob	5	19	26	+6.80	2	15	13	-12.19	0	2	-	-2.00
Sam Thomas	2	10	20	-1.17	1	10	10	-8.09	2	3	67	+8.00
Timmy Murphy	1	7	14	-5.80	2	5	40	+6.25	0	2	-	-2.00

By month

	Hurdles				Chases				Bumpers			
	W	R	%	£1 stake	W	R	%	£1 stake	W	R	%	£1 stake
May 2010	3	14	21	-1.15	1	9	11	-5.75	2	2	100	+6.75
June	1	8	13	-2.00	1	7	14	-2.50	0	1	-	-1.00
July	2	3	67	+34.50	1	4	25	-2.27	0	0	-	+0.00
August	4	10	40	+2.11	3	4	75	+6.50	1	1	100	+0.44
September	1	5	20	+0.50	0	3	-	-3.00	0	0	-	+0.00
October	10	31	32	+4.75	3	15	20	-0.75	1	7	14	-5.47
November	12	48	25	-5.81	12	42	29	-1.21	2	6	33	+1.50
December	4	18	22	-6.78	6	20	30	+13.77	2	8	25	+3.00
January 2011	8	48	17	-26.02	6	29	21	-11.36	0	5	-	-5.00
February	8	37	22	-10.06	8	26	31	+3.92	0	5	-	-5.00
March	10	38	26	+8.46	3	36	8	-26.10	1	6	17	-3.50
April	7	36	19	-17.62	9	40	23	-17.63	1	8	13	-5.25

By horse

	Wins-Runs	%	£1 level stakes	Win prize	Total prize
Big Buck's	4-4	100	+2.02	£256,379.40	£256,379.40
Master Minded	4-5	80	+6.81	£220,901.50	£220,901.50
Poquelin	2-5	40	+14.10	£108,319.00	£139,842.58
Denman	0-3	-	-3.00	£0.00	£129,697.50
Zarkandar	3-3	100	+15.17	£125,727.82	£125,727.82
Silviniaco Conti	3-5	60	+6.83	£69,828.25	£89,631.25
Kauto Star	0-2	-	-2.00	£0.00	£72,828.00
Al Ferof	3-5	60	+8.39	£65,639.50	£69,388.00
Neptune Collonges	1-5	20	+1.50	£51,309.00	£53,721.00
Tchico Polos	1-6	17	-2.00	£39,907.00	£52,325.00
Ghizao	2-5	40	+6.25	£22,957.50	£50,672.96
Rock On Ruby	2-5	40	+3.75	£11,850.80	£44,478.80
Celestial Halo	1-7	14	-4.50	£18,528.25	£42,001.65
Meanus Dandy	1-5	20	+1.00	£39,907.00	£40,948.75
What A Friend	0-4	-	-4.00	£0.00	£38,437.00

PAUL NICHOLLS

All runners

	Wins	Runs	%	Win prize	Total prize	£1 Stake
Hurdle	71	298	24	£809,964.66	£1,031,694.53	-17.11
Chase	53	236	22	£774,821.09	£1,359,810.19	-47.37
Bumper	10	49	20	£23,100.02	£32,554.70	-13.52
TOTAL	134	583	23	£1,607,885.77	£2,424,059.42	-77.99

By course – last four seasons

	Hurdles				Chases				Bumpers			
	W	R	%	£1 stake	W	R	%	£1 stake	W	R	%	£1 stake
Aintree	10	55	18	-21.43	9	83	11	-38.68	1	10	10	-7.25
Ascot	6	37	16	-17.94	9	46	20	-20.61	2	7	29	+1.75
Ayr	3	17	18	-5.40	0	18	-	-18.00	1	1	100	+1.50
Bangor-On-Dee	3	11	27	+6.75	2	11	18	-5.50	0	3	-	-3.00
Carlisle	0	0	-	+0.00	0	1	-	-1.00	0	0	-	+0.00
Cheltenham	25	151	17	-9.32	26	202	13	-79.10	3	12	25	+3.25
Chepstow	24	111	22	-1.82	9	52	17	-28.60	6	22	27	-4.75
Doncaster	4	16	25	-2.08	5	22	23	-2.25	0	1	-	-1.00
Exeter	17	59	29	+4.71	20	48	42	+2.45	0	6	-	-6.00
Fakenham	1	5	20	-3.09	8	13	62	+5.11	0	0	-	+0.00
Ffos Las	2	9	22	-3.45	1	3	33	-0.80	0	3	-	-3.00
Folkestone	0	1	-	-1.00	2	4	50	-0.19	0	0	-	+0.00
Fontwell	9	34	26	-3.75	14	34	41	-4.10	5	16	31	+0.13
Haydock	3	16	19	-2.59	5	20	25	+2.72	0	0	-	+0.00
Hereford	3	22	14	-10.09	3	13	23	-7.86	2	7	29	-1.00
Huntingdon	2	4	50	+1.07	1	8	13	-6.64	0	1	-	-1.00
Kempton	11	55	20	+1.76	15	56	27	-12.43	1	9	11	-6.80
Kempton (A.W)	0	0	-	+0.00	0	0	-	+0.00	2	7	29	+4.00
Leicester	0	1	-	-1.00	1	2	50	+1.00	0	0	-	+0.00
Lingfield	2	5	40	-0.67	0	4	-	-4.00	0	0	-	+0.00
Lingfield (A.W)	0	0	-	+0.00	0	0	-	+0.00	0	1	-	-1.00
Ludlow	2	13	15	-5.67	1	9	11	-7.80	0	7	-	-7.00
Market Rasen	1	5	20	-3.50	0	7	-	-7.00	0	0	-	+0.00
Newbury	20	91	22	-20.67	25	82	30	+28.06	3	15	20	-2.50
Newcastle	0	0	-	+0.00	0	1	-	-1.00	0	0	-	+0.00
Newton Abbot	13	51	25	+17.68	20	55	36	-1.24	7	13	54	+9.83
Perth	1	3	33	+0.00	1	1	100	+1.50	0	0	-	+0.00
Plumpton	6	16	38	+8.07	1	10	10	-7.00	1	4	25	-1.75
Sandown	11	44	25	+12.48	23	65	35	+9.31	1	4	25	+1.00
Southwell	0	0	-	+0.00	1	1	100	+0.91	0	0	-	+0.00
Stratford	3	20	15	-11.19	5	25	20	-11.05	5	8	63	+17.63
Taunton	37	109	34	-8.55	12	33	36	-7.55	7	12	58	+10.12
Towcester	0	0	-	+0.00	1	1	100	+2.25	0	0	-	+0.00
Uttoxeter	1	8	13	-4.00	3	12	25	-5.01	2	5	40	+3.25
Warwick	1	8	13	-5.80	3	15	20	-9.52	0	2	-	-2.00
Wetherby	0	3	-	-3.00	1	4	25	+4.00	0	0	-	+0.00
Wincanton	27	106	25	-36.71	15	54	28	+22.50	3	21	14	-13.96
Worcester	7	19	37	+20.54	4	18	22	-7.29	2	5	40	-1.65

By race type

	Hurdles				Chases			
	W	R	%	£1 stake	W	R	%	£1 stake
Handicap	17	139	12	-20.75	11	101	11	-28.92
Novice	31	146	21	-24.68	8	51	16	-31.45
Maiden	7	44	16	-25.57	1	4	25	-0.88

By jockey

	Hurdles				Chases				Bumpers			
	W	R	%	£1 stake	W	R	%	£1 stake	W	R	%	£1 stake
Jason Maguire	39	161	24	-13.74	16	95	17	-37.16	7	32	22	-3.72
Henry Brooke	8	36	22	+2.40	1	4	25	-0.50	2	5	40	+2.75
Adrian Lane	5	92	5	-65.12	4	19	21	+0.13	2	13	15	-1.50
A P McCoy	4	12	33	+4.81	0	3	-	-3.00	0	0	-	+0.00
Graham Lee	2	11	18	-5.28	2	7	29	-2.83	0	0	-	+0.00
Timmy Murphy	0	4	-	-4.00	2	5	40	-1.47	0	1	-	-1.00
Mr J Hamer	1	11	9	-3.00	1	8	13	-4.00	0	2	-	-2.00
John Kington	0	17	-	-17.00	1	5	20	+4.00	1	10	10	+5.00
Sam Thomas	0	0	-	+0.00	1	2	50	+0.10	0	0	-	+0.00
Brian Harding	0	3	-	-3.00	1	9	11	+1.00	0	0	-	+0.00

By month

	Hurdles				Chases				Bumpers			
	W	R	%	£1 stake	W	R	%	£1 stake	W	R	%	£1 stake
May 2010	7	37	19	-13.79	4	18	22	-1.42	0	7	-	-7.00
June	5	21	24	+2.85	0	11	-	-11.00	0	2	-	-2.00
July	0	13	-	-13.00	1	7	14	-3.00	0	0	-	+0.00
August	1	14	7	-6.00	1	4	25	+0.00	0	0	-	+0.00
September	2	7	29	-2.09	0	1	-	-1.00	0	0	-	+0.00
October	6	34	18	+0.40	2	18	11	-8.00	2	8	25	+3.50
November	8	38	21	-4.80	5	22	23	-5.01	3	10	30	+2.13
December	1	11	9	-9.00	2	9	22	-5.50	2	12	17	+0.00
January 2011	9	46	20	-21.31	3	19	16	-4.72	0	1	-	-1.00
February	10	41	24	+10.18	5	22	23	-2.72	1	4	25	-2.60
March	8	54	15	-21.95	2	20	10	-15.21	2	12	17	-4.25
April	1	36	3	-34.43	4	14	29	+5.83	2	8	25	+9.75

By horse

	Wins-Runs	%	£1 level stakes	Win prize	Total prize
Ballabriggs	3-4	75	+17.43	£540,013.75	£542,788.75
Peddlers Cross	2-4	50	+0.42	£61,066.50	£141,281.50
Overturn	0-5	-	-5.00	£0.00	£39,316.00
Any Given Day	1-7	14	+1.00	£17,103.00	£36,702.00
Son Of Flicka	2-10	20	+5.00	£11,849.45	£28,619.55
Fiendish Flame	1-9	11	-5.50	£16,040.84	£25,160.59
Tara Royal	1-5	20	-1.75	£9,107.00	£22,660.20
Reindeer Dippin	2-5	40	+10.50	£9,965.15	£18,521.15
Alegralil	1-4	25	+0.50	£17,103.00	£17,317.40
Drill Sergeant	2-10	20	-5.99	£4,965.25	£15,907.75
Alderley Rover	3-10	30	+0.77	£10,841.12	£15,893.17
Wymott	3-4	75	+2.62	£15,444.00	£15,444.00
Gilsland	2-3	67	+4.33	£13,010.00	£14,920.00
Chamirey	2-6	33	-2.47	£12,751.80	£13,601.80
Inventor	1-5	20	-1.00	£12,524.00	£13,132.40

DONALD McCAIN

All runners

	Wins	Runs	%	Win prize	Total prize	£1 Stake
Hurdle	59	357	17	£268,534.01	£515,629.36	-113.93
Chase	29	167	17	£665,208.61	£738,629.10	-53.74
Bumper	12	64	19	£20,713.55	£31,874.96	-1.47
TOTAL	100	588	17	£954,456.17	£1,286,133.42	-169.14

By course – last four seasons

	Hurdles				Chases				Bumpers		
	W	R	%	£1 stake	W	R	%	£1 stake	W	R	%	£1 stake
Aintree	8	64	13	+20.98	1	25	4	-10.00	0	16	-	-16.00
Ascot	2	7	29	+11.50	1	7	14	-1.00	0	0	-	+0.00
Ayr	10	37	27	-9.60	10	28	36	+17.54	0	3	-	-3.00
Bangor-On-Dee	22	178	12	-77.54	13	68	19	-2.26	7	33	21	+0.50
Carlisle	6	45	13	-23.88	6	51	12	-34.33	2	13	15	-4.00
Cartmel	5	33	15	-14.88	4	16	25	+2.00	0	0	-	+0.00
Catterick	6	38	16	+12.90	4	19	21	+6.25	1	10	10	-4.50
Cheltenham	2	35	6	-6.00	1	23	4	-13.00	0	5	-	-5.00
Chepstow	2	17	12	-3.00	2	8	25	-2.00	0	2	-	-2.00
Doncaster	2	29	7	+1.00	3	15	20	-4.04	0	1	-	-1.00
Exeter	2	9	22	-3.80	2	7	29	+0.00	1	1	100	+14.00
Fakenham	0	1	-	-1.00	0	1	-	-1.00	0	0	-	+0.00
Ffos Las	2	10	20	-1.33	0	6	-	-6.00	0	0	-	+0.00
Fontwell	1	3	33	+0.00	2	2	100	+3.60	1	1	100	+5.00
Haydock	14	58	24	+5.58	7	30	23	+10.83	2	12	17	-5.38
Hereford	7	41	17	-13.06	0	8	-	-8.00	0	3	-	-3.00
Hexham	7	51	14	-20.76	4	15	27	+2.91	1	8	13	-6.39
Huntingdon	1	15	7	-13.39	1	4	25	-0.75	0	0	-	+0.00
Kelso	6	37	16	-0.58	4	30	13	-16.29	0	6	-	-6.00
Kempton	1	5	20	-2.50	1	3	33	+2.00	0	0	-	+0.00
Leicester	4	19	21	+17.10	1	10	10	-6.75	0	0	-	+0.00
Lingfield	0	1	-	-1.00	0	0	-	+0.00	0	0	-	+0.00
Ludlow	2	17	12	-5.00	1	12	8	-8.00	0	3	-	-3.00
Market Rasen	2	28	7	-18.00	6	26	23	+8.38	2	7	29	+5.50
Musselburgh	2	20	10	-15.26	2	13	15	-7.83	0	3	-	-3.00
Newbury	2	19	11	-11.42	1	9	11	+1.00	1	1	100	+14.00
Newcastle	5	28	18	-8.95	2	16	13	-11.00	0	1	-	-1.00
Newton Abbot	1	2	50	+0.25	0	1	-	-1.00	0	0	-	+0.00
Perth	2	8	25	-3.09	2	5	40	+13.50	0	2	-	-2.00
Plumpton	0	0	-	+0.00	0	2	-	-2.00	0	1	-	-1.00
Sandown	0	13	-	-13.00	1	6	17	-3.75	0	0	-	+0.00
Sedgefield	9	51	18	-18.69	4	25	16	-11.29	1	8	13	-5.25
Southwell	0	14	-	-14.00	1	11	9	-7.50	0	1	-	-1.00
Southwell (A.W)	0	0	-	+0.00	0	0	-	+0.00	2	10	20	+2.00
Stratford	3	22	14	-4.89	0	2	-	-2.00	0	4	-	-4.00
Taunton	0	7	-	-7.00	0	4	-	-4.00	0	1	-	-1.00
Towcester	4	37	11	-11.63	3	19	16	-14.47	0	10	-	-10.00
Uttoxeter	20	122	16	-1.92	6	41	15	-28.94	3	27	11	-0.50
Warwick	1	9	11	-5.25	0	4	-	-4.00	0	1	-	-1.00
Wetherby	8	51	16	-21.02	8	29	28	+7.40	1	7	14	-5.60
Wincanton	1	7	14	-2.67	1	5	20	-1.50	0	0	-	+0.00
Worcester	4	26	15	-5.73	2	11	18	+2.00	0	5	-	-5.00

By race type

| | Hurdles | | | | Chases | | | |
	W	R	%	£1 stake	W	R	%	£1 stake
Handicap	21	167	13	+3.58	29	255	11	-34.69
Novice	19	121	16	-7.22	13	66	20	-8.16
Maiden	8	37	22	+81.50	0	0	-	+0.00

By jockey

| | Hurdles | | | | Chases | | | | Bumpers | | | |
	W	R	%	£1 stake	W	R	%	£1 stake	W	R	%	£1 stake
Paddy Brennan	22	149	15	-13.42	24	121	20	+14.89	3	19	16	+36.50
Sam T-Davies	23	146	16	+96.08	13	132	10	-48.08	1	25	4	-19.00
Mr W T-Davies	1	8	13	-6.00	3	11	27	-3.01	0	3	-	-3.00
Tom Molloy	2	6	33	-1.31	2	15	13	+4.50	0	4	-	-4.00
David England	1	16	6	-1.00	1	23	4	-12.00	0	5	-	-5.00
Graham Lee	0	0	-	+0.00	1	1	100	+9.00	0	0	-	+0.00
Brian Hughes	0	0	-	+0.00	0	1	-	-1.00	0	0	-	+0.00
Daryl Jacob	0	1	-	-1.00	0	0	-	+0.00	0	0	-	+0.00
Mr B Connell	0	0	-	+0.00	0	0	-	+0.00	0	1	-	-1.00
Mr D O'Connor	0	0	-	+0.00	0	1	-	-1.00	0	0	-	+0.00

By month

| | Hurdles | | | | Chases | | | | Bumpers | | | |
	W	R	%	£1 stake	W	R	%	£1 stake	W	R	%	£1 stake
May 2010	3	26	12	-16.82	2	20	10	+1.00	0	4	-	-4.00
June	1	17	6	-6.00	5	18	28	+2.88	0	1	-	-1.00
July	2	9	22	-0.75	3	12	25	+2.33	0	1	-	-1.00
August	6	13	46	+28.83	5	18	28	+12.78	0	2	-	-2.00
September	4	23	17	-6.08	6	16	38	+6.29	2	3	67	+1.50
October	10	38	26	+86.83	5	41	12	-19.89	0	4	-	-4.00
November	5	44	11	-32.44	7	45	16	+5.41	0	3	-	-3.00
December	3	25	12	-3.50	2	25	8	-1.00	0	5	-	-5.00
January 2011	3	33	9	-13.97	1	32	3	-26.00	0	5	-	-5.00
February	3	33	9	+15.50	3	29	10	-13.01	2	9	22	+48.00
March	5	45	11	+13.75	3	35	9	-7.50	0	12	-	-12.00
April	3	21	14	+3.00	2	28	7	-14.00	0	9	-	-9.00

By horse

	Wins-Runs	%	£1 level stakes	Win prize	Total prize
Imperial Commander	1-2	50	-0.09	£112,660.00	£112,660.00
Little Josh	2-4	50	+19.25	£93,930.00	£99,022.00
Grand Slam Hero	4-8	50	+17.88	£57,462.05	£57,462.05
Hello Bud	1-3	33	+5.50	£56,378.58	£56,378.58
Ballyfitz	0-7	-	-7.00	£0.00	£41,899.65
Baby Run	3-5	60	+2.99	£26,680.45	£41,674.45
Billie Magern	4-10	40	+2.08	£24,593.00	£31,632.00
Banjaxed Girl	1-6	17	-3.50	£9,121.60	£21,161.60
Astracad	3-8	38	+3.25	£14,458.30	£20,284.30
Ollie Magern	1-3	33	+12.00	£13,010.00	£20,253.50
Amber Brook	1-5	20	+4.00	£9,393.00	£16,343.25
Ammunition	3-5	60	+22.00	£14,143.00	£14,663.75
Kayf Aramis	0-8	-	-8.00	£0.00	£14,471.90
C'Monthehammers	1-5	20	+6.00	£12,674.00	£14,011.00
Major Malarkey	2-6	33	+17.00	£8,781.75	£13,844.15

NIGEL TWISTON-DAVIES

All runners

	Wins	Runs	%	Win prize	Total prize	£1 Stake
Hurdle	49	332	15	£152,481.44	£269,584.13	+67.36
Chase	44	320	14	£509,707.65	£704,127.80	-51.71
Bumper	4	59	7	£6,781.80	£14,713.19	+2.50
TOTAL	97	711	14	£668,970.89	£988,425.12	+18.15

By course – last four seasons

	Hurdles				Chases				Bumpers			
	W	R	%	£1 stake	W	R	%	£1 stake	W	R	%	£1 stake
Aintree	3	32	9	-6.50	9	73	12	-14.50	0	4	-	-4.00
Ascot	1	27	4	-22.67	1	29	3	-24.50	0	3	-	-3.00
Ayr	1	2	50	+0.50	2	6	33	+9.88	0	0	-	+0.00
Bangor-On-Dee	4	32	13	-20.92	3	28	11	-16.83	0	5	-	-5.00
Carlisle	0	2	-	-2.00	4	21	19	+8.25	0	0	-	+0.00
Cartmel	1	2	50	+2.33	0	3	-	-3.00	0	0	-	+0.00
Catterick	0	0	-	+0.00	0	0	-	+0.00	0	1	-	-1.00
Cheltenham	14	129	11	+121.25	20	192	10	-41.96	0	17	-	-17.00
Chepstow	6	64	9	-16.38	4	49	8	-19.00	0	12	-	-12.00
Doncaster	3	16	19	+7.00	0	10	-	-10.00	0	3	-	-3.00
Exeter	5	27	19	+32.83	4	32	13	+4.50	0	3	-	-3.00
Fakenham	0	1	-	-1.00	0	0	-	+0.00	0	0	-	+0.00
Ffos Las	4	23	17	+5.00	5	26	19	-5.18	0	8	-	-8.00
Folkestone	1	10	10	-1.00	0	8	-	-8.00	1	2	50	+0.63
Fontwell	2	10	20	+18.00	4	16	25	+0.25	0	4	-	-4.00
Haydock	3	22	14	+10.50	3	28	11	-19.48	0	6	-	-6.00
Hereford	5	36	14	+10.91	2	20	10	-15.00	0	14	-	-14.00
Hexham	0	0	-	+0.00	0	0	-	+0.00	1	1	100	+1.25
Huntingdon	5	34	15	-4.71	4	39	10	-17.89	1	8	13	-4.50
Kelso	0	5	-	-5.00	5	14	36	+4.90	0	0	-	+0.00
Kempton	2	27	7	-17.00	4	36	11	-9.88	1	1	100	+5.00
Leicester	1	12	8	-10.47	3	20	15	+7.25	0	0	-	+0.00
Lingfield	2	11	18	-8.27	2	9	22	-4.84	0	0	-	+0.00
Lingfield (A.W)	0	0	-	+0.00	0	0	-	+0.00	0	2	-	-2.00
Ludlow	6	55	11	-16.50	4	48	8	-19.63	1	13	8	-3.00
Market Rasen	6	34	18	-1.63	10	35	29	+5.00	0	4	-	-4.00
Musselburgh	0	1	-	-1.00	0	0	-	+0.00	0	0	-	+0.00
Newbury	2	48	4	+1.00	5	58	9	-32.63	0	9	-	-9.00
Newcastle	0	0	-	+0.00	1	4	25	+11.00	0	0	-	+0.00
Newton Abbot	6	15	40	+23.75	4	12	33	+16.33	0	3	-	-3.00
Perth	15	50	30	+16.14	12	50	24	-6.09	5	6	83	+9.37
Plumpton	1	9	11	-2.00	0	8	-	-8.00	1	4	25	-1.00
Sandown	2	19	11	-8.50	1	31	3	-26.00	0	3	-	-3.00
Sedgefield	0	2	-	-2.00	0	2	-	-2.00	0	0	-	+0.00
Southwell	6	26	23	+24.58	2	16	13	-5.00	0	4	-	-4.00
Stratford	9	45	20	+69.32	7	60	12	-32.25	1	11	9	-8.00
Taunton	1	17	6	+0.00	0	8	-	-8.00	0	1	-	-1.00
Towcester	4	51	8	-21.32	9	41	22	+6.96	1	11	9	-5.50
Uttoxeter	18	73	25	+38.78	6	45	13	-20.65	4	20	20	-8.79
Warwick	7	35	20	+2.68	7	34	21	+0.48	2	13	15	+44.00
Wetherby	2	10	20	-2.00	5	13	38	+11.74	1	3	33	+0.25
Wincanton	2	16	13	+2.00	3	27	11	-10.25	0	4	-	-4.00
Worcester	8	48	17	-11.44	3	27	11	-8.50	1	10	10	-4.50

By race type

	Hurdles				Chases			
	W	R	%	£1 stake	W	R	%	£1 stake
Handicap	29	214	14	-8.63	33	264	13	-54.35
Novice	12	113	11	-68.89	14	77	18	-18.39
Maiden	4	45	9	-0.42	0	3	-	-3.00

By jockey

	Hurdles				Chases				Bumpers			
	W	R	%	£1 stake	W	R	%	£1 stake	W	R	%	£1 stake
A P McCoy	25	151	17	-60.82	28	171	16	-47.64	3	15	20	-6.53
Richie McLernon	12	123	10	+6.89	14	117	12	-14.92	0	8	-	-8.00
Mr A J Berry	2	26	8	-14.00	5	32	16	+6.41	0	4	-	-4.00
Anthony Freeman	0	3	-	-3.00	0	0	-	+0.00	1	1	100	+28.00
Miss Jenny Carr	0	4	-	-4.00	1	3	33	+4.00	0	0	-	+0.00
Sam Thomas	1	6	17	+9.00	0	4	-	-4.00	0	1	-	-1.00
Dominic Elsworth	0	8	-	-8.00	1	7	14	-1.50	0	1	-	-1.00
Dougie Costello	1	8	13	+21.00	0	7	-	-7.00	0	1	-	-1.00
Andrew Tinkler	0	1	-	-1.00	0	0	-	+0.00	0	0	-	+0.00
Barry Keniry	0	0	-	+0.00	0	1	-	-1.00	0	0	-	+0.00

By month

	Hurdles				Chases				Bumpers			
	W	R	%	£1 stake	W	R	%	£1 stake	W	R	%	£1 stake
May 2010	2	30	7	-13.09	4	31	13	-11.59	0	2	-	-2.00
June	9	23	39	+36.35	3	34	9	-19.75	0	2	-	-2.00
July	4	26	15	+19.08	4	26	15	+8.10	0	0	-	+0.00
August	1	23	4	-19.00	5	28	18	+7.00	0	2	-	-2.00
September	2	16	13	-6.50	3	19	16	-5.00	0	0	-	+0.00
October	4	38	15	-18.10	2	37	5	-13.00	2	6	33	-1.27
November	7	46	15	-23.53	9	44	20	+0.12	0	6	-	-6.00
December	2	29	7	-19.25	4	38	11	-18.75	1	1	100	+2.75
January 2011	2	41	5	-34.63	5	33	15	-6.38	0	2	-	-2.00
February	1	25	4	+4.00	1	21	5	-19.20	0	1	-	-1.00
March	1	29	3	-26.00	5	34	15	-7.70	1	5	20	+24.00
April	6	25	24	+25.73	2	13	15	-5.50	0	3	-	-3.00

By horse

	Wins-Runs	%	£1 level stakes	Win prize	Total prize
Albertas Run	1-5	20	+2.00	£154,896.20	£195,553.50
Don't Push It	0-5	-	-5.00	£0.00	£100,890.00
Synchronised	1-4	25	+2.00	£45,608.00	£54,563.30
Backspin	2-3	67	+6.75	£23,368.62	£24,703.62
Rock Noir	2-6	33	+2.75	£12,837.50	£19,135.13
Galaxy Rock	3-8	38	-0.70	£14,626.95	£17,897.95
Sea Wall	2-7	29	+24.00	£13,851.40	£16,565.80
Get Me Out Of Here	0-5	-	-5.00	£0.00	£16,458.20
Sunnyhillboy	0-3	-	-3.00	£0.00	£16,065.00
Yellow Flag	2-5	40	+3.75	£7,984.62	£15,510.62
Tarvini	2-10	20	+9.00	£14,271.75	£14,961.75
In The Zone	2-9	22	+4.50	£6,455.51	£12,125.51
Ringaroses	0-3	-	-3.00	£0.00	£10,695.00
Isn't That Lucky	1-5	20	-0.50	£7,604.40	£9,790.25
Mister Hyde	2-6	33	-0.75	£7,806.00	£9,535.60

JONJO O'NEILL

All runners

	Wins	Runs	%	Win prize	Total prize	£1 Stake
Hurdle	41	358	11	£140,477.43	£215,914.88	-81.93
Chase	49	361	14	£379,809.92	£635,787.61	-84.65
Bumper	4	31	13	£6,318.15	£10,032.68	+6.48
TOTAL	94	750	13	£526,605.50	£861,735.17	-160.11

By course – last four seasons

	Hurdles				Chases				Bumpers			
	W	R	%	£1 stake	W	R	%	£1 stake	W	R	%	£1 stake
Aintree	5	29	17	-2.51	4	38	11	+1.00	0	6	-	-6.00
Ascot	1	17	6	-6.00	4	17	24	+5.50	0	6	-	-6.00
Ayr	0	2	-	-2.00	0	3	-	-3.00	0	0	-	+0.00
Bangor-On-Dee	12	87	14	-36.18	15	76	20	-16.34	0	5	-	-5.00
Carlisle	0	10	-	-10.00	5	28	18	-8.40	0	1	-	-1.00
Cartmel	1	4	25	+0.00	0	2	-	-2.00	0	0	-	+0.00
Catterick	0	1	-	-1.00	0	3	-	-3.00	0	0	-	+0.00
Cheltenham	2	67	3	-49.00	9	78	12	-17.88	0	7	-	-7.00
Chepstow	3	60	5	-45.50	8	40	20	+16.88	1	12	8	-9.63
Doncaster	1	16	6	+13.00	1	8	13	-5.75	0	0	-	+0.00
Exeter	8	56	14	-1.75	5	42	12	+7.00	1	5	20	-1.25
Fakenham	5	24	21	-10.69	3	11	27	-3.25	0	0	-	+0.00
Ffos Las	5	32	16	-17.96	7	36	19	+0.50	0	7	-	-7.00
Folkestone	1	24	4	-14.00	4	17	24	+3.10	0	2	-	-2.00
Fontwell	11	44	25	+15.85	7	40	18	+2.18	1	2	50	+3.00
Haydock	1	20	5	-8.00	2	27	7	-12.67	1	3	33	+26.00
Hereford	8	60	13	-14.38	5	33	15	-4.00	0	9	-	-9.00
Huntingdon	7	78	9	-25.60	5	40	13	-7.05	1	6	17	-4.20
Kempton	2	38	5	-27.25	2	26	8	-17.25	0	4	-	-4.00
Leicester	1	16	6	-11.50	7	31	23	+6.86	0	0	-	+0.00
Lingfield	4	18	22	-0.38	2	18	11	-12.58	0	0	-	+0.00
Lingfield (A.W)	0	0	-	+0.00	0	0	-	+0.00	1	2	50	+0.38
Ludlow	7	28	25	+23.25	12	46	26	+20.13	0	2	-	-2.00
Market Rasen	8	85	9	-56.38	23	76	30	+29.70	1	7	14	-1.00
Musselburgh	0	0	-	+0.00	0	0	-	+0.00	0	1	-	-1.00
Newbury	4	44	9	-23.00	2	38	5	-20.13	0	5	-	-5.00
Newcastle	0	0	-	+0.00	0	2	-	-2.00	0	0	-	+0.00
Newton Abbot	6	49	12	+9.48	5	40	13	-19.29	0	1	-	-1.00
Perth	0	1	-	-1.00	0	4	-	-4.00	0	0	-	+0.00
Plumpton	3	24	13	+9.38	0	11	-	-11.00	0	1	-	-1.00
Sandown	3	25	12	-3.50	2	19	11	-10.50	0	4	-	-4.00
Sedgefield	2	5	40	+0.50	0	6	-	-6.00	0	0	-	+0.00
Southwell	6	44	14	-25.80	8	31	26	-1.07	0	6	-	-6.00
Stratford	6	53	11	-28.73	10	67	15	-9.33	0	6	-	-6.00
Taunton	0	19	-	-19.00	0	9	-	-9.00	0	0	-	+0.00
Towcester	14	64	22	+24.33	14	58	24	+15.48	0	6	-	-6.00
Uttoxeter	13	125	10	-66.01	8	95	8	-61.22	3	18	17	-7.25
Warwick	3	26	12	-11.08	4	37	11	-14.50	0	8	-	-8.00
Wetherby	7	13	54	+32.04	4	19	21	-10.18	0	3	-	-3.00
Wincanton	5	23	22	+19.25	1	7	14	-2.50	0	1	-	-1.00
Worcester	23	84	27	+29.97	13	62	21	+1.73	3	10	30	-3.70

By race type

	Hurdles				Chases			
	W	R	%	£1 stake	W	R	%	£1 stake
Handicap	15	171	9	-96.47	19	124	15	-40.41
Novice	20	115	17	-6.35	12	51	24	-11.01
Maiden	5	44	11	-7.77	0	0	-	+0.00

By jockey

	Hurdles				Chases				Bumpers			
	W	R	%	£1 stake	W	R	%	£1 stake	W	R	%	£1 stake
Tom Scudamore	2	14	14	+4.50	2	5	40	+0.16	0	2	-	-2.00
Dean Coleman	3	13	23	+0.25	1	10	10	-8.00	0	2	-	-2.00
Daryl Jacob	0	2	-	-2.00	3	5	60	+4.47	0	0	-	+0.00
Richard Killoran	1	29	3	-25.75	2	11	18	-3.77	0	7	-	-7.00
Jason Maguire	1	2	50	+2.50	0	1	-	-1.00	0	0	-	+0.00
Robert Thornton	1	3	33	+0.75	0	0	-	+0.00	0	2	-	-2.00
Johnny Farrelly	0	3	-	-3.00	0	1	-	-1.00	1	2	50	+24.00
Dougie Costello	0	2	-	-2.00	1	5	20	-1.25	0	0	-	+0.00
Michael Murphy	0	3	-	-3.00	1	5	20	+3.50	0	2	-	-2.00
C O'Farrell	0	0	-	+0.00	0	1	-	-1.00	0	0	-	+0.00

By month

	Hurdles				Chases				Bumpers			
	W	R	%	£1 stake	W	R	%	£1 stake	W	R	%	£1 stake
May 2010	4	22	18	-8.20	9	19	47	+7.99	1	5	20	+21.00
June	11	39	28	-4.47	4	19	21	-8.20	2	4	50	+2.00
July	8	30	27	+8.49	2	16	13	-8.09	0	0	-	+0.00
August	8	49	16	-14.85	3	22	14	-10.75	0	1	-	-1.00
September	5	23	22	-5.12	1	11	9	-7.75	0	0	-	+0.00
October	1	28	4	-24.25	1	14	7	-12.27	0	3	-	-3.00
November	1	18	6	-16.71	1	10	10	-1.50	1	4	25	-0.75
December	0	9	-	-9.00	1	4	25	-0.25	0	6	-	-6.00
January 2011	4	38	11	-23.25	2	13	15	+15.00	0	8	-	-8.00
February	5	25	20	+14.41	3	13	23	-0.07	2	7	29	+0.25
March	0	25	-	-25.00	1	17	6	-13.25	1	9	11	-6.50
April	1	20	5	+14.00	3	11	27	+6.33	1	6	17	-4.09

By horse

	Wins-Runs	%	£1 level stakes	Win prize	Total prize
Beshabar	2-4	50	+5.80	£106,043.50	£120,106.00
Saint Are	1-5	20	+29.00	£56,520.00	£58,239.00
Grand Lahou	2-11	18	-0.50	£10,890.50	£21,451.00
The Ferbane Man	4-11	36	-1.46	£14,779.41	£20,786.34
Architrave	3-6	50	+1.69	£15,160.75	£15,311.55
Destroyer Deployed	2-3	67	+4.25	£2,927.25	£14,691.75
Ben's Folly	3-4	75	+9.00	£13,920.70	£13,920.70
Baily Storm	3-4	75	+5.47	£13,310.00	£13,310.00
Lord Gunnerslake	3-7	43	+5.25	£10,888.95	£12,130.15
Dead Or Alive	1-7	14	-2.50	£6,505.00	£10,889.20
House Of Bourbon	2-5	40	+3.00	£7,220.55	£9,161.95
Holoko Heights	3-8	38	+2.42	£7,519.50	£9,118.35
Quo Video	2-9	22	+14.00	£6,505.00	£9,027.37
Ruby Isabel	2-5	40	-0.17	£6,801.00	£8,416.05
Isle Of Inishmore	3-6	50	+10.33	£7,671.74	£7,905.74

TIM VAUGHAN

All runners

	Wins	Runs	%	Win prize	Total prize	£1 Stake
Hurdle	50	333	15	£193,054.65	£250,263.81	-94.21
Chase	33	173	19	£222,217.96	£294,531.76	-29.31
Bumper	8	57	14	£12,332.15	£29,265.57	-10.09
TOTAL	91	563	16	£427,604.76	£574,061.14	-133.61

By course – last four seasons

	Hurdles				Chases				Bumpers			
	W	R	%	£1 stake	W	R	%	£1 stake	W	R	%	£1 stake
Aintree	1	5	20	+29.00	1	8	13	-6.00	0	3	-	-3.00
Ascot	0	2	-	-2.00	0	1	-	-1.00	0	0	-	+0.00
Ayr	1	2	50	+0.25	1	3	33	+5.50	0	1	-	-1.00
Bangor-On-Dee	10	38	26	+7.97	1	19	5	-14.67	3	9	33	+6.83
Carlisle	0	2	-	-2.00	0	0	-	+0.00	0	0	-	+0.00
Cartmel	3	16	19	-0.63	1	8	13	-3.00	0	0	-	+0.00
Catterick	0	1	-	-1.00	0	0	-	+0.00	0	0	-	+0.00
Cheltenham	0	19	-	-19.00	0	11	-	-11.00	0	1	-	-1.00
Chepstow	1	44	2	-39.50	4	24	17	-2.90	2	11	18	+23.00
Doncaster	1	4	25	+0.50	1	1	100	+0.30	0	0	-	+0.00
Exeter	2	17	12	+3.50	1	7	14	-4.13	1	2	50	-0.09
Fakenham	5	21	24	-10.67	4	12	33	-0.46	0	3	-	-3.00
Ffos Las	4	59	7	-36.21	4	28	14	-8.38	4	19	21	-6.50
Folkestone	1	3	33	-0.50	1	3	33	+0.75	1	2	50	+0.75
Fontwell	8	42	19	-11.06	6	25	24	-5.34	1	10	10	-6.50
Haydock	0	2	-	-2.00	0	0	-	+0.00	0	1	-	-1.00
Hereford	2	37	5	-11.90	2	25	8	-15.00	1	10	10	+16.00
Hexham	3	12	25	-5.50	1	6	17	-4.78	0	0	-	+0.00
Huntingdon	2	23	9	-17.75	4	13	31	+4.23	0	1	-	-1.00
Kempton	0	4	-	-4.00	0	1	-	-1.00	0	0	-	+0.00
Leicester	2	13	15	+7.73	1	8	13	-6.33	0	0	-	+0.00
Lingfield	2	4	50	+8.00	0	2	-	-2.00	0	0	-	+0.00
Lingfield (A.W)	0	0	-	+0.00	0	0	-	+0.00	0	5	-	-5.00
Ludlow	3	27	11	-16.25	2	12	17	-7.50	1	8	13	+2.00
Market Rasen	12	43	28	-0.16	4	22	18	+10.13	0	6	-	-6.00
Musselburgh	1	5	20	-3.43	0	1	-	-1.00	0	1	-	-1.00
Newbury	2	7	29	+11.00	1	3	33	+5.00	0	3	-	-3.00
Newcastle	0	3	-	-3.00	2	3	67	+3.03	0	1	-	-1.00
Newton Abbot	10	61	16	-21.27	3	22	14	-12.43	2	14	14	-6.75
Perth	3	8	38	-0.43	1	6	17	-1.00	0	1	-	-1.00
Plumpton	4	25	16	+7.00	3	9	33	-2.82	0	9	-	-9.00
Sandown	0	3	-	-3.00	0	1	-	-1.00	0	1	-	-1.00
Sedgefield	4	19	21	-7.16	1	11	9	-9.17	0	1	-	-1.00
Southwell	8	35	23	-14.13	9	18	50	+9.96	0	3	-	-3.00
Southwell (A.W)	0	0	-	+0.00	0	0	-	+0.00	0	5	-	-5.00
Stratford	8	48	17	-0.09	4	26	15	+5.25	2	7	29	+18.33
Taunton	3	22	14	+9.25	1	5	20	+0.50	0	1	-	-1.00
Towcester	4	20	20	-4.25	4	15	27	-3.00	1	7	14	-3.25
Uttoxeter	13	64	20	-11.44	4	21	19	+0.75	1	8	13	+18.00
Warwick	2	6	33	+3.00	0	3	-	-3.00	0	2	-	-2.00
Wetherby	3	19	16	-11.13	2	7	29	-3.33	0	0	-	+0.00
Wincanton	5	21	24	+16.95	2	7	29	+1.83	0	1	-	-1.00
Worcester	8	64	13	-10.00	8	27	30	+0.84	3	12	25	+8.38

By race type

| | Hurdles | | | | Chases | | | |
	W	R	%	£1 stake	W	R	%	£1 stake
Handicap	16	178	9	-26.68	25	172	15	-14.04
Novice	12	99	12	-30.86	14	78	18	-0.06
Maiden	8	40	20	+0.28	0	1	-	-1.00

By jockey

| | Hurdles | | | | Chases | | | | Bumpers | | | |
	W	R	%	£1 stake	W	R	%	£1 stake	W	R	%	£1 stake
Paul Moloney	32	194	16	-8.55	25	141	18	-10.82	2	8	25	-3.28
D P Fahy	6	53	11	-6.63	5	26	19	+0.75	0	1	-	-1.00
Adam Wedge	2	22	9	-2.00	5	21	24	+17.13	0	0	-	+0.00
A P McCoy	4	13	31	-1.92	0	1	-	-1.00	0	0	-	+0.00
Aodhagan Conlon	2	13	15	-3.09	2	13	15	-2.00	0	1	-	-1.00
Jonathan England	0	14	-	-14.00	2	10	20	-0.50	0	0	-	+0.00
Graham Lee	0	0	-	+0.00	1	1	100	+2.50	0	0	-	+0.00
Miss I Tompsett	1	2	50	+3.50	0	0	-	+0.00	0	0	-	+0.00
Tom O'Brien	1	2	50	+15.00	0	1	-	-1.00	0	0	-	+0.00
Ashley Bird	0	1	-	-1.00	0	0	-	+0.00	0	0	-	+0.00

By month

| | Hurdles | | | | Chases | | | | Bumpers | | | |
	W	R	%	£1 stake	W	R	%	£1 stake	W	R	%	£1 stake
May 2010	8	29	28	+22.30	3	22	14	-3.75	0	1	-	-1.00
June	8	33	24	+15.16	7	17	41	+23.25	0	0	-	+0.00
July	2	25	8	-20.33	2	12	17	+4.25	0	0	-	+0.00
August	2	29	7	-21.63	2	21	10	-9.00	0	0	-	+0.00
September	2	25	8	-16.63	3	21	14	-6.75	0	0	-	+0.00
October	2	31	6	-20.33	3	16	19	+2.75	1	2	50	+0.63
November	7	33	21	-3.51	5	24	21	-3.99	0	0	-	+0.00
December	1	6	17	-1.50	1	10	10	-0.50	0	0	-	+0.00
January 2011	5	41	12	+39.50	4	21	19	-2.68	0	0	-	+0.00
February	2	24	8	-17.90	1	21	5	-16.00	0	0	-	+0.00
March	7	40	18	-0.69	5	30	17	-3.52	1	8	13	-5.90
April	2	16	13	-11.13	1	17	6	-12.00	0	0	-	+0.00

By horse

	Wins-Runs	%	£1 level stakes	Win prize	Total prize
State Of Play	0-1	-	-1.00	£0.00	£50,445.00
Tiger O'Toole	3-6	50	+42.00	£37,425.30	£38,307.80
West With The Wind	4-6	67	+10.88	£35,683.50	£37,020.50
Deep Purple	0-4	-	-4.00	£0.00	£34,785.00
Courella	3-9	33	+5.50	£12,875.60	£17,117.65
Dantari	0-10	-	-10.00	£0.00	£16,543.40
Warpath	2-4	50	+13.00	£13,368.90	£14,421.90
Ajman	3-12	25	+14.00	£11,852.00	£14,040.75
William's Wishes	3-4	75	+1.09	£13,126.82	£13,126.82
Postmaster	1-7	14	+0.00	£10,139.20	£13,054.60
Tarkari	0-5	-	-5.00	£0.00	£12,433.50
Blacktoft	1-10	10	+3.00	£6,970.70	£11,721.55
Lucaindubai	2-8	25	-2.63	£6,309.85	£11,680.35
Oursininlaw	2-9	22	+6.00	£8,781.75	£10,756.50
Mutual Respect	2-6	33	+1.25	£8,781.75	£10,619.60

EVAN WILLIAMS

All runners

	Wins	Runs	%	Win prize	Total prize	£1 Stake
Hurdle	48	345	14	£167,532.25	£287,140.06	-49.68
Chase	40	237	17	£184,215.05	£354,608.90	-17.94
Bumper	2	13	15	£3,903.00	£5,698.40	-8.28
TOTAL	90	595	15	£355,650.30	£647,447.36	-75.90

By course – last four seasons

	Hurdles				Chases				Bumpers			
	W	R	%	£1 stake	W	R	%	£1 stake	W	R	%	£1 stake
Aintree	0	6	-	-6.00	0	14	-	-14.00	0	0	-	+0.00
Ascot	3	13	23	+46.67	2	16	13	-9.75	0	0	-	+0.00
Ayr	0	0	-	+0.00	1	1	100	+1.88	0	0	-	+0.00
Bangor-On-Dee	5	56	9	-44.94	0	15	-	-15.00	0	1	-	-1.00
Carlisle	0	1	-	-1.00	0	1	-	-1.00	0	0	-	+0.00
Cartmel	3	31	10	-18.75	3	17	18	-8.00	0	0	-	+0.00
Catterick	0	1	-	-1.00	0	2	-	-2.00	0	1	-	-1.00
Cheltenham	3	53	6	-31.75	1	17	6	-2.00	0	2	-	-2.00
Chepstow	8	78	10	-1.50	1	33	3	-28.50	0	7	-	-7.00
Doncaster	0	1	-	-1.00	0	0	-	+0.00	0	0	-	+0.00
Exeter	7	35	20	+12.94	0	13	-	-13.00	1	3	33	-1.56
Fakenham	8	23	35	+22.35	3	11	27	-0.38	0	0	-	+0.00
Ffos Las	7	82	9	-38.75	14	76	18	-1.42	0	12	-	-12.00
Folkestone	0	1	-	-1.00	0	1	-	-1.00	0	0	-	+0.00
Fontwell	8	68	12	-35.01	7	38	18	-5.80	0	4	-	-4.00
Haydock	1	10	10	+2.00	0	5	-	-5.00	0	0	-	+0.00
Hereford	7	86	8	+36.25	12	52	23	-5.12	0	7	-	-7.00
Hexham	5	10	50	+12.11	0	6	-	-6.00	0	0	-	+0.00
Huntingdon	4	24	17	+12.40	1	16	6	-3.00	0	0	-	+0.00
Kempton	2	9	22	+8.50	1	9	11	-5.25	0	2	-	-2.00
Leicester	3	18	17	-5.25	2	13	15	-8.53	0	0	-	+0.00
Lingfield	1	8	13	-5.13	1	4	25	+11.00	0	0	-	+0.00
Lingfield (A.W)	0	0	-	+0.00	0	0	-	+0.00	0	3	-	-3.00
Ludlow	19	122	16	-33.86	14	91	15	-21.78	2	20	10	-14.38
Market Rasen	8	42	19	+3.75	2	27	7	-10.00	0	1	-	-1.00
Musselburgh	1	2	50	+2.00	1	1	100	+3.00	0	1	-	-1.00
Newbury	1	12	8	-9.25	0	9	-	-9.00	0	0	-	+0.00
Newton Abbot	14	78	18	-18.10	3	41	7	-19.00	0	0	-	+0.00
Perth	0	8	-	-8.00	0	4	-	-4.00	0	0	-	+0.00
Plumpton	7	46	15	-3.71	4	17	24	-0.17	0	2	-	-2.00
Sandown	0	19	-	-19.00	0	13	-	-13.00	0	2	-	-2.00
Sedgefield	2	20	10	-17.05	3	12	25	+6.88	0	0	-	+0.00
Southwell	7	36	19	-8.12	5	35	14	-18.92	0	1	-	-1.00
Stratford	10	67	15	+12.86	5	38	13	-9.93	2	5	40	+0.10
Taunton	9	45	20	+14.98	3	22	14	-14.58	2	3	67	+13.00
Towcester	1	17	6	-6.00	0	9	-	-9.00	0	0	-	+0.00
Uttoxeter	10	79	13	-25.15	6	43	14	-3.55	0	3	-	-3.00
Warwick	0	13	-	-13.00	1	11	9	-7.25	0	0	-	+0.00
Wetherby	4	20	20	-8.84	3	15	20	-2.50	0	0	-	+0.00
Wincanton	4	37	11	-0.25	1	16	6	-11.67	0	1	-	-1.00
Worcester	7	58	12	-11.13	9	48	19	+26.63	0	3	-	-3.00

By race type

	Hurdles				Chases			
	W	R	%	£1 stake	W	R	%	£1 stake
Handicap	18	149	12	-48.71	14	155	9	-60.63
Novice	18	105	17	-27.87	15	53	28	-9.06
Maiden	5	33	15	-15.27	0	1	-	-1.00

By jockey

	Hurdles				Chases				Bumpers			
	W	R	%	£1 stake	W	R	%	£1 stake	W	R	%	£1 stake
Richard Johnson	24	140	17	-54.79	24	116	21	-5.08	7	20	35	+17.28
Tom O'Brien	9	57	16	-5.05	5	57	9	-31.89	2	9	22	-2.50
Rhys Flint	3	31	10	-11.75	1	28	4	-22.50	0	4	-	-4.00
Chris Davies	3	15	20	+15.50	0	0	-	+0.00	0	0	-	+0.00
Giles Hawkins	3	27	11	-13.92	0	10	-	-10.00	0	2	-	-2.00
Mr J A Best	0	1	-	-1.00	2	3	67	+3.25	0	1	-	-1.00
A P McCoy	1	3	33	-0.13	1	3	33	+2.00	0	0	-	+0.00
C P Geoghegan	1	5	20	-2.50	0	0	-	+0.00	0	0	-	+0.00
Mr S Parish	0	1	-	-1.00	0	0	-	+0.00	0	0	-	+0.00
Seamus Durack	0	0	-	+0.00	0	0	-	+0.00	0	1	-	-1.00

By month

	Hurdles				Chases				Bumpers			
	W	R	%	£1 stake	W	R	%	£1 stake	W	R	%	£1 stake
May 2010	4	28	14	-13.79	3	17	18	-10.07	0	5	-	-5.00
June	0	8	-	-8.00	0	12	-	-12.00	0	0	-	+0.00
July	2	7	29	+7.00	0	6	-	-6.00	0	0	-	+0.00
August	2	6	33	+2.08	0	6	-	-6.00	0	0	-	+0.00
September	2	12	17	-7.72	2	8	25	+0.00	1	1	100	+1.00
October	13	35	37	+19.25	5	31	16	-6.53	3	6	50	+6.25
November	7	40	18	-11.83	3	29	10	-18.38	0	5	-	-5.00
December	2	22	9	-17.85	2	22	9	-15.14	0	0	-	+0.00
January 2011	5	39	13	-11.27	5	25	20	+8.50	2	4	50	+3.50
February	1	25	4	-18.50	2	18	11	-7.60	2	8	25	-0.97
March	2	44	5	-36.00	5	27	19	+4.75	1	3	33	+12.00
April	3	24	13	+9.50	6	21	29	-0.75	0	7	-	-7.00

By horse

	Wins-Runs	%	£1 level stakes	Win prize	Total prize
Menorah	2-3	67	+6.75	£142,525.00	£152,441.00
Captain Chris	2-6	33	+2.40	£87,453.34	£108,851.14
Wishfull Thinking	3-6	50	+5.00	£84,220.10	£106,651.10
Quinz	3-5	60	+8.98	£70,483.00	£71,870.50
Nearby	3-9	33	+21.50	£50,999.05	£61,832.05
Kilcrea Kim	4-7	57	+9.50	£30,457.25	£33,483.75
Cheltenian	2-2	100	+14.53	£33,068.25	£33,068.25
Triggerman	2-11	18	+0.00	£15,174.60	£28,323.60
Planet Of Sound	0-2	-	-2.00	£0.00	£26,064.00
Fair Along	1-4	25	+3.00	£18,528.25	£25,746.25
Balthazar King	4-8	50	+2.50	£21,188.64	£25,004.64
Safari Journey	1-5	20	+6.00	£17,103.00	£23,503.00
Tarablaze	2-6	33	-2.39	£15,926.50	£20,738.00
Lacdoudal	1-2	50	+3.50	£15,655.00	£19,817.50
Cockney Trucker	2-9	22	-2.25	£10,327.33	£19,429.83

PHILIP HOBBS

All runners

	Wins	Runs	%	Win prize	Total prize	£1 Stake
Hurdle	44	291	15	£373,141.32	£502,837.55	-85.63
Chase	33	226	15	£397,671.40	£607,470.72	-73.21
Bumper	9	39	23	£46,430.08	£52,742.27	+4.78
TOTAL	86	556	15	£817,242.80	£1,163,050.54	-154.06

By course – last four seasons

	Hurdles				Chases				Bumpers			
	W	R	%	£1 stake	W	R	%	£1 stake	W	R	%	£1 stake
Aintree	5	44	11	-11.00	2	24	8	-7.75	1	11	9	-6.50
Ascot	4	46	9	-23.63	7	46	15	+5.29	2	7	29	+10.00
Ayr	0	7	-	-7.00	1	8	13	-2.00	0	0	-	+0.00
Bangor-On-Dee	7	30	23	+11.37	5	21	24	+10.00	0	5	-	-5.00
Cartmel	0	0	-	+0.00	0	1	-	-1.00	0	0	-	+0.00
Catterick	0	1	-	-1.00	0	0	-	+0.00	0	0	-	+0.00
Cheltenham	13	127	10	-39.00	15	124	12	-35.75	3	12	25	+28.50
Chepstow	11	86	13	+19.33	12	61	20	+3.10	2	8	25	-2.42
Doncaster	1	16	6	-12.75	2	12	17	-1.50	0	0	-	+0.00
Exeter	17	103	17	-29.74	18	71	25	-11.47	4	16	25	+13.00
Ffos Las	6	29	21	-2.75	3	20	15	-6.38	2	4	50	+2.50
Folkestone	0	7	-	-7.00	1	8	13	-2.50	0	0	-	+0.00
Fontwell	5	26	19	-11.65	3	14	21	-6.78	1	2	50	+0.38
Haydock	8	35	23	+4.25	0	15	-	-15.00	1	3	33	+0.75
Hereford	4	25	16	-9.66	5	12	42	+8.41	2	7	29	-2.73
Huntingdon	5	34	15	-8.27	8	23	35	+19.80	1	3	33	+1.00
Kempton	11	63	17	-23.51	8	47	17	+15.27	2	10	20	+8.53
Leicester	2	9	22	+3.50	2	17	12	-3.89	0	0	-	+0.00
Lingfield	1	5	20	-3.27	2	5	40	-0.73	0	0	-	+0.00
Ludlow	4	40	10	-26.46	9	31	29	+6.85	0	3	-	-3.00
Market Rasen	4	22	18	-4.97	2	14	14	-5.63	0	2	-	-2.00
Musselburgh	0	2	-	-2.00	0	0	-	+0.00	0	0	-	+0.00
Newbury	17	89	19	+6.55	5	57	9	-28.13	1	7	14	+10.00
Newton Abbot	9	58	16	-21.58	7	34	21	+1.00	1	4	25	-1.00
Perth	1	13	8	-10.90	4	17	24	+1.08	1	1	100	+2.50
Plumpton	1	16	6	-14.60	0	3	-	-3.00	1	1	100	+5.00
Sandown	9	41	22	+12.35	2	31	6	+16.00	1	6	17	-2.25
Sedgefield	0	0	-	+0.00	0	1	-	-1.00	0	0	-	+0.00
Southwell	3	11	27	+1.75	1	4	25	-2.50	0	0	-	+0.00
Stratford	4	33	12	-12.93	2	40	5	-30.75	0	2	-	-2.00
Taunton	13	89	15	-31.55	6	19	32	+3.39	1	3	33	-1.00
Towcester	1	12	8	-9.25	0	9	-	-9.00	0	1	-	-1.00
Uttoxeter	8	39	21	-11.21	1	24	4	-19.50	1	8	13	-2.50
Warwick	3	29	10	-14.29	5	18	28	-2.89	0	5	-	-5.00
Wetherby	3	5	60	+11.00	1	6	17	-2.00	0	0	-	+0.00
Wincanton	23	97	24	+29.85	6	57	11	-20.42	0	11	-	-11.00
Worcester	3	26	12	-15.04	3	24	13	-15.13	1	8	13	-6.00

By race type

	Hurdles				Chases			
	W	R	%	£1 stake	W	R	%	£1 stake
Handicap	14	143	10	-59.58	18	96	19	+27.63
Novice	22	155	14	-55.55	14	58	24	-7.59
Maiden	5	30	17	-7.00	0	1	-	-1.00

By jockey

	Hurdles				Chases				Bumpers			
	W	R	%	£1 stake	W	R	%	£1 stake	W	R	%	£1 stake
Robert Thornton	20	168	12	-80.83	14	76	18	-12.55	6	48	13	-21.89
Wayne Hutchinson	16	92	17	-16.47	13	44	30	+19.77	0	20	-	-20.00
Peter Hatton	4	16	25	+15.75	0	0	-	+0.00	0	2	-	-2.00
Sam Thomas	1	12	8	-10.60	1	5	20	-0.50	1	1	100	+3.00
Gerard Tumelty	0	12	-	-12.00	0	0	-	+0.00	2	9	22	+11.50
Jack Doyle	0	0	-	+0.00	1	2	50	+5.50	0	0	-	+0.00
Mr J Banks	0	0	-	+0.00	1	2	50	+13.00	0	0	-	+0.00
Mr S Waley-Cohen	1	4	25	-1.50	0	0	-	+0.00	0	0	-	+0.00
A P McCoy	1	4	25	+2.00	0	1	-	-1.00	0	0	-	+0.00
Jimmy McCarthy	1	9	11	-7.00	0	4	-	-4.00	0	0	-	+0.00

By month

	Hurdles				Chases				Bumpers			
	W	R	%	£1 stake	W	R	%	£1 stake	W	R	%	£1 stake
May 2010	0	16	-	-16.00	1	9	11	-1.50	1	5	20	-3.09
June	0	7	-	-7.00	0	1	-	-1.00	0	1	-	-1.00
July	0	4	-	-4.00	0	1	-	-1.00	0	0	-	+0.00
August	0	0	-	+0.00	0	0	-	+0.00	0	0	-	+0.00
September	0	3	-	-3.00	1	1	100	+3.50	0	0	-	+0.00
October	3	25	12	-10.50	1	6	17	-4.80	0	0	-	+0.00
November	12	54	22	+12.68	4	22	18	+8.50	0	10	-	-10.00
December	5	23	22	+18.33	2	12	17	+3.50	2	15	13	-1.63
January 2011	7	59	12	-28.96	3	24	13	+1.38	0	11	-	-11.00
February	8	64	13	-27.00	10	27	37	+12.03	1	20	5	-16.00
March	6	65	9	-51.53	7	29	24	-0.39	4	15	27	+5.32
April	3	37	8	-27.33	1	16	6	-14.00	1	12	8	-1.00

By horse

	Wins-Runs	%	£1 level stakes	Win prize	Total prize
Medermit	3-7	43	+0.20	£34,338.20	£62,871.20
Bensalem	1-4	25	+2.00	£42,757.50	£52,389.25
Mille Chief	2-6	33	+1.21	£49,300.00	£51,847.60
Karabak	1-5	20	+1.00	£19,953.50	£41,713.00
Montbazon	1-3	33	-0.38	£34,585.48	£41,501.73
Kumbeshwar	1-5	20	+3.50	£2,602.00	£40,140.48
West End Rocker	2-4	50	+20.00	£40,060.50	£40,060.50
Blazing Bailey	2-5	40	+12.50	£28,404.00	£28,839.50
Salden Licht	1-4	25	-1.00	£8,238.10	£27,154.10
Mister Stickler	2-7	29	+3.00	£15,352.20	£19,143.70
Bakbenscher	1-4	25	+0.33	£12,674.00	£17,535.50
King Troy	1-2	50	+5.50	£10,019.20	£16,445.20
Midnight Appeal	4-5	80	+9.25	£13,474.35	£13,474.35
Smad Place	2-4	50	+6.25	£8,944.37	£12,692.87
Jetnova	3-8	38	+18.50	£10,550.40	£12,099.75

ALAN KING

All runners

	Wins	Runs	%	Win prize	Total prize	£1 Stake
Hurdle	45	360	13	£211,981.44	£453,074.63	-145.65
Chase	30	149	20	£264,220.95	£376,970.25	+5.22
Bumper	9	91	10	£51,820.95	£71,283.96	-40.39
TOTAL	84	600	14	£528,023.34	£901,328.84	-180.82

By course – last four seasons

	Hurdles				Chases				Bumpers			
	W	R	%	£1 stake	W	R	%	£1 stake	W	R	%	£1 stake
Aintree	7	60	12	-24.10	5	19	26	+0.48	0	16	-	-16.00
Ascot	7	58	12	+13.38	4	25	16	+0.20	0	7	-	-7.00
Ayr	0	10	-	-10.00	0	13	-	-13.00	0	3	-	-3.00
Bangor-On-Dee	7	59	12	-30.27	11	24	46	+15.98	4	15	27	+5.50
Cheltenham	16	154	10	-55.75	6	78	8	-18.00	1	19	5	-8.00
Chepstow	8	77	10	-52.61	1	21	5	-17.25	1	16	6	-11.50
Doncaster	12	63	19	-9.80	4	27	15	-13.68	2	10	20	-5.71
Exeter	6	54	11	-24.13	5	28	18	+12.33	4	12	33	+11.13
Fakenham	0	1	-	-1.00	1	5	20	-3.09	1	5	20	-1.00
Ffos Las	0	14	-	-14.00	2	10	20	+12.50	1	8	13	-5.63
Folkestone	5	22	23	+57.60	4	9	44	+1.49	1	3	33	+0.25
Fontwell	15	60	25	+6.17	6	16	38	+5.92	1	7	14	-5.09
Haydock	2	23	9	-17.25	3	18	17	-0.50	1	4	25	-1.90
Hereford	5	49	10	-27.00	3	14	21	-7.19	2	10	20	-2.75
Hexham	0	0	-	+0.00	1	1	100	+0.50	0	0	-	+0.00
Huntingdon	15	99	15	-39.45	6	36	17	-13.72	8	26	31	+6.50
Kempton	17	87	20	+27.67	7	45	16	-16.61	2	14	14	-3.50
Kempton (A.W)	0	0	-	+0.00	0	0	-	+0.00	0	6	-	-6.00
Leicester	4	28	14	-7.92	2	12	17	-8.80	0	0	-	+0.00
Lingfield	5	21	24	+8.53	1	7	14	-2.50	0	0	-	+0.00
Lingfield (A.W)	0	0	-	+0.00	0	0	-	+0.00	3	9	33	+1.88
Ludlow	5	26	19	-6.45	0	8	-	-8.00	0	5	-	-5.00
Market Rasen	7	51	14	-23.91	4	19	21	+0.87	2	12	17	-6.84
Newbury	11	107	10	-43.00	4	53	8	-9.00	3	25	12	+21.50
Newcastle	0	1	-	-1.00	0	1	-	-1.00	0	0	-	+0.00
Newton Abbot	2	22	9	-16.80	2	4	50	+2.38	0	4	-	-4.00
Plumpton	10	28	36	+14.95	6	17	35	-0.08	0	2	-	-2.00
Sandown	7	54	13	-4.17	4	25	16	-1.75	1	11	9	-7.25
Southwell	6	35	17	-8.42	1	19	5	-17.38	4	16	25	-3.89
Stratford	5	20	25	-6.95	2	15	13	-3.17	0	3	-	-3.00
Taunton	12	79	15	-29.76	6	17	35	+10.17	1	10	10	-2.50
Towcester	9	37	24	-7.34	1	4	25	-0.25	5	18	28	+23.75
Uttoxeter	9	59	15	-15.61	3	23	13	-9.75	5	33	15	-9.88
Warwick	13	52	25	-0.46	6	24	25	+18.04	6	31	19	+1.58
Wetherby	3	19	16	-2.00	0	4	-	-4.00	0	2	-	-2.00
Wincanton	15	78	19	-16.30	6	38	16	-14.38	2	17	12	-3.50
Worcester	1	8	13	-6.70	0	2	-	-2.00	0	6	-	-6.00

By race type

	Hurdles				Chases			
	W	R	%	£1 stake	W	R	%	£1 stake
Handicap	24	185	13	-43.24	18	149	12	-55.53
Novice	8	76	11	-23.80	6	24	25	+6.59
Maiden	2	24	8	-10.00	0	0	-	+0.00

By jockey

	Hurdles				Chases				Bumpers			
	W	R	%	£1 stake	W	R	%	£1 stake	W	R	%	£1 stake
Tom Scudamore	15	144	10	-58.68	16	99	16	-26.51	2	14	14	-9.30
C O'Farrell	9	36	25	+7.97	1	12	8	+14.00	0	0	-	+0.00
Danny Cook	2	26	8	-15.40	4	16	25	-2.37	0	2	-	-2.00
Johnny Farrelly	2	33	6	-22.75	1	20	5	-16.00	1	5	20	+46.00
A P McCoy	2	7	29	+0.50	1	5	20	-2.80	0	0	-	+0.00
Timmy Murphy	2	18	11	+13.00	1	12	8	-7.50	0	0	-	+0.00
Hadden Frost	1	14	7	-6.00	1	4	25	+0.00	0	0	-	+0.00
Mr J J Codd	0	0	-	+0.00	1	2	50	+2.33	0	0	-	+0.00
S Clements	1	1	100	+0.62	0	1	-	-1.00	0	0	-	+0.00
Barry Geraghty	1	2	50	+15.00	0	1	-	-1.00	0	0	-	+0.00

By month

	Hurdles				Chases				Bumpers			
	W	R	%	£1 stake	W	R	%	£1 stake	W	R	%	£1 stake
May 2010	6	32	19	+12.00	3	13	23	-4.46	0	0	-	+0.00
June	2	33	6	-24.92	0	9	-	-9.00	0	1	-	-1.00
July	1	19	5	-15.00	1	7	14	-2.00	0	1	-	-1.00
August	2	16	13	+0.00	0	9	-	-9.00	0	0	-	+0.00
September	0	9	-	-9.00	3	11	27	-1.13	0	0	-	+0.00
October	0	18	-	-18.00	2	14	14	-2.63	0	0	-	+0.00
November	2	29	7	-20.50	2	21	10	-14.13	1	2	50	+0.50
December	2	22	9	-3.50	2	12	17	-3.00	1	5	20	+46.00
January 2011	7	40	18	+4.90	5	21	24	-7.79	0	3	-	-3.00
February	3	30	10	-18.34	1	11	9	-6.50	2	6	33	-1.30
March	4	32	13	-3.04	5	28	18	+29.33	0	5	-	-5.00
April	6	22	27	+8.66	2	22	9	-16.56	0	0	-	+0.00

By horse

	Wins-Runs	%	£1 level stakes	Win prize	Total prize
Grands Crus	3-5	60	+6.50	£78,085.50	£155,089.50
Battle Group	5-11	45	+40.83	£45,795.80	£57,449.10
Massini's Maguire	1-1	100	+8.00	£56,330.00	£56,330.00
Buena Vista	1-8	13	+13.00	£39,907.00	£55,550.00
Minella Four Star	1-5	20	+21.00	£41,770.80	£50,056.80
Faasel	0-3	-	-3.00	£0.00	£39,321.00
Junior	1-3	33	+1.33	£30,010.00	£38,140.00
Swing Bill	2-11	18	-1.50	£19,941.25	£36,714.75
Matuhi	2-6	33	+0.88	£28,179.00	£35,337.00
Great Endeavour	0-4	-	-4.00	£0.00	£34,899.00
I'msingingtheblues	0-10	-	-10.00	£0.00	£25,932.00
Raslan	1-13	8	-4.50	£18,666.00	£24,933.50
Dan Breen	2-7	29	-1.56	£7,071.50	£21,864.66
Hunterview	1-6	17	-2.25	£15,655.00	£17,541.80
Frosted Grape	4-15	27	-1.13	£12,200.01	£15,900.90

DAVID PIPE

All runners

	Wins	Runs	%	Win prize	Total prize	£1 Stake
Hurdle	35	303	12	£282,856.86	£460,744.88	-87.74
Chase	26	178	15	£257,030.04	£520,367.29	-46.85
Bumper	4	23	17	£5,984.60	£18,829.39	+35.20
TOTAL	65	504	13	£545,871.50	£999,941.56	-99.39

By course – last four seasons

	Hurdles				Chases				Bumpers			
	W	R	%	£1 stake	W	R	%	£1 stake	W	R	%	£1 stake
Aintree	2	34	6	-14.38	3	36	8	-5.00	0	3	-	-3.00
Ascot	6	32	19	+33.91	6	31	19	+15.27	1	1	100	+1.75
Ayr	1	7	14	-2.00	0	9	-	-9.00	0	0	-	+0.00
Bangor-On-Dee	4	35	11	+2.00	3	21	14	-5.50	1	4	25	+5.00
Carlisle	0	0	-	+0.00	0	2	-	-2.00	0	0	-	+0.00
Cartmel	0	0	-	+0.00	1	4	25	+4.50	0	0	-	+0.00
Cheltenham	10	143	7	-24.50	12	121	10	-16.47	0	5	-	-5.00
Chepstow	9	52	17	-1.08	2	25	8	-2.50	1	2	50	-0.20
Doncaster	2	8	25	+4.00	2	9	22	+4.00	0	3	-	-3.00
Exeter	8	106	8	-81.65	5	40	13	+9.75	0	6	-	-6.00
Fakenham	1	4	25	-2.56	1	2	50	+0.20	0	0	-	+0.00
Ffos Las	4	21	19	+10.41	1	12	8	-7.00	0	2	-	-2.00
Folkestone	1	16	6	-13.00	2	8	25	+2.38	0	0	-	+0.00
Fontwell	11	61	18	-12.11	5	26	19	-6.13	2	5	40	+3.83
Haydock	3	29	10	-16.97	2	13	15	+12.00	1	2	50	+1.00
Hereford	3	29	10	-21.37	2	12	17	-4.63	0	3	-	-3.00
Hexham	2	6	33	+1.50	1	2	50	+0.25	0	0	-	+0.00
Huntingdon	4	30	13	-10.00	1	12	8	-5.50	0	1	-	-1.00
Kelso	1	2	50	-0.09	1	4	25	-2.60	0	0	-	+0.00
Kempton	3	27	11	-14.38	3	24	13	-5.88	0	0	-	+0.00
Kempton (A.W)	0	0	-	+0.00	0	0	-	+0.00	0	1	-	-1.00
Leicester	1	6	17	-3.13	3	10	30	+3.00	0	0	-	+0.00
Lingfield	0	8	-	-8.00	2	9	22	+1.03	0	0	-	+0.00
Ludlow	7	36	19	-5.25	0	13	-	-13.00	0	4	-	-4.00
Market Rasen	5	31	16	-6.97	2	25	8	-15.39	1	1	100	+2.50
Musselburgh	1	1	100	+2.75	0	0	-	+0.00	1	1	100	+1.50
Newbury	3	45	7	-28.67	5	43	12	+10.58	1	3	33	+48.00
Newcastle	1	3	33	+3.00	1	3	33	+9.00	1	1	100	+1.20
Newton Abbot	21	157	13	-34.88	9	50	18	+5.00	2	6	33	+5.25
Perth	3	11	27	+4.33	1	8	13	+5.00	0	0	-	+0.00
Plumpton	5	34	15	-18.20	2	14	14	-4.17	0	0	-	+0.00
Sandown	9	37	24	+13.32	3	21	14	-3.25	0	1	-	-1.00
Sedgefield	3	9	33	+5.58	0	3	-	-3.00	0	0	-	+0.00
Southwell	3	15	20	-0.75	2	13	15	-9.09	0	0	-	+0.00
Southwell (A.W)	0	0	-	+0.00	0	0	-	+0.00	0	1	-	-1.00
Stratford	10	45	22	+16.20	7	26	27	-0.75	0	1	-	-1.00
Taunton	10	124	8	-25.75	3	20	15	-8.70	0	2	-	-2.00
Towcester	5	38	13	-10.38	5	21	24	+6.62	1	4	25	+0.33
Uttoxeter	15	88	17	+7.37	10	43	23	+26.52	1	7	14	-4.50
Warwick	7	28	25	+4.60	5	15	33	+25.50	1	5	20	+3.00
Wetherby	1	10	10	-8.20	1	5	20	-3.56	0	0	-	+0.00
Wincanton	9	90	10	-48.26	7	51	14	-25.29	0	5	-	-5.00
Worcester	7	58	12	-32.90	5	20	25	-4.53	1	4	25	+17.00

Top trainers 2010-11 by winners

Won	Ran	%	Trainer	Won	Ran	%	Won	Ran	%
	All runs				First time out			Horses	
153	612	25	Nicky Henderson	56	200	28	93	200	47
134	583	23	Paul Nicholls	43	186	23	84	186	45
100	588	17	Donald McCain	25	138	18	62	138	45
97	711	14	Nigel Twiston-Davies	29	173	17	66	173	38
94	750	13	Jonjo O'Neill	15	189	8	67	189	35
91	563	16	Tim Vaughan	28	164	17	62	164	38
90	595	15	Evan Williams	20	150	13	56	150	37
86	556	15	Philip Hobbs	28	152	18	56	152	37
84	600	14	Alan King	25	171	15	60	171	35
65	504	13	David Pipe	19	133	14	44	133	33
60	368	16	Howard Johnson	25	130	19	46	130	35
60	384	16	Peter Bowen	12	70	17	34	70	49
45	390	12	Gary Moore	14	102	14	30	102	29
44	233	19	Charlie Longsdon	13	61	21	26	61	43
41	328	13	Colin Tizzard	9	74	12	26	74	35
41	343	12	Lucinda Russell	8	78	10	33	78	42
40	361	11	Sue Smith	4	83	5	23	83	28
38	372	10	Venetia Williams	6	108	6	27	108	25
38	200	19	Kim Bailey	12	53	23	26	53	49
35	123	28	Gordon Elliott	17	61	28	21	61	34
32	311	10	Milton Harris	3	53	6	23	53	43
30	206	15	Emma Lavelle	15	64	23	21	64	33
29	321	9	Ferdy Murphy	3	84	4	25	84	30
28	203	14	Paul Webber	10	63	16	23	63	37
28	150	19	Rebecca Curtis	12	42	29	21	42	50
27	125	22	Alan Swinbank	7	41	17	16	41	39
26	208	13	Malcolm Jefferson	6	59	10	18	59	31
26	145	18	Victor Dartnall	5	39	13	17	39	44
26	166	16	Richard Lee	9	39	23	19	39	49
26	143	18	Lawney Hill	10	46	22	18	46	39
25	199	13	Ian Williams	7	62	11	20	62	32
24	213	11	Oliver Sherwood	7	52	13	17	52	33
22	108	20	Dr Richard Newland	6	24	25	14	24	58
22	222	10	Brendan Powell	3	48	6	14	48	29
22	164	13	Keith Reveley	5	42	12	14	42	33
21	108	19	Brian Ellison	4	28	14	12	28	43
21	206	10	Neil Mulholland	1	46	2	10	46	22
21	234	9	Seamus Mullins	6	61	10	15	61	25
21	154	14	Jim Goldie	3	39	8	14	39	36
20	202	10	Charlie Mann	1	50	2	16	50	32
20	179	11	Alison Thorpe	5	43	12	13	43	30
20	71	28	David Arbuthnot	4	19	21	9	19	47
19	176	11	Martin Keighley	6	43	14	16	43	37
19	129	15	Micky Hammond	6	28	21	12	28	43
19	110	17	Jim Best	6	39	15	12	39	31
18	224	8	Tom George	5	70	7	16	70	23
18	189	10	Nicky Richards	3	52	6	14	52	27
18	145	12	Robin Dickin	3	37	8	12	37	32

Top trainers 2010-11 by prize-money

Total prizemoney	Trainer	Win prizemoney	Wins	Class 1-3 Won	Class 1-3 Ran	Class 1-3 %	Class 4-6 Won	Class 4-6 Ran	Class 4-6 %
£2,424,059	Paul Nicholls	£1,607,886	134	69	358	19	65	225	29
£2,210,465	Nicky Henderson	£1,591,676	153	76	355	21	77	257	30
£1,286,133	Donald McCain	£954,456	100	26	187	14	74	401	18
£1,163,051	Philip Hobbs	£817,243	86	42	311	14	44	245	18
£999,942	David Pipe	£545,872	65	26	262	10	39	242	16
£988,425	Nigel Twiston-Davies	£668,971	97	29	335	9	68	376	18
£901,329	Alan King	£528,023	84	37	281	13	47	319	15
£861,735	Jonjo O'Neill	£526,606	94	18	243	7	76	507	15
£647,447	Evan Williams	£355,650	90	23	212	11	67	383	17
£574,061	Tim Vaughan	£427,605	91	12	93	13	79	470	17
£524,195	Howard Johnson	£330,615	60	24	174	14	36	194	19
£483,874	W P Mullins	£318,454	4	4	35	11	0	0	—
£436,281	Colin Tizzard	£248,666	41	15	111	14	26	217	12
£396,962	Peter Bowen	£271,237	60	22	146	15	38	238	16
£392,034	Ferdy Murphy	£219,089	29	10	110	9	19	211	9
£365,016	Gordon Elliott	£280,026	35	13	56	23	22	67	33
£352,498	Nick Williams	£247,711	17	11	83	13	6	33	18
£341,862	Tom George	£228,764	18	6	66	9	12	158	8
£323,903	Lucinda Russell	£227,531	41	11	112	10	30	231	13
£304,187	Gary Moore	£171,450	45	13	143	9	32	247	13
£264,405	Venetia Williams	£164,601	38	12	162	7	26	210	12
£258,496	Sue Smith	£197,878	40	12	109	11	28	252	11
£258,091	Charlie Longsdon	£177,548	44	19	88	22	25	145	17
£257,910	Emma Lavelle	£188,293	30	12	91	13	18	115	16
£256,818	Paul Webber	£161,252	28	9	74	12	19	129	15
£228,602	Henry De Bromhead	£207,480	2	2	11	18	0	0	—
£223,407	Brian Ellison	£129,160	21	9	55	16	12	53	23
£222,214	Milton Harris	£114,520	32	8	131	6	24	180	13
£202,968	Neil Mulholland	£119,174	21	4	35	11	17	171	10
£201,590	M M Lynch	£0	0	0	1	—	0	0	—
£183,900	Malcolm Jefferson	£105,581	26	6	60	10	20	148	14
£183,438	Kim Bailey	£141,015	38	10	69	14	28	131	21
£175,966	Ian Williams	£106,146	25	10	63	16	15	136	11
£162,431	Victor Dartnall	£92,197	26	5	48	10	21	97	22
£151,872	Richard Lee	£95,928	26	10	60	17	16	106	15
£148,147	Patrick Rodford	£101,658	12	5	17	29	7	43	16
£147,165	Charlie Mann	£91,852	20	5	77	6	15	125	12
£146,207	Rebecca Curtis	£89,872	28	4	62	6	24	88	27
£143,866	Nicky Richards	£108,204	18	6	44	14	12	145	8
£138,637	Jennie Candlish	£79,291	15	5	32	16	10	79	13
£133,813	Henrietta Knight	£25,899	6	2	46	4	4	104	4
£133,691	Dr Richard Newland	£102,200	22	8	46	17	14	62	23
£128,270	John Wade	£90,634	13	7	18	39	6	98	6
£128,175	Brendan Powell	£78,166	22	7	63	11	15	159	9
£121,933	Lawney Hill	£86,850	26	5	32	16	21	111	19
£117,058	Oliver Sherwood	£75,862	24	2	55	4	22	158	14
£116,840	Martin Keighley	£68,347	19	5	55	9	14	121	12
£112,832	Keith Reveley	£68,257	22	5	38	13	17	126	13

Top jockeys 2010-11

all rides			chases		hurdles		Jockey	best trainer	for best trainer	
W	R	%	W	R	W	R			W	R
218	885	25	66	319	125	479	A P McCoy	Jonjo O'Neill	56	337
151	784	19	57	285	79	423	Richard Johnson	Tim Vaughan	58	231
95	490	19	22	160	63	274	Jason Maguire	Donald McCain	62	288
70	631	16	00	195	43	310	Paul Moloney	Evan Williams	59	343
78	535	15	38	212	32	279	Paddy Brennan	Nigel Twiston-Davies	49	289
77	606	13	32	237	35	322	Graham Lee	Ferdy Murphy	21	206
74	466	16	27	155	38	245	Tom O'Brien	Peter Bowen	22	134
65	541	12	27	196	27	287	Brian Hughes	Howard Johnson	25	206
63	556	11	29	195	31	312	Tom Scudamore	David Pipe	33	257
61	235	26	21	84	33	123	Barry Geraghty	Nicky Henderson	58	208
61	491	12	26	203	34	267	Aidan Coleman	Venetia Williams	33	267
59	487	12	25	200	31	248	Sam Twiston-Davies	N Twiston-Davies	37	303
57	366	16	22	111	33	212	Dougie Costello	John Quinn	16	59
56	427	13	31	150	19	231	Daryl Jacob	David Arbuthnot	14	42
52	375	14	18	99	27	215	Robert Thornton	Alan King	40	292
47	417	11	16	146	31	238	Jamie Moore	Gary Moore	36	249
42	323	13	21	122	19	176	Nick Scholfield	Paul Nicholls	15	66
41	284	14	14	71	23	168	Wayne Hutchinson	Alan King	29	156
39	448	9	12	149	21	237	Leighton Aspell	Oliver Sherwood	23	169
39	245	16	21	102	15	123	Felix De Giles	Charlie Longsdon	19	84
36	340	11	15	128	10	172	Sam Thomas	Emma Lavelle	7	46
36	319	11	22	144	12	142	Jimmy Derham	Seamus Mullins	19	149
35	304	12	20	112	12	155	James Reveley	Keith Reveley	19	138
35	378	9	17	132	16	210	Denis O'Regan	Victor Dartnall	11	46
35	328	11	14	102	16	180	Andrew Tinkler	Nicky Henderson	20	130
35	354	10	19	154	14	182	Richie McLernon	Jonjo O'Neill	26	248
34	295	12	6	70	22	183	Barry Keniry	Micky Hammond	11	69
33	234	14	6	51	21	153	David Bass	Nicky Henderson	14	76
32	283	11	14	92	13	143	Timmy Murphy	Howard Johnson	3	8
31	150	21	16	64	11	75	Noel Fehily	Paul Nicholls	17	46
30	285	11	17	110	13	159	Peter Toole	Charlie Mann	12	105
29	206	14	7	64	20	121	Harry Skelton	Paul Nicholls	21	96
29	314	9	16	106	12	181	Campbell Gillies	Lucinda Russell	19	118
28	258	11	17	125	9	98	Joe Tizzard	Colin Tizzard	28	239
28	304	9	17	141	11	151	Peter Buchanan	Lucinda Russell	21	204
27	206	13	16	73	10	114	Jack Doyle	Emma Lavelle	15	99
26	106	25	6	42	19	57	R Walsh	Paul Nicholls	23	95
26	193	13	11	59	11	105	Paul Gallagher	Howard Johnson	12	45
26	281	9	9	89	15	161	Richie McGrath	Kate Walton	10	67
25	309	8	3	70	20	203	Rhys Flint	Steve Gollings	5	19
25	256	10	9	73	15	168	Sean Quinlan	Kim Bailey	21	102
24	209	11	4	49	16	139	Donal Devereux	Peter Bowen	20	143
24	241	10	6	70	17	155	Ryan Mania	Howard Johnson	7	24
24	237	10	10	67	11	136	Charlie Poste	Robin Dickin	12	70
23	224	10	5	37	14	164	Warren Marston	Martin Keighley	11	81
22	275	8	4	67	15	180	Will Kennedy	Paul Webber	10	66
22	394	6	14	163	8	193	Andrew Thornton	Caroline Bailey	6	96
22	235	9	15	86	7	128	Wilson Renwick	Howard Johnson	11	56

Big Races, Fixtures and Track Facts

Fixtures

Key - **Jumps**, Flat

October

1 Saturday...Ascot, **Fontwell**, Redcar, Wolverhampton
2 Sunday..**Huntingdon**, **Kelso**, **Uttoxeter**
3 Monday ....Pontefract, Warwick, Windsor
4 Tuesday...Catterick, Leicester, Southwell
5 Wednesday ....Kempton, **Ludlow**, Nottingham, **Towcester**
6 Thursday ....Ayr, **Exeter**, Wolverhaampton, **Worcester**
7 Friday ....**Carlisle**, Newmarket, Wolverhampton, York
8 Saturday ....**Chepstow**, **Hexham**, Newmarket, Wolverhampton, York
9 Sunday..**Ffos Las**, Goodwood
10 Monday ....Salisbury, Windsor, Yarmouth
11 Tuesday...**Huntingdon**, Leicester, Newcastle
12 Wednesday.....................................Kempton, Lingfield, Nottingham, **Wetherby**
13 Thursday ....Brighton, Kempton, **Uttoxeter**, **Wincanton**
14 Friday ....**Cheltenham**, Haydock, Redcar, Wolverhampton
15 Saturday ....Ascot, Catterick, **Cheltenham**, **Kelso**, Wolverhampton
16 Sunday..Bath, **Kempton**
17 Monday ....**Plumpton**, Pontefract, Windsor
18 Tuesday ....**Exeter**, Lingfield, Yarmouth
19 Wednesday ....**Fontwell**, Kempton, Newmarket, **Worcester**
20 Thursday ....Brighton, **Carlisle**, **Ludlow**, Wolverhampton
21 Friday.....................................Doncaster, **Fakenham**, Newbury, Wolverhampton
22 Saturday...........................**Aintree**, **Chepstow**, Doncaster, Newbury, **Stratford**,
    ....Wolverhampton
23 Sunday..**Aintree**, **Wincanton**
24 Monday...Leicester, Redcar, Leicester, Southwell
25 Tuesday..Catterick, **Taunton**, Yarmouth
26 Wednesday ....**Haydock**, Kempton, Musselburgh, Nottingham
27 Thursday ....**Fontwell**, Kempton, Lingfield, **Stratford**
28 Friday.............................Newmarket, **Uttoxeter**, **Wetherby**, Wolverhampton
29 Saturday...........................**Ascot**, Ayr, Newmarket, **Wetherby**, Wolverhampton
30 Sunday ....**Carlisle**, **Huntingdon**
31 Monday ....**Kempton**, **Plumpton**, Wolverhampton

November

1 Tuesday ....**Exeter**, Kempton, Redcar
2 Wednesday ....**Chepstow**, Kempton, Nottingham, **Warwick**
3 Thursday ....**Musselburgh**, Southwell, **Towcester**, Wolverhampton
4 Friday.............................Ffos Las, **Fontwell**, **Hexham**, Wolverhampton
5 Saturday..........................Doncaster, **Kelso**, **Sandown**, **Wincanton**
6 Sunday ....**Ffos Las**, **Market Rasen**
7 Monday ....**Carlisle**, **Hereford**, **Southwell**
8 Tuesday...**Huntingdon**, Lingfield, **Sedgefield**
9 Wednesday ....**Bangor**, **Exeter**, Kempton, Southwell
10 Thursday...Kempton, **Ludlow**, Southwell, **Taunton**
11 Friday................................**Cheltenham**, Lingfield, **Newcastle**, Wolverhampton
12 Saturday...........**Cheltenham**, Lingfield, **Uttoxeter**, **Wetherby**, Wolverhampton

13 Sunday ....**Cheltenham, Fontwell**
14 Monday.............................**Leicester, Plumpton,** Wolverhampton
15 Tuesday............................**Fakenham, Folkestone,** Southwell
16 Wednesday ....**Hexham,** Kempton, Lingfield, **Warwick**
17 Thursday ....**Hereford,** Kempton, **Market Rasen, Wincanton**
18 Friday ....**Ascot, Haydock,** Kempton, Wolverhampton
19 Saturday ....**Ascot, Haydock, Huntingdon,** Lingfield, Wolverhampton
20 Sunday ....**Exeter, Towcester**
21 Monday..**Ffos Las, Kempton, Ludlow**
22 Tuesday..............................**Lingfield, Sedgefield,** Southwell
23 Wednesday ....**Fontwell,** Kempton, Lingfield, **Wetherby**
24 Thursday ....Kempton, **Newbury, Taunton, Uttoxeter**
25 Friday ....**Doncaster, Musselburgh, Newbury,** Wolverhampton
26 Saturday ....**Bangor, Newbury, Newcastle, Towcester,** Wolverhampton
27 Sunday ....**Carlisle, Leicester**
28 Monday.........................**Ffos Las, Folkestone,** Wolverhampton
29 Tuesday...**Ayr,** Lingfield, **Southwell**
30 Wednesday ....**Catterick, Hereford,** Kempton, **Uttoxeter**

December

1 Thursday.....................**Leicester, Market Rasen, Wincanton,** Wolverhampton
2 Friday ....**Exeter,** Lingfield, **Sandown,** Wolverhampton
3 Saturday ....**Aintree, Chepstow, Sandown, Wetherby,** Wolverhampton
4 Sunday ....**Kelso, Warwick**
5 Monday...............................Lingfield, **Musselburgh, Plumpton**
6 Tuesday ....**Fontwell, Sedgefield,** Southwell
7 Wednesday ....**Hexham,** Kempton, **Leicester,** Lingfield
8 Thursday ....**Huntingdon,** Kempton, **Ludlow, Taunton**
9 Friday.............................**Cheltenham, Doncaster,** Southwell, Wolverhampton
10 Saturday ....**Cheltenham, Doncaster, Lingfield,** Southwell, Wolverhampton
11 Sunday ....**Hereford,** Southwell
12 Monday..**Fakenham,** Wolverhampton
13 Tuesday..............................**Catterick, Folkestone,** Southwell
14 Wednesday ....**Bangor,** Kempton, Lingfield, **Newbury**
15 Thursday.....................**Exeter,** Kempton, Southwell, **Towcester**
16 Friday.............................**Ascot,** Southwell, **Uttoxeter,** Wolverhampton
17 Saturday..............................**Ascot, Haydock,** Lingfield, **Newcastle**
18 Sunday..**Carlisle,** Kempton
19 Monday.............................**Bangor, Plumpton,** Wolverhampton
20 Tuesday ....Kempton, **Musselburgh, Taunton**
21 Wednesday ....**Ffos Las,** Kempton, **Ludlow,** Wolverhampton
22 Thursday ....**Hereford, Sedgefield,** Southwell
26 Monday..............**Ffos Las, Fontwell, Huntingdon, Kempton, Market Rasen,**
   ....**Towcester, Wetherby, Wincanton,** Wolverhampton
27 Tuesday ....**Chepstow, Kempton,** Southwell, **Wetherby**
28 Wednesday............................**Catterick, Leicester,** Lingfield, Wolverhampton
29 Thursday ....**Doncaster, Kelso,** Kempton, Southwell
30 Friday.............................**Haydock,** Lingfield, **Taunton,** Wolverhampton
31 Saturday.............................Lingfield, **Newbury, Uttoxeter, Warwick**

The 2012 fixture list had not been released at the time of going to press – apologies for the inconvenience

2011 big-race dates

November

1	Exeter	Haldon Gold Cup
5	Wincanton	Elite Hurdle
11	Cheltenham	Sharp Novices' Hurdle
12	Cheltenham	Paddy Power Gold Cup
13	Cheltenham	November Novices' Chase
13	Cheltenham	Greatwood Handicap Hurdle
19	Ascot	Ascot Hurdle
19	Ascot	Amlin 1965 Chase
19	Haydock	Betfair Chase
19	Huntingdon	Peterborough Chase
25	Newbury	Berkshire Novices' Chase
26	Newbury	Long Distance Hurdle
26	Newbury	Hennessy Cognac Gold Cup
26	Newcastle	Fighting Fifth Hurdle
26	Newcastle	Rehearsal Chase

December

2	Sandown	Winter Novices' Hurdle
3	Sandown	Tingle Creek Trophy
3	Sandown	Henry VIII Novices' Chase
3	Sandown	Sandown Park Handicap Hurdle
3	Aintree	Becher Chase
10	Cheltenham	Bristol Novices' Hurdle
10	Cheltenham	International Hurdle
10	Cheltenham	Relkeel Hurdle
10	Cheltenham	Boylesports Gold Cup
10	Lingfield	December Novices' Chase
10	Lingfield	Summit Junior Hurdle
16	Ascot	Noel Novices' Chase
16	Ascot	Kennel Gate Novices' Hurdle
17	Ascot	Long Walk Hurdle
17	Ascot	Silver Cup Chase
17	Ascot	Ladbroke Handicap Hurdle
26	Kempton	Christmas Hurdle
26	Kempton	Feltham Novices' Chase
26	Kempton	King George VI Chase
26	Wetherby	Rowland Meyrick Handicap Chase
27	Kempton	Wayward Lad Novices' Chase
27	Kempton	Desert Orchid Chase
27	Chepstow	Finale Junior Hurdle
27	Chepstow	Welsh National
31	Newbury	Challow Novices' Hurdle

Outlook

Big race records

Year	Form	Winner	Age-weight	Trainer	Jockey	SP	Ran

Charlie Hall Chase (3m110yds) Wetherby

Year	Form	Winner	Age-weight	Trainer	Jockey	SP	Ran
2001	-13	Sackville	8-11-5	F Crowley	D Casey	5-1	9
2002	-	Marlborough	10-11-0	N Henderson	M Fitzgerald	7-2	8
2003	-	Ballybough Rasher	8-11-0	H Johnson	G Lee	40-1	6
2004	-	Grey Abbey	10-11-6	H Johnson	G Lee	5-1	6
2005	-	Ollie Magern	7-11-5	N Twiston-Davies	C Llewellyn	11-4f	8
2006	-	Our Vic	8-11-10	D Pipe	T Murphy	6-1	10
2007	-	Ollie Magern	9-11-6	N Twiston-Davies	P Brennan	11-4	7
2008	-	State Of Play	8-11-0	E Williams	P Moloney	5-2f	6
2009	-	Deep Purple	8-11-5	E Williams	P Moloney	9-2	5
2010	-	Nacarat	9-11-0	T George	S Thomas	6-1	8

Traditionally a race for small fields, and while there have been only two winning favourites in nine years it has still proven profitable to focus on those near the front of the market with only two winners returning bigger than 6-1 since 1998. At this stage of the season a good proportion of the runners may be some way short of peak fitness, and it pays to look for trainers who can be relied on to have their horse ready with Evan Williams, Nigel Twiston-Davies and Howard Johnson both winning twice in the last eight years. The small fields mean front-runners like Grey Abbey and Ollie Magern can often get their own way.

Paddy Power Gold Cup (2m4f110yds) Cheltenham

Year	Form	Winner	Age-weight	Trainer	Jockey	SP	Ran
2001	-1	Shooting Light	8-11-3	M Pipe	A McCoy	9-4f	14
2002	-	Cyfor Malta	9-11-9	M Pipe	B Geraghty	16-1	15
2003	-	Fondmort	7-10-13	N Henderson	M Fitzgerald	3-1f	9
2004	-	Celestial Gold	6-10-2	M Pipe	T Murphy	12-1	14
2005	-	Our Vic	7-11-7	M Pipe	T Murphy	9-2f	18
2006	-2	Exotic Dancer	6-11-2	J O'Neill	A McCoy	16-1	16
2007	-1	L'Antartique	7-10-13	F Murphy	G Lee	13-2	20
2008	-	Imperial Commander	7-10-7	N Twiston-Davies	P Brennan	13-2	19
2009	-1	Tranquil Sea	7-10-13	E O'Grady	A McNamara	11-2f	16
2010	-1	Little Josh	8-10-8	N Twiston-Davies	S T-Davies (3)	20-1	18

AKA 'The Thomas Pink', 'The Murphys','The Mackeson'. A Martin Pipe benefit in the last ten years of his career, with seven winners coming from his Nicholashayne yard, but it's been slightly trickier for punters to work out since then. That said, Tranquil Sea made it six winning favourites in 12 years when winning in 2009 while L'Antartique and Imperial Commander were also well fancied. The best pointer is course form – of the last 15 winners, only Little Josh, Tranquil Sea, Our Vic (third in the SunAlliance) and Senor El Betrutti hadn't previously won at Cheltenham, though that admittedly includes the last two winners.

Hennessy Cognac Gold Cup Handicap Chase (3m2f) Newbury

2001	-	**What's Up Boys**	7-10-12	P Hobbs	P Flynn	14-1	14
2002	-3	**Gingembre**	8-10-13	L Taylor	A Thornton	16-1	25
2003	-F1	**Strong Flow**	6-11-0	P Nicholls	R Walsh	5-1jf	21
2004	-1	**Celestial Gold**	6-10-5	M Pipe	T Murphy	9-4f	14
2005	-	**Trabolgan**	7-11-12	N Henderson	M Fitzgerald	13-2	19
2006	-	**State Of Play**	6-11-4	E Williams	P Moloney	10-1	16
2007	-	**Denman**	7-11-12	P Nicholls	S Thomas	5-1	18
2008	-6	**Madison Du Berlais**	7-11-4	D Pipe	T Scudamore	25-1	15
2009	-	**Denman**	9-11-12	P Nicholls	R Walsh	11-4f	19
2010	-	**Diamond Harry**	7-10-0	N Williams	D Jacob	6-1	18

Just about the most high-quality handicap of the season, won by some very special horses and twice by Denman. This has been a great race for second-season chasers recently, with Diamond Harry, Denman, State Of Play, Trabolgan (when the first six home had just lost novice status), Celestial Gold, What's Up Boys, King's Road and Ever Blessed fitting the bill since 1999, while Strong Flow was a novice. Be My Royal was also a winning novice in 2002 but was disqualified due to a banned substance. Relatively low weights are traditionally favoured, but six of the last eight winners defied 11st or more.

Fighting Fifth Hurdle (2m) Newcastle

2001	-	**Landing Light**	6-11-8	N Henderson	M Fitzgerald	4-5f	5
2002	-11	**Intersky Falcon**	5-11-8	J O'Neill	L Cooper	11-10f	6
2003	-71	**The French Furze**	9-11-0	N Richards	B Harding	25-1	8
2004	-31	**Harchibald**	5-11-7	N Meade	P Carberry	9-4jf	8
2005	-	**Arcalis**	5-11-7	H Johnson	T Dobbin	9-4f	9
2006	-	**Straw Bear**	5-11-7	N Gifford	A McCoy	Evsf	9
2007	-	**Harchibald**	8-11-7	N Meade	P Carberry	4-1	8
2008	-	**Punjabi**	5-11-7	N Henderson	B Geraghty	8-11f	6
2009	-12	**Go Native**	6-11-7	N Meade	D Condon	25-1	7
2010*	-	**Peddlers Cross**	5-11-7	D McCain	J Maguire	9-4	5

run at Newbury

Firmly back on the radar as a leading Champion Hurdle trial after a brief and unsuccessful period as a limited handicap in the 90s. The small field helps the cream rise to the top, with several top-class hurdlers winning at short prices and nine triumphant favourites in 13 years, and Go Native of course made a nonsense of his 25-1 quote by immediately adding another Grade 1 triumph after his win in 2009.

Tingle Creek Trophy Chase (2m) Sandown

2001	-	**Flagship Uberalles**	7-11-7	P Hobbs	R Widger	7-2	6
2002	-	**Cenkos**	8-11-7	P Nicholls	R Walsh	6-1	6
2003	-1	**Moscow Flyer**	9-11-7	J Harrington	B Geraghty	6-4f	7
2004	-1	**Moscow Flyer**	10-11-7	J Harrington	B Geraghty	2-1	7
2005	-2	**Kauto Star**	5-11-7	P Nicholls	M Fitzgerald	5-2jf	7
2006	-11	**Kauto Star**	6-11-7	P Nicholls	R Walsh	4-9f	7
2007	-1	**Twist Magic**	5-11-7	P Nicholls	S Thomas	5-1	8
2008	-	**Master Minded**	5-11-7	P Nicholls	A McCoy	4-7f	7
2009	-3	**Twist Magic**	7-11-7	P Nicholls	R Walsh	9-4	5
2010*	-1	**Master Minded**	7-11-7	P Nicholls	N Fehily	10-11f	9

run at Cheltenham

Changed from a handicap to a conditions event prior to the 1994 renewal and grew to rank alongside the Champion Chase in terms of quality, with Moscow Flyer beating Well Chief and Azertyuiop in a 2004 epic. Remarkably, no winner has returned bigger than 7-1 in the last 15 years, and that was on the only occasion when the field was bigger than eight. Only four horses older than nine have ever triumphed.

betinternet.com Handicap Hurdle (2m) Sandown

2001	-1431	**Rob Leach**	4-9-12	G L Moore	F Keniry (3)	14-1	11
2002	-	**Spirit Leader**	6-10-0	J Harrington	N Williamson	9-2	12
2003	-111	**Overstrand**	4-10-6	M Reveley	R Walsh	9-1	14
2004	-11	**Monte Cinto**	4-10-5	P Nicholls	R Walsh	8-1	21
2005	-1	**Verasi**	4-10-13	G Moore	J Moore	12-1	19
2006	-1	**Overstrand**	7-10-12	Dr R Newland	S Jones (7)	8-1	17
2007	-1	**Ring The Boss**	6-10-0	P Hobbs	T O'Brien	7-4f	13
2008	-311	**Sunnyhillyboy**	5-10-12	J O'Neill	A McCoy	9-2jf	12
2009	-0	**Tasheba**	4-11-12	N Henderson	B Geraghty	8-1	9
2010		*Abandoned*					

AKA 'The William Hill Hurdle'. Often run on dead ground or going with some give, exaggerating the effect of weight carried, so top-weights have an even worse record than in other competitive handicaps, making Tasheba's effort in 2009, when the first to defy 11st or more in more than 15 years as well as the second since 1998 who hadn't won last time out, all the more remarkable. Four-year-olds have won six of the last ten runnings.

Boylesports.com Gold Cup Chase (2m5f) Cheltenham

2001		*Abandoned*					
2002	-3	**Fondmort**	6-10-5	N Henderson	M Fitzgerald	5-1	9
2003	-11	**Iris Royal**	7-10-13	N Henderson	M Fitzgerald	7-1	17
2004	-132	**Monkerhostin**	7-10-2	P Hobbs	R Johnson	4-1	13
2005	-54	**Sir Oj**	8-10-0	N Meade	P Carberry	16-1	16
2006	-21	**Exotic Dancer**	6-11-4	J O'Neill	A Dobbin	8-1	12
2007	-31	**Tamarinbleu**	7-11-8	D Pipe	D O'Regan	22-1	16
2008		*Abandoned*					
2009	-12	**Poquelin**	6-11-8	P Nicholls	R Walsh	7-2f	17
2010	-25	**Poquelin**	7-11-12	P Nicholls	I Popham (5)	16-1	16

AKA 'The Massey-Ferguson', 'The Tripleprint'. Not surprisingly, the Paddy Power Gold Cup, held at the same venue four weeks earlier, is traditionally the most useful guide to this event. In the mid-90s Senor El Betrutti did the double while Addington Boy and Another Coral stepped up on placed efforts, and more recently Monkerhostin and Poquelin (for his 2009 win) improved on their second-place efforts and Exotic Dancer pulled off the double. A prior outing is essential, and not necessarily a winning one.

Boylesports.com International Hurdle (2m1f) Cheltenham

2001		*Abandoned*					
2002	-11	**Rooster Booster**	8-11-4	P Hobbs	R Johnson	11-8f	9
2003	-24FF112141	**Rigmarole**	5-11-4	P Nicholls	R Thornton	25-1	7
2004	-12	**Back In Front**	7-11-8	E J O'Grady	D N Russell	5-2f	7
2005	-13	**Harchibald**	6-11-8	N Meade	P Carberry	10-11f	9
2006	-1	**Detroit City**	4-11-8	P Hobbs	R Johnson	4-6f	4
2007	-2	**Osana**	5-11-0	D Pipe	P Brennan	7-1	8
2008*	-1	**Binocular**	4-11-4	N Henderson	A McCoy	Evsf	5

DETROIT CITY: completed the now common Greatwood/International double

| 2009 | -1 | **Khyber Kim** | 7-11-4 | N Twiston-Davies | P Brennan | 12-1 | 7 |
| 2010 | -1 | **Menorah** | 5-11-4 | P Hobbs | R Johnson | 7-4f | 9 |

*run at Ascot

AKA 'The Bula'. A Cheltenham specialist is absolutely vital in this race, and that has made the Greatwood Hurdle, run at the Paddy Power meeting over course and distance, a key trial with Detroit City, Khyber Kim and Menorah all pulling off the double and Osana improving on his second place in the last five years. In fact, of the last 13 winners at Cheltenham (Binocular's 2008 win was at Ascot) only Geos, Harchibald and Osana hadn't previously won at Prestbury Park, and the latter pair had both come second there. Four of the last five winners were four or five and there have been six winning favourites in eight runnings.

Long Walk Hurdle (3m1f110yds) Ascot

2001	-1	**Baracouda**	6-11-7	F Doumen	T Doumen	2-5f	5
2002	-23	**Deano's Beeno**	10-11-7	M Pipe	A McCoy	14-1	5
2003	-1	**Baracouda**	8-11-7	F Doumen	T Doumen	2-7f	6
2004*	-1	**Baracouda**	9-11-7	F Doumen	A P McCoy	8-13f	8
2005**	-2	**My Way De Solzen**	5-11-7	A King	R Thornton	12-1	8
2006	-2	**Mighty Man**	6-11-7	H Daly	R Johnson	8-11f	9
2007	-733	**Lough Derg**	7-11-7	D Pipe	T Scudamore	14-1	9
2008	-1	**Punchestowns**	5-11-7	N Henderson	B Geraghty	3-1f	11
2009***	-1	**Big Buck's**	6-11-7	P Nicholls	R Walsh	1-2f	8
2010***	-1	**Big Buck's**	7-11-7	P Nicholls	A McCoy	2-13f	6

*run at Windsor   **run at Chepstow   ***run at Newbury

A top-quality Grade 1 hurdle and a massive pointer to Cheltenham. Of the last 11 winners, only Deano's Beeno and Lough Derg didn't finish first or second in the World Hurdle at some point in their career. Four-year-olds struggle but still fare better than they do at Cheltenham aged five, with Silver Wedge and Ocean Hawk successful in the 90s.

Silver Cup Handicap Chase (3m110yds) Ascot

2001	-11	**Shooting Light**	8-11-6	M Pipe	A McCoy	5-2f	9
2002	-6	**Behrajan**	7-11-12	H Daly	R Johnson	7-1	7
2003	-2	**Horus**	8-10-1	M Pipe	J Moore (3)	11-2	8
2004*	-134	**Spring Grove**	9-10-11	R Alner	A Thornton	8-1	8
2005		*Abandoned*					
2006	-5	**Billyvoddan**	7-10-12	H Daly	L Aspell	25-1	18
2007	-0	**Vodka Bleu**	8-10-3	D Pipe	T Murphy	12-1	10
2008	-3	**Niche Market**	7-10-0	R Buckler	H Skelton (5)	33-1	14
2009		*Abandoned*					
2010		*Abandoned*					

*run at Windsor

AKA 'The SGB', 'The Betterware Gold Cup'. The traditional centrepiece of Ascot's big December meeting has been won by some top-class horses in its time, subsequent Gold Cup hero Cool Dawn among them. It no longer tends to be a particularly classy contest but, prior to the last two abandonments, it had attracted bigger fields since Ascot's redevelopment, with all three winners since then returned at double-figure prices, while the last five winners all carried 11st or less after a run of success for top weights.

King George VI Chase (3m) Kempton

2001	-31	**Florida Pearl**	9-11-10	W Mullins	A Maguire	8-1	8
2002	-1	**Best Mate**	7-11-10	H Knight	A McCoy	11-8f	10
2003	-111	**Edredon Bleu**	11-11-10	H Knight	J Culloty	25-1	12
2004	-121	**Kicking King**	6-11-10	T J Taaffe	B Geraghty	3-1	13
2005*	-23	**Kicking King**	7-11-10	T J Taaffe	B Geraghty	11-8f	9
2006	-111	**Kauto Star**	6-11-10	P Nicholls	R Walsh	8-13f	9
2007	-21	**Kauto Star**	7-11-10	P Nicholls	R Walsh	4-6f	7
2008	-1U	**Kauto Star**	8-11-10	P Nicholls	R Walsh	10-11f	10
2009	-1	**Kauto Star**	9-11-10	P Nicholls	R Walsh	8-13f	13
2010**	-3	**Long Run**	6-11-10	N Henderson	Mr S W-Cohen	9-2	9

*run at Sandown   **run in January 2011

A race which the best performers often manage to win several times, with Kauto Star, Kicking King, See More Business and One Man all multiple winners since the days of the legendary Desert Orchid. Kempton's sharp three miles provides less of a stamina test than other major tracks, particularly Cheltenham, so those who have just failed to see out the Gold Cup trip often make amends here, such as One Man and Florida Pearl. There were also stamina doubts about Kicking King prior to his first win, while Edredon Bleu was a two-mile performer stepping into the unknown.

Christmas Hurdle (2m) Kempton

2001	-1	**Landing Light**	6-11-7	N Henderson	M Fitzgerald	5-4f	5
2002	-11	**Intersky Falcon**	5-11-7	J O'Neill	C Swan	Evensf	6
2003	-13	**Intersky Falcon**	6-11-7	J O'Neill	L Cooper	11-4	6
2004	-311	**Harchibald**	5-11-7	N Meade	P Carberry	8-11f	7
2005	-11	**Feathard Lady**	5-11-0	C Murphy	R Walsh	6-4f	7
2006	-1	**Jazz Messenger**	6-11-7	N Meade	N Madden	10-1	7
2007	-6	**Straw Bear**	6-11-7	N Gifford	A McCoy	9-2	6
2008	-	**Harchibald**	9-11-7	N Meade	P Carberry	7-1	7
2009	-121	**Go Native**	6-11-7	N Meade	D Condon	5-2	7

| 2010* | -3 | **Binocular** | 7-11-7 | N Henderson | A McCoy | 13-8f | 6 |

run in January 2011

Forget Harchibald's trend-busting win in 2008 as this sharp two miles is ideal for young, improving types, and each of the ten other winners since 1999 would have been aged five or six had Binocular's win not been forced over into 2011 by bad weather. Every winner from 1999 to 2006 had a prior win under their belt, but since then Binocular, Harchibald and Straw Bear were all getting off the mark for the season.

Welsh National Handicap Chase (3m5f110yds) Chepstow

2001	-14	**Supreme Glory**	8-10-0	P Murphy	L Aspell	10-1	13
2002	-4	**Mini Sensation**	9-10-4	J O'Neill	A Dobbin	8-1	16
2003	-F2	**Bindaree**	9-10-9	N Twiston Davies	C Llewellyn	10-1	14
2004	-1	**Silver Birch**	7-10-1	P Nicholls	R Walsh	4-1f	14
2005	-64	**L'Aventure**	6-10-4	P Nicholls	L Aspell	14-1	18
2006	-1	**Halcon Genelardais**	6-11-3	A King	W Hutchinson	7-1	18
2007	-2	**Miko De Beauchene**	7-10-5	R Alner	A Thornton	13-2	18
2008	-41	**Notre Pere**	7-11-0	T Dreaper	A Lynch	16-1	20
2009	-2	**Dream Alliance**	8-10-8	P Hobbs	T O'Brien	20-1	18
2010	-56	**Synchronised**	8-11-6	J O'Neill	A McCoy	5-1	18

run in January 2011

As with most staying handicap chases that are often run in the mud, horses at the foot of the weights are massively favoured, underlining Halcon Genelardais' achievements in winning in 2006 and coming second 12 months later and providing a big clue to Notre Pere's subsequent Grade 1 success. What, then, should we expect from Synchronised, who remarkably became the third horse in five years to defy the 11st barrier last year? Generally punters should not even rule out anything from out of the handicap – Kendal Cavalier was even 13lb wrong in 1997. Only three winners have carried 11st 10lb or more in more than 50 runnings, and Silver Birch was a rare winning favourite in 2004.

Rowland Meyrick Chase (3m1f) Wetherby

2001	-332	**Behrajan**	6-11-10	H Daly	M Bradburne	5-2f	12
2002		*Abandoned*					
2003	-P	**Gunner Welburn**	11-10-0	A Balding	R McGrath	10-1	8
2004	-44	**Truckers Tavern**	9-11-2	F Murphy	K J Mercer	8-1	7
2005	-00	**Therealbandit**	8-10-6	M Pipe	A Glassonbury	9-1	10
2006	-00	**Leading Man**	6-10-0	F Murphy	G Lee	9-1	10
2007	-313	**Lothian Falcon**	8-10-7	P Maddison	R Walford	2-1f	6
2008	-U	**Nozic**	7-10-8	P Nicholls	H Skelton (5)	7-1	8
2009		*Abandoned*					
2010		*Abandoned*					

A race that has often been disrupted by small fields and abandonments, and most recent renewals didn't take a great deal of winning any more as four of the last six winners looked to be either past their best or bang out of form. The 2008 race was a classic, though, as lightly-weighted Nozic ran the finish out of Arkle winner Tidal Bay.

MCR Handicap Hurdle (2m) Leopardstown

2002	-54	**Adamant Approach**	8-11-1	W Mullins	R Walsh	8-1	26
2003	-2	**Xenophon**	7-10-11	A Martin	M Fitzgerald	12-1	28
2004	-01	**Dromlease Express**	6-10-4	C Byrnes	J Allen (7)	6-1jf	19
2005	-	**Essex**	5-10-8	M J P O'Brien	B Geraghty	5-1f	21

2006	-1252132	**Studmaster**	6-10-3	Mrs J Harrington	T Treacy	12-1	27
2007	-2	**Spring The Que**	8-10-10	R Tyner	P Enright (7)	16-1	30
2008	-411	**Barker**	7-10-6	J Barrett	T Murphy	10-1	28
2009	-5P4	**Penny's Bill**	7-9-12	Miss E Boyle	S Flanagan (3)	50-1	30
2010	-222	**Puyol**	8-10-10	J Mulhern	J Cullen	16-1	30
2011	-5	**Final Approach**	5-10-9	W Mullins	P Townend	6-1	26

AKA 'The Ladbroke', 'The Pierse'. Still Ireland's hottest handicap despite losing Ladbrokes' sponsorship and its Grade 1 status after the 2000 race. The Irish really like to keep the prize at home – there has only been one British winner in more than 20 years (Master Tribe in 1997). The strongest trends won't rule out that much of the field, but the winners tend to be either five, six or seven (Puyol was only the fifth older winner in 2010 and no four-year-old has won since 1977) carrying less than 11st. Favourites had had a dismal record until Dromlease Express and Essex scored in 2004 and 2005.

Totesport Trophy Handicap Hurdle (2m110yds) Newbury

2002	-21	**Copeland**	7-11-7	M Pipe	A McCoy	13-2	16
2003	-2315	**Spirit Leader**	7-10-0	J Harrington	N Williamson	14-1	27
2004	-2	**Geos**	9-10-9	N Henderson	M Foley	16-1	25
2005	-2611	**Essex**	5-11-6	M J P O'Brien	B Geraghty	4-1f	25
2006		*Abandoned*					
2007	-030020	**Heathcote**	5-10-6	G Moore	J Moore	50-1	20
2008	-13	**Wingman**	6-10-0	G Moore	J Moore	14-1	24
2009		*Abandoned*					
2010	-111	**Get Me Out Of Here**	6-10-6	J O'Neill	A McCoy	6-1	23
2011	-1211	**Recession Proof**	5-10-8	J Quinn	D Costello	12-1	15

AKA 'The Schweppes'. A race at a cross-roads for punters with trends possibly changing again. Between 1970 and 1996 only three winners carried more than 11st, before the pattern turned full circle with a big increase in prize-money encouraging more genuine Champion Hurdle horses to race and six out of nine winners racing from near the top of the weights – Rooster Booster deserved to make it seven in 2004 but was just edged out by Geos in one of the greatest weight-carrying performances of the modern age. However, victories for two lightly-weighted Gary Moore inmates, Heathcote and Wingman, plus novices Get Me Out Of Here and Recession Proof, suggest that the traditional Champion Hurdle trials are hitting back, and the light-weights and the plot horses are having their time again.

Blue Square Gold Cup Handicap Chase (3m4f) Haydock

2002		*Abandoned*					
2003	-	**Shotgun Willy**	9-11-12	P Nicholls	R Walsh	10-1	17
2004	-1452	**Jurancon II**	7-10-6	M Pipe	J Elliott (5)	10-1	10
2005	-1	**Forest Gunner**	11-10-10	R Ford	P Buchanan (3)	12-1	11
2006	-613	**Ossmoses**	9-10-0	D Forster	R McGrath	14-1	14
2007	-13201	**Heltornic**	7-10-0	M Scudamore	T Scudamore	12-1	16
2008	-21	**Miko de Beauchene**	8-11-12	R Alner	A Thornton	17-2	16
2009	-5651	**Rambling Minster**	11-11-0	K Reveley	J Reveley (3)	18-1	16
2010	-512	**Silver By Nature**	8-10-11	Miss L Russell	P Buchanan	7-1	14
2011	-07	**Silver By Nature**	9-11-12	Miss L Russell	P Buchanan	10-1	14

AKA 'The Greenalls'. This race is usually run on soft ground and can be a real test of stamina, too much for most of the market leaders in recent years with no winning favourite (and only two winners in double figures) since Frantic Tan in 2001. It may be overrated as a Grand National trial, with Silver By Nature, Rambling Minster, Forest Gunner, Jurancon II and Shotgun Willy all beaten when well fancied at Aintree.

Eider Handicap Chase (4m1f) Newcastle

2002	-301	**This Is Serious**	8-11-2	C Swan	A Dobbin	4-1f	15
2003		*Abandoned*					
2004	-22P217	**Tyneandthyneagain**	9-11-12	R Guest	H Oliver	28-1	20
2005		*Abandoned*					
2006	-0FP2	**Philson Run**	10-11-6	N Williams	G Lee	10-1	17
2007	-3464	**Nil Desperandum**	10-11-12	V Williams	T Scudamore	6-1	16
2008	-0P2	**Comply Or Die**	9-11-12	D Pipe	T Murphy	11-1	18
2009	-56172	**Merigo**	8-11-1	A Parker	T Murphy	5-1	13
2010	-4	**Gidam Gidam**	8-11-0	J Mackie	P Kinsella	16-1	16
2011	-P6	**Companero**	11-11-0	H Johnson	P Buchanan	16-1	12

AKA 'The Northern National'. It will take more than Comply Or Die's double to convince trends followers that this is a strong National pointer as most winners are dour stayers without the pace and class for Aintree, shown by three of the last six winners being aged in double figures. Weight is no barrier to success as each of the last nine winners carried at least 11st and three of the last six were top-weight.

Racing Post Handicap Chase (3m) Kempton

2002	-2221	**Gunther McBride**	7-10-3	P Hobbs	R Johnson	5-1	14
2003	-211111	**La Landiere**	8-11-7	R Phillips	W Marston	5-1j	14
2004	-235	**Marlborough**	12-11-12	N Henderson	R Walsh	8-1	11
2005	-1F2F41	**Farmer Jack**	9-11-12	P Hobbs	R Johnson	5-1	16
2006*	-11	**Innox**	10-11-0	F Doumen	A McCoy	8-1	15
2007	-5261	**Simon**	8-11-5	J Spearing	A Thornton	11-2	10
2008	-361	**Gungadu**	8-11-12	P Nicholls	R Walsh	4-1f	15
2009	-21	**Nacarat**	8-10-13	T George	A McCoy	10-1	20
2010	-01240	**Razor Royale**	8-10-5	N Twiston-Davies	P Brennan	11-1	13
2011	-113	**Quinz**	7-11-0	P Hobbs	R Johnson	8-1	16

*run at Sandown

Once again it's remarkable how many horses manage to defy welter burdens to win this top prize – Gloria Victis, Marlborough, Farmer Jack and Gungadu all carried 11st 10lb or more to victory in the last 12 years, and six others defied in excess of 10st 13lb. There's little for trends followers in terms of age (Gloria Victis was six when he won in 2000, Marlborough 12 in 2004, and every age in between has been successful since 1997). Clearly it's wrong to look beyond the first few in the betting with no winner bigger than 11-1 since 1997, and Richard Johnson knows his way around Kempton's three miles well having won five of the last 11 runnings to be held at the venue.

Imperial Cup Handicap Hurdle (2m) Sandown

2002	-2221	**Polar Red**	5-11-1	M Pipe	A McCoy	6-4f	16
2003	-25053141	**Korelo**	5-11-6	M Pipe	A McCoy	9-4f	17
2004	-62	**Scorned**	9-10-3	A Balding	B Fenton	14-1	23
2005	-10311	**Medison**	5-10-1	M Pipe	T Murphy	9-2f	19
2006	-00013P	**Victram**	6-10-3	A McGuinness	A Lynch	8-1	21
2007	-11	**Gaspara**	4-10-5	D Pipe	A McCoy	11-4f	22
2008	-141	**Ashkazar**	4-10-12	D Pipe	T Murphy	10-3f	22
2009	-10	**Dave's Dream**	6-10-13	N Henderson	B Geraghty	12-1	19

| 2010 | -06611 | **Qaspal** | 6-10-3 | P Hobbs | A McCoy | 11-4f | 23 |
| 2011 | -1322 | **Alarazi** | 7-10-3 | L Wadham | D Elsworth | 10-1 | 24 |

This falls on the eve of the festival and, with the sponsors putting up a bonus for horses doubling up, a strong and competitive field is always assured. Martin Pipe was the master in this race, winning three of the last five runnings in which he had runners, and David Pipe has maintained his record with Gaspara and Ashkazar. Both of those were four-year-olds, and five-year-olds also have an outstanding record with six winning in 14 years, so it clearly takes a real youngster to be sufficiently ahead of the handicapper. Indeed, Alarazi was last year only the second winner to be older than six since 2000.

Supreme Novices' Hurdle (2m110yds) Cheltenham

2002	-1111	**Like-A-Butterfly**	8-11-3	C Roche	C Swan	7-4f	28
2003	-211	**Back In Front**	6-11-8	E O'Grady	N Williamson	3-1f	19
2004	-111	**Brave Inca**	6-11-7	C Murphy	B Cash	7-2f	19
2005	-111143	**Arcalis**	5-11-7	H Johnson	G Lee	20-1	20
2006	-3111	**Noland**	5-11-7	P Nicholls	R Walsh	6-1	20
2007	-21	**Ebaziyan**	6-11-7	W Mullins	D Condon	40-1	22
2008	-11	**Captain Cee Bee**	7-11-7	E Harty	R Thornton	17-2	22
2009	-12121	**Go Native**	6-11-7	N Meade	P Carberry	12-1	20
2010	-11212	**Menorah**	5-11-7	P Hobbs	R Johnson	12-1	18
2011	-F311	**Al Ferof**	6-11-7	P Nicholls	R Walsh	10-1	15

Al Ferof and Menorah were rare British winners of this race, with Go Native's win in 2009 at the time making it eight winners in 11 renewals for the Irish. Generally, though, it has always paid to look beyond their most fancied runner, with three successive winning favourites between 2002 and 2004 – Like-A-Butterfly, Back In Front and Brave Inca – something of a rarity in this race which has seen warm market leaders Cousin Vinny, Dunguib and even main British hope Cue Card turned over since. Tellingly, all three of those had won the previous year's Champion Bumper, and no winner of that has followed up since Montelado in 1992. Noland was a big trend-buster in 2006, being trained by Paul Nicholls (whose record with novices at this meeting is wretched) and a winner of the Tolworth Hurdle at Sandown (which tends to be a terrible guide), but both those facts still ring true overall.

Arkle Trophy (2m) Cheltenham

2002	-111F	**Moscow Flyer**	8-11-8	J Harrington	B Geraghty	11-2	12
2003	-111	**Azertyuiop**	6-11-8	P Nicholls	R Walsh	5-4f	9
2004	-151	**Well Chief**	5-11-3	M Pipe	A McCoy	9-1	16
2005	-2213	**Contraband**	7-11-3	M Pipe	T Murphy	9-1	19
2006	-1111	**Voy Por Ustedes**	5-11-2	A King	R Thornton	15-2	14
2007	-21211	**My Way De Solzen**	7-11-7	A King	R Thornton	7-2	13
2008	-1112	**Tidal Bay**	7-11-7	H Johnson	D O'Regan	6-1	14
2009	-1222	**Forpadydeplasterer**	7-11-7	T Cooper	B Geraghty	8-1	17
2010	-1111	**Sizing Europe**	8-11-7	H de Bromhead	A Lynch	6-1	12
2011	-22221	**Captain Chris**	7-11-7	P Hobbs	R Johnson	6-1	10

A typical Arkle winner tends to be relatively well fancied with plenty of wins under his belt earlier in the season, yet favourites still have an awful record. Plenty of high-class horses have been turned over, with only Azertyuiop doing the business. French-breds have a great record, helped by once generous five-year-olds' weight-for-age allowances, but with that abolished normality has been restored with the last five winners aged at least seven.

Spinal Research Handicap (3m110yds) Cheltenham

2002	-133	**Frenchman's Creek**	8-10-5	H Morrison	P Carberry	8-1	23
2003	-131	**Youlneverwalkalone**	9-10-11	C Roche	B Geraghty	7-1	18
2004	-31U21	**Fork Lightning**	8-10-5	A King	R Thornton	7-1	11
2005	-0003F43	**Kelami**	7-10-2	F Doumen	R Thornton	8-1	20
2006	-511111	**Dun Doire**	7-10-9	A Martin	R Walsh	7-1	21
2007	-00	**Joes Edge**	10-10-6	F Murphy	D Russell	50-1	23
2008	-P61	**An Accordion**	7-10-12	D Pipe	T Scudamore	7-1	14
2009	-121	**Wichita Lineman**	8-10-9	J O'Neill	A McCoy	5-1f	21
2010	-3001	**Chief Dan George**	10-10-10	J Moffatt	P Aspell	33-1	24
2011	-52	**Bensalem**	8-11-2	A King	R Thornton	5-1	19

AKA 'The Ritz Club'. After some older, heavily-weighted victors in the 90s, winners now look easier to find in this competitive handicap with only two winners bigger than 8-1 since 1999. That said, favourites have a shocking record with just three successful in three decades. A strong stayer is absolutely essential as Bensalem was only the third winner out of the last 17 to lack previous winning form at three miles or further, and all three had been placed over that trip on soft ground. Runners carrying less than 11st also have a distinct advantage, with Bensalem the first to defy such a burden since 1998.

Champion Hurdle (2m110yds) Cheltenham

2002	-2331	**Hors La Loi III**	7-12-0	J Fanshawe	D Gallagher	10-1	15
2003	-1111	**Rooster Booster**	9-12-0	P Hobbs	R Johnson	9-2	17
2004	-2022	**Hardy Eustace**	7-11-10	D Hughes	C O'Dwyer	33-1	14
2005	-2331	**Hardy Eustace**	8-11-10	D Hughes	C O'Dwyer	7-2jf	14
2006	-1311	**Brave Inca**	8-11-10	C Murphy	A McCoy	7-4f	18
2007	-1	**Sublimity**	7-11-10	J Carr	P Carberry	16-1	10
2008	-1321	**Katchit**	5-11-10	A King	R Thornton	10-1	15
2009	-1F3	**Punjabi**	6-11-10	N Henderson	B Geraghty	22-1	23
2010	-531	**Binocular**	6-11-10	N Henderson	A McCoy	9-1	12
2011	-111	**Hurricane Fly**	7-11-10	W Mullins	R Walsh	11-4f	11

It used to be straightforward narrowing down the list of contenders for this race – look for horses with plenty of form and experience, having had at least four runs that season and a win last time out – but much has changed in recent years with younger horses, many of whom had been kept largely under wraps, coming to the fore. Katchit defied the biggest trend of all as a winning five-year-old in 2008 and five others – Zaynar, Celestial Halo, Binocular, Punjabi and Afsoun – have been placed in the last five years. Still, Punjabi was only the fourth winner in 26 years to have been beaten on his previous start.

National Hunt Chase Challenge Cup (4m) Cheltenham

2002	-32232212	**Rith Dubh**	10-11-11	J O'Neill	Mr JT McNamara	10-1	26
2003	-FF342	**Sudden Shock**	8-11-7	J O'Neill	Mr D Cullen	25-1	24
2004	-2212	**Native Emperor**	8-11-11	J O'Neill	Mr R Widger	5-1jf	22
2005	-22F4	**Another Rum**	7-11-7	I A Duncan	Mr M J O'Hare	40-1	20
2006	-5361	**Hot Weld**	7-11-11	F Murphy	Mr R Harding	33-1	22
2007	-3111430	**Butler's Cabin**	7-12-0	J O'Neill	Mr A Berry	33-1	19
2008	-27322	**Old Benny**	7-11-7	A King	C Huxley	9-1	20
2009	-42212	**Tricky Trickster**	6-11-11	N Twiston-Davies	Mr S W-Cohen	11-1	19
2010	-2051	**Poker De Sivola**	7-11-6	F Murphy	Ms K Walsh	14-1	18
2011	-313211F25	**Chicago Grey**	8-11-6	G Elliott	Mr D O'Connor	5-1f	16

A marathon novice chase for amateur riders, this is dangerous territory for punters, underlined by hot favourite Stormez's short-priced defeat in 2003 and the subsequent long-shots Another Rum, Hot Weld and Butler's Cabin storming home. The key factor is experience – horses simply must have run at least four times in the campaign and three winners since 2002 had between seven and nine runs to their name.

Neptune Investments Novices' Hurdle (2m5f) Cheltenham

Year	Form	Horse	Age/Weight	Trainer	Jockey	SP	Ran
2002	-1	**Galileo**	6-11-7	T George	J Maguire	12-1	14
2003	-51112	**Hardy Eustace**	6-11-7	D Hughes	K Kelly	6-1	19
2004	-12	**Fundamentalist**	6-11-7	N Twiston-Davies	C Llewellyn	12-1	15
2005	-310121	**No Refuge**	5-11-7	H Johnson	G Lee	17-2	20
2006	-1F221	**Nicanor**	5-11-7	N Meade	P Carberry	17-2	17
2006	-121U53	**Massini's Maguire**	6-11-7	P Hobbs	R Johnson	20-1	15
2008	-1	**Fiveforthree**	6-11-7	W Mullins	R Walsh	7-1	15
2009	-1111	**Mikael D'Haguenet**	5-11-7	W Mullins	R Walsh	5-2f	14
2010	-111	**Peddlers Cross**	5-11-7	D McCain	J Maguire	7-1	17
2011	-4131	**First Lieutenant**	6-11-7	M Morris	D Russell	7-1	12

This often throws up a supposed good thing, but Mikael D'Haguenet was the first winning favourite since Monsignor in 2000 and several short-priced jollies had been turned over in the meantime, joined since by Rite Of Passage and So Young. There have been five wins in nine renewals for Ireland as they transfer their dominance of the Supreme Novices' Hurdle. For more than a decade up to 2002 all winners had had at least four runs over hurdles, and five of the last seven winners also ticked that box.

RSA Chase (3m1f) Cheltenham

Year	Form	Horse	Age/Weight	Trainer	Jockey	SP	Ran
2002	-21F2	**Hussard Collonges**	7-11-4	P Beaumont	R Garritty	33-1	19
2003	-1311	**One Knight**	7-11-4	P Hobbs	R Johnson	15-2	9
2004	-F1332	**Rule Supreme**	8-11-4	W Mullins	D Casey	25-1	10
2005	-122	**Trabolgan**	7-11-4	N Henderson	M Fitzgerald	5-1	9
2006	-1231	**Star De Mohaison**	5-10-8	P Nicholls	B Geraghty	14-1	9
2007	-1111	**Denman**	7-11-4	P Nicholls	R Walsh	6-5f	17
2008	-1211	**Albertas Run**	7-11-4	J O'Neill	A McCoy	4-1f	11
2009	-131	**Cooldine**	7-11-4	W Mullins	R Walsh	9-4f	15
2010	-3F112	**Weapon's Amnesty**	7-11-4	C Byrnes	D Russell	10-1	9
2011	-21411	**Bostons Angel**	7-11-4	Mrs J Harrington	R Power	16-1	12

This had become known as a race for upsets before Denman, Albertas Run and Cooldine hit back for favourite backers. Nonetheless, despite Albertas Run's victory, the Reynoldstown Chase at Ascot remains a desperately poor guide and that has been responsible for seeing several fancied runners turned over. Stamina is the key asset, though surprisingly some dodgy jumpers, most notably One Knight and Rule Supreme, have won. The Irish have also won each of the last three renewals.

Queen Mother Champion Chase (2m) Cheltenham

Year	Form	Horse	Age/Weight	Trainer	Jockey	SP	Ran
2002	-1	**Flagship Uberalles**	8-12-0	P Hobbs	R Johnson	7-4f	12
2003	-1U11	**Moscow Flyer**	9-12-0	J Harrington	B Geraghty	7-4f	11
2004	-221	**Azertyuiop**	7-11-10	P Nicholls	R Walsh	15-8	8
2005	-111	**Moscow Flyer**	11-11-10	J Harrington	B Geraghty	6-4f	8
2006	-431	**Newmill**	8-11-10	J J Murphy	A McNamara	16-1	12
2007	-21U	**Voy Por Ustedes**	6-11-10	A King	R Thornton	5-1	10
2008	-U11	**Master Minded**	5-11-10	P Nicholls	R Walsh	3-1	8

2009	-11	**Master Minded**	6-11-10	P Nicholls	R Walsh	4-11f	12
2010	-141	**Big Zeb**	9-11-10	C Murphy	B Geraghty	10-1	9
2011	-3223	**Sizing Europe**	9-11-10	H de Bromhead	A Lynch	10-1	11

Newmill was only the fourth winner in over 40 runnings to return at a double-figure price, and while it would be wrong to say that was easy to predict it was nonetheless forecast in the pages of the *RFO* – Nick Watts tipped Newmill ante-post at 100-1! Newmill was also only the second winner since Martha's Son in 1997 to return bigger than 7-2, but since then Big Zeb and Sizing Europe were also double-figure prices. The latter upheld the remarkable record of Arkle winners as Moscow Flyer, Azertyuiop and Voy Por Ustedes have also followed up since 2003 and the last 13 to step up the following year all got placed at worst. However, defending champions have a poor record.

Coral Cup (2m5f) Cheltenham

2002	-54U	**Ilnamar**	6-10-5	M Pipe	R Greene	25-1	27
2003	-21	**Xenophon**	7-11-0	A Martin	M Fitzgerald	4-1f	27
2004	-134231	**Monkerhostin**	7-10-8	P Hobbs	R Johnson	13-2	27
2005	-1626	**Idole First**	6-10-10	Miss V Williams	B Geraghty	33-1	29
2006	-50121	**Sky's The Limit**	5-11-12	E O'Grady	B Geraghty	11-1	30
2007	-023521	**Burntoakboy**	9-10-3	Dr R P Newland	S Jones (5)	10-1	28
2008	-71	**Naiad Du Misselot**	7-10-13	F Murphy	D Russell	7-1	24
2009	-4511	**Ninetieth Minute**	6-10-3	T Taaffe	P W Flood	14-1	27
2010	-510	**Spirit River**	5-11-2	N Henderson	B Geraghty	14-1	28
2011	-2102	**Carlito Brigante**	5-11-0	G Elliott	D Russell	16-1	22

The Irish love to lay one out for this, but with constant bickering over how their raiders are assessed by the handicapper it is tough to know when their horses have been nicely treated and when they are best left alone. For example, they had four of the first five in 1998, the first five in 1999, a massively-punted winner in 2003 in Xenophon and the first two (well clear of the remainder) in 2006. Yet it's far from one-way traffic, with eight British winners in the last 14 runnings. Sky's The Limit was the first ever winning five-year-old, but he has since been joined by Spirit River and Carlito Brigante.

Weatherbys Champion Bumper (2m110yds) Cheltenham

2002	-1	**Pizarro**	5-11-6	E O'Grady	J Spencer	14-1	23
2003	-12	**Liberman**	5-11-6	M Pipe	A McCoy	2-1f	25
2004	-311	**Total Enjoyment**	5-10-12	T Cooper	J Culloty	7-1	24
2005	-11	**Missed That**	6-11-5	W Mullins	R Walsh	7-2f	24
2006	-2131	**Hairy Molly**	6-11-5	J Crowley	P Carberry	33-1	23
2007	-111	**Cork All Star**	5-11-5	J Harrington	B Geraghty	11-2	24
2008	-1	**Cousin Vinny**	5-11-5	W Mullins	Mr P Mullins	12-1	23
2009	-11	**Dunguib**	6-11-5	P Fenton	Mr B O'Connell	9-2	24
2010	-1	**Cue Card**	4-10-12	C Tizzard	J Tizzard	40-1	24
2011	-21	**Cheltenian**	5-11-5	P Hobbs	R Johnson	14-1	24

Bonanza time for the Irish, winners of 14 of the 19 runnings, though it could be that wins for Cue Card and Cheltenian represent a turning of the tide. Willie Mullins led the way for Ireland in jaw-dropping style around the turn of the century, winning four renewals out of five from 1996 to 2000, but he always did best when he had only one contender with just a single prior outing and that was the pointer to Cousin Vinny in 2008. Five-year-olds tend to dominate, but Missed That, Hairy Molly and Dunguib have redressed the balance for six-year-olds and Cue Card was the first successful four-year-old since Dato Star in 1995.

Pertemps Final Handicap Hurdle (3m1f110yds) Cheltenham

2002	-341	Freetown	6-11-2	L Lungo	A Dobbin	20-1	24
2003	-	Inching Closer	6-11-2	J O'Neill	B Geraghty	6-1f	24
2004	-380P6	Creon	9-10-0	J O'Neill	T Murphy	50-1	24
2005	-4421102	Oulart	6-10-2	D T Hughes	P Carberry	10-1	22
2006	-50505	Kadoun	9-11-7	M O'Brien	T Ryan (3)	50-1	24
2007	-2F0	Oscar Park	8-10-9	D Arbuthnot	T Doyle	14-1	24
2008	-1271	Ballyfitz	8-10-8	N Twiston-Davies	P Brennan	18-1	24
2009	-242611	Kayf Aramis	7-10-5	Miss V Williams	A Coleman	16-1	22
2010	-0500	Buena Vista	9-10-4	D Pipe	H Frost (3)	16-1	24
2011	-728700	Buena Vista	10-10-3	D Pipe	C O'Farrell (5)	20-1	23

A race that has regained its reputation as a desperately tricky puzzle in recent years. There was a decent spell of success for punters around the turn of the century, when the winning formula had been to back in-form horses with recent winning form carrying over 11st, thereby missing out all the bad-value plot horses laid out for the race. However, the bookmakers hit back with the 50-1 wins of Creon and Kadoun, and since then all five winners were among the lower weights priced at least 14-1.

Ladbrokes World Hurdle (3m) Cheltenham

2002*	-111	Baracouda	7-11-10	F Doumen	T Doumen	13-8f	16
2003*	-12	Baracouda	8-11-10	F Doumen	T Doumen	9-4j	11
2004*	-2	Iris's Gift	7-11-10	J O'Neill	B Geraghty	9-2	10
2005	-2211	Inglis Drever	6-11-10	H Johnson	G Lee	5-1	12
2006	-211	My Way De Solzen	6-11-10	A King	R Thornton	8-1	20
2007	-12	Inglis Drever	8-11-10	H Johnson	P Brennan	5-1	14
2008	-11	Inglis Drever	9-11-10	H Johnson	D O'Regan	11-8f	17
2009	-U11	Big Buck's	6-11-10	P Nicholls	R Walsh	6-1	14
2010	-11	Big Buck's	7-11-10	P Nicholls	R Walsh	5-6f	14
2011	-11	Big Buck's	8-11-10	P Nicholls	R Walsh	10-11f	13

Run over 3m1f as the Stayers' Hurdle

An amazing race for former champions with three horses – Big Buck's, Inglis Drever and Baracouda – sharing eight of the last ten renewals between them. That trio were all good enough to defy the trends, but as far as first-time winners are concerned there seems a slim career window in which a horse can win this, with six or seven-year-olds ideal. No five-year-old has ever won and only five eight-year-olds have scored, including the three legends. Even Baracouda was thrice outspeeded by younger rivals (Iris's Gift, Inglis Drever and My Way De Solzen) attempting further wins. Winners tend to have run well in some of the season's major staying hurdles, particularly the Long Walk Hurdle, and the last ten hadn't been out of the first two all season over hurdles.

Byrne Group Plate H'cap Chase (2m4f110yds) Cheltenham

2002	-P5	Blowing Wind	9-10-9	M Pipe	R Walsh	25-1	21
2003	-	Young Spartacus	10-10-9	H Daly	R Johnson	16-1	19
2004	-322141	Tikram	7-10-0	G Moore	T Murphy	16-1	12
2005	-2304	Liberthine	6-10-1	N Henderson	S Waley-Cohen(7)	25-1	22
2006	-433	Non So	8-11-3	N Henderson	M Fitzgerald	14-1	24
2007	-134	Idole First	8-10-7	Miss V Williams	A O'Keeffe	12-1	23
2008	-01437U5	Mister McGoldrick	11-11-7	Mrs S Smith	D Elsworth	66-1	22
2009	-20272	Something Wells	8-10-7	Miss V Williams	W Biddick	33-1	23

| 2010 | -3144 | **Great Endeavour** | 6-10-4 | D Pipe | D Cook (3) | 18-1 | 24 |
| 2011 | -45152F1 | **Holmwood Legend** | 10-10-9 | P Rodford | K Burke (3) | 25-1 | 20 |

AKA 'The Mildmay of Flete'. A terrible race for punters as, with so many top handicaps at Cheltenham over this trip over the course of a season, many of the leading contenders are far too exposed, allowing rivals with less obvious claims to make hay. Because of this the last 11 winners were 12-1 or bigger, and shock 66-1 victor Mister McGoldrick even defied the trend of horses with 11st or less winning, which has otherwise obliged in ten of the other 11 most recent renewals.

Fulke Walwyn Kim Muir H'cap Chase (3m110yds) Cheltenham

2002	-1	**The Bushkeeper**	8-11-2	N Henderson	Mr D Crosse	9-2f	23
2003	-	**Royal Predica**	9-10-13	M Pipe	Mr S McHugh (7)	33-1	23
2004	-42P9	**Maximize**	10-10-6	M Pipe	Mr D Edwards	40-1	22
2005	-31522	**Juveigneur**	8-11-7	N Henderson	Mr R Burton	12-1	24
2006	-P3621P	**You're Special**	9-10-12	F Murphy	Mr R Harding	33-1	21
2007	-36120	**Cloudy Lane**	7-10-11	D McCain	Mr R Burton	15-2f	24
2008	-43P	**High Chimes**	9-10-10	E Williams	Mr J Tudor (3)	14-1	24
2009	-14339	**Character Building**	9-11-12	J Quinn	Mr J J Codd	16-1	24
2010	-0311	**Ballabriggs**	9-11-12	D McCain	Mr R Harding	9-1	24
2011	-32	**Junior**	8-11-6	D Pipe	Mr J Codd	10-3f	24

A fairly tough handicap, with three of the last nine winners coming in at 33-1 or 40-1, though three favourites have also triumphed in the last decade. It's also important to note that two of the shock winners were trained by Martin Pipe and the other by Ferdy Murphy – horsemanship counts for plenty in this amateur race and the best jockeys tend to be attached to top yards, so don't discount anything from a traditional jumping stable. That's more of a factor than a light weights as Junior was the third successive winner to defy more than 11st last season, making it five out of the last ten in all.

Triumph Hurdle (2m1f) Cheltenham

2002	-1	**Scolardy**	4-11-0	W Mullins	C Swan	16-1	28
2003	-01141B41	**Spectroscope**	4-11-0	J O'Neill	B Geraghty	20-1	27
2004	-331	**Made In Japan**	4-11-0	P Hobbs	R Johnson	20-1	23
2005	-111	**Penzance**	4-11-0	A King	R Thornton	9-1	23
2006	-011	**Detroit City**	4-11-0	P Hobbs	R Johnson	7-2f	17
2007	-112111	**Katchit**	4-11-0	A King	R Thornton	11-2	23
2008	-12	**Celestial Halo**	4-11-0	P Nicholls	R Walsh	5-1	14
2009	-11	**Zaynar**	4-11-0	N Henderson	B Geraghty	11-2	18
2010	-4211	**Soldatino**	4-11-0	N Henderson	B Geraghty	6-1	17
2011	-1	**Zarkandar**	4-11-0	P Nicholls	D Jacob	13-2	23

Incredibly, 13 of the last 14 winners had won on their most recent outing, so that helps to narrow the race down for punters immediately, and since the advent of the Fred Winter Hurdle it has become far more predictable still with Zarkandar the biggest-priced winner in six years at just 13-2. There is a pronounced trend against home-breds, which was flagged up in the *RFO* prior to the 2002 running when all nine missed the frame, and that still applies despite Penzance's 2005 win with just three placed efforts since then.

County Handicap Hurdle (2m1f) Cheltenham

2002	-55422	**Rooster Booster**	8-11-1	P Hobbs	R Johnson	8-1	21
2003	-23151	**Spirit Leader**	7-11-7	J Harrington	B Geraghty	10-1	28
2004	-1238	**Sporazene**	5-10-13	P Nicholls	R Walsh	7-1f	23

AMERICAN TRILOGY: one of eight winning five-year-olds in 12 years

2005	-0P660048	**Fontanesi**	5-10-0	M Pipe	T Murphy	16-1	30
2006	-221U1131	**Desert Quest**	6-10-10	P Nicholls	R Walsh	4-1jf	29
2007	-1013	**Pedrobob**	9-10-0	A Mullins	PA Carberry	12-1	28
2008	-5202233	**Silver Jaro**	5-10-13	T Hogan	N Fehily	50-1	22
2009	-1349	**American Trilogy**	5-11-0	P Nicholls	R Walsh	20-1	27
2010	-100440110	**Thousand Stars**	6-10-5	W Mullins	Ms K Walsh	20-1	28
2011	-51	**Final Approach**	5-10-12	W Mullins	R Walsh	10-1	26

Much like the Imperial Cup, another fiercely competitive 2m handicap hurdle, young horses have a big edge and Final Approach was the eighth winning five-year-old in the last 12 years. He was also the fourth winner in five years for the Irish, which is remarkable given that Pedrobob was only the second in 20 years when he won in 2007. No horse has carried more than 11st to victory since Spirit Leader in 2003.

Cheltenham Gold Cup (3m2f110yds) Cheltenham

2002	-122	**Best Mate**	7-12-0	H Knight	J Culloty	7-1	18
2003	-11	**Best Mate**	8-12-0	H Knight	J Culloty	13-8f	15
2004	-21	**Best Mate**	9-11-10	H Knight	J Culloty	8-11f	10
2005	-1211	**Kicking King**	7-11-10	T Taaffe	B Geraghty	4-1f	15
2006	-1152	**War Of Attrition**	7-11-10	M Morris	C O'Dwyer	15-2	22
2007	-1111	**Kauto Star**	7-11-10	P Nicholls	R Walsh	5-4f	18
2008	-111	**Denman**	8-11-10	P Nicholls	S Thomas	9-4	12
2009	-1U1	**Kauto Star**	9-11-10	P Nicholls	R Walsh	7-4f	16
2010	-25	**Imperial Commander**	9-11-10	N Twiston-Davies	P Brennan	7-1	11
2011	-31	**Long Run**	6-11-10	N Henderson	Mr S W-Cohen	7-2f	13

As the Gold Cup increasingly becomes the be-all and end-all for top staying chasers, epitomised by how Best Mate was wrapped in cotton wool to pull off his hat-trick, so the race is being dominated by the established class acts. Best Mate joined the immortals of steeplechasing and became the first triple winner since Arkle (1964-66) in 2004, since when Kauto Star has also become the first ever horse to regain the crown. Each twice won as favourite, while Kicking King and Long Run were other winning jollies, so this is no longer a race in which chancing an outsider is worthwhile despite victories for Cool Ground, Mr Mulligan, Cool Dawn and See More Business in the 90s at 16-1 or bigger. Strong stayers can still make the frame at fancy prices, though, as Neptune Collonges, Turpin Green, Hedgehunter, Sir Rembrandt, Harbour Pilot (twice) and Truckers Tavern showed in recent years. Any runner older than ten can be discounted and even ten-year-olds struggle – none have won since Cool Dawn including Kauto Star and Denman twice – while it would be wrong to rule out any horse as too young because, although Long Run was the first six-year-old to win since Mill House, The Fellow was beaten a short-head in 1991 and ill-fated Gloria Victis still in the front rank when falling two out in 2000.

Christie's Foxhunter Chase (3m2f110yds) Cheltenham

2002	-3	**Last Option**	10-12-0	R Tate	Mrs F Needham	20-1	20
2003	-1	**Kingscliff**	6-12-0	S Alner	Mr R Young	11-4f	24
2004	-1P2	**Earthmover**	13-12-0	P Nicholls	Miss A Goschen	14-1	24
2005	-U1	**Sleeping Night**	9-12-0	P Nicholls	Mr C J Sweeney	7-2f	24
2006	-4U	**Whyso Mayo**	9-12-0	R Hurley	Mr D Murphy	20-1	24
2007	-	**Drombeag**	9-12-0	J O'Neill	Mr J T McNamara	20-1	24
2008	-P	**Amicelli**	9-12-0	C Coward	Mr O Greenall	33-1	23
2009	-	**Cappa Bleu**	7-12-0	Mrs E Crow	Mr R Burton	11-2	24
2010	-21	**Baby Run**	10-12-0	N Twiston-Davies	S Twiston-Davies	9-2jf	24
2011	-21	**Zemsky**	8-12-0	I Ferguson	Mr D O'Connor	33-1	24

This is regarded as a lottery by many punters, with four of the last six winners coming in at 20-1 or bigger, but it's much easier than that if you simply rule out any horse older than ten, thereby wiping out three-quarters of the field at a stroke in most years. Veterans dropping back into hunter chases quite simply have a shocking record, with Earthmover's win in 2004 a dreadful return for the last ten years given how many have gone off at short prices in that time. Cappa Bleu was very unusual in winning on his debut under rules, while Whyso Mayo was a rare Irish winner in 2006.

Grand Annual Handicap Chase (2m110yds) Cheltenham

2002	-321	**Fadoudal Du Cochet**	9-10-0	A Moore	D Casey	6-1	18
2003	-2231	**Palarshan**	5-10-0	H Daly	M Bradburne	8-1	21
2004	-614	**St Pirran**	9-10-1	P Nicholls	R Walsh	4-1f	21
2005	-3212	**Fota Island**	9-10-1	M Morris	P Carberry	7-1f	24
2006	-5	**Greenhope**	8-10-11	N Henderson	A Tinkler	20-1	23
2007	-333	**Andreas**	7-10-11	P Nicholls	R Thornton	12-1	23
2008	-836	**Tiger Cry**	10-10-6	A Moore	D Russell	15-2	17
2009	-1423F2	**Oh Crick**	6-10-0	A King	W Hutchinson	7-1	18
2010	-2F222F5	**Pigeon Island**	7-10-1	N Twiston-Davies	P Brennan	16-1	19
2011	-U6483	**Oiseau De Nuit**	9-11-6	C Tizzard	S Clements (7)	40-1	23

Lightly-weighted horses have a big edge in this contest, with Oiseau De Nuit the first to carry 11st or more since the mighty Edredon Bleu in 1998, and seven in the interim carried either 10st or 10st 1lb. Novices have an exceptional record, with Samakaan, Palarshan, Fota Island, Oh Crick and Pigeon Island all successful in their first chasing season after Sound Reveille in the mid-90s. Victory last time out was once essential but no longer as none of the last eight winners won on their previous outing.

Totesport Bowl Chase (3m1f) Aintree

2002	-31140	**Florida Pearl**	10-11-12	W Mullins	B Geraghty	5-2	6
2003	-373P	**First Gold**	10-11-2	F Doumen	T Doumen	14-1	7

2004	-422F3	**Tiutchev**	11-11-12	M Pipe	A McCoy	11-2	8
2005	-115	**Grey Abbey**	11-11-12	J H Johnson	G Lee	7-2	8
2006	-U	**Celestial Gold**	8-11-8	M Pipe	T Murphy	8-1	9
2007	-211212	**Exotic Dancer**	7-11-12	J O'Neill	A McCoy	6-4f	5
2008	-221	**Our Vic**	10-11-10	D Pipe	T Murphy	9-1	5
2009	-6118	**Madison Du Berlais**	8-11-10	D Pipe	T Scudamore	12-1	10
2010	-21	**What A Friend**	7-11-7	P Nicholls	R Walsh	5-2	5
2011	-1443	**Nacarat**	10-11-7	T George	P Brennan	7-?	6

AKA 'The Martell Cup'. A dramatic uplift in prize-money improved the quality of this race greatly around the turn of the decade as Florida Pearl won almost twice as much in 2002 as Macgeorge had three years earlier, and it's even attracted Gold Cup winners in Kauto Star, Denman and Imperial Commander. Tellingly, though, all three were beaten, including Denman twice, and in his case it may not necessarily be because of the lack of freshness. Despite being left-handed, Aintree's flat, sharp Mildmay course has much more in common with Kempton than Cheltenham and form there seems to be key – seven of the nine winners from 2000 to 2008 had previously been first or second in the King George, dual winner Docklands Express twice won the Racing Post Chase, a race also won by Nacarat, and Madison Du Berlais's best run had come at the Sunbury track when beating Denman.

Grand National Handicap Chase (4m4f) Aintree

2002	-753367	**Bindaree**	8-10-4	N Twiston-Davies	J Culloty	20-1	40
2003	3P631364	**Monty's Pass**	10-10-7	J Mangan	B Geraghty	16-1	40
2004	-342P5	**Amberleigh House**	12-10-10	D McCain	G Lee	16-1	39
2005	-924061	**Hedgehunter**	9-11-1	W Mullins	R Walsh	7-1f	40
2006	-04B443	**Numbersixvalverde**	10-10-8	M Brassil	N Madden	11-1	40
2007	-0242	**Silver Birch**	10-10-6	G Elliott	R Power	33-1	40
2008	-0P21	**Comply Or Die**	9-10-9	D Pipe	T Murphy	7-1jf	40
2009	-218278	**Mon Mome**	9-11-0	Miss V Williams	L Treadwell	100-1	40
2010	-423P	**Don't Push It**	10-11-5	J O'Neill	A McCoy	10-1jf	40
2011	-112	**Ballabriggs**	10-11-0	D McCain	J Maguire	14-1	40

A light weight used to be the key National trend, but efforts by the handicapper to attract more and more class horses have led to the weights becoming more condensed in recent years, so more horses carry 11st or more and Hedgehunter, Mon Mome, Don't Push It and Ballabriggs all defied such a burden. Winners still tend to have hidden their ability from the handicapper that season – seven of the last 12 winners hadn't won at all over fences (Ballabriggs was campaigned over hurdles to protect his mark), and none of the last 12 more than once. Forget the old adage about class horses with winning form over 2m4f; even with the modified fences, this race is a severe test of stamina and proven ability to last home over three miles or further is essential. Look for horses who have run with credit in other major staying handicaps, but be careful with Hennessy form as Newbury winners Suny Bay and What's Up Boys were beaten by the handicapper in second. Don't back at starting price but take the best available odds 'with a run' in the days before the race as prices tend to shorten dramatically close to start time.

Scottish Grand National Handicap Chase (4m120yds) Ayr

2002	-36P4P5	**Take Control**	8-10-6	M Pipe	R Walsh	20-1	18
2003	-31223	**Ryalux**	10-10-5	A Crook	R McGrath	15-2	19
2004	-611	**Grey Abbey**	10-11-12	J H Johnson	G Lee	12-1	28
2005	-1222P1	**Joes Edge**	8-10-0	F Murphy	K J Mercer (3)	20-1	20
2006	-10402	**Run For Paddy**	10-10-2	C Llewellyn	C Llewellyn	33-1	30

2007	-PPP6	Hot Weld	8-10-0	F Murphy	P McDonald (5)	14-1	23
2008	-P313	Iris De Balme	8-10-0	S Curran	C Huxley (7)	66-1	24
2009	-116P1	Hello Bud	11-10-9	N Twiston-Davies	P Brennan	12-1	17
2010	-72d61	Merigo	9-10-0	A Parker	T Murphy	18-1	30
2011	-B12	Beshabar	9-10-4	T Vaughan	R Johnson	15-2	28

This has been a lean race for punters, with no winning favourites since Paris Pike in 2000 and some real skinners in that time, topped by 66-1 shot Iris De Balme romping to victory in 2008. The first mistake is backing horses who had a hard race in the Grand National as very few manage to reproduce their best form. The ground tends to be fast as well, rendering soft-ground winter form redundant. There are no conclusive trends with regard to weight – ten of the last 23 winners carried the minimum of 10st, ranging up to 26lb out of the handicap, but four of the last 13 winners carried more than 11st and class acts Young Kenny and Grey Abbey defied welter burdens.

Irish Grand National Handicap Chase (3m5f) Fairyhouse

2002	-5312F1	The Bunny Boiler	8-9-9	N Meade	R Geraghty (5)	12-1	17
2003	-P24	Timbera	9-10-12	D Hughes	J Culloty	11-1	21
2004	-UP34	Granit D'Estruval	10-10-0	F. Murphy	B Harding	33-1	28
2005	-8231513	Numbersixvalverde	9-10-1	M Brassil	R Walsh	9-1	26
2006	-60006	Point Barrow	8-10-8	P Hughes	P Carberry	20-1	26
2007	-31114301	Butler's Cabin	7-10-4	J O'Neill	A McCoy	14-1	29
2008	-057	Hear The Echo	7-10-0	M Morris	P Flood	33-1	23
2009	-3148	Niche Market	8-10-5	R Buckler	H Skelton (5)	33-1	28
2010	-P2	Bluesea Cracker	8-10-4	J Motherway	AJ McNamara	25-1	26
2011	-76312	Organisedconfusion	6-9-13	A Moore	Miss N Carberry	12-1	25

A race whose history is littered with great winners, Desert Orchid one of 11 horses since the war to shoulder more than 11st 10lb to victory, but the class of the race has decreased in recent years and light weights have dominated, with the last 11 winners carrying 10st 12lb or less. British raiders have traditionally had an awful record, but that's changed in recent times with Granit d'Estruval winning in 2004, Butler's Cabin leading a British one-two in 2007, and Niche Market also triumphant in 2009. Young, improving chasers are the order of the day, with Commanche Court, Davids Lad and Numbersixvalverde going on to bigger things, and this has become a top Aintree National trial.

Bet365 Gold Cup Handicap Chase (3m5f) Sandown

2002	32143356	Bounce Back	6-10-9	M Pipe	A McCoy	14-1	20
2003	-51233U	Ad Hoc	9-10-10	P Nicholls	R Walsh	7-1	16
2004	-1211415UU	Puntal	8-11-4	M Pipe	D Howard (3)	25-1	18
2006	-16134022	Lacdoudal	7-11-5	P Hobbs	R Johnson	10-1	18
2007	-PPP61	Hot Weld	8-10-0	F Murphy	G Lee	6-1	10
2008	-33P	Monkerhostin	11-10-13	P Hobbs	R Johnson	25-1	19
2009	-165	Hennessy	8-10-7	C Llewellyn	A McCoy	13-2	14
2010	-0025400	Church Island	11-10-5	M Hourigan	A Heskin (7)	20-1	19
2011	-76U	Poker De Sivola	8-10-12	F Murphy	T Murphy	11-1	18

AKA 'The Whitbread'. As in so many staying chases, light weights are favoured – 14 of the last 22 winners have carried 10st 6lb or less. However, the fast ground at this late stage of the season also gives the quality horses more of a chance, as Puntal and Lacdoudal showed. Six of the last 17 winners had run in the Grand National, but Mr Frisk in 1990 remains the only horse ever to win both races. Hot Weld was also the first horse to follow up from the Scottish National in 2007.

Track Facts

YOU WANT course statistics? Look no further – this section contains all the numbers you'll need for every jumps track in the country.

Course by course, we've set out four-year trainer and jockey statistics, favourites records, winning pointers and three-dimensional racecourse maps, plus details of how to get there and every fixture date for the new season.

Following this, from page 222, we've got details of course record times, plus standard times for each track.

Note that we have been unable to produce standard times in a very small number of cases, as there have not been enough recent races over the trip at the track in question.

See also our statistical assessment of last season's records from Britain's top ten trainers (page 123).

AINTREE	177-178	LEICESTER	200
ASCOT	179	LINGFIELD	201
AYR	180	LUDLOW	202
BANGOR	181	MARKET RASEN	203
CARLISLE	182	MUSSELBURGH	204
CARTMEL	183	NEWBURY	205
CATTERICK	184	NEWCASTLE	206
CHELTENHAM	185-186	NEWTON ABBOT	207
CHEPSTOW	187	PERTH	208
DONCASTER	188	PLUMPTON	209
EXETER	189	SANDOWN	210-211
FAKENHAM	190	SEDGEFIELD	212
FFOS LAS	191	SOUTHWELL	213
FOLKESTONE	192	STRATFORD	214
FONTWELL	193	TAUNTON	215
HAYDOCK	194	TOWCESTER	216
HEREFORD	195	UTTOXETER	217
HEXHAM	196	WARWICK	218
HUNTINGDON	197	WETHERBY	219
KELSO	198	WINCANTON	220
KEMPTON	199	WORCESTER	221

Ormskirk Rd, Liverpool,
L9 5AS. Tel: 0151 523 2600

AINTREE

How to get there Road: M6,
M62, M57, M58. Rail: Liverpool
Lime Street and taxi.

Features The left-handed 2m2f
giant triangular Grand National
course is perfectly flat. Inside it,
the sharp left-handed Mildmay
course is 1m4f in circumference.

2011 Fixtures October 22-23,
December 3

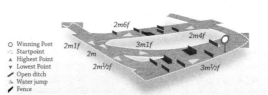

O	Winning Post
⌐	Startpoint
▲	Highest Point
▼	Lowest Point
✎	Open ditch
▓	Water jump
✦	Fence

Trainers	Wins-Runs	%	Hurdles	Chases	£1 level stks
Paul Nicholls	20-148	14	10-55	9-83	-67.36
Peter Bowen	15-86	17	10-40	4-39	+114.55
Nicky Henderson	14-98	14	7-50	5-35	+16.78
Nigel Twiston-Davies	12-109	11	3-32	9-73	-25.00
Alan King	12-95	13	7-60	5-19	-39.62
Howard Johnson	11-100	11	2-47	9-48	-30.91
Donald McCain	9-105	9	8-64	1-25	-5.02
Jonjo O'Neill	9-73	12	5-29	4-38	-7.51
Philip Hobbs	8-79	10	5-44	2-24	-25.25
John Quinn	6-34	18	2-13	4-20	+8.88
David Pipe	5-73	7	2-34	3-36	-22.38
Ian Williams	5-33	15	4-22	1-9	+10.50
Venetia Williams	4-75	5	1-40	3-33	+76.00
Sue Smith	4-50	8	2-27	1-21	+34.58
Lucinda Russell	4-36	11	2-21	2-13	+71.75

Jockeys	Wins-Rides	%	£1 level stks	Best Trainer	W-R
R Walsh	19-88	22	-15.86	Paul Nicholls	17-79
A P McCoy	15-123	12	-21.13	Jonjo O'Neill	8-46
Paddy Brennan	11-108	10	-16.50	Nigel Twiston-Davies	7-68
Robert Thornton	11-83	13	-28.82	Alan King	11-69
Tom O'Brien	10-66	15	+4.93	Peter Bowen	5-30
Dougie Costello	9-48	19	+15.88	John Quinn	6-24
Denis O'Regan	8-92	9	-53.91	Howard Johnson	7-64
Richard Johnson	8-73	11	+18.75	Philip Hobbs	5-42
Barry Geraghty	8-60	13	+1.41	Nicky Henderson	6-40
Jason Maguire	6-72	8	-22.02	Donald McCain	6-51
Brian Hughes	5-52	10	-4.50	Howard Johnson	2-14
Tom Scudamore	4-45	9	-12.88	David Pipe	2-25
Graham Lee	3-100	3	-82.75	Ferdy Murphy	2-62
Aidan Coleman	3-57	5	-7.00	Venetia Williams	3-42
Timmy Murphy	3-47	6	-25.25	David Pipe	2-16

Favourites

Hurdle	32.2%	-13.26	Chase	22.9%	-33.32	TOTAL	27.9%	-51.59

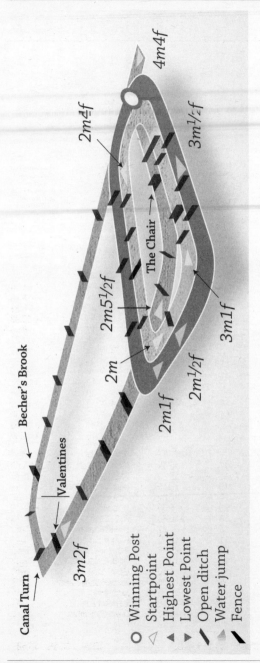

Canal Turn

3m2f

Becher's Brook

Valentines

2m4½f

2m5½f

The Chair

2m

2m1f

4m4f

3m½f

3m1f

2m½f

Aintree's Grand National course – used in the Becher Chase, the Grand Sefton Chase, the Topham Chase, the Foxhunters' Chase and the Grand National

○ Winning Post
▽ Startpoint
◀ Highest Point
▶ Lowest Point
╱ Open ditch
▲ Water jump
▰ Fence

Ascot, Berkshire SL5 7JX
0870 7227 227

ASCOT

How to get there Road: M4
junction 6 or M3 junction 3 on to
A332. Rail: Frequent service from
Reading or Waterloo

Features Right-handed

2011 Fixtures October 29,
November 18-19, December
16-17

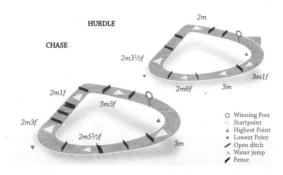

Trainers	Wins-Runs	%	Hurdles	Chases	£1 level stks
Nicky Henderson	35-116	30	22-80	9-26	+4.89
Paul Nicholls	17-90	19	6-37	9-46	-36.79
Philip Hobbs	13-99	13	4-46	7-46	-8.33
David Pipe	13-64	20	6-32	6-31	+50.93
Alan King	11-90	12	7-58	4-25	+6.58
Gary Moore	7-61	11	2-33	4-25	-4.25
Emma Lavelle	6-53	11	4-38	2-13	-24.33
Brendan Powell	6-39	15	3-25	3-10	+2.88
Jonjo O'Neill	5-40	13	1-17	4-17	-6.50
Evan Williams	5-29	17	3-13	2-16	+36.92
Henrietta Knight	4-36	11	0-15	4-18	+1.00
Henry Daly	4-30	13	2-7	2-21	-13.38
Venetia Williams	3-40	8	1-15	2-24	-4.50
Charlie Mann	3-35	9	2-26	1-9	-17.63
Donald McCain	3-14	21	2-7	1-7	+10.50

Jockeys	Wins-Rides	%	£1 level stks	Best Trainer	W-R
Barry Geraghty	22-54	41	+16.11	Nicky Henderson	20-48
Richard Johnson	10-88	11	-15.83	Philip Hobbs	10-65
A P McCoy	10-60	17	-25.19	Nicky Henderson	4-12
Noel Fehily	10-49	20	+12.04	Paul Nicholls	3-6
R Walsh	10-44	23	-15.53	Paul Nicholls	8-32
Tom Scudamore	8-44	18	+40.88	David Pipe	8-28
Paul Moloney	8-31	26	+51.67	Evan Williams	5-12
Timmy Murphy	7-63	11	-11.92	Barney Curley	1-1
Robert Thornton	6-59	10	-26.93	Alan King	6-50
Paddy Brennan	6-59	10	-15.67	Nigel Twiston-Davies	2-38
Jamie Moore	6-53	11	+1.50	Gary Moore	6-40
Mick Fitzgerald	5-19	26	-6.46	Nicky Henderson	3-7
Wayne Hutchinson	4-36	11	+16.75	Alan King	3-19
Liam Treadwell	3-33	9	+26.50	Eoin Griffin	1-1
Aidan Coleman	3-32	9	-9.50	David Arbuthnot	1-1

Favourites

Hurdle	38.2%	-11.26	Chase	38.4%	-5.68	TOTAL	38.6%	-16.68

AYR

Whitletts Road, Ayr, KA8 0JE
Tel: 01292 264 179

How to get there Road: south from Glasgow on A77 or A75, A70, A76. Rail: Ayr

Features Left-handed 1m4f oval, easy turns, slight uphill finish

2011 Fixtures 29 November

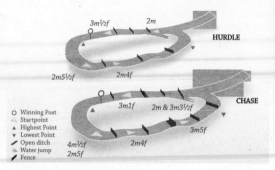

Trainers	Wins-Runs	%	Hurdles	Chases	£1 level stks
Lucinda Russell	25-206	12	7-118	16-73	-5.18
Donald McCain	20-68	29	10-37	10-28	+4.94
Jim Goldie	19-133	14	9-86	8-41	+41.25
Nicky Richards	13-120	11	9-81	4-31	-46.77
Howard Johnson	12-81	15	7-43	4-31	-41.30
P Monteith	11-67	16	7-37	4-30	+2.63
Ferdy Murphy	8-72	11	2-27	6-42	-19.90
Nicky Henderson	8-34	24	4-16	2-16	+1.38
Pauline Robson	8-22	36	3-9	5-13	+40.00
William Amos	6-44	14	5-29	0-7	+42.67
L Lungo	6-30	20	2-15	4-10	+4.07
J J Lambe	5-36	14	3-26	2-9	+41.00
Keith Reveley	5-29	17	2-15	3-12	-10.80
Lisa Harrison	5-13	38	4-12	0-0	+39.00
Alistair Whillans	4-52	8	0-25	4-19	-39.46

Jockeys	Wins-Rides	%	£1 level stks	Best Trainer	W-R
Graham Lee	24-132	18	+31.23	Ferdy Murphy	5-40
Peter Buchanan	20-143	14	+30.73	Lucinda Russell	19-121
Richie McGrath	20-117	17	+56.75	Jim Goldie	11-65
Brian Harding	17-95	18	+35.26	Nicky Richards	5-26
Denis O'Regan	12-62	19	-25.67	Howard Johnson	10-42
James Reveley	11-80	14	-17.80	Keith Reveley	5-27
Jason Maguire	11-35	31	-2.13	Donald McCain	10-27
Campbell Gillies	9-90	10	-38.73	Lucinda Russell	5-61
Harry Haynes	8-52	15	+51.69	Lisa Harrison	3-5
Brian Hughes	7-93	8	-24.00	Ann Hamilton	2-4
Timmy Murphy	7-37	19	+40.00	Andrew Parker	2-3
Ryan Mania	6-55	11	-26.13	P Monteith	3-11
Barry Geraghty	6-26	23	-5.63	Nicky Henderson	6-21
Wilson Renwick	5-73	7	-31.00	L Lungo	3-16
Jan Faltejsek	4-36	11	+29.00	William Amos	2-11

Favourites

Hurdle	39.7%	-2.48	Chase	36.3%	-3.30	TOTAL	37.8%	-10.97

Bangor-on-Dee, nr Wrexham,
Clwyd. Tel: 01948 860 438

BANGOR

How to get there Road: A525.
Rail: Wrexham

Features Left-handed, 1m4f
round, quite sharp, final fence
gets plenty of fallers

2011 Fixtures November 9, 26,
December 14, 19

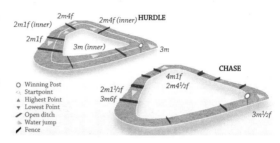

Trainers	Wins-Runs	%	Hurdles	Chases	£1 level stks
Donald McCain	42-279	15	22-178	13-68	-79.30
Jonjo O'Neill	27-168	16	12-87	15-76	-57.52
Alan King	22-98	22	7-59	11-24	-8.80
Tim Vaughan	14-66	21	10-38	1-19	+0.13
Venetia Williams	13-89	15	7-47	6-35	-24.43
Philip Hobbs	12-56	21	7-30	5-21	+16.37
Nicky Henderson	10-40	25	7-21	1-8	-5.91
Henry Daly	9-49	18	4-18	4-21	+43.25
David Pipe	8-60	13	4-35	3-21	+1.50
Rebecca Curtis	8-34	24	4-20	2-8	+2.54
Nigel Twiston-Davies	7-65	11	4-32	3-28	-42.75
Charlie Longsdon	7-35	20	3-17	3-15	+34.75
Ian Williams	6-49	12	3-36	3-11	-16.42
Charlie Mann	6-33	18	4-18	2-14	+0.25
Evan Williams	5-72	7	5-56	0-15	-60.94

Jockeys	Wins-Rides	%	£1 level stks	Best Trainer	W-R
Jason Maguire	35-162	22	-14.80	Donald McCain	33-134
A P McCoy	32-159	20	-44.88	Jonjo O'Neill	18-87
Richard Johnson	20-81	25	+2.90	Tim Vaughan	8-25
Sam Thomas	11-64	17	-18.72	Venetia Williams	3-21
Tom O'Brien	11-60	18	-4.38	Philip Hobbs	7-22
Robert Thornton	11-55	20	-7.54	Alan King	10-33
Aidan Coleman	10-61	16	+9.13	Venetia Williams	7-41
Graham Lee	9-60	15	+24.00	Jim Goldie	2-5
Noel Fehily	9-57	16	-8.00	Charlie Mann	4-19
Tom Scudamore	8-70	11	-26.50	David Pipe	3-30
Wayne Hutchinson	8-66	12	-18.38	Alan King	7-32
Andrew Tinkler	8-61	13	-16.17	Nicky Henderson	3-14
Paddy Brennan	7-60	12	-34.75	Nigel Twiston-Davies	4-26
Mark Bradburne	6-46	13	+36.50	Henry Daly	3-17
Will Kennedy	5-32	16	+125.00	Alex Hales	2-6

Favourites

Hurdle	38.4%	-6.47	Chase	32.9%	-25.29	TOTAL	36.3% -27.19

CARLISLE

Blackwell, Carlisle, CA2 4TS
Tel: 01228 522 973

How to get there Road: M6 Jctn 42. Rail: 2m from Citadel Station, Carlisle

Features Pear-shaped, 1m5f circuit, right-handed, undulating, uphill home straight

2011 Fixtures October 7, 20, 30, November 7, 27, December 18

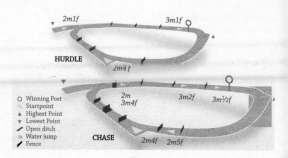

Trainers	Wins-Runs	%	Hurdles	Chases	£1 level stks
Howard Johnson	40-152	26	15-49	23-90	+58.27
Sue Smith	20-132	15	3-29	17-94	+26.56
Donald McCain	14-109	13	6-45	6-51	-62.21
Lucinda Russell	13-123	11	2-43	11-77	-4.75
Ferdy Murphy	10-96	10	2-29	8-63	-51.25
Nicky Richards	9-58	16	2-20	7-32	-5.05
P Monteith	6-48	13	2-10	4-38	+19.25
Keith Reveley	5-51	10	3-16	1-25	-16.59
Jonjo O'Neill	5-39	13	0-10	5-28	-19.40
L Lungo	5-27	19	0-10	5-14	-0.63
Micky Hammond	5-23	22	3-6	2-17	+28.88
William Amos	5-22	23	1-11	2-6	+109.00
Martin Todhunter	4-59	7	1-15	3-43	-1.50
James Ewart	4-49	8	1-13	3-30	-18.50
Chris Grant	4-39	10	1-13	3-23	-15.00

Jockeys	Wins-Rides	%	£1 level stks	Best Trainer	W-R
Denis O'Regan	26-95	27	+45.40	Howard Johnson	24-79
Wilson Renwick	13-72	18	+35.71	L Lungo	4-18
Graham Lee	12-125	10	-71.63	Ferdy Murphy	9-58
Peter Buchanan	12-114	11	-8.88	Lucinda Russell	11-93
Ryan Mania	12-79	15	-14.58	Dianne Sayer	3-14
James Reveley	10-63	16	+23.03	Keith Reveley	4-27
Brian Harding	9-95	9	-0.54	Alan Mactaggart	4-11
Jason Maguire	9-55	16	-26.88	Donald McCain	9-49
Brian Hughes	7-76	9	-28.60	Howard Johnson	4-18
Richie McGrath	6-104	6	-79.89	Jonjo O'Neill	2-7
Fearghal Davis	6-69	9	-24.00	Nicky Richards	3-14
Campbell Gillies	6-40	15	+101.50	William Amos	3-10
Tjade Collier	6-35	17	-14.29	Sue Smith	5-31
Shane Byrne	6-24	25	+53.50	Sue Smith	6-24
Dougie Costello	5-51	10	-2.75	Lucy Normile	2-3

Favourites

Hurdle	27.4%	-19.53		Chase	37.7%	+8.99		TOTAL	33.9%	-15.42

Grange-over-Sands, Penrith, CA10
2HG. Tel: 01593 536 340

CARTMEL

How to get there Road: M6
Jctn 36, A591. Rail: Cark-in-
Cartmel or Grange-over-Sands

Features Tight, left-handed 1m
circuit, undulating, half-mile run-in
from last (longest in country)

2011 Fixtures None

HURDLE

CHASE

2m 1½f
3m2f

2m6f

3m6f

2m1½f
3m2f

○ Winning Post
＼ Startpoint
▲ Highest Point
▼ Lowest Point
╱ Open ditch
▨ Water jump
▮ Fence

Trainers	Wins-Runs	%	Hurdles	Chases	£1 level stks
Donald McCain	9-49	18	5-33	4-16	-12.88
Richard Ford	9-33	27	4-22	5-11	+34.50
Peter Bowen	8-41	20	4-24	4-17	-5.14
Evan Williams	6-48	13	3-31	3-17	-26.75
J J Lambe	6-42	14	4-30	2-12	+7.00
P Monteith	5-28	18	3-13	2-15	+16.00
George Moore	5-20	25	5-17	0-3	+30.56
Michael Chapman	4-63	6	3-40	1-23	-26.50
Tim Vaughan	4-24	17	3-16	1-8	-3.63
Richard Guest	4-24	17	2-14	2-10	+6.50
Dianne Sayer	4-18	22	3-12	1-6	-0.25
George Charlton	4-14	29	2-8	2-6	-0.33
Martin Todhunter	3-33	9	2-20	1-13	-3.00
Sue Smith	3-33	9	1-15	2-18	-15.00
Nicky Richards	3-11	27	2-9	1-2	+4.00

Jockeys	Wins-Rides	%	£1 level stks	Best Trainer	W-R
Graham Lee	14-70	20	-0.11	Richard Ford	4-12
Brian Hughes	7-72	10	-29.70	Alan Swinbank	3-7
Tom O'Brien	7-27	26	+8.74	Peter Bowen	6-19
Ryan Mania	5-33	15	+10.25	P Monteith	3-12
A P McCoy	5-27	19	-0.38	Edgar Byrne	1-1
Campbell Gillies	5-23	22	-0.85	Lucinda Russell	2-5
Jason Maguire	5-20	25	+0.38	Donald McCain	4-19
Timmy Murphy	5-17	29	+14.50	George Charlton	1-1
Richie McGrath	4-37	11	-5.27	Aytach Sadik	1-1
Barry Keniry	4-35	11	+12.06	George Moore	4-16
Keith Mercer	4-34	12	+4.50	Roger Fisher	2-12
Paul Moloney	4-29	14	-18.20	Evan Williams	2-22
Paddy Aspell	3-50	6	-20.50	John Dixon	2-7
Brian Harding	3-36	8	-23.50	Dianne Sayer	2-5
Denis O'Regan	3-29	10	+1.00	Martin Todhunter	3-11

Favourites

Hurdle	39.1%	+13.09	Chase	28.4%	-12.61	TOTAL	34.8%	+0.48

CATTERICK

Catterick Bridge, Richmond, N Yorks
DL10 7PE. Tel: 01748 811 478

How to get there Road: A1.
Rail: Darlington

Features Left-handed, 1m2f
oval, undulating, sharp turns,
favours small, handy horses

2011 Fixtures November 30,
December 13, 28

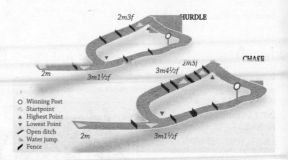

○ Winning Post
⌐ Startpoint
▲ Highest Point
▼ Lowest Point
✎ Open ditch
≋ Water jump
⌐ Fence

Trainers	Wins-Runs	%	Hurdles	Chases	£1 level stks
Howard Johnson	14-102	14	5-51	8-37	-18.34
Sue Smith	13-105	12	5-45	7-40	-15.13
Donald McCain	11-67	16	6-38	4-19	+14.65
Ferdy Murphy	10-76	13	4-29	5-41	-24.54
Keith Reveley	10-70	14	4-28	5-27	+49.17
Alan Swinbank	10-36	28	3-15	0-4	+11.10
Micky Hammond	7-41	17	4-21	2-16	+29.25
Chris Grant	5-58	9	3-29	2-22	+6.33
James Ewart	4-26	15	0-6	3-13	+0.25
Brian Ellison	4-9	44	3-8	1-1	+19.50
Tim Easterby	3-32	9	0-11	3-13	-6.50
John Wade	3-31	10	1-10	1-15	-0.50
Evelyn Slack	3-28	11	2-9	1-19	-15.25
Nicky Richards	3-16	19	2-12	1-3	-6.75
Tom Tate	3-4	75	3-3	0-0	+8.88

Jockeys	Wins-Rides	%	£1 level stks	Best Trainer	W-R
Denis O'Regan	12-80	15	-9.71	Howard Johnson	9-47
Graham Lee	10-93	11	-33.44	Ferdy Murphy	6-51
Brian Hughes	10-83	12	-16.52	Alan Swinbank	5-12
Jason Maguire	10-42	24	+16.15	Donald McCain	8-37
James Reveley	9-72	13	+43.17	Keith Reveley	8-47
Keith Mercer	8-66	12	-11.63	Tom Tate	3-3
Fearghal Davis	7-66	11	-9.25	Micky Hammond	2-11
Dougie Costello	7-45	16	+4.63	Alan Swinbank	2-5
Barry Keniry	6-46	13	+0.00	Alan Swinbank	2-6
Richie McGrath	5-55	9	-16.50	Kate Walton	2-9
Tjade Collier	5-46	11	-21.38	Sue Smith	5-37
Henry Oliver	5-22	23	+17.25	Sue Smith	4-19
Campbell Gillies	4-40	10	+13.33	Chris Grant	2-14
Wilson Renwick	3-44	7	+23.00	Stuart Coltherd	1-2
James O'Farrell	3-41	7	-10.00	Dianne Sayer	1-4

Favourites

Hurdle 28.6% -27.73		Chase 30.3% -9.31		TOTAL 28.9% -45.94

Prestbury Park, Cheltenham,
GL50 4SH. Tel: 01242 513 014

CHELTENHAM

How to get there Road: A435,
five miles north of M5 Jctns 9,
10, 11

Features There are two left-
handed courses – the Old Course
is 1m4f around, the New Course
slightly longer. Both are undulating
and end with a testing uphill finish

2011 Fixtures October 14-15,
November 11-13, December 9-10

*BACCALAUREATE (left): 100-1 win in January 2010
was a massive boost to Nigel Twiston-Davies's profit*

New Course

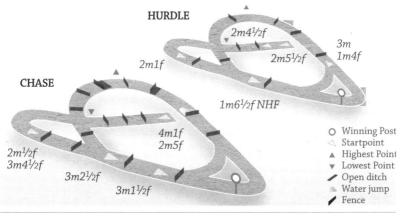

HURDLE

2m4½f

2m5½f

3m
1m4f

2m1f

1m6½f NHF

CHASE

4m1f
2m5f

2m½f
3m4½f

3m2½f

3m1½f

○	Winning Post
△	Startpoint
▲	Highest Point
▼	Lowest Point
✦	Open ditch
⬛	Water jump
✦	Fence

185

Old Course

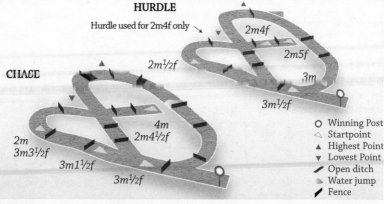

HURDLE

Hurdle used for 2m4f only

2m4f

2m5f

2m½f

3m

CHASE

3m½f

4m

2m4½f

2m

3m3½f

3m1½f

3m½f

O Winning Post
△ Startpoint
▲ Highest Point
▼ Lowest Point
◢ Open ditch
▨ Water jump
▰ Fence

Trainers	Wins-Runs	%	Hurdles	Chases	£1 level stks
Paul Nicholls	54-365	15	25-151	26-202	-85.17
Nicky Henderson	36-279	13	27-161	5-97	-45.05
Nigel Twiston-Davies	34-338	10	14-129	20-192	+62.29
Philip Hobbs	31-263	12	13-127	15-124	-46.25
Alan King	23-251	9	16-154	6-78	-81.75
David Pipe	22-269	8	10-143	12-121	-45.97
Jonjo O'Neill	11-152	7	2-67	9-78	-73.88
W P Mullins	11-88	13	9-46	1-25	-11.67
Colin Tizzard	11-72	15	2-22	8-45	+76.36
Venetia Williams	10-123	8	3-47	7-76	+8.75
Gordon Elliott	8-50	16	5-32	3-18	+23.38
Ferdy Murphy	6-68	9	1-15	5-53	-17.00
Nick Williams	6-56	11	3-30	3-26	-19.84
Charlie Mann	6-56	11	2-23	4-33	-3.75
Ian Williams	6-52	12	0-29	6-22	-6.00

Jockeys	Wins-Rides	%	£1 level stks	Best Trainer	W-R
R Walsh	45-195	23	+22.86	Paul Nicholls	37-161
Paddy Brennan	29-248	12	+58.69	Nigel Twiston-Davies	23-200
Barry Geraghty	28-157	18	+22.62	Nicky Henderson	25-127
Richard Johnson	27-199	14	-19.13	Philip Hobbs	24-144
A P McCoy	23-235	10	-96.46	Jonjo O'Neill	9-79
Robert Thornton	19-178	11	-48.25	Alan King	17-151
Timmy Murphy	13-152	9	-71.82	David Pipe	7-66
Noel Fehily	12-102	12	+20.73	Charlie Mann	5-31
Joe Tizzard	10-67	15	+40.37	Colin Tizzard	10-62
Tom Scudamore	9-138	7	-73.00	David Pipe	7-100
Aidan Coleman	9-96	9	+1.75	Venetia Williams	9-69
D N Russell	7-63	11	+27.50	C Byrnes	2-4
Daryl Jacob	5-82	6	-42.50	Nick Williams	4-46
Rhys Flint	5-58	9	-11.50	Philip Hobbs	4-34
P Carberry	5-58	9	-11.13	Gordon Elliott	3-9

Favourites

Hurdle	30.6%	-19.42	Chase	27.8%	-33.21	TOTAL	28.6%	-60.37

*Stats are for both courses

Chepstow, Gwent, NP6 5YH
Tel: 01291 622 260

CHEPSTOW

How to get there Road: three miles west of Severn Bridge (M4). Rail: Chepstow

Features Left-handed, undulating oval, nearly 2m round, suits long-striding front-runners

2011 Fixtures October 8, 22, November 2, December 3, 27

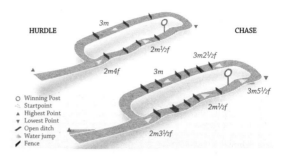

○ Winning Post
↖ Startpoint
▲ Highest Point
▼ Lowest Point
⟋ Open ditch
≋ Water jump
𝆑 Fence

Trainers	Wins-Runs	%	Hurdles	Chases	£1 level stks
Paul Nicholls	39-185	21	24-111	9-52	-35.17
Philip Hobbs	25-155	16	11-86	12-61	+20.02
Jonjo O'Neill	12-112	11	3-60	8-40	-38.25
Colin Tizzard	12-87	14	4-21	6-52	-19.63
David Pipe	12-79	15	9-52	2-25	-3.78
Victor Dartnall	11-58	19	2-22	6-26	+0.83
Nigel Twiston-Davies	10-125	8	6-64	4-49	-47.38
Alan King	10-114	9	8-77	1-21	-81.36
Venetia Williams	10-67	15	3-34	7-29	-19.51
Evan Williams	9-118	8	8-78	1-33	-37.00
Tim Vaughan	7-79	9	1-44	4-24	-19.40
Bernard Llewellyn	7-51	14	5-38	2-11	+59.00
C Roberts	7-47	15	1-23	6-15	+16.75
Peter Bowen	6-59	10	3-33	1-17	-13.70
Tom George	6-44	14	6-27	0-12	-9.88

Jockeys	Wins-Rides	%	£1 level stks	Best Trainer	W-R
Richard Johnson	24-145	17	+14.62	Philip Hobbs	14-86
R Walsh	24-72	33	+11.96	Paul Nicholls	24-72
Sam Thomas	16-86	19	-8.29	Paul Nicholls	9-38
Tom O'Brien	15-79	19	+55.25	Philip Hobbs	9-33
Paddy Brennan	11-91	12	-7.63	Nigel Twiston-Davies	7-62
A P McCoy	11-52	21	+3.08	Jonjo O'Neill	3-21
Rhys Flint	10-61	16	-8.63	Keith Goldsworthy	3-8
Joe Tizzard	9-100	9	-55.63	Colin Tizzard	8-66
Aidan Coleman	9-63	14	-11.75	Venetia Williams	5-28
Jack Doyle	9-32	28	+25.12	Emma Lavelle	4-12
Timmy Murphy	8-37	22	+14.71	Emma Lavelle	2-6
Noel Fehily	7-49	14	+6.50	Jonjo O'Neill	2-11
Daryl Jacob	6-76	8	-26.30	Nick Williams	5-20
Sean Quinlan	6-47	13	-18.58	David Rees	3-7
Michael Murphy	6-44	14	-4.75	C Roberts	4-7

Favourites

Hurdle	32.6%	-22.85	Chase 32.9% -9.58	TOTAL	33.1% -35.62

DONCASTER

Grand Street, Leger Way, Doncaster
DN2 6BB. Tel: 01302 320 666/7

How to get there Road: M18
Jctn 3, A638, A18 towards Hull.
Rail: Doncaster Central

Features Left-handed, flat, 2m
round, run-in of just over a
furlong, rarely heavy, favours
speed horses

2011 Fixtures November 25,
December 9-10, 29

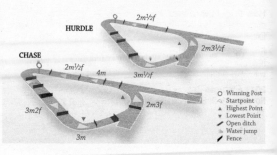

Trainers	Wins-Runs	%	Hurdles	Chases	£1 level stks
Alan King	18-100	18	12-63	4-27	-29.19
Nicky Henderson	10-55	18	6-33	2-14	-8.00
Paul Nicholls	9-39	23	4-16	5-22	-5.33
Howard Johnson	8-58	14	6-28	2-27	-3.15
Henry Daly	7-44	16	3-18	3-22	-0.32
Keith Reveley	6-63	10	3-28	3-25	-33.54
Sue Smith	5-71	7	2-27	3-40	-30.50
Ferdy Murphy	5-65	8	1-25	4-38	-29.75
Donald McCain	5-45	11	2-29	3-15	-4.04
Tony Carroll	5-14	36	5-13	0-1	+43.50
Malcolm Jefferson	4-53	8	2-32	1-16	-22.00
John Quinn	4-38	11	2-23	2-11	-5.00
Paul Webber	4-28	14	2-16	2-6	-1.13
David Pipe	4-20	20	2-8	2-9	+5.00
Nigel Twiston-Davies	3-29	10	3-16	0-10	-6.00

Jockeys	Wins-Rides	%	£1 level stks	Best Trainer	W-R
Robert Thornton	12-46	26	+23.23	Alan King	10-39
Dougie Costello	9-66	14	+22.80	John Quinn	4-32
Wayne Hutchinson	8-51	16	-5.33	Alan King	6-41
Graham Lee	7-83	8	-30.64	Ferdy Murphy	4-38
James Reveley	6-63	10	-32.38	Keith Reveley	5-42
Andrew Tinkler	6-61	10	-27.29	Nicky Henderson	5-24
Denis O'Regan	6-52	12	+17.85	Howard Johnson	4-20
Richard Johnson	6-34	18	-13.72	Tim Vaughan	2-2
Phil Kinsella	5-51	10	-1.67	Malcolm Jefferson	3-18
A P McCoy	5-18	28	-4.65	Paul Webber	1-1
Mark Bradburne	4-28	14	-8.82	Lucy Wadham	1-1
Dominic Elsworth	4-16	25	+2.25	Jeremy Scott	1-1
Christian Williams	4-14	29	+7.50	Paul Nicholls	3-5
Brian Hughes	3-63	5	-47.38	Howard Johnson	2-9
Keith Mercer	3-46	7	-15.00	Tom Tate	2-7

Favourites

Hurdle	32.7%	-11.19	Chase	39.1%	+13.49	TOTAL	35.9%	+6.30

Kennford, nr Exeter, Devon
EX6 7XS. Tel: 01392 832 599

EXETER

How to get there Road: five
miles south of M5, A38. Rail:
Exeter Central or Exeter St Davids

Features Right-handed, 2m,
hilly, stiff half-mile home straight
with 300-yard run-in

2011 Fixtures October 6, 18,
November 1, 9, 20, December 2,
15

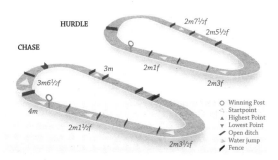

Trainers	Wins-Runs	%	Hurdles	Chases	£1 level stks
Philip Hobbs	39-190	21	17-103	18-71	-28.21
Paul Nicholls	37-113	33	17-59	20-48	+1.15
Victor Dartnall	19-93	20	10-52	9-35	-10.26
Alan King	15-94	16	6-54	5-28	-0.67
Jonjo O'Neill	14-103	14	8-56	5-42	+4.00
David Pipe	13-152	9	8-106	5-40	-77.90
R H & Mrs S Alner	10-83	12	4-33	6-50	-16.52
Chris Down	9-110	8	8-77	1-24	+21.25
Nigel Twiston-Davies	9-62	15	5-27	4-32	+34.33
Jeremy Scott	9-47	19	8-39	0-5	-0.22
Emma Lavelle	9-47	19	6-32	3-13	+5.54
James Frost	8-137	6	6-100	2-31	-67.00
Evan Williams	8-51	16	7-35	0-13	-1.61
Nick Williams	8-36	22	4-19	4-16	-1.78
Seamus Mullins	7-73	10	4-42	3-22	+5.75

Jockeys	Wins-Rides	%	£1 level stks	Best Trainer	W-R
Richard Johnson	31-151	21	-37.78	Philip Hobbs	24-111
A P McCoy	17-89	19	+2.19	Jonjo O'Neill	8-42
Daryl Jacob	15-118	13	+1.44	Nick Williams	6-23
Robert Thornton	15-70	21	+13.00	Alan King	9-50
R Walsh	14-32	44	+1.48	Paul Nicholls	14-32
Christian Williams	13-72	18	-18.95	Victor Dartnall	6-18
Sam Thomas	12-84	14	-24.01	Paul Nicholls	8-20
Tom O'Brien	11-98	11	-38.93	Philip Hobbs	8-42
Nick Scholfield	10-65	15	-3.72	Jeremy Scott	6-17
Tom Scudamore	9-107	8	-18.75	David Pipe	6-75
Paddy Brennan	9-80	11	-1.78	Nigel Twiston-Davies	3-33
Jack Doyle	9-54	17	+6.27	Victor Dartnall	3-17
Felix De Giles	8-34	24	+16.48	Tom George	2-3
Noel Fehily	7-53	13	+2.54	Paul Nicholls	3-6
Jason Maguire	7-40	18	+0.33	Donald McCain	3-12

Favourites

Hurdle	33.5%	-43.12		Chase	38.5%	-16.87		TOTAL	35.8%	-63.47

FAKENHAM

Fakenham, Norfolk, NR21 7NY
Tel: 01328 862 388

How to get there Road:
A1065 from Swaffham, A148
King's Lynn, A1067 from
Norwich. Rail: Kings Lynn,
Norwich

Features Left-handed, 1m
circuit, undulating, unsuitable for
long-striding horses

2011 Fixtures October 21,
November 15, December 12

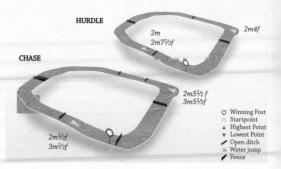

Trainers	Wins-Runs	%	Hurdles	Chases	£1 level stks
Nicky Henderson	14-35	40	5-16	6-12	+4.05
Evan Williams	11-34	32	8-23	3-11	+21.98
Tim Vaughan	9-36	25	5-21	4-12	-14.13
Paul Nicholls	9-18	50	1-5	8-13	+2.02
Jonjo O'Neill	8-35	23	5-24	3-11	-13.94
Lucy Wadham	8-32	25	1-13	7-16	+11.46
Milton Harris	7-62	11	6-35	1-26	-28.08
Neil King	6-93	6	3-59	3-25	-48.00
Jim Best	6-27	22	6-25	0-1	-5.87
Pam Sly	5-26	19	2-15	2-8	+3.33
Michael Quinlan	5-13	38	5-12	0-1	+12.00
Richard Guest	4-31	13	1-10	3-21	-9.75
Caroline Bailey	4-23	17	2-16	2-7	-4.25
Alex Hales	4-16	25	3-13	1-2	+2.25
Renee Robeson	4-15	27	0-4	4-5	+9.13

Jockeys	Wins-Rides	%	£1 level stks	Best Trainer	W-R
A P McCoy	17-42	40	+2.32	Jonjo O'Neill	6-15
Richard Johnson	13-36	36	+12.20	Tim Vaughan	6-16
Sam Thomas	9-21	43	+8.27	Paul Nicholls	5-9
Barry Geraghty	7-12	58	+6.58	Nicky Henderson	7-12
Paul Moloney	6-34	18	+1.91	Evan Williams	5-15
Felix De Giles	6-22	27	+2.94	Nicky Henderson	4-6
Dominic Elsworth	5-24	21	-6.01	Lucy Wadham	4-9
Christian Williams	5-21	24	-0.81	Paul Nicholls	2-4
Dougie Costello	4-26	15	-10.13	Tim Pitt	1-1
Adam Pogson	4-25	16	-10.50	Caroline Bailey	2-6
Leighton Aspell	4-24	17	+13.00	Lucy Wadham	2-11
Peter Toole	4-23	17	+17.00	Charlie Mann	2-12
Mr J Owen	4-10	40	+7.99	J M Turner	3-6
Mattie Batchelor	4-9	44	+3.68	Mark Bradstock	2-4
David England	4-8	50	+18.33	Pam Sly	4-5

Favourites

Hurdle	44.2%	+5.49		Chase	41.6%	-9.37		TOTAL	43.9%	+1.11

Trimsaran, Carmarthenshire
SA17 4DE. Tel: 01554 811 092

FFOS LAS

How to get there Road: M4
Jctn 48, follow A4138 to Llanelli.
Rail: Llanelli, Kidwelly, Carmarthen

Features Left-handed, flat,
galloping

2011 Fixtures October 9,
November 6, 21, 28, December
21, 26

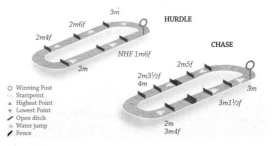

Trainers	Wins-Runs	%	Hurdles	Chases	£1 level stks
Evan Williams	21-170	12	7-82	14-76	-52.17
Rebecca Curtis	13-59	22	7-38	2-13	-20.31
Nicky Henderson	13-35	37	7-19	4-10	+12.05
Tim Vaughan	12-106	11	4-59	4-28	-51.09
Jonjo O'Neill	12-75	16	5-32	7-36	-24.46
Peter Bowen	11-95	12	6-53	3-26	-31.50
Philip Hobbs	11-53	21	6-29	3-20	-6.63
Keith Goldsworthy	10-74	14	3-38	3-17	+37.75
Nigel Twiston-Davies	9-57	16	4-23	5-26	-8.18
David Pipe	5-35	14	4-21	1-12	+1.41
Alan King	3-32	9	0-14	2-10	-7.13
Charlie Mann	3-15	20	2-10	1-4	+29.75
Paul Nicholls	3-15	20	2-9	1-3	-7.25
Gordon Elliott	3-14	21	2-8	1-5	+1.00
Richard Lee	3-11	27	0-5	2-5	+5.25

Jockeys	Wins-Rides	%	£1 level stks	Best Trainer	W-R
A P McCoy	29-91	32	-5.21	Jonjo O'Neill	9-36
Richard Johnson	21-99	21	-5.09	Philip Hobbs	10-35
Paul Moloney	13-91	14	-26.17	Evan Williams	11-77
Tom O'Brien	11-62	18	+5.00	Peter Bowen	6-32
Paddy Brennan	9-45	20	-3.43	Nigel Twiston-Davies	6-25
Barry Geraghty	9-23	39	-1.34	Nicky Henderson	7-12
Tom Scudamore	8-53	15	+10.91	David Pipe	4-27
Jason Maguire	6-43	14	-9.26	Peter Bowen	1-1
Sam Twiston-Davies	5-29	17	+8.25	Nigel Twiston-Davies	3-25
Aodhagan Conlon	5-28	18	+1.88	Rebecca Curtis	2-14
Timmy Murphy	5-14	36	+3.88	Alan Fleming	2-2
Jimmy McCarthy	4-22	18	+30.00	Michael Blanshard	2-6
Johnny Farrelly	4-21	19	+18.25	Richard Lee	2-3
Peter Toole	4-14	29	+69.00	Heather Main	1-1
Wayne Hutchinson	3-22	14	+4.50	Ian Williams	1-1

Favourites

Hurdle	38.9%	-11.15		Chase	39.3%	+0.38		TOTAL	40.1%	-4.79

FOLKESTONE

Westenhanger, Hythe, Kent
Tel: 01303 266 407

How to get there Road: M20
Jctn 11, A20 Westenhanger. Rail:
Westenhanger

Features Right-handed, 1m3f
circuit, easy turns, undulating

2011 Fixtures November 15,
28, December 13

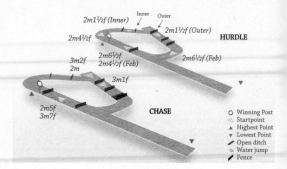

Trainers	Wins-Runs	%	Hurdles	Chases	£1 level stks
Gary Moore	12-63	19	8-39	4-23	-4.89
Alan King	10-34	29	5-22	4-9	+59.34
Oliver Sherwood	8-32	25	4-19	2-9	+16.50
Nick Gifford	7-34	21	1-18	6-14	+18.05
Richard Rowe	6-49	12	4-23	2-23	-22.38
Jim Best	6-33	18	4-24	2-7	-10.65
Warren Greatrex	6-13	46	4-8	1-2	+9.30
Venetia Williams	5-43	12	3-21	2-17	-16.75
Jonjo O'Neill	5-43	12	1-24	4-17	-12.90
Carl Llewellyn	5-26	19	3-17	1-6	+11.88
Emma Lavelle	5-25	20	2-14	1-6	+5.25
Nicky Henderson	5-14	36	2-4	3-9	-2.33
Peter Bowen	5-11	45	2-5	3-6	+12.94
Anna Newton-Smith	4-38	11	0-15	4-16	-18.50
Charlie Mann	4-26	15	2-13	2-12	-6.72

Jockeys	Wins-Rides	%	£1 level stks	Best Trainer	W-R
Jamie Moore	12-60	20	+8.28	Gary Moore	9-36
Noel Fehily	9-35	26	+35.90	Charlie Mann	3-16
Richard Johnson	9-34	26	+24.75	Tim Vaughan	3-4
Robert Thornton	9-32	28	-3.83	Alan King	8-26
Paddy Brennan	7-34	21	-8.83	Warren Greatrex	2-2
Dominic Elsworth	7-30	23	+2.63	Oliver Sherwood	4-10
Aidan Coleman	6-34	18	-8.00	Venetia Williams	4-17
Tom O'Brien	6-28	21	-4.74	Peter Bowen	3-4
A P McCoy	6-25	24	-4.65	Jonjo O'Neill	2-11
Tom Scudamore	5-41	12	-19.63	David Pipe	2-16
Sam Thomas	5-36	14	-15.51	Emma Lavelle	2-5
Leighton Aspell	5-33	15	+5.50	Oliver Sherwood	3-14
Daryl Jacob	5-29	17	-11.15	Alison Batchelor	1-1
Mr P York	5-28	18	-15.69	P York	4-9
Felix De Giles	4-23	17	+2.75	Anna Newton-Smith	3-9

Favourites

Hurdle	40%	-8.80	Chase	45.5%	+7.64	TOTAL	42.9%	-3.97

Fontwell Park, nr Arundel, W Sussex
BN18 0SX. Tel: 01243 543 335

FONTWELL

How to get there Road: A29
to Bognor Regis. Rail: Barnham

Features Left-handed, 1m4f
circuit, quite sharp

2011 Fixtures October 1, 19,
27, November 4, 13, 23,
December 6, 26

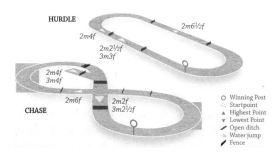

HURDLE
2m4f
2m2½f
3m3f
2m6½f

2m4f
3m4f

2m6f
CHASE
2m2f
3m2½f

○ Winning Post
◦ Startpoint
▲ Highest Point
▼ Lowest Point
╱ Open ditch
◣ Water jump
╱ Fence

Trainers	Wins-Runs	%	Hurdles	Chases	£1 level stks
Gary Moore	53-243	22	35-148	16-78	-22.80
Paul Nicholls	28-84	33	9-34	14-34	-7.72
Alan King	22-83	27	15-60	6-16	+7.00
Brendan Powell	20-224	9	10-130	9-76	-85.57
Nick Gifford	20-106	19	3-51	11-40	+7.66
Jonjo O'Neill	19-86	22	11-44	7-40	+21.03
David Pipe	18-92	20	11-61	5-26	-14.40
Chris Gordon	15-160	9	11-107	3-43	+53.00
Evan Williams	15-110	14	8-68	7-38	-44.81
Tim Vaughan	15-77	19	8-42	6-25	-22.90
Charlie Mann	12-65	18	6-36	5-25	-7.71
Oliver Sherwood	11-55	20	8-39	2-9	+48.92
Alison Thorpe	9-66	14	4-50	5-15	-19.13
Colin Tizzard	9-55	16	3-16	3-26	+19.38
Venetia Williams	9-46	20	7-25	2-17	-8.43

Jockeys	Wins-Rides	%	£1 level stks	Best Trainer	W-R
Jamie Moore	42-214	20	-32.29	Gary Moore	37-147
A P McCoy	33-126	26	-15.71	Jonjo O'Neill	11-41
Richard Johnson	22-100	22	-15.79	Tim Vaughan	9-31
Robert Thornton	21-109	19	-25.17	Alan King	16-54
Leighton Aspell	16-116	14	+29.83	Oliver Sherwood	6-18
Daryl Jacob	14-116	12	+40.33	Nick Williams	3-8
Tom Scudamore	13-84	15	-25.25	David Pipe	10-44
Paul Moloney	13-74	18	-14.15	Evan Williams	7-37
Aidan Coleman	12-84	14	-18.10	Venetia Williams	7-30
Noel Fehily	12-77	16	-2.83	Charlie Mann	7-36
Tom O'Brien	12-69	17	+22.60	Philip Hobbs	3-11
Christian Williams	11-80	14	-13.64	Paul Nicholls	3-7
Timmy Murphy	11-66	17	-13.08	Nick Gifford	2-6
Jack Doyle	11-44	25	+28.67	Emma Lavelle	7-21
Sam Jones	10-88	11	-15.50	Brendan Powell	6-40

Favourites

Hurdle	29.5%	-87.08	Chase	47%	+50.70	TOTAL	37.8%	-27.11

HAYDOCK

Newton-Le-Willows, Lancashire
WA12 0HQ. Tel: 01942 725 963

How to get there Road: M6
Jctn 23 on A49 to Wigan. Rail:
Wigan or Warrington Bank Quay
(main line)

Features Flat, left handed, 1m5f
circuit, quarter-mile run-in, chase
track much sharper (like hurdles
track) since introduction of
portable fences

2011 Fixtures October 26,
November 18-19, December 17,
30

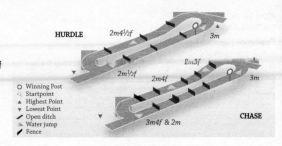

Trainers	Wins-Runs	%	Hurdles	Chases	£1 level stks
Donald McCain	23-100	23	14-58	7-30	+11.04
Sue Smith	10-98	10	1-42	8-49	-29.89
Philip Hobbs	9-53	17	8-35	0-15	-10.00
Paul Nicholls	8-36	22	3-16	5-20	+0.13
Nigel Twiston-Davies	6-56	11	3-22	3-28	-14.98
Alan King	6-45	13	2-23	3-18	-19.65
David Pipe	6-44	14	3-29	2-13	-3.97
Malcolm Jefferson	6-35	17	3-21	3-12	+4.50
Venetia Williams	5-46	11	3-18	2-27	-27.38
Nick Williams	5-15	33	2-7	3-7	+10.83
Jonjo O'Neill	4-50	8	1-20	2-27	+5.33
Keith Reveley	4-48	8	2-23	1-18	-13.42
Ferdy Murphy	4-45	9	2-17	1-21	-18.67
Nicky Henderson	4-44	9	2-34	0-4	-22.12
Lucinda Russell	4-29	14	0-13	4-14	+4.00

Jockeys	Wins-Rides	%	£1 level stks	Best Trainer	W-R
Jason Maguire	18-64	28	+19.19	Donald McCain	17-51
Graham Lee	9-84	11	-32.97	Ferdy Murphy	4-36
Brian Hughes	9-33	27	+62.00	Alan Swinbank	3-7
Paddy Brennan	7-47	15	-13.39	Nigel Twiston-Davies	4-29
Richie McGrath	6-44	14	-1.59	Tim Easterby	2-9
Tom Scudamore	6-41	15	-14.97	David Pipe	3-23
Sam Thomas	6-39	15	-11.70	Paul Nicholls	4-18
Robert Thornton	5-28	18	-6.50	Alan King	4-17
Richard Johnson	5-27	19	+2.38	Philip Hobbs	3-17
Timmy Murphy	5-21	24	+5.00	David Arbuthnot	1-1
Tom O'Brien	4-36	11	-5.25	Philip Hobbs	3-21
Barry Geraghty	4-14	29	-1.30	David Arbuthnot	1-1
Tjade Collier	3-46	7	-22.50	Sue Smith	3-46
A P McCoy	3-44	7	-39.29	Donald McCain	1-2
James Reveley	3-36	8	-3.67	Keith Reveley	3-30

Favourites

Hurdle	39.8%	+5.25	Chase	26.3%	-19.17	TOTAL 33.7% -16.56

Roman Road, Holmer, Hereford
HR4 9QU. Tel: 01981 250 436

HEREFORD

How to get there Road: A49
north of Hereford. Rail: Hereford

Features Right-handed, 1m4f
circuit, fences trickier than those
at most minor tracks

2011 Fixtures November 7, 17,
30, December 11, 22

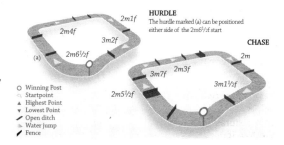

Trainers	Wins-Runs	%	Hurdles	Chases	£1 level stks
Evan Williams	19-145	13	7-86	12-52	+24.13
Venetia Williams	14-80	18	8-50	5-26	-14.88
Jonjo O'Neill	13-102	13	8-60	5-33	-27.38
Philip Hobbs	11-44	25	4-25	5-12	-3.97
Rebecca Curtis	11-35	31	4-21	2-7	+11.80
Nicky Henderson	11-33	33	7-25	1-2	-1.25
Alan King	10-73	14	5-49	3-14	-36.94
Richard Lee	10-55	18	3-21	7-31	+25.96
Paul Nicholls	8-42	19	3-22	3-13	-18.95
Henry Daly	8-38	21	1-15	6-16	-9.84
Peter Bowen	8-36	22	0-16	3-12	+31.18
Nigel Twiston-Davies	7-70	10	5-36	2-20	-18.09
Donald McCain	7-52	13	7-41	0-8	-24.06
Charlie Longsdon	6-30	20	4-17	2-10	+48.63
Jim Best	6-12	50	6-12	0-0	+13.10

Jockeys	Wins-Rides	%	£1 level stks	Best Trainer	W-R
A P McCoy	30-100	30	+2.08	Jonjo O'Neill	10-49
Richard Johnson	20-100	20	-18.73	Philip Hobbs	8-20
Aidan Coleman	13-77	17	-3.88	Venetia Williams	8-43
Robert Thornton	10-65	15	-3.54	Alan King	6-42
Paul Moloney	9-83	11	-52.12	Evan Williams	8-55
Paddy Brennan	8-66	12	-22.11	Tom George	3-20
Jason Maguire	8-65	12	-31.88	Donald McCain	4-30
Jamie Moore	8-33	24	+17.99	Gary Moore	4-6
Sam Thomas	7-56	13	-12.50	Venetia Williams	3-15
Warren Marston	6-54	11	-1.00	Martin Keighley	4-24
Tom O'Brien	6-52	12	-25.82	Peter Bowen	4-11
Harry Skelton	6-42	14	-17.97	Evan Williams	2-2
Charlie Poste	5-85	6	-48.38	Richard Lee	4-25
Tom Scudamore	5-71	7	-46.17	David Pipe	2-27
Christian Williams	5-52	10	-32.40	Bernard Llewellyn	1-1

Favourites

Hurdle	32.7%	-29.47	Chase	36.2%	-9.59	TOTAL	34.9%	-40.38

HEXHAM

High Yarridge, Hexham, Northumberland
NE46 2JP. Tel: 01434 606 881

How to get there Road: A69.
Rail: Hexham

Features Left-handed, 1m4f
circuit, very stiff, back straight
runs nearly all downhill before
steep uphill run from home turn

2011 Fixtures October 8,
November 4, 16, December 7

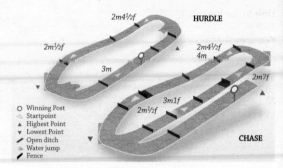

○ Winning Post
△ Startpoint
▲ Highest Point
▼ Lowest Point
✐ Open ditch
⚬ Water jump
✦ Fence

Trainers	Wins-Runs	%	Hurdles	Chases	£1 level stks
Howard Johnson	26-117	22	17-69	6-32	+2.11
Sue Smith	18-116	16	7-49	9-52	+5.38
Lucinda Russell	13-121	11	5-54	8-62	-52.13
Ferdy Murphy	13-81	16	8-38	4-39	-16.68
J J Lambe	13-54	24	10-40	2-12	+3.86
Donald McCain	12-74	16	7-51	4-15	-24.24
Malcolm Jefferson	10-70	14	6-36	4-21	-26.97
Martin Todhunter	8-93	9	2-52	6-38	-45.25
Maurice Barnes	7-65	11	7-51	0-8	+148.75
Micky Hammond	7-56	13	5-33	2-22	-25.17
Nicky Richards	7-53	13	5-37	2-14	-24.58
P Monteith	7-49	14	3-22	4-25	-5.70
Evelyn Slack	6-37	16	3-18	3-18	+18.75
James Ewart	6-29	21	2-12	4-14	+14.20
Alan Swinbank	6-28	21	4-16	1-3	-10.84

Jockeys	Wins-Rides	%	£1 level stks	Best Trainer	W-R
Graham Lee	26-143	18	-32.83	Ferdy Murphy	8-46
Denis O'Regan	21-99	21	-3.32	Howard Johnson	14-49
Richie McGrath	15-101	15	-1.50	Kate Walton	5-22
Brian Hughes	13-126	10	-69.47	Alan Swinbank	5-21
Peter Buchanan	11-118	9	-59.38	Lucinda Russell	6-72
Brian Harding	10-109	9	-55.44	Nicky Richards	3-17
Dougie Costello	9-71	13	-22.87	John Quinn	4-16
Campbell Gillies	8-78	10	+0.13	Lucinda Russell	5-29
Tjade Collier	8-59	14	+15.75	Sue Smith	6-45
Tom Messenger	8-50	16	+46.50	Micky Hammond	2-3
Michael McAlister	7-79	9	+134.75	Maurice Barnes	7-55
Fearghal Davis	7-78	9	-39.64	Evelyn Slack	3-11
Phil Kinsella	7-72	10	-24.15	Malcolm Jefferson	4-20
Harry Haynes	7-62	11	+4.80	James Ewart	5-18
Jason Maguire	7-43	16	-3.24	Donald McCain	7-36

Favourites

Hurdle	39.7%	-2.33		Chase	29.1%	-36.22		TOTAL	35.4%	-38.59

Brampton, Huntingdon, Cambs
PE18 8NN. Tel: 01480 453 373

HUNTINGDON

How to get there Road: Follow signs off A14. Rail: Huntingdon

Features Right-handed, flat track, short run-in of around 200 yards

2011 Fixtures October 2, 11, 30, November 8, 19, December 8, 26

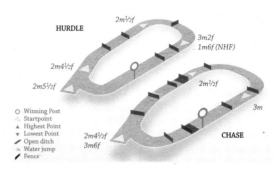

Trainers	Wins-Runs	%	Hurdles	Chases	£1 level stks
Nicky Henderson	34-94	36	20-54	7-22	-1.73
Alan King	29-161	18	15-99	6-36	-46.67
Brendan Powell	16-95	17	9-44	7-40	+0.90
Philip Hobbs	14-60	23	5-34	8-23	+12.53
Neil King	13-130	10	7-87	5-33	-45.38
Jonjo O'Neill	13-124	10	7-78	5-40	-36.85
Charlie Mann	12-44	27	9-26	3-13	+4.95
Gary Moore	11-104	11	4-57	7-44	-30.04
Nigel Twiston-Davies	10-81	12	5-34	4-39	-27.10
Henry Daly	10-66	15	5-25	5-37	-25.89
Charlie Longsdon	10-54	19	6-30	4-22	-0.04
Don Cantillon	9-27	33	1-16	7-7	+35.35
Pam Sly	8-53	15	5-29	3-20	+4.00
Henrietta Knight	8-52	15	2-22	5-24	-16.38
Emma Lavelle	8-48	17	2-19	5-26	-3.00

Jockeys	Wins-Rides	%	£1 level stks	Best Trainer	W-R
A P McCoy	27-124	22	+1.34	Jonjo O'Neill	10-68
Richard Johnson	24-119	20	-6.61	Philip Hobbs	9-35
Robert Thornton	21-114	18	-32.28	Alan King	16-88
Noel Fehily	14-60	23	+20.57	Charlie Mann	9-28
Wayne Hutchinson	12-63	19	-9.07	Alan King	8-33
Jamie Moore	11-118	9	-55.41	Gary Moore	7-70
Barry Geraghty	11-27	41	-2.17	Nicky Henderson	11-25
Paul Moloney	10-75	13	-3.29	Henrietta Knight	2-6
Dominic Elsworth	10-62	16	-20.20	Lucy Wadham	3-14
Richard Killoran	10-33	30	+25.10	Nicky Henderson	4-7
Alex Merriam	9-107	8	-58.25	Neil King	9-76
Warren Marston	8-58	14	+0.88	Henrietta Knight	2-2
Felix De Giles	8-37	22	+2.35	Nicky Henderson	3-9
Sam Jones	7-79	9	-47.54	Brendan Powell	2-15
Paddy Brennan	7-68	10	-29.64	Nigel Twiston-Davies	6-43

Favourites

Hurdle 37.5% -10.29   Chase 36.8% -16.64   TOTAL 38.3% -17.04

KELSO

Kelso, Roxburghshire.
Tel: 01668 281 611

How to get there Road: 1m
north of Kelso on B6461 to
Ednam. Rail: Berwick on Tweed

Features Tight, left-handed,
1m3f circuit

2011 Fixtures October 2, 15,
November 5, December 4, 29

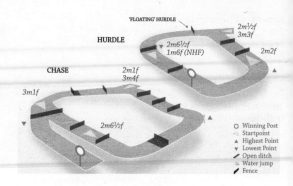

O Winning Post
Startpoint
▲ Highest Point
▼ Lowest Point
Open ditch
Water jump
Fence

Trainers	Wins-Runs	%	Hurdles	Chases	£1 level stks
Howard Johnson	23-135	17	13-86	7-35	-2.00
Nicky Richards	20-127	16	7-77	11-40	-43.91
P Monteith	17-150	11	7-87	9-59	-41.86
Lucinda Russell	17-143	12	13-76	4-56	+14.88
James Ewart	13-77	17	8-45	4-25	+13.82
Ferdy Murphy	11-82	13	7-38	4-44	-34.27
George Charlton	10-84	12	6-54	2-17	-26.73
Donald McCain	10-73	14	6-37	4-30	-22.88
Alan Swinbank	10-39	26	8-25	1-3	+11.79
Jim Goldie	8-55	15	7-37	1-17	+8.23
Malcolm Jefferson	7-45	16	2-20	2-16	-3.95
Sue Bradburne	6-57	11	0-33	6-24	-16.25
Keith Reveley	6-52	12	3-16	3-27	-7.25
Maurice Barnes	5-63	8	4-54	1-7	-16.90
James Moffatt	5-52	10	3-43	1-3	+0.75

Jockeys	Wins-Rides	%	£1 level stks	Best Trainer	W-R
Graham Lee	26-174	15	-23.71	Ferdy Murphy	8-58
Richie McGrath	19-147	13	-9.02	Pauline Robson	5-11
Denis O'Regan	19-117	16	-32.33	Howard Johnson	15-69
Ryan Mania	17-128	13	-14.54	P Monteith	5-42
Peter Buchanan	13-155	8	-43.88	Lucinda Russell	12-103
Brian Hughes	13-139	9	-26.42	Alan Swinbank	6-24
Wilson Renwick	12-135	9	-31.25	P Monteith	5-53
Harry Haynes	12-71	17	+16.39	James Ewart	6-36
Barry Keniry	10-85	12	-14.04	George Moore	4-26
Phil Kinsella	9-77	12	-11.45	Malcolm Jefferson	5-20
Paddy Aspell	8-131	6	-69.38	Ann Hamilton	2-14
Brian Harding	8-130	6	-60.57	Nicky Richards	4-27
Campbell Gillies	8-71	11	+8.75	William Amos	3-8
Jason Maguire	8-44	18	-5.25	Donald McCain	8-36
Jan Faltejsek	7-62	11	-21.98	George Charlton	7-49

Favourites

Hurdle	33.3%	-24.59		Chase	44.8%	+25.78		TOTAL	36.7%	-17.05

Staines Rd East, Sunbury-on-Thames
TW16 5AQ. Tel: 01932 782 292

KEMPTON

How to get there Road: M3
Jctn 1, A308 towards
Kingston-on-Thames. Rail:
Kempton Park from Waterloo

Features A sharp right-handed
track with the emphasis very
much on speed

2011 Fixtures October 16, 31,
November 21, December 26-27

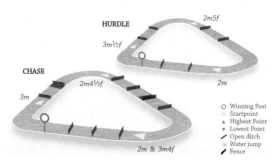

Trainers	Wins-Runs	%	Hurdles	Chases	£1 level stks
Nicky Henderson	51-179	28	23-100	21-61	+0.42
Paul Nicholls	27-120	23	11-55	15-56	-17.47
Alan King	26-146	18	17-87	7-45	+7.56
Philip Hobbs	21-120	18	11-63	8-47	+0.30
Gary Moore	11-128	9	2-79	8-46	-40.94
Andy Turnell	8-44	18	5-25	3-16	+23.83
Nigel Twiston-Davies	7-64	11	2-27	4-36	-21.88
Emma Lavelle	7-50	14	4-28	2-14	-5.84
David Pipe	6-51	12	3-27	3-24	-20.25
R H & Mrs S Alner	6-41	15	1-6	4-27	+9.50
Venetia Williams	5-57	9	2-29	3-28	-26.75
Paul Webber	5-48	10	2-30	3-12	-17.50
David Arbuthnot	5-16	31	4-11	0-3	+19.96
Jonjo O'Neill	4-68	6	2-38	2-26	-48.50
Nick Gifford	4-51	8	2-29	2-19	-24.00

Jockeys	Wins-Rides	%	£1 level stks	Best Trainer	W-R
Barry Geraghty	27-82	33	-7.71	Nicky Henderson	27-80
R Walsh	20-60	33	+11.83	Paul Nicholls	20-56
Richard Johnson	15-105	14	-9.95	Philip Hobbs	13-65
A P McCoy	14-100	14	-44.40	Nicky Henderson	4-16
Robert Thornton	14-100	14	-50.14	Alan King	14-83
Mick Fitzgerald	12-33	36	+18.90	Nicky Henderson	11-26
Paddy Brennan	11-87	13	-16.38	Nigel Twiston-Davies	6-47
Jamie Moore	11-79	14	+16.33	Gary Moore	8-53
Wayne Hutchinson	8-45	18	+80.50	Alan King	5-21
Noel Fehily	7-67	10	-25.34	Emma Lavelle	3-5
Daryl Jacob	7-43	16	-1.54	David Arbuthnot	3-5
Timmy Murphy	6-58	10	-28.95	Alan Fleming	2-11
Jack Doyle	6-50	12	-3.55	Emma Lavelle	3-31
Nick Scholfield	6-40	15	-6.50	Paul Nicholls	3-10
Rhys Flint	6-34	18	+5.88	Philip Hobbs	3-10

Favourites

Hurdle	37.4%	-14.22	Chase	38.9%	-8.49	TOTAL	38.8%	-18.51

LEICESTER

Leicester, LE2 4AL
Tel: 0116 271 6515

How to get there Road: M1
Jctn 21, 2m south of city centre
on A6. Rail: Leicester

Features Right-handed, 1m6f
circuit, stiff uphill run-in

2011 Fixtures November 14,
27, December 1, 7, 28

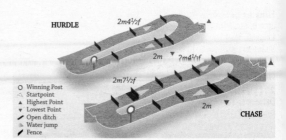

HURDLE · 2m4½f · 2m · 2m4½f · 2m7½f · 2m · CHASE

O Winning Post
◔ Startpoint
▲ Highest Point
▼ Lowest Point
✎ Open ditch
⚓ Water jump
✔ Fence

Trainers	Wins-Runs	%	Hurdles	Chases	£1 level stks
Nicky Henderson	9-19	47	2-5	7-14	+11.39
Caroline Bailey	8-48	17	2-17	6-31	+11.25
Jonjo O'Neill	8-47	17	1-16	7-31	-4.64
Alan King	6-40	15	4-28	2-12	-16.72
Venetia Williams	6-31	19	3-17	3-14	-10.14
Evan Williams	5-31	16	3-18	2-13	-13.78
Donald McCain	5-29	17	4-19	1-10	+10.35
Richard Lee	5-25	20	1-7	4-18	+15.83
Brendan Powell	5-23	22	1-6	4-17	+40.49
Nigel Twiston-Davies	4-32	13	1-12	3-20	-3.22
Paul Webber	4-27	15	1-10	3-17	-0.83
Philip Hobbs	4-26	15	2-9	2-17	-0.39
Tom George	4-21	19	2-5	2-16	+12.25
Neil King	4-20	20	4-15	0-5	+6.00
David Pipe	4-16	25	1-6	3-10	-0.13

Jockeys	Wins-Rides	%	£1 level stks	Best Trainer	W-R
A P McCoy	12-40	30	+6.40	Jonjo O'Neill	5-20
Andrew Thornton	7-54	13	-3.25	Caroline Bailey	6-25
Richard Johnson	7-45	16	-10.83	Richard Lee	3-6
Dominic Elsworth	7-39	18	+3.67	Paul Webber	3-11
Wayne Hutchinson	7-30	23	+23.24	Tony Carroll	3-12
Robert Thornton	7-26	27	+5.92	Alan King	4-20
Andrew Tinkler	6-35	17	-3.86	Nicky Henderson	3-6
Paddy Brennan	6-27	22	+0.03	Tom George	2-5
Graham Lee	6-23	26	+5.21	Ferdy Murphy	3-11
Noel Fehily	5-39	13	-12.19	Charlie Mann	2-9
Aidan Coleman	5-37	14	-18.64	Venetia Williams	3-16
Charlie Poste	5-36	14	-0.75	Robin Dickin	2-9
Paul Moloney	4-27	15	-8.87	David Evans	1-1
Jamie Moore	4-23	17	-2.67	Gary Moore	2-12
Tom O'Brien	4-22	18	+0.30	Caroline Keevil	2-2

Favourites

Hurdle	42.4%	+4.31	Chase	40%	+8.47	TOTAL	41%	+12.78

Lingfield, Surrey, RH7 6PQ
Tel: 01342 834 800

LINGFIELD

How to get there Road: M25
Jctn 6, south on A22. Rail:
Lingfield from London Bridge and
Victoria

Features Left-handed, 1m4f
circuit, hilly

2011 Fixtures November 8, 22,
December 10

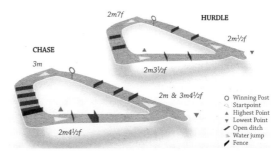

Trainers	Wins-Runs	%	Hurdles	Chases	£1 level stks
Gary Moore	9-68	13	6-33	3-35	+6.25
Jonjo O'Neill	6-36	17	4-18	2-18	-12.96
Alan King	6-28	21	5-21	1-7	+6.03
Charlie Mann	6-15	40	3-6	3-9	+8.20
Nick Gifford	5-21	24	2-13	3-8	+16.75
Tom George	5-16	31	1-4	4-12	-2.51
Nigel Twiston-Davies	4-20	20	2-11	2-9	-13.11
Richard Phillips	3-19	16	2-11	1-8	-3.00
Philip Hobbs	3-10	30	1-5	2-5	-4.00
Nicky Henderson	3-9	33	1-7	2-2	-4.00
Paul Webber	3-7	43	3-5	0-2	+17.00
Venetia Williams	2-23	9	0-14	2-9	-16.25
Brendan Powell	2-23	9	1-17	1-5	-14.00
David Pipe	2-17	12	0-8	2-9	-6.97
Chris Gordon	2-16	13	0-9	2-7	+8.00

Jockeys	Wins-Rides	%	£1 level stks	Best Trainer	W-R
A P McCoy	9-30	30	-2.96	Jonjo O'Neill	5-18
Robert Thornton	7-24	29	+12.30	Alan King	3-16
Richard Johnson	6-23	26	+2.50	Tim Vaughan	2-2
Jamie Moore	5-59	8	-25.50	Gary Moore	5-40
Paddy Brennan	5-25	20	-15.78	Nigel Twiston-Davies	3-12
Noel Fehily	5-23	22	-8.80	Charlie Mann	5-7
Liam Treadwell	5-21	24	+5.25	Nick Gifford	4-13
Andrew Thornton	4-35	11	-14.75	Anna Newton-Smith	1-1
Dominic Elsworth	4-15	27	+104.00	Heather Main	1-1
Warren Marston	3-26	12	+0.00	Nick Gifford	1-1
Tom Scudamore	3-20	15	-1.75	Richard Lee	1-1
Paul Moloney	3-19	16	+1.75	Evan Williams	2-7
Daryl Jacob	3-18	17	+11.00	Charlie Mann	1-2
Mattie Batchelor	3-15	20	+36.50	Jamie Poulton	2-4
Joshua Moore	3-9	33	+5.75	Gary Moore	3-6

Favourites

Hurdle	43.8%	+0.75		Chase	35%	-7.99		TOTAL	39.2%	-8.23

LUDLOW

Bromfield, Ludlow, Shrewsbury, Shropshire. Tel: 01981 250 052

How to get there Road: 2m north of Ludlow on A49. Rail: Ludlow

Features Flat, right-handed, has sharp turns and a tooting run in of 450 yards

2011 Fixtures October 5, 20, November 10, 21, December 8, 21

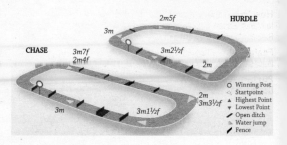

Trainers	Wins-Runs	%	Hurdles	Chases	£1 level stks
Evan Williams	35-233	15	19-122	14-91	-70.01
Nicky Henderson	31-83	37	19-50	4-13	+20.59
Jonjo O'Neill	19-76	25	7-28	12-46	+41.38
Philip Hobbs	13-74	18	4-40	9-31	-22.61
Venetia Williams	12-52	23	1-14	11-38	+21.03
Nigel Twiston-Davies	11-116	9	6-55	4-48	-39.13
Henry Daly	10-109	9	4-50	4-47	-52.44
Keith Goldsworthy	8-40	20	3-24	3-10	+94.92
David Pipe	7-53	13	7-36	0-13	-22.25
Richard Lee	7-50	14	1-13	6-37	+0.25
Charlie Mann	7-33	21	4-18	3-10	+6.50
Tim Vaughan	6-47	13	3-27	2-12	-21.75
David Evans	5-55	9	3-40	2-13	-29.94
Ann Price	5-54	9	0-9	5-45	+21.00
Henrietta Knight	5-53	9	1-20	1-17	-11.04

Jockeys	Wins-Rides	%	£1 level stks	Best Trainer	W-R
A P McCoy	30-101	30	-1.35	Nicky Henderson	8-19
Richard Johnson	24-140	17	-33.52	Philip Hobbs	8-46
Paul Moloney	22-140	16	-63.26	Evan Williams	22-119
Noel Fehily	12-60	20	+13.13	Charlie Mann	6-21
Barry Geraghty	11-27	41	+11.03	Nicky Henderson	8-22
Aidan Coleman	9-53	17	-16.80	Venetia Williams	7-25
Jamie Moore	9-41	22	+6.67	Gary Moore	3-17
Sam Thomas	8-54	15	+18.96	Henrietta Knight	4-15
Andrew Tinkler	7-69	10	-14.83	Nicky Henderson	3-12
Charlie Poste	7-59	12	+8.13	Robin Dickin	3-10
Felix De Giles	7-28	25	+2.61	Nicky Henderson	6-10
Paddy Brennan	6-86	7	-39.50	Nigel Twiston-Davies	5-61
Lee Stephens	6-82	7	-3.75	Ann Price	5-39
Tom O'Brien	6-68	9	-44.50	Philip Hobbs	2-15
Daryl Jacob	6-50	12	-19.22	Nick Williams	2-9

Favourites

Hurdle	38.6%	-12.41	Chase	41.7%	+18.96	TOTAL	39.6%	+1.28

Legsby Road, LN8 3EA
Tel: 01673 843 434

MARKET RASEN

How to get there Road: A46
to Market Rasen, course on A631.
Rail: Market Rasen (1m walk)

Features Right-handed, easy
fences, run-in of 250 yards

2011 Fixtures November 6, 17,
December 1, 26

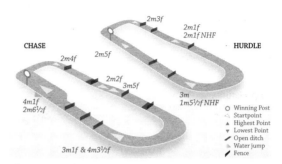

Trainers	Wins-Runs	%	Hurdles	Chases	£1 level stks
Jonjo O'Neill	32-168	19	8-85	23-76	-27.67
Malcolm Jefferson	20-120	17	13-66	3-31	+13.10
Steve Gollings	16-110	15	14-79	1-19	-17.92
Nigel Twiston-Davies	16-73	22	6-34	10-35	-0.63
Tim Vaughan	16-71	23	12-43	4-22	+3.97
Peter Bowen	15-100	15	4-43	9-48	+31.88
Sue Smith	13-144	9	6-61	7-70	-8.90
Alan King	13-82	16	7-51	4-19	-29.89
Alan Swinbank	13-43	30	8-18	1-5	+3.39
Evan Williams	10-70	14	8-42	2-27	-7.25
Donald McCain	10-61	16	2-28	6-26	-4.13
David Pipe	8-57	14	5-31	2-25	-19.85
John Quinn	8-47	17	5-33	3-11	+3.69
Charlie Mann	8-47	17	3-25	5-21	-8.08
Nicky Henderson	8-26	31	4-18	2-5	-8.28

Jockeys	Wins-Rides	%	£1 level stks	Best Trainer	W-R
A P McCoy	43-157	27	-4.33	Jonjo O'Neill	23-80
Richard Johnson	19-102	19	+13.43	Tim Vaughan	10-33
Brian Hughes	18-109	17	-27.27	Alan Swinbank	11-28
Paddy Brennan	16-63	25	+3.88	Nigel Twiston-Davies	12-39
Dougie Costello	13-133	10	-58.93	John Quinn	8-42
Keith Mercer	13-81	16	+17.36	Steve Gollings	6-31
Noel Fehily	12-50	24	+20.42	Charlie Mann	8-32
Graham Lee	10-123	8	-38.67	Malcolm Jefferson	3-12
James Halliday	9-67	13	+1.50	Malcolm Jefferson	8-43
Tom Messenger	8-94	9	-1.25	Chris Bealby	5-43
Denis O'Regan	8-82	10	-33.55	Howard Johnson	3-25
Rhys Flint	8-40	20	-8.47	Steve Gollings	4-22
Robert Thornton	7-74	9	-51.41	Alan King	5-50
Adam Pogson	7-69	10	-30.73	Charles Pogson	7-46
Tom Scudamore	7-68	10	-20.50	David Pipe	5-36

Favourites

Hurdle	33.1%	-50.98	Chase	34.9%	-1.60	TOTAL	34%	-54.39

MUSSELBURGH

East Lothian
Tel: 01316 652 859

How to get there Road: A1 out of Edinburgh. Rail: Musselburgh from Edinburgh

Features Right-handed, 1m2f circuit, very flat with sharp turns

2011 Fixtures November 3, 25, December 5, 20

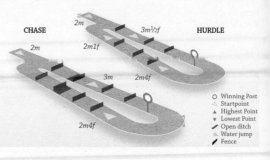

Trainers	Wins-Runs	%	Hurdles	Chases	£1 level stks
Howard Johnson	37-148	25	25-96	7-35	+19.83
Ferdy Murphy	14-95	15	6-55	8-36	-12.49
Lucinda Russell	11-69	16	4-33	7-29	-13.12
Jim Goldie	9-75	12	6-53	1-16	+10.92
Nicky Richards	6-56	11	3-34	1-16	+5.67
Keith Reveley	6-42	14	2-20	4-14	-9.67
Gordon Elliott	6-20	30	3-13	1-4	+2.58
Richard Fahey	5-35	14	5-30	0-1	-18.45
P Monteith	4-42	10	2-27	2-14	-17.09
James Ewart	4-38	11	3-22	1-7	-19.83
Donald McCain	4-36	11	2-20	2-13	-26.09
Alan Swinbank	4-21	19	2-11	0-0	-8.15
Nicky Henderson	4-11	36	3-7	0-2	+0.48
Sue Bradburne	3-65	5	0-31	3-29	-40.00
John Wade	3-24	13	0-11	2-7	+4.90

Jockeys	Wins-Rides	%	£1 level stks	Best Trainer	W-R
Denis O'Regan	24-93	26	-2.37	Howard Johnson	22-75
Graham Lee	20-144	14	-49.33	Ferdy Murphy	12-72
Brian Hughes	15-114	13	-21.95	Howard Johnson	6-28
Richie McGrath	10-71	14	+21.33	Jim Goldie	5-23
Jason Maguire	10-51	20	-0.64	Gordon Elliott	6-15
James Reveley	9-74	12	-27.93	Keith Reveley	5-35
Peter Buchanan	7-87	8	-45.87	Lucinda Russell	6-51
Dougie Costello	7-61	11	+0.50	Geoffrey Harker	1-1
Campbell Gillies	7-40	18	-1.65	Lucinda Russell	5-14
Paddy Aspell	4-58	7	-18.50	Christopher Wilson	1-2
Fearghal Davis	3-51	6	-19.50	Evelyn Slack	2-10
Mark Bradburne	3-42	7	-19.63	Jim Goldie	1-1
Harry Haynes	3-39	8	+21.67	James Ewart	2-21
Keith Mercer	3-36	8	-26.75	Tom Tate	2-7
Ewan Whillans	3-26	12	-1.50	Alistair Whillans	2-9

Favourites

Hurdle	38.5%	-8.12	Chase	29.3%	-11.33

TOTAL 35.9% -18.94

Newbury, Berkshire, RG14 7NZ
Tel: 01635 400 15 or 414 85

NEWBURY

How to get there Road: Follow signs from M4 or A34. Rail: Newbury Racecourse

Features Flat, left-handed, 1m6f circuit, suits galloping sorts with stamina, tough fences

2011 Fixtures November 24-26, December 14, 31

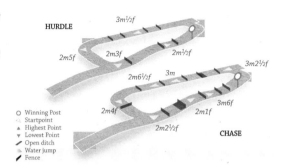

Trainers	Wins-Runs	%	Hurdles	Chases	£1 level stks
Nicky Henderson	51-221	23	27-127	15-68	-22.71
Paul Nicholls	48-188	26	20-91	25-82	+4.88
Philip Hobbs	23-153	15	17-89	5-57	-11.58
Alan King	18-185	10	11-107	4-53	-30.50
Tom George	11-58	19	4-29	7-27	+27.58
David Pipe	9-91	10	3-45	5-43	+29.92
Colin Tizzard	9-58	16	4-14	5-35	+23.25
Gary Moore	8-100	8	6-69	1-23	+40.00
Oliver Sherwood	8-35	23	4-21	4-12	+54.71
Nigel Twiston-Davies	7-115	6	2-48	5-58	-40.63
Jonjo O'Neill	6-87	7	4-44	2-38	-48.13
Nick Williams	6-26	23	3-12	2-13	-1.29
Venetia Williams	4-74	5	2-32	2-42	-52.84
Emma Lavelle	4-62	6	2-36	2-14	-22.50
Paul Webber	4-54	7	2-25	2-20	-28.00

Jockeys	Wins-Rides	%	£1 level stks	Best Trainer	W-R
A P McCoy	35-128	27	+20.98	Nicky Henderson	16-25
Barry Geraghty	26-105	25	-17.85	Nicky Henderson	24-95
Richard Johnson	23-135	17	+37.88	Philip Hobbs	17-85
R Walsh	22-70	31	+2.67	Paul Nicholls	22-67
Paddy Brennan	16-158	10	+2.63	Tom George	7-24
Sam Thomas	14-116	12	-62.64	Paul Nicholls	9-45
Dominic Elsworth	11-83	13	+12.33	Oliver Sherwood	4-18
Robert Thornton	9-120	8	-66.00	Alan King	8-107
Timmy Murphy	8-67	12	-24.67	Nick Williams	3-4
Jamie Moore	6-64	9	+51.00	Gary Moore	5-40
Wayne Hutchinson	6-41	15	+18.00	Alan King	5-29
Noel Fehily	5-69	7	-42.75	Charlie Mann	3-19
Aidan Coleman	5-54	9	-2.50	Venetia Williams	2-36
Nick Scholfield	5-52	10	-20.09	Paul Nicholls	4-17
Mick Fitzgerald	5-31	16	-9.63	Nicky Henderson	4-20

Favourites

Hurdle	35.7%	-18.13	Chase	38.5%	+3.52	TOTAL	36.6%	-24.20

NEWCASTLE

High Gosforth Park, Newcastle
NE3 5HP. Tel: 01912 362 020

How to get there Road: Follow signs from A1. Rail: 4m from Newcastle Central

Features Left-handed, 1m6f circuit, tough fences, half-mile straight is all uphill

2011 Fixtures November 11, 26, December 17

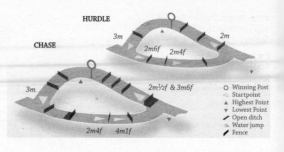

HURDLE	
CHASE	

O Winning Post
⤺ Startpoint
▲ Highest Point
▼ Lowest Point
◢ Open ditch
✤ Water jump
✦ Fence

Trainers	Wins-Runs	%	Hurdles	Chases	£1 level stks
Howard Johnson	17-123	14	7-75	9-36	-34.40
Nicky Richards	13-86	15	7-60	5-20	-3.52
Keith Reveley	13-83	16	5-53	6-18	-5.07
Sue Smith	11-108	10	4-47	4-48	-1.00
Lucinda Russell	10-94	11	2-44	8-45	-52.63
Chris Grant	9-58	16	5-38	4-13	-15.92
Malcolm Jefferson	9-48	19	5-26	4-13	+36.75
James Ewart	7-53	13	2-27	4-17	-14.62
Donald McCain	7-45	16	5-28	2-16	-20.95
George Charlton	5-39	13	5-25	0-5	+0.50
Donald Whillans	5-38	13	5-36	0-0	+13.00
Alistair Whillans	5-38	13	4-25	1-9	-16.25
Tim Easterby	5-32	16	3-16	1-13	-17.05
Jim Goldie	5-31	16	3-24	2-6	+4.50
Henry Hogarth	5-30	17	1-11	4-18	-10.50

Jockeys	Wins-Rides	%	£1 level stks	Best Trainer	W-R
James Reveley	13-101	13	-12.93	Keith Reveley	11-58
Richie McGrath	12-111	11	-41.97	Jim Goldie	3-13
Graham Lee	12-102	12	-47.38	Ann Hamilton	2-3
Dougie Costello	12-71	17	-4.13	Malcolm Jefferson	3-4
Brian Hughes	11-125	9	-59.37	John Wade	4-24
Brian Harding	10-103	10	-11.38	Alistair Whillans	3-9
Denis O'Regan	10-72	14	-12.30	Howard Johnson	7-50
Barry Keniry	8-57	14	-7.25	George Moore	3-18
Wilson Renwick	7-77	9	-29.93	Henry Hogarth	1-2
Ryan Mania	7-48	15	+55.25	Sandy Thomson	2-3
Peter Buchanan	6-114	5	-77.38	Lucinda Russell	5-68
Harry Haynes	6-62	10	-25.59	James Ewart	4-30
Garry Whillans	6-24	25	+52.50	Donald Whillans	4-15
Tony Dobbin	6-24	25	-1.07	Nicky Richards	4-13
Timmy Murphy	6-24	25	+27.50	Karen McLintock	1-1

Favourites

Hurdle	35.6%	-1.65	Chase	33.7%	-11.53	TOTAL	34%	-20.06

Devon, TQ12 3AF
Tel: 01626 532 35

NEWTON ABBOT

How to get there Road: On A380 from Newton Abbot to Torquay. Rail: Newton Abbot

Features Tight, left-handed, 1m1f circuit

2011 Fixtures None

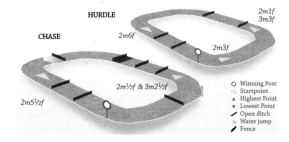

Trainers	Wins-Runs	%	Hurdles	Chases	£1 level stks
Paul Nicholls	40-119	34	13-51	20-55	+26.27
David Pipe	32-213	15	21-157	9-50	-24.63
Evan Williams	17-119	14	14-78	3-41	-37.10
Philip Hobbs	17-96	18	9-58	7-34	-21.58
Tim Vaughan	15-97	15	10-61	3-22	-40.45
Peter Bowen	14-103	14	8-53	3-37	-35.17
Alison Thorpe	14-66	21	11-52	3-13	+27.23
Jonjo O'Neill	11-90	12	6-49	5-40	-10.82
James Frost	10-143	7	10-117	0-17	-81.13
Nigel Twiston-Davies	10-30	33	6-15	4-12	+37.08
Tom George	9-41	22	3-17	6-22	-4.71
Colin Tizzard	8-84	10	2-41	6-39	-11.50
Liam Corcoran	8-59	14	7-45	1-7	-2.17
Nicky Henderson	7-25	28	7-20	0-1	-3.24
Seamus Mullins	6-55	11	4-36	2-17	+6.50

Jockeys	Wins-Rides	%	£1 level stks	Best Trainer	W-R
A P McCoy	39-167	23	-49.71	Jonjo O'Neill	8-49
Richard Johnson	30-175	17	-64.24	Tim Vaughan	11-54
Tom Scudamore	24-181	13	-42.46	David Pipe	22-131
Tom O'Brien	19-99	19	+42.67	Peter Bowen	5-35
Paddy Brennan	14-75	19	+11.17	Nigel Twiston-Davies	4-18
Paul Moloney	13-83	16	+1.43	Evan Williams	8-56
Aidan Coleman	11-67	16	+36.25	Susan Gardner	2-13
Nick Scholfield	10-83	12	-46.95	Paul Nicholls	7-18
Harry Skelton	10-74	14	-12.50	Paul Nicholls	6-27
Sam Thomas	10-58	17	-28.27	Paul Nicholls	6-14
Sam Twiston-Davies	10-21	48	+58.33	Nigel Twiston-Davies	6-9
Daryl Jacob	9-88	10	-21.13	David Arbuthnot	2-3
Seamus Durack	9-58	16	-16.13	Peter Bowen	4-12
Danny Cook	9-48	19	+45.83	David Pipe	7-15
Robert Thornton	8-64	13	-13.18	Alan King	3-24

Favourites

Hurdle 37.7% -18.37   Chase 41.1% +15.73   TOTAL 39.2% -4.52

PERTH

Scone Palace Park, Perth
PH2 6BB. Tel: 01683 220 131

How to get there Road: A93.
Rail: Free bus service from Perth

Features Flat, right-handed,
1m2f circuit

2011 Fixtures None

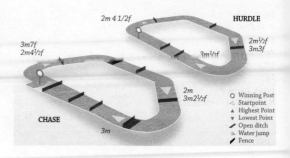

Trainers	Wins-Runs	%	Hurdles	Chases	£1 level stks
Gordon Elliott	52-179	29	31-104	16-65	+9.70
Nigel Twiston-Davies	32-106	30	15-50	12-50	+19.42
Lucinda Russell	16-173	9	9-93	6-74	-45.64
P Monteith	15-108	14	4-56	11-49	+4.92
Jim Goldie	14-82	17	12-60	2-21	-3.62
Nicky Richards	12-97	12	7-58	5-33	-32.26
I R Ferguson	9-41	22	6-20	1-14	+26.13
Ferdy Murphy	8-53	15	3-24	5-26	-3.88
A J Martin	7-40	18	5-26	1-13	+3.50
S R B Crawford	6-33	18	2-17	0-6	-6.50
Philip Hobbs	6-31	19	1-13	4-17	-7.32
Sue Smith	6-31	19	3-11	3-20	+19.75
Chris Grant	6-23	26	1-10	4-12	+32.60
Harriet Graham	5-44	11	1-20	4-18	-13.75
Alison Thorpe	5-21	24	4-14	1-6	+23.00

Jockeys	Wins-Rides	%	£1 level stks	Best Trainer	W-R
Graham Lee	26-155	17	+12.46	Ferdy Murphy	8-42
Paddy Brennan	24-92	26	+8.72	Nigel Twiston-Davies	21-76
Jason Maguire	24-84	29	+29.71	Gordon Elliott	19-64
Peter Buchanan	14-172	8	-59.25	Lucinda Russell	13-133
P Carberry	12-45	27	-6.87	Gordon Elliott	11-37
Campbell Gillies	10-80	13	-28.64	S R B Crawford	4-10
Timmy Murphy	10-62	16	-11.02	P Monteith	6-28
Richard Johnson	10-51	20	-14.60	Philip Hobbs	4-20
Brian Hughes	9-125	7	-70.79	Gordon Elliott	4-15
Richie McGrath	9-94	10	-41.90	Jim Goldie	4-31
Denis O'Regan	8-89	9	-30.25	I R Ferguson	3-10
Wilson Renwick	7-98	7	-21.50	P Monteith	4-27
K M Donoghue	7-24	29	-3.33	Gordon Elliott	6-16
A P McCoy	6-24	25	-4.22	Gordon Elliott	3-7
Sam Twiston-Davies	6-21	29	+3.83	Nigel Twiston-Davies	6-18

Favourites

Hurdle	37.3%	-10.96	Chase	28.4%	-35.35	TOTAL 34.5% -42.07

Plumpton, Sussex
Tel: 01273 890 383

PLUMPTON

How to get there Road: A274
or A275 to B2116. Rail: Plumpton

Features Quirky, undulating,
left-handed 1m1f circuit, uphill
straight, has several course
specialists

2011 Fixtures October 17, 31,
November 14, December 5, 19

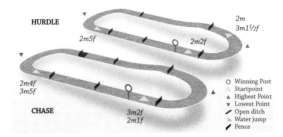

Trainers	Wins-Runs	%	Hurdles	Chases	£1 level stks
Gary Moore	27-168	16	19-113	7-52	-30.25
Alan King	16-47	34	10-28	6-17	+12.87
Nick Gifford	15-65	23	5-36	6-22	+8.00
Seamus Mullins	12-96	13	4-42	7-40	-2.87
Evan Williams	11-65	17	7-46	4-17	-5.87
Anna Newton-Smith	10-68	15	4-37	6-30	-13.67
Jim Best	10-66	15	9-58	1-7	-31.58
Neil King	9-45	20	5-27	2-14	+48.32
Charlie Mann	9-36	25	5-21	4-14	+9.67
Venetia Williams	8-47	17	3-26	3-16	-19.25
Paul Nicholls	8-30	27	6-16	1-10	-0.68
Michael Madgwick	7-48	15	4-17	3-27	+53.75
David Pipe	7-48	15	5-34	2-14	-22.37
Tim Vaughan	7-43	16	4-25	3-9	-4.82
Colin Tizzard	7-41	17	2-16	5-21	+17.77

Jockeys	Wins-Rides	%	£1 level stks	Best Trainer	W-R
Jamie Moore	18-122	15	-16.30	Gary Moore	16-88
Richard Johnson	18-84	21	-10.67	Tim Vaughan	4-19
Robert Thornton	14-48	29	-0.16	Alan King	13-31
A P McCoy	12-58	21	-19.59	Nicky Henderson	3-12
Liam Treadwell	12-58	21	-9.67	Nick Gifford	11-35
Paul Moloney	11-55	20	-6.23	Evan Williams	5-21
Noel Fehily	11-46	24	+32.80	Charlie Mann	6-14
Philip Hide	10-70	14	-17.65	Gary Moore	7-42
Aidan Coleman	9-63	14	-6.13	Venetia Williams	7-34
Paddy Brennan	9-57	16	-20.51	Suzy Smith	2-2
Mattie Batchelor	8-83	10	-46.38	Jamie Poulton	5-21
Marc Goldstein	8-77	10	+26.49	Michael Madgwick	6-39
Alex Merriam	8-55	15	+31.75	Neil King	6-33
Tom Scudamore	7-61	11	-30.35	David Pipe	3-26
Andrew Thornton	7-56	13	-0.25	Seamus Mullins	2-8

Favourites

Hurdle	35.4%	-39.01	Chase	39.2%	+12.13	TOTAL 36.6% -34.56

SANDOWN

Esher, Surrey, KT10 9AJ
Tel: 01372 463 072 or 464 348

How to get there Road: M25 anti-clockwise Jctn 10 and A3, M25 clockwise Jctn 9 and A224. Rail: Esher (from Waterloo)

Features Right-handed, 1m5f circuit, tough fences and stiff uphill finish

2011 Fixtures November 5, December 2-3

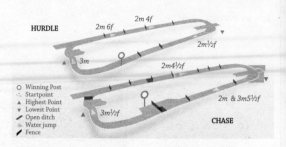

Trainers	Wins-Runs	%	Hurdles	Chases	£1 level stks
Paul Nicholls	35-113	31	11-44	23-65	+22.79
Nicky Henderson	25-116	22	18-79	7-27	-15.17
Alan King	12-90	13	7-54	4-25	-13.17
Philip Hobbs	12-78	15	9-41	2-31	+26.10
David Pipe	12-59	20	9-37	3-21	+9.07
Gary Moore	7-107	7	5-80	1-23	-40.00
Charlie Longsdon	6-26	23	2-12	4-11	+16.25
Jonjo O'Neill	5-48	10	3-25	2-19	-18.00
Charlie Mann	5-37	14	2-21	3-14	-1.75
Venetia Williams	4-55	7	2-27	2-27	-23.75
Nick Williams	4-21	19	2-13	1-7	+25.00
David Arbuthnot	4-15	27	2-8	1-5	+12.36
Nigel Twiston-Davies	3-53	6	2-19	1-31	-37.50
Emma Lavelle	3-42	7	2-26	1-12	-34.30
Lucy Wadham	3-19	16	3-15	0-0	+12.00

Jockeys	Wins-Rides	%	£1 level stks	Best Trainer	W-R
A P McCoy	20-80	25	-9.20	Nicky Henderson	4-12
R Walsh	16-47	34	+22.41	Paul Nicholls	16-46
Barry Geraghty	13-40	33	+23.01	Nicky Henderson	13-36
Timmy Murphy	11-49	22	+11.65	David Pipe	7-19
Sam Thomas	10-42	24	-6.77	Paul Nicholls	10-22
Robert Thornton	9-54	17	-5.17	Alan King	8-42
Jamie Moore	6-86	7	-38.25	Gary Moore	4-61
Richard Johnson	6-77	8	-15.75	Philip Hobbs	5-43
Aidan Coleman	6-46	13	+7.11	Venetia Williams	3-32
Noel Fehily	6-40	15	+3.45	Brendan Powell	1-1
Daryl Jacob	5-46	11	-6.00	Nick Williams	3-17
Dominic Elsworth	5-45	11	-11.67	Lucy Wadham	2-10
Wayne Hutchinson	5-43	12	+22.25	Alan King	3-27
Tom O'Brien	5-24	21	+4.35	Philip Hobbs	3-9
Paddy Brennan	3-59	5	-38.00	Tom George	2-8

Favourites

Hurdle	36.6%	-5.62	Chase	35.4%	-8.94	TOTAL	35.1%	-18.06

BARRY GERAGHTY: has an outstanding strike-rate at Sandown

SEDGEFIELD

Sedgefield, Cleveland, TS21 2HW
Tel: 01740 621 925

How to get there Road: 2m from A1 on A689. Rail: Stockton, Darlington

Features Left-handed, 1m2f circuit, sharp and undulating, no water jump

2011 Fixtures November 8, 22, December 6, 22

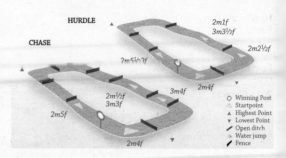

Trainers	Wins-Runs	%	Hurdles	Chases	£1 level stks
Ferdy Murphy	29-169	17	13-73	16-85	+7.39
Howard Johnson	22-133	17	9-82	13-41	-63.80
Donald McCain	14-84	17	9-51	4-25	-35.23
George Moore	13-81	16	10-62	1-12	-7.63
Alan Swinbank	13-56	23	5-25	1-13	-15.45
Sue Smith	12-140	9	5-61	6-73	-67.25
John Wade	11-124	9	2-54	9-60	-47.25
Martin Todhunter	11-87	13	10-59	1-25	-21.88
Evelyn Slack	9-76	12	4-30	5-46	-20.67
Chris Grant	8-62	13	7-39	1-16	+16.38
J J Lambe	8-50	16	7-39	1-10	-9.14
Tim Walford	8-40	20	3-20	5-18	+0.63
Robert Johnson	7-100	7	2-54	5-42	+16.50
Micky Hammond	7-69	10	3-40	4-27	-12.00
Malcolm Jefferson	7-66	11	3-28	4-31	-16.75

Jockeys	Wins-Rides	%	£1 level stks	Best Trainer	W-R
Brian Hughes	32-226	14	-39.42	Alan Swinbank	8-42
Graham Lee	30-178	17	-31.64	Ferdy Murphy	19-90
Denis O'Regan	22-107	21	-21.78	Howard Johnson	13-62
Barry Keniry	16-118	14	-22.01	George Moore	9-51
A P McCoy	13-39	33	-1.18	J J Lambe	4-6
Tjade Collier	12-86	14	-3.25	Sue Smith	8-50
Jason Maguire	12-57	21	-23.10	Donald McCain	9-36
Fearghal Davis	11-129	9	-38.32	Evelyn Slack	6-36
Wilson Renwick	11-96	11	-32.10	L Lungo	3-9
Richie McGrath	10-122	8	-37.92	Kate Walton	5-23
Dougie Costello	9-111	8	-64.57	Tim Walford	2-5
James Reveley	9-58	16	+10.83	Keith Reveley	6-24
Paddy Aspell	8-136	6	-30.00	Ann Hamilton	3-17
Ryan Mania	8-93	9	+18.25	Dianne Sayer	4-24
Michael O'Connell	8-61	13	+15.75	Ferdy Murphy	4-15

Favourites

Hurdle	38%	-21.04	Chase	30.1% -27.39	TOTAL 34% -57.36

Rolleston, nr Newark, Notts
NG25 0TS. Tel: 01636 814 481

SOUTHWELL

How to get there Road: A1 to
Newark and A617 to Southwell or
A52 to Nottingham (off M1) and
A612 to Southwell. Rail: Rolleston

Features Flat, left-handed, 1m2f
circuit

2011 Fixtures November 7, 29

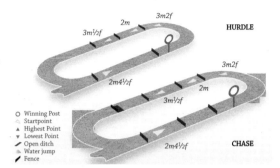

O Winning Post
⌁ Startpoint
▲ Highest Point
▼ Lowest Point
✐ Open ditch
🌢 Water jump
⫟ Fence

Trainers	Wins-Runs	%	Hurdles	Chases	£1 level stks
Tim Vaughan	17-56	30	8-35	9-18	-7.17
Jonjo O'Neill	14-81	17	6-44	8-31	-32.86
Evan Williams	12-72	17	7-36	5-35	-28.04
Charlie Mann	12-36	33	7-19	5-16	+22.75
Alan King	11-70	16	6-35	1-19	-29.69
Sue Smith	9-82	11	6-39	3-35	+17.00
Nigel Twiston-Davies	8-46	17	6-26	2-16	+15.58
Heather Dalton	8-16	50	2-4	6-11	+38.50
John Cornwall	5-43	12	0-9	5-34	-11.00
Peter Bowen	5-31	16	1-12	2-16	+12.50
David Pipe	5-28	18	3-15	2-13	-9.84
Nicky Henderson	5-24	21	4-14	1-5	-7.16
Oliver Sherwood	5-22	23	1-10	2-4	-0.04
Chris Bealby	4-35	11	2-21	1-7	-11.63
Keith Reveley	4-29	14	2-12	1-7	-7.17

Jockeys	Wins-Rides	%	£1 level stks	Best Trainer	W-R
A P McCoy	26-99	26	-18.25	Jonjo O'Neill	13-48
Richard Johnson	19-68	28	-2.68	Tim Vaughan	10-30
Noel Fehily	13-53	25	-7.00	Charlie Mann	9-24
Paul Moloney	12-75	16	-0.26	Evan Williams	7-46
Robert Thornton	8-69	12	-37.05	Alan King	7-46
Paddy Brennan	6-48	13	+13.75	Nigel Twiston-Davies	3-20
Brian Hughes	6-45	13	-14.75	Alan Swinbank	2-4
Joe Cornwall	6-44	14	+0.00	John Cornwall	5-42
Aidan Coleman	6-41	15	+10.12	Venetia Williams	3-13
Tjade Collier	6-41	15	+42.00	Sue Smith	5-34
Tom O'Brien	6-38	16	+34.41	Renee Robeson	2-2
Tom Scudamore	6-34	18	-13.68	David Pipe	3-16
Felix De Giles	6-27	22	+17.50	James Evans	2-6
James Reveley	6-21	29	+12.83	Keith Reveley	4-16
Sam Thomas	5-24	21	+9.91	Ian Williams	1-1

Favourites

Hurdle	42.3%	+9.19	Chase	39.7%	+2.77	TOTAL	42.5%	+25.80

STRATFORD

Luddington Road, Stratford
CV37 9SE. Tel: 01789 267 949

How to get there Road: M40
Jctn 15, A3400, B439, A46.

Features Sharp, left-handed,
1m2f circuit

£2011 Fixtures October 22, 27

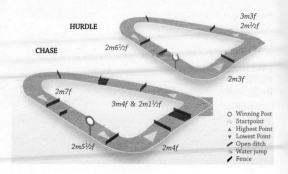

Trainers	Wins-Runs	%	Hurdles	Chases	£1 level stks
Nigel Twiston-Davies	17-116	15	9-45	7-60	+29.07
Evan Williams	17-110	15	10-67	5-38	+3.04
David Pipe	17-72	24	10-45	7-26	+14.45
Jonjo O'Neill	16-126	13	6-53	10-67	-44.06
Tim Vaughan	14-81	17	8-48	4-26	+23.49
Paul Nicholls	13-53	25	3-20	5-25	-4.62
Peter Bowen	12-76	16	8-30	4-36	-3.59
Charlie Longsdon	10-41	24	4-16	6-21	+22.99
Nicky Henderson	9-40	23	8-25	0-11	-9.23
Milton Harris	7-94	7	4-58	3-34	-37.09
Alison Thorpe	7-45	16	6-36	1-9	-11.75
Ian Williams	7-45	16	7-33	0-9	+7.00
Alan King	7-38	18	5-20	2-15	-13.12
Keith Goldsworthy	7-28	25	3-14	3-11	+14.23
Tony Carroll	6-79	8	6-62	0-12	-36.50

Jockeys	Wins-Rides	%	£1 level stks	Best Trainer	W-R
A P McCoy	26-138	19	-32.53	Jonjo O'Neill	11-63
Richard Johnson	20-148	14	-42.05	Tim Vaughan	7-39
Paddy Brennan	16-114	14	-27.87	Nigel Twiston-Davies	9-68
Tom Scudamore	16-94	17	-11.97	David Pipe	13-51
Tom O'Brien	14-79	18	-6.40	Peter Bowen	7-26
Robert Thornton	14-78	18	-7.67	Alan King	5-27
Aidan Coleman	10-67	15	+30.75	Venetia Williams	2-16
Nick Scholfield	10-62	16	+66.50	Peter Hiatt	2-4
Christian Williams	9-70	13	+16.48	Paul Nicholls	4-9
Paul Moloney	9-69	13	-24.18	Evan Williams	7-40
Noel Fehily	9-61	15	+9.25	Jonjo O'Neill	3-11
Jack Doyle	8-51	16	+7.25	Emma Lavelle	4-18
Timmy Murphy	7-45	16	-8.38	David Pipe	2-7
D P Fahy	7-38	18	+1.42	Evan Williams	5-26
Felix De Giles	7-33	21	-3.72	Charlie Longsdon	4-5

Favourites

Hurdle 32.6% -52.33   Chase 28.9% -36.68   TOTAL 31.5% -90.24

Orchard Portman, Taunton, Somerset
TA3 7BL. Tel: 01823 337 172

TAUNTON

How to get there Road: M5
Jctn 25. Rail: Taunton

Features Right-handed, 1m2f
circuit

2011 Fixtures October 25,
November 10, 24, December 8,
20, 30

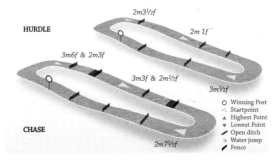

Trainers	Wins-Runs	%	Hurdles	Chases	£1 level stks
Paul Nicholls	56-154	36	37-109	12-33	-5.98
Philip Hobbs	20-111	18	13-89	6-19	-29.16
Alan King	19-106	18	12-79	6-17	-22.09
Venetia Williams	15-67	22	11-45	4-20	+20.56
Evan Williams	14-70	20	9-45	3-22	+13.40
David Pipe	13-146	9	10-124	3-20	-36.45
Victor Dartnall	11-47	23	7-32	3-13	+62.23
Nicky Henderson	7-33	21	4-22	2-5	-12.73
Charlie Mann	7-31	23	1-16	6-14	+15.00
Ron Hodges	6-92	7	3-51	3-38	-62.92
Emma Lavelle	6-28	21	2-12	3-15	+8.85
Colin Tizzard	5-82	6	0-31	5-43	-46.50
Patrick Rodford	5-29	17	0-5	4-21	-4.78
James Frost	4-81	5	3-63	1-12	-38.50
Bob Buckler	4-44	9	0-19	3-19	-19.50

Jockeys	Wins-Rides	%	£1 level stks	Best Trainer	W-R
Sam Thomas	22-85	26	+37.33	Paul Nicholls	11-33
R Walsh	20-39	51	+11.64	Paul Nicholls	20-39
Daryl Jacob	14-111	13	-17.92	Nick Williams	4-24
Richard Johnson	14-79	18	-3.56	Philip Hobbs	10-49
Robert Thornton	9-61	15	-22.88	Alan King	9-53
Paul Moloney	9-59	15	+2.76	Evan Williams	9-36
Timmy Murphy	9-58	16	+6.23	Ron Hodges	3-10
Wayne Hutchinson	9-51	18	-11.33	Alan King	8-34
Christian Williams	8-47	17	-22.23	Paul Nicholls	4-8
Noel Fehily	8-35	23	-5.34	Paul Nicholls	3-4
Jack Doyle	8-35	23	-5.43	Emma Lavelle	4-10
Tom O'Brien	7-60	12	-3.34	Philip Hobbs	4-26
Keiran Burke	7-45	16	+36.35	Patrick Rodford	4-25
Tom Scudamore	6-79	8	-36.00	David Pipe	5-54
Harry Skelton	6-51	12	-8.16	Paul Nicholls	4-16

Favourites

Hurdle   38.9%   -12.46   Chase   32.2%   -36.75   TOTAL   36.5% -52.28

TOWCESTER

Easton Newston, Towcester
NN12 7HS. Tel: 01327 353 414

How to get there Road: M1
Jctn 15a, A43 West. Rail:
Northampton (8m) and bus
service

Features Right-handed, 1m6f
circuit, uphill from back straight

2011 Fixtures October 5,
November 3, 20, 26, December
15, 26

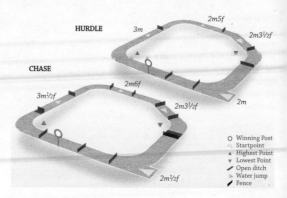

Trainers	Wins-Runs	%	Hurdles	Chases	£1 level stks
Jonjo O'Neill	28-128	22	14-64	14-58	+33.82
Venetia Williams	17-101	17	8-47	6-43	+9.54
Alan King	15-59	25	9-37	1-4	+16.16
Nigel Twiston-Davies	14-103	14	4-51	9-41	-19.86
Nicky Henderson	12-39	31	6-20	3-6	+13.10
David Pipe	11-63	17	5-38	5-21	-3.43
Kim Bailey	11-60	18	4-24	7-36	+7.74
Robin Dickin	9-102	9	3-41	6-53	-34.38
Henry Daly	9-66	14	6-37	2-23	-16.68
Jim Old	9-42	21	3-26	6-14	+13.75
Tim Vaughan	9-42	21	4-20	4-15	-10.50
Oliver Sherwood	8-45	18	1-26	5-13	+14.00
Brendan Powell	7-73	10	4-42	3-24	-13.38
Donald McCain	7-66	11	4-37	3-19	-36.09
Peter Pritchard	7-56	13	2-21	5-30	+20.50

Jockeys	Wins-Rides	%	£1 level stks	Best Trainer	W-R
A P McCoy	23-100	23	-12.27	Jonjo O'Neill	10-46
Jason Maguire	20-95	21	+22.88	Jim Old	8-21
Aidan Coleman	14-101	14	+5.66	Venetia Williams	10-56
Robert Thornton	13-49	27	+4.26	Alan King	7-26
Paddy Brennan	12-88	14	-21.49	Nigel Twiston-Davies	9-52
Richard Johnson	11-64	17	-14.17	Tim Vaughan	5-12
Tom Scudamore	10-79	13	-26.86	David Pipe	7-43
Richie McLernon	10-55	18	+3.83	Jonjo O'Neill	10-38
Andrew Thornton	9-116	8	-37.38	Caroline Bailey	4-40
Noel Fehily	9-41	22	+23.88	Alex Hales	2-2
Felix De Giles	8-66	12	-32.91	Nicky Henderson	2-6
Sean Quinlan	8-53	15	-5.14	Kim Bailey	4-10
Mark Bradburne	8-52	15	+20.48	Henry Daly	5-21
Charlie Poste	7-86	8	-25.88	Robin Dickin	4-27
Warren Marston	7-84	8	-17.17	Martin Keighley	4-36

Favourites

Hurdle	33.3%	-27.17	Chase	34%	-6.85	TOTAL	32%	-57.70

Wood Lane, Uttoxeter, Staffs
ST14 8BD. Tel: 01889 562 561

UTTOXETER

How to get there Road: M6
Jctn 14. Rail: Uttoxeter

Features Left-handed, 1m2f
circuit, undulating with sweeping
curves, suits galloping types

2011 Fixtures October 2, 13,
28, November 12, 24, 30,
December 16, 31

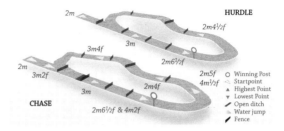

Trainers	Wins-Runs	%	Hurdles	Chases	£1 level stks
Donald McCain	29-190	15	20-122	6-41	-31.35
Nigel Twiston-Davies	28-138	20	18-73	6-45	+9.34
David Pipe	26-138	19	15-88	10-43	+29.39
Jonjo O'Neill	24-238	10	13-125	8-95	-134.47
Tim Vaughan	18-93	19	13-64	4-21	+7.31
Alan King	17-115	15	9-59	3-23	-35.23
Evan Williams	16-125	13	10-79	6-43	-31.70
Kim Bailey	16-84	19	8-43	7-32	+26.54
Peter Bowen	14-106	13	10-68	3-25	-12.36
Venetia Williams	13-100	13	5-48	7-44	-41.97
Nicky Henderson	11-38	29	7-25	1-4	+9.63
Philip Hobbs	10-71	14	8-39	1-24	-33.21
Alison Thorpe	10-67	15	8-58	1-6	+2.50
Charlie Mann	10-39	26	4-24	6-14	+5.20
Renee Robeson	10-38	26	6-24	3-9	+6.40

Jockeys	Wins-Rides	%	£1 level stks	Best Trainer	W-R
A P McCoy	36-202	18	-96.39	Jonjo O'Neill	12-105
Jason Maguire	35-161	22	+15.85	Donald McCain	20-98
Richard Johnson	22-161	14	-45.86	Tim Vaughan	12-43
Paddy Brennan	21-126	17	-35.13	Nigel Twiston-Davies	16-62
Tom Scudamore	19-161	12	-61.11	David Pipe	13-83
Noel Fehily	17-91	19	+18.28	Charlie Mann	6-21
Robert Thornton	16-117	14	-37.04	Alan King	10-64
Paul Moloney	14-104	13	+0.00	Evan Williams	8-57
Tom O'Brien	13-107	12	-11.95	Peter Bowen	6-41
Sam Thomas	12-112	11	-35.31	Venetia Williams	3-38
Aidan Coleman	12-101	12	-26.38	Lawney Hill	3-9
Christian Williams	11-106	10	+1.08	Lawney Hill	3-17
Andrew Thornton	9-74	12	-10.00	Simon Earle	3-4
Jimmy McCarthy	9-74	12	-29.10	Renee Robeson	4-18
Warren Marston	8-87	9	-24.00	Martin Keighley	3-24

Favourites

Hurdle	38.6%	+1.32		Chase	34.1%	-14.37		TOTAL	36.8%	-13.02

WARWICK

Hampton Street, Warwick
CV34 6HN. Tel: 01926 491 553

How to get there Road: M40 Jctn 15 on to A429 and follow signs to town centre. Rail: Warwick

Features Left handed, 1m0f circuit, undulating

2011 Fixtures November 2, 16, December 4, 31

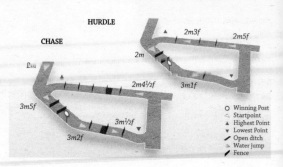

HURDLE

CHASE

2m3f
2m5f
2m
2m4½f
3m1f
3m5f
3m½f
3m2f

○ Winning Post
⚐ Startpoint
▲ Highest Point
▼ Lowest Point
⚫ Open ditch
Water jump
Fence

Trainers	Wins-Runs	%	Hurdles	Chases	£1 level stks
Alan King	25-107	23	13-52	6-24	+19.15
Nigel Twiston-Davies	16-82	20	7-35	7-34	+47.16
David Pipe	13-48	27	7-28	5-15	+33.10
Nicky Henderson	10-31	32	4-13	4-11	-2.20
Philip Hobbs	8-52	15	3-29	5-18	-22.18
Jonjo O'Neill	7-71	10	3-26	4-37	-33.58
Venetia Williams	7-49	14	6-29	1-17	-8.35
Neil King	6-28	21	2-18	4-9	+7.07
Ian Williams	5-46	11	3-32	2-7	+2.50
Henry Daly	5-40	13	2-19	3-13	-4.00
Colin Tizzard	5-25	20	0-4	4-14	+23.50
Richard Lee	5-22	23	2-9	2-10	+17.25
Richard Phillips	4-43	9	2-28	2-11	-6.00
Charlie Mann	4-25	16	1-12	3-13	-9.83
Paul Nicholls	4-25	16	1-8	3-15	-17.32

Jockeys	Wins-Rides	%	£1 level stks	Best Trainer	W-R
Robert Thornton	18-83	22	+0.85	Alan King	17-67
A P McCoy	14-61	23	+2.64	Jonjo O'Neill	6-33
Paddy Brennan	12-54	22	+57.68	Nigel Twiston-Davies	11-35
Richard Johnson	8-50	16	-7.29	Philip Hobbs	5-20
Aidan Coleman	7-48	15	+16.13	Venetia Williams	4-24
Andrew Tinkler	6-41	15	-9.00	Nicky Henderson	3-9
Sam Thomas	6-35	17	-19.08	Venetia Williams	2-10
Andrew Thornton	5-47	11	-13.13	Caroline Bailey	3-20
Jason Maguire	5-44	11	+34.75	Jim Old	2-21
Wayne Hutchinson	5-38	13	-12.35	Alan King	5-19
Will Kennedy	5-38	13	+10.25	Alex Hales	2-13
Timmy Murphy	5-37	14	-17.15	Henrietta Knight	1-1
Noel Fehily	5-35	14	-8.27	Charlie Mann	2-11
Paul Moloney	5-33	15	-10.28	Matt Sheppard	1-1
Daryl Jacob	5-28	18	-9.83	David Arbuthnot	2-3

Favourites

Hurdle	41.9%	+11.53	Chase	36.5%	-9.17	TOTAL	36.8%	-12.06

York Road, Wetherby, West Yorks
L22 5EJ. Tel: 01937 582 035

WETHERBY

How to get there Road: A1,
A58 from Leeds, B1224 from
York. Rail: Leeds, Harrogate, York

Features Long, left-handed
circuit (1m4f chases, 1m2f
hurdles), suits galloping types

2011 Fixtures October 12,
28-29, November 12, 23,
December 3, 26-27

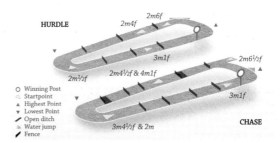

Trainers	Wins-Runs	%	Hurdles	Chases	£1 level stks
Howard Johnson	39-196	20	22-126	14-59	+35.25
Donald McCain	17-87	20	8-51	8-29	-19.22
Sue Smith	15-147	10	4-70	11-69	-42.34
Micky Hammond	12-162	7	5-110	7-41	-89.29
Jonjo O'Neill	11-35	31	7-13	4-19	+18.87
Tim Easterby	9-77	12	4-45	5-29	+3.63
George Moore	8-82	10	6-56	1-16	-23.75
Ferdy Murphy	8-74	11	2-30	6-39	-38.07
John Quinn	8-45	18	6-33	1-9	-4.25
Alan Swinbank	8-36	22	3-18	1-5	-0.23
Nigel Twiston-Davies	8-26	31	2-10	5-13	+9.99
Chris Grant	7-53	13	4-38	3-10	-18.17
Evan Williams	7-35	20	4-20	3-15	-11.34
Brian Ellison	7-19	37	3-12	4-7	+12.50
Keith Reveley	6-61	10	4-43	1-6	-41.43

Jockeys	Wins-Rides	%	£1 level stks	Best Trainer	W-R
Brian Hughes	25-160	16	-27.58	Alan Swinbank	8-28
Denis O'Regan	24-145	17	-3.87	Howard Johnson	23-101
Graham Lee	18-117	15	-18.56	Ferdy Murphy	5-38
A P McCoy	18-37	49	+5.94	Jonjo O'Neill	6-11
Dougie Costello	15-110	14	-11.54	John Quinn	8-35
Jason Maguire	15-66	23	-12.47	Donald McCain	13-49
Richie McGrath	14-115	12	-30.15	Tim Easterby	5-26
Barry Keniry	10-137	7	-68.29	Micky Hammond	6-54
Fearghal Davis	10-87	11	-27.88	Micky Hammond	4-19
Phil Kinsella	10-73	14	+47.15	Keith Reveley	5-22
Keith Mercer	8-61	13	+11.38	Brian Ellison	2-2
Peter Buchanan	7-70	10	+11.00	Lucinda Russell	2-32
Ryan Mania	7-47	15	+9.50	Howard Johnson	5-10
Richard Johnson	7-18	39	+3.55	Richard Phillips	2-3
Paddy Brennan	6-23	26	-2.38	Nigel Twiston-Davies	5-14

Favourites

Hurdle	37.2%	-17.41	Chase	34.5% -17.95	TOTAL	36.4% -27.84

WINCANTON

Wincanton, Somerset
BA9 8BJ. Tel: 01963 323 44

How to get there Road: A303 to Wincanton, course on B3081, 1m from town centre. Rail: Gillingham

Features Right handed, 1m4f circuit, dries fast

2011 Fixtures October 13, 23, November 5, 17, December 1, 26

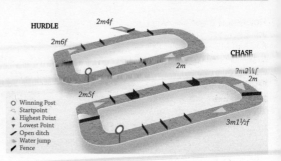

HURDLE 2m4f 2m6f 2m5f 2m CHASE 2m 2m3f 3m1½f

O Winning Post
⊰ Startpoint
▲ Highest Point
▼ Lowest Point
⟋ Open ditch
🟑 Water jump
⟋ Fence

Trainers	Wins-Runs	%	Hurdles	Chases	£1 level stks
Paul Nicholls	45-181	25	27-106	15-54	-28.17
Philip Hobbs	29-165	18	23-97	6-57	-1.57
Alan King	23-133	17	15-78	6-38	-34.18
Colin Tizzard	17-143	12	4-63	12-70	-33.38
David Pipe	16-146	11	9-90	7-51	-78.55
Venetia Williams	11-78	14	2-40	9-38	-29.62
Andy Turnell	10-54	19	8-38	1-14	-1.72
Nicky Henderson	8-54	15	6-38	2-12	-27.22
Victor Dartnall	8-38	21	5-24	3-11	+7.25
R H & Mrs S Alner	7-69	10	2-34	5-30	-7.50
Gary Moore	7-44	16	6-33	1-10	+2.55
Tim Vaughan	7-29	24	5-21	2-7	+17.78
Seamus Mullins	6-103	6	1-65	4-34	-11.75
Charlie Mann	6-45	13	2-30	4-15	-14.67
Emma Lavelle	6-36	17	2-23	2-8	-9.92

Jockeys	Wins-Rides	%	£1 level stks	Best Trainer	W-R
Richard Johnson	28-121	23	-6.14	Philip Hobbs	18-77
Robert Thornton	20-100	20	-23.64	Alan King	16-74
Sam Thomas	17-79	22	-23.49	Paul Nicholls	11-30
Nick Scholfield	14-82	17	+9.14	Paul Nicholls	6-27
Daryl Jacob	13-133	10	+10.58	R H & Mrs S Alner	5-28
Aidan Coleman	13-71	18	+35.51	Venetia Williams	5-28
Joe Tizzard	12-139	9	-59.13	Colin Tizzard	12-108
A P McCoy	12-49	24	-1.86	Jim Best	2-3
Timmy Murphy	11-75	15	-25.94	David Pipe	3-11
Harry Skelton	11-62	18	+14.91	Paul Nicholls	6-23
R Walsh	11-35	31	-5.02	Paul Nicholls	11-35
Jack Doyle	8-36	22	+2.00	Emma Lavelle	5-16
Tom O'Brien	7-64	11	+1.38	Philip Hobbs	4-28
Paul Moloney	7-54	13	+10.58	Evan Williams	5-31
Liam Heard	6-77	8	-11.38	Anthony Honeyball	2-8

Favourites

Hurdle	41.2%	-10.29		Chase	33.5%	-17.36		TOTAL	37.2%	-37.61

Pitchcroft, Worcester
WR1 3EJ. Tel: 01905 253 64

WORCESTER

How to get there Road: M5
Jctn 6 from north, M5 Jctn 7 or
A38 from south. Rail: Worcester
(Forgate Street)

Features Left-handed, 1m5f
circuit, subject to flooding

2011 Fixtures October 6, 19

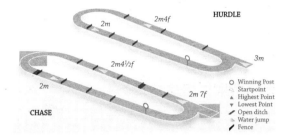

Trainers	Wins-Runs	%	Hurdles	Chases	£1 level stks
Jonjo O'Neill	39-156	25	23-84	13-62	+28.00
Tim Vaughan	19-103	18	8-64	8-27	-0.78
Evan Williams	16-109	15	7-58	9-48	+12.50
David Pipe	13-82	16	7-58	5-20	-20.42
Paul Nicholls	13-42	31	7-19	4-18	+11.60
Nigel Twiston-Davies	12-85	14	8-48	3-27	-24.44
Nicky Henderson	8-28	29	5-21	1-2	+1.38
Philip Hobbs	7-58	12	3-26	3-24	-36.17
Anthony Honeyball	7-21	33	5-14	0-2	+60.41
Donald McCain	6-42	14	4-26	2-11	-8.73
Ian Williams	6-40	15	4-24	2-14	-20.92
Lawney Hill	6-25	24	2-13	2-5	+54.50
Peter Bowen	5-70	7	2-42	3-23	-36.50
Alison Thorpe	5-58	9	4-45	1-13	-9.14
Tony Carroll	5-34	15	4-23	1-10	+16.00

Jockeys	Wins-Rides	%	£1 level stks	Best Trainer	W-R
A P McCoy	60-203	30	+23.19	Jonjo O'Neill	33-105
Richard Johnson	19-151	13	-22.42	Tim Vaughan	8-55
Tom Scudamore	16-105	15	+13.40	David Pipe	10-57
Paul Moloney	11-72	15	+2.25	Evan Williams	10-45
Aidan Coleman	9-68	13	+28.13	Lawney Hill	4-5
Noel Fehily	8-43	19	-8.18	Charlie Mann	2-11
Paddy Brennan	7-72	10	-32.30	Nigel Twiston-Davies	5-38
Tom O'Brien	7-63	11	-11.00	Philip Hobbs	2-13
Robert Thornton	7-58	12	-15.78	Ian Williams	2-3
Harry Skelton	7-41	17	+2.85	Paul Nicholls	5-13
Daryl Jacob	7-38	18	+29.00	R H & Mrs S Alner	2-5
Rachael Green	7-11	64	+70.41	Anthony Honeyball	7-11
Charlie Poste	5-52	10	+33.00	Richard Lee	2-9
D P Fahy	5-35	14	+19.50	Evan Williams	4-33
Richie McLernon	5-32	16	+12.50	Jonjo O'Neill	5-30

Favourites

Hurdle	38.5%	-8.65	Chase	32.9%	-23.70	TOTAL	36.4%	-39.40

Record and standard times

Course

Distance (obstacles)	Record holder (date set)	record time	standard time

Aintree, Mildmay course

Distance (obstacles)	Record holder (date set)	record time	standard time
2m Ch (12)	Nohalmdun (7 Apr 1990)	3m45.30s	3m48s
2m110yds Hdl (9)	Spinning (3 Apr 1993)	3m44.80s	3m50s
2m1f Hdl (9)	The Jigsaw Man (14 May 2010)	4m09.30s	3m57s
2m1f110yds Ch (14)	Pats Minstrel (17 Nov 1995)	4m21.90s	/
2m4f Ch (16)	Wind Force (2 Apr 1993)	4m46.60s	4m48s
2m4f Hdl (11)	Gallateen (2 Apr 1993)	4m37.10s	4m40s
3m110yds Hdl (13)	Andrew's First (1 Apr 1993)	5m50.70s	5m51s
3m1f Ch (19)	Cab On Target (2 Apr 1993)	6m03.40s	6m06s

Aintree, Grand National course

Distance (obstacles)	Record holder (date set)	record time	standard time
2m5f110yds Ch (18)	Always Waining (8 Apr 2011)	5m19.30s	5m21s
2m6f Ch (18)	Sirrah Jay (1 Apr 1993)	5m26.50s	5m29s
3m2f Ch (22)	Eurotrek (19 Nov 2006)	6m46.60s	6m34s
3m3f Ch (22)	Young Hustler (18 Nov 1995)	6m54.50s	6m49s
4m4f Ch (30)	Mr Frisk (7 Apr 1990)	8m47.80s	9m05s

Ascot

Distance (obstacles)	Record holder (date set)	record time	standard time
2m Hdl (8)	Kanad (3 Nov 2007)	3m40.10s	3m39s
	Ultravox (10 Apr 2011)	3m40.10s	
2m1f Ch (13)	Crossbow Creek (28 Oct 2006)	4m03.00s	4m02s
2m3f Ch (15)	Bedarra Boy (10 Apr 2011)	4m40.10s	4m34s
2m3f110yds Hdl (11)	Zaynar (21 Nov 2009)	4m34.30s	4m33s
2m5f110yds Ch (17)	Kew Jumper (11 Apr 2008)	5m12.60s	5m14s
3m Ch (20)	See You Sometime (28 Oct 2006)	5m53.50s	5m56s
3m Hdl (14)	Scots Dragoon (11 Apr 2008)	5m46.60s	5m39s
3m1f Hdl (15)	Lough Derg (22 Dec 2007)	5m57.30s	5m53s

Ayr

Distance (obstacles)	Record holder (date set)	record time	standard time
2m Ch (12)	Clay County (12 Oct 1991)	3m38.60s	3m43s
2m Hdl (9)	Secret Ballot (19 Apr 1980)	3m27.40s	3m37s
2m4f Ch (17)	Chandigar (15 May 1972)	4m44.10s	4m44s
2m4f Hdl (11)	Moss Royal (19 Apr 1974)	4m35.00s	4m36s
2m5f Ch (18)	Even Flo (17 Apr 2009)	5m17.20s	4m58s
2m5f110yds Ch (18)	Star To The North (9 May 2001)	5m10.20s	5m06s
2m5f110yds Hdl (12)	Spring Breeze (21 Apr 2007)	5m06.60s	5m00s
3m110yds Hdl (12)	Nautical Lad (6 Apr 1964)	5m42.00s	5m43s
3m1f Ch (19)	Top 'N' Tale (12 May 1982)	5m57.70s	5m59s
3m2f110yds Hdl (14)	Meditator (18 Apr 1997)	6m26.90s	6m14s
3m3f110yds Ch (21)	Joacci (15 Apr 2005)	6m50.20s	6m39s
4m110yds Ch (27)	Hot Weld (21 Apr 2007)	7m55.10s	7m57s
4m1f Ch (27)	Young Ash Leaf (17 Apr 1971)	8m00.40s	8m04s

Bangor

Distance (obstacles)	Record holder (date set)	record time	standard time
2m1f Hdl (9)	Andy Rew (24 Apr 1982)	3m44.50s	3m50s
2m1f110yds Ch (12)	Vintage Gold (3 Aug 2007)	4m07.00s	4m09s
2m4f Hdl (11)	Smithy's Choice (25 Apr 1987)	4m34.10s	4m34s
2m4f110yds Ch (15)	Apollo Creed (22 Jul 2008)	4m52.50s	4m57s

ALWAYS WAINING: stormed to a new course record at Aintree last season

2m7f110yds Hdl (12)	Desperate (12 Apr 1993)	5m41.00s	5m25s
3m Hdl (12)	General Pershing (20 Apr 1991)	5m34.00s	5m32s
3m110yds Ch (18)	Hehasalife (8 Sep 2006)	5m54.60s	5m58s
3m6f Ch (21)	Kaki Crazy (23 May 2001)	7m34.10s	7m24s
4m1f Ch (24)	Nazzaro (13 Dec 1995)	8m50.60s	8m14s

Carlisle

2m Ch (12)	Cape Felix (20 Apr 1981)	3m55.80s	3m58s
2m1f Hdl (9)	Supertop (25 Oct 1997)	4m02.60s	4m05s
2m4f Ch (16)	New Alco (12 Nov 2007)	5m00.40s	4m58s
2m4f Hdl (11)	Gods Law (29 Sep 1990)	4m50.60s	4m47s
2m5f Ch (16)	Isn't That Lucky (11 Apr 2009)	5m24.40s	5m14s
3m110yds Ch (18)	Ripalong Lad (9 Oct 2009)	6m00.70s	6m07s
3m1f Hdl (12)	Mr Preacher Man (25 Oct 2007)	6m13.50s	6m00s
3m2f Ch (19)	Lady Of Gortmerron (6 Oct 2000)	6m40.40s	6m33s
3m4f Ch (21)	See You There (19 Feb 2007)	7m42.20s	7m04s

Cartmel

2m1f110yds Ch (12)	Clever Folly (27 May 1992)	4m07.50s	4m10s
2m1f110yds Hdl (8)	Sayeh (28 Aug 1999)	3m57.90s	3m59s
	Indian Jockey (24 May 1997)	3m57.90s	
	Kalshan (26 May 1990)	3m57.90s	
2m5f110yds Ch (14)	Corrarder (30 May 1994)	5m06.50s	5m09s
2m6f Hdl (11)	Browneyes Blue (28 May 2007)	5m13.90s	5m06s
3m2f Ch (18)	Better Times Ahead (28 Aug 1999)	6m13.40s	6m16s
3m2f Hdl (12)	Portonia (30 May 1994)	5m58.00s	6m04s

3m6f Ch (20)	Chabrimal Minster (26 May 2007)	7m12.00s	7m16s

Catterick

2m Ch (12)	Preston Deal (18 Dec 1971)	3m44.60s	3m47s
2m Hdl (8)	Lunar Wind (22 Apr 1982)	3m36.50s	3m39s
2m3f Ch (15)	Fear Siuil (24 Nov 2001)	4m41.90s	4m37s
2m3f Hdl (10)	Sovereign State (1 Dec 2004)	4m34.00s	4m23s
3m1f110yds Ch (19)	Clever General (7 Nov 1981)	6m14.00s	6m15s
3m1f110yds Hdl (12)	Coamus O'Flynn (8 Nov 1986)	6m03.80s	6m04s
3m4f110yds Ch (21)	The Wilk (10 Jan 1990)	7m15.30s	7m03s
3m6f Ch (23)	General Hardi (13 Nov 2011)	7m41.80s	7m26s

Cheltenham, New Course

2m110yds Ch (14)	Samakaan (16 Mar 2000)	3m52.40s	3m55s
2m1f Hdl (8)	Detroit City (17 Mar 2006)	3m51.20s	3m55s
2m4f110yds Hdl (9)	Sir Dante (15 Apr 1997)	4m45.00s	4m46s
2m5f Ch (17)	Barnbrook Again (18 Apr 1990)	5m01.60s	5m04s
2m5f110yds Hdl (10)	Fashion House (19 Sep 1968)	4m53.60s	5m01s
3m Hdl (12)	Bacchanal (16 Mar 2000)	5m36.60s	5m39s
3m1f110yds Ch (21)	Bigsun (15 Mar 1990)	6m13.40s	6m18s
3m2f110yds Ch (22)	Long Run (18 Mar 2011)	6m29.70s	6m34s
3m4f110yds Ch (24)	Gentle Ranger (16 Apr 2010)	7m14.50s	7m04s
4m1f Ch (27)	Hot Weld (16 Mar 2006)	8m33.20s	8m17s

Cheltenham, Old Course

2m Ch (12)	Edredon Bleu (15 Mar 2000)	3m44.70s	3m50s
2m110yds Hdl (8)	Istabraq (14 Mar 2000)	3m48.10s	3m51s
2m4f110yds Ch (15)	Dark Stranger (15 Mar 2000)	4m49.60s	5m00s
2m5f Hdl (10)	Monsignor (15 Mar 2000)	4m52.00s	4m59s

SIZING AUSTRALIA: lowered the mark at Cheltenham's cross-country course

3m110yds Ch (19)	Marlborough (14 Mar 2000)	5m59.70s	6m06s
3m1f110yds Hdl (13)	Rubhahunish (14 Mar 2000)	6m03.40s	6m10s
3m2f Ch (19)	The Pooka (26 Sep 1973)	6m20.60s	6m30s
3m3f110yds Ch (21)	Shardam (15 Nov 2003)	7m01.00s	6m54s
4m Ch (24)	Relaxation (15 Mar 2000)	8m00.60s	8m04s

Cheltenham, Cross-Country Course

3m1f Ch (25)	Linden's Lotto (1 Jan 1999)	6m59.30s	/
3m7f Ch (32)	Sizing Australia (15 Mar 2011)	8m06.22s	/

Chepstow

2m110yds Ch (12)	Panto Prince (9 Apr 1989)	3m54.10s	3m58s
2m110yds Hdl (8)	Tingle Bell (4 Oct 1986)	3m43.20s	3m45s
2m3f110yds Ch (16)	Armala (14 May 1996)	4m45.00s	4m47s
2m4f Hdl (11)	Court Appeal (8 May 1990)	4m38.80s	4m32s
3m Ch (18)	Broadheath (4 Oct 1986)	5m47.90s	5m51s
3m Hdl (12)	Chucklestone (11 May 1993)	5m33.60s	5m35s
3m2f110yds Ch (22)	Jaunty Jane (26 May 1975)	6m39.40s	6m39s
3m5f110yds Ch (22)	Creeola (27 Apr 1957)	7m24.00s	7m31s

Doncaster

2m110yds Ch (12)	Itsgottabealright (28 Jan 1989)	3m51.90s	3m57s
2m110yds Hdl (8)	Good For A Loan (24 Feb 1993)	3m46.60s	3m49s
2m3f Ch (15)	Watch My Back (12 Dec 2009)	4m41.80s	4m38s
2m3f110yds Hdl (10)	Bobby Ewing (11 Dec 2009)	4m33.00s	4m32s
3m Ch (18)	Dalkey Sound (26 Jan 1991)	5m52.40s	5m54s
3m110yds Hdl (11)	Pondolfi (4 Nov 1972)	5m45.30s	5m39s
3m2f Ch (19)	Always Right (5 Mar 2011)	6m11.80s	6m24s
3m4f Ch (21)	Shraden Leader (5 Mar 1994)	7m04.80s	6m56s

Exeter

2m1f Hdl (8)	Et Maintenant (6 May 2008)	3m46.40s	3m54s
2m1f110yds Ch (12)	Bushwacker (3 May 2011)	3m58.10s	4m07s
2m3f Hdl (9)	Il Capitano (9 Oct 2002)	4m16.50s	4m20s
2m3f110yds Ch (15)	James Pigg (25 Aug 1995)	4m31.50s	4m36s
2m5f110yds Hdl (10)	Miss Saffron (7 Oct 2010)	5m15.20s	4m59s
2m6f110yds Ch (17)	James Pigg (6 Sep 1995)	5m22.70s	5m23s
2m6f110yds Hdl (11)	Presenting Express (4 Oct 2006)	5m18.50s	5m13s
2m7f110yds Ch (17)	Mister Gloss (14 May 2008)	5m30.10s	5m36s
2m7f110yds Hdl (11)	Very Cool (4 May 2010)	5m26.20s	5m28s
3m Ch (17)	Dennis The Legend (13 May 2009)	5m42.80s	5m43s
3m110yds Hdl (12)	Il Capitano (1 Oct 2002)	5m42.30s	5m42s
3m1f110yds Ch (19)	Radnor Lad (14 May 2008)	6m03.00s	6m08s
3m2f Ch (19)	The Leggett (24 Mar 1993)	6m30.70s	6m07s
3m6f110yds Ch (21)	The Bandit (18 Apr 2006)	7m23.40s	7m27s
4m Ch (21)	Lancastrian Jet (7 Dec 2001)	8m17.90s	7m52s

Fakenham

2m Hdl (9)	Cobbet (9 May 2001)	3m45.70s	3m42s
2m110yds Ch (12)	Cheekie Ora (23 Apr 1984)	3m44.90s	3m56s
2m110yds Hdl (9)	Tom Clapton (25 May 1992)	3m47.80s	3m50s
2m4f Hdl (11)	Ayem (16 May 1999)	4m41.20s	4m42s
2m5f Hdl (11)	Lobric (21 Apr 1992)	4m51.80s	4m57s
2m5f110yds Ch (16)	Skipping Tim (25 May 1992)	5m10.30s	5m12s
2m7f110yds Hdl (13)	Laughing Gas (20 May 1995)	5m37.10s	5m34s

3m Ch (18)	Saldatore (23 Apr 1984)	5m55.70s	5m50s
3m110yds Ch (18)	Specialize (16 May 1999)	5m56.90s	5m58s

Ffos Las

2m Ch (13)	West With The Wind (17 Jun 2010)	3m46.60s	3m43s
2m Hdl (8)	Valain (28 Aug 2009)	3m33.60s	3m35s
2m3f110yds Ch (15)	Cold Harbour (31 May 2011)	4m37.34s	4m35s
2m4f Hdl (10)	Plunkett (18 Jun 2009)	4m39.40s	4m33s
2m5f Ch (17)	Putney Bridge (17 Jun 2010)	5m09.70s	4m58s
2m6f Hdl (11)	Akbabend (7 Jun 2011)	5m16.18s	5m02s
3m Ch (18)	Sea Wall (18 Jun 2009)	5m49.60s	5m44s
3m Hdl (12)	Quattrocento (18 Jun 2009)	5m41.50s	5m35s
3m1f110yds Ch (19)	Backstage (28 Aug 2009)	6m07.10s	6m07s

Folkestone

2m Ch (12)	High Gale (30 Apr 1999)	3m48.80s	3m50s
2m1f110yds Hdl (9)	Super Tek (14 Nov 1983)	3m56.20s	4m05s
2m4f110yds Hdl (10)	Circus Colours (2 Apr 1996)	4m57.00s	4m50s
2m5f Ch (15)	Captain Knock (12 May 2011)	5m05.70s	5m07s
2m6f110yds Hdl (11)	Royalty Miss (30 Apr 1985)	5m18.20s	5m20s
3m1f Ch (18)	Highland (23 May 2001)	6m11.40s	6m10s
3m2f Ch (19)	Ide No Ide (12 May 2011)	6m18.90s	6m26s
3m4f Hdl (13)	North West (25 Nov 1985)	6m43.20s	6m46s

Fontwell

2m2f Ch (13)	A Thousand Dreams (3 Jun 2002)	4m14.50s	4m18s
2m2f110yds Hdl (9)	Hyperion Du Moulin II (3 Jun 2002)	4m06.80s	4m11s
2m3f Ch (14)	Connaught Cracker (3 May 1999)	4m32.00s	4m33s
2m4f Ch (15)	Chalcedony (3 Jun 2002)	4m38.10s	4m46s
2m4f Hdl (10)	Hillswick (27 Aug 1999)	4m30.50s	4m33s
2m6f Ch (16)	Contes (3 Jun 2002)	5m13.90s	5m17s
2m6f110yds Hdl (11)	Mister Pickwick (3 Jun 2002)	5m06.70s	5m09s
3m2f110yds Ch (19)	Il Capitano (6 May 2002)	6m24.30s	6m25s
3m3f Hdl (13)	Lord of The Track (18 Aug 2003)	6m21.60s	6m19s
3m4f Ch (21)	Strolling Vagabond (18 Mar 2007)	7m11.10s	6m46s

Haydock

2m Ch (13)	Incorporation (28 Oct 2009)	4m00.10s	3m55s
2m Hdl (8)	She's Our Mare (1 May 1999)	3m32.30s	3m40s
2m4f Ch (15)	Etxalar (28 Oct 2009)	4m49.90s	4m57s
2m4f Hdl (10)	Moving Out (6 May 1995)	4m35.30s	4m41s
2m6f Hdl (12)	Peter the Butchers (3 May 1982)	5m12.70s	5m13s
2m7f110yds Hdl (12)	Boscean Chieftain (3 May 1993)	5m32.30s	5m37s
3m Ch (18)	Catch The Perk (28 Oct 2009)	5m55.30s	6m03s
3m4f Ch (22)	Dom D'Orgeval (23 Apr 2011)	7m26.60s	7m11s

Hereford

2m Ch (12)	Smolensk (21 Mar 1998)	3m46.10s	3m48s
2m1f Hdl (8)	Tasty Son (11 Sep 1973)	3m42.20s	3m45s
2m3f Ch (14)	Kings Wild (28 Sep 1990)	4m30.00s	4m31s
2m3f110yds Hdl (10)	Polden Pride (6 May 1995)	4m22.20s	4m23s
2m4f Hdl (11)	Pigeon Island (3 Jun 2007)	4m38.09s	4m30s
2m5f110yds Ch (16)	Fealing Real (20 Jun 2010)	5m06.90s	5m07s
2m6f110yds Hdl (12)	Rivermouth (28 Apr 2011)	5m19.80s	5m06s
3m1f110yds Ch (19)	Gilston Lass (8 Apr 1995)	6m10.60s	6m11s

| 3m2f Hdl (13) | Wee Danny (10 Sep 2003) | 6m02.80s | 6m06s |

Hexham

2m110yds Ch (12)	Adamatic (17 Jun 2000)	3m53.60s	3m56s
2m110yds Hdl (8)	Francies Fancy (19 June 2005)	3m57.80s	3m53s
2m4f110yds Ch (15)	Mr Laggan (14 Sep 2003)	4m55.40s	4m57s
2m4f110yds Hdl (10)	Pappa Charlie (27 May 1997)	4m31.50s	4m50s
3m Hdl (12)	Fingers Crossed (29 Apr 1991)	5m45.50s	5m46s
3m1f Ch (19)	Silent Snipe (1 Jun 2002)	6m07.60s	6m06s
4m Ch (25)	Simply Smashing (18 Mar 2010)	8m34.00s	8m00s

Huntingdon

2m110yds Ch (12)	No Greater Love (23 May 2007)	3m53.30s	3m55s
2m110yds Hdl (8)	Weather Front (31 Aug 2009)	3m32.70s	3m38s
2m4f110yds Ch (16)	Peccadillo (26 Dec 2004)	4m46.40s	4m52s
2m4f110yds Hdl (10)	Sabre Hongrois (4 Oct 2009)	4m30.20s	4m36s
2m5f110yds Hdl (10)	Sound of Laughter (14 Apr 1984)	4m45.80s	4m50s
3m Ch (19)	Ozzie Jones (18 Sep 1998)	5m44.40s	5m48s
3m2f Hdl (12)	Orchard King (31 Aug 2009)	5m50.20s	5m59s
3m6f110yds Ch (25)	Kinnahalla (24 Nov 2001)	8m02.70s	7m33s

Kelso

2m110yds Hdl (8)	The Premier Expres (2 May 1995)	3m39.60s	3m42s
2m1f Ch (12)	Mr Coggy (2 May 1984)	4m02.40s	4m04s
2m2f Hdl (10)	All Welcome (15 Oct 1994)	4m11.40s	4m07s
2m6f110yds Ch (17)	Bas De Laine (13 Nov 1996)	5m29.60s	5m26s
2m6f110yds Hdl (11)	Hit The Canvas (30 Sep 1995)	5m12.20s	5m13s
3m1f Ch (19)	McGregor The Third (19 Sep 1999)	6m01.20s	6m03s
3m3f Hdl (13)	Dook's Delight (19 May 1995)	6m10.10s	6m15s
3m4f Ch (21)	Seven Towers (2 Dec 1996)	7m02.30s	6m53s
4m Ch (24)	Seven Towers (17 Jan 1997)	8m07.50s	7m58s

Kempton

2m Ch (13)	Hoo La Baloo (21 Oct 2007)	3m48.30s	3m45s
2m Hdl (8)	Australia Day (17 Oct 2010)	3m40.40s	3m43s
2m4f110yds Ch (17)	Beat The Boys (13 Nov 2007)	5m14.80s	4m59s
2m5f Hdl (10)	Glacial Sunset (7 Nov 2006)	5m09.10s	4m58s
3m Ch (19)	Harry's Dream (14 Oct 2006)	6m01.50s	5m50s
3m110yds Hdl (12)	Carole's Legacy (22 Nov 2010)	6m06.90s	5m53s

Leicester

2m Ch (12)	William's Wishes (15 Nov 2010)	3m54.50s	3m57s
2m Hdl (9)	Ryde Again (20 Nov 1989)	3m39.60s	3m41s
2m1f Ch (12)	Noon (2 Nov 1971)	4m10.20s	4m12s
2m4f110yds Ch (15)	Prairie Minstrel (4 Dec 2003)	5m00.50s	5m06s
2m4f110yds Hdl (12)	Prince of Rheims (5 Dec 1989)	4m45.50s	4m47s
2m7f110yds Ch (18)	Bubble Boy (9 Dec 2009)	5m47.70s	5m51s
3m Hdl (13)	King Tarquin (1 Apr 1967)	5m48.00s	5m44s

Lingfield

2m Ch (12)	Rapide Plaisir (28 Sep 2007)	3m48.70s	3m54s
2m110yds Hdl (8)	Va Utu (19 Mar 1993)	3m48.00s	3m51s
2m3f110yds Hdl (10)	Bellezza (20 Mar 1993)	4m37.30s	4m39s
2m4f110yds Ch (14)	Copsale Lad (29 Oct 2005)	5m04.00s	5m03s
2m7f Hdl (12)	Herecomestanley (28 Sep 2007)	5m31.90s	5m30s

| 3m Ch (18) | Mighty Frolic (19 Mar 1993) | 5m58.40s | 5m57s |

Ludlow

2m Ch (13)	Pearl King (5 Apr 2007)	3m47.30s	3m52s
2m Hdl (9)	Desert Fighter (11 Oct 2001)	3m36.40s	3m36s
2m4f Ch (17)	Handy Money (5 Apr 2007)	4m47.30s	4m49s
2m5f Hdl (11)	Willy Willy (11 Oct 2001)	4m54.70s	4m49s
3m Ch (19)	Rodalko (4 March 2004)	5m50.50s	5m49s
3m Hdl (12)	Rift Valley (12 May 2005)	5m36.60s	5m34s
3m1f110yds Ch (20)	Moving Earth (12 May 2005)	6m17.30s	6m10s
3m2f110yds Hdl (13)	Gysart (9 Oct 1997)	6m07.50s	6m10s
3m3f110yds Ch (22)	Act In Time (13 Dec 2001)	6m58.50s	6m40s

Market Rasen

2m1f Hdl (8)	Australia Day (17 Jul 2010)	3m57.40s	3m53s
2m2f Ch (12)	Viable (17 Jul 2010)	4m17.20s	4m21s
2m3f Hdl (10)	Problema Tic (23 Jan 2011)	4m28.60s	4m25s
2m4f Ch (15)	Fleeting Mandate (24 Jul 1999)	4m42.80s	4m51s
2m5f Hdl (10)	Apache Chant (23 Jan 2011)	5m04.00s	4m56s
2m6f110yds Ch (15)	Annas Prince (19 Oct 1979)	5m24.20s	5m27s
3m Hdl (12)	Trustful (21 May 1977)	5m38.80s	5m40s
3m1f Ch (19)	Allerlea (1 May 1985)	6m01.00s	6m06s
3m4f110yds Ch (21)	Cromwell (5 Oct 2003)	7m17.50s	7m01s
4m1f Ch (23)	Barkin (23 Nov 1991)	8m51.20s	8m12s

Musselburgh

2m Ch (12)	Sonsie Mo (6 Dec 1993)	3m48.10s	3m49s
2m Hdl (9)	Joe Bumpas (11 Dec 1989)	3m35.90s	3m38s
2m1f Hdl (9)	Bodfari Signet (3 Apr 2001)	4m04.60s	3m54s
2m4f Ch (16)	Bohemian Spirit (18 Dec 2005)	4m44.50s	4m53s
2m4f Hdl (12)	Pyracantha (19 Nov 2010)	4m37.80s	4m41s
3m Ch (18)	Snowy (18 Dec 2005)	5m47.70s	5m52s
3m110yds Hdl (13)	Magnificent Seven (20 Dec 2006)	5m57.00s	5m47s

Newbury

2m110yds Hdl (8)	Dhofar (25 Oct 1985)	3m45.20s	3m49s
2m1f Ch (13)	Barnbrook Again (25 Nov 1989)	3m58.20s	4m01s
2m2f110yds Ch (15)	Rubberdubber (4 Mar 2006)	4m31.90s	4m24s
2m3f Hdl (11)	Schapiro (2 Apr 2005)	4m30.50s	4m27s
2m4f Ch (16)	Espy (25 Oct 1991)	4m47.90s	4m49s
2m5f Hdl (12)	Penneyrose Bay (2 Apr 2005)	4m51.20s	4m57s
2m6f110yds Ch (17)	Von Origny (3 Mar 2006)	5m35.50s	5m27s
	Pennyrose Bay (24 Mar 2007)		
3m Ch (18)	Red Devil Robert (2 Apr 2005)	5m43.50s	5m49s
3m110yds Hdl (13)	Landsdowne (25 Oct 1996)	5m45.40s	5m48s
3m2f110yds Ch (21)	Topsham Bay (26 Mar 1993)	6m27.10s	6m29s

Newcastle

2m Hdl (9)	Padre Mio (25 Nov 1995)	3m40.70s	3m42s
2m110yds Ch (14)	Greenheart (7 May 1990)	3m56.70s	3m58s
2m4f Ch (17)	Snow Blessed (19 May 1984)	4m46.70s	4m51s
2m4f Hdl (11)	Mils Mij (13 May 1989)	4m42.00s	4m42s
2m6f Hdl (12)	Bygones Of Brid (28 Nov 2009)	5m24.90s	5m12s
3m Ch (20)	Even Swell (30 Oct 1975)	5m48.10s	5m51s
3m Hdl (13)	Withy Bank (29 Nov 1986)	5m40.10s	5m42s

| 3m6f Ch (25) | Charlie Potheen (28 Apr 1973) | 7m30.00s | 7m30s |
| 4m1f Ch (27) | Domaine Du Pron (21 Feb 1998) | 8m30.40s | 8m20s |

Newton Abbot

2m110yds Ch (13)	Noble Comic (24 Jun 2000)	3m53.20s	3m51s
	Norborne Bandit (22 Aug 2009)	3m53.20s	
2m1f Hdl (8)	Windbound Lass (1 Aug 1988)	3m45.00s	3m48s
2m3f Hdl	There's No Panic (17 Jul 2010)	4m16.40s	4m18s
2m5f110yds Ch (16)	Karadin (13 Aug 2002)	5m06.30s	5m04s
2m6f Hdl (10)	Virbian (30 Jun 1983)	4m55.40s	4m58s
3m2f110yds Ch (20)	Just In Business (14 May 2001)	6m21.50s	6m19s
3m3f Hdl (12)	La Carotte (31 Jul 1989)	6m17.60s	6m18s

Perth

2m Ch (12)	Beldine (22 Aug 1992)	3m47.50s	3m50s
2m110yds Hdl (8)	Molly Fay (23 Sep 1971)	3m40.40s	3m44s
2m4f110yds Ch (15)	Ball O Malt (6 Jul 2006)	4m53.50s	4m57s
2m4f110yds Hdl (10)	Valiant Dash (19 May 1994)	4m41.20s	4m43s
3m Ch (18)	Montreal (6 Jun 2004)	5m52.00s	5m56s
3m110yds Hdl (12)	Mystic Memory (20 Aug 1994)	5m43.10s	5m45s
3m3f Hdl (14)	Noir Et Vert (28 Apr 2006)	6m37.20s	6m24s
3m7f Ch (23)	General Wolfe (25 Apr 2002)	7m58.90s	7m48s

Plumpton

2m Hdl (9)	Royal Derbi (19 Sep 1988)	3m31.00s	3m40s
2m1f Ch (12)	Janiture (19 Apr 2003)	4m05.90s	4m04s
2m1f Hdl (10)	Striding Edge (7 Aug 1992)	3m58.60s	3m54s
2m2f Ch (14)	Pats Minstrel (15 Apr 1995)	4m24.10s	4m19s
2m4f Ch (14)	Blakeney Coast (8 May 2005)	4m48.20s	4m49s
2m4f Hdl (12)	Director's Choice (30 Apr 1994)	4m37.60s	4m38s
2m5f Hdl (12)	Son Of Greek Myth (17 Sep 2006)	4m50.10s	4m52s
3m1f110yds Hdl (14)	Take The Stand (16 Oct 2006)	5m57.60s	6m01s
3m2f Ch (18)	Sunday Habits (19 Apr 2003)	6m23.50s	6m21s
3m5f Ch (21)	Ecuyer Du Roi (15 Apr 02)	7m19.80s	7m08s

Sandown

2m Ch (13)	Dempsey (28 Apr 2007)	3m43.40s	3m49s
2m110yds Hdl (8)	Olympian (13 Mar 1993)	3m42.00s	3m47s
2m4f Hdl (9)	Oslot (28 Apr 2007)	4m35.70s	4m39s
2m4f110yds Ch (17)	Coulton (29 Apr 1995)	4m57.10s	4m58s
2m6f Hdl (11)	Kintbury (5 Nov 1983)	5m05.60s	5m08s
3m Hdl (12)	Rostropovich (27 Apr 2002)	5m39.10s	5m38s
3m110yds Ch (22)	Arkle (6 Nov 1965)	5m59.00s	6m00s
3m5f110yds Ch (24)	Cache Fleur (29 Apr 1995)	7m09.10s	7m15s

Sedgefield

2m110yds Ch (13)	Suas Leat (16 Sep 1997)	3m53.60s	3m54s
2m1f Hdl (8)	Country Orchid (5 Sep 1997)	3m45.70s	3m48s
2m4f Ch (15)	Polar Gale (23 May 2007)	4m48.00s	4m46s
2m4f Hdl (9)	Ad Murum (11 Aug 2006)	4m38.30s	4m29s
2m5f Ch (16)	Pennybridge (30 Sep 1997)	4m59.20s	5m00s
2m5f110yds Hdl (10)	Palm House (4 Sep 1992)	4m46.30s	4m50s
3m3f Ch (21)	The Gallopin' Major (14 Sep 1996)	6m29.30s	6m31s
3m3f110yds Hdl (13)	Pikestaff (25 Jul 2005)	6m19.70s	6m21s
3m4f Ch (22)	Mister Muddypaws (5 May 2000)	6m46.50s	6m46s

Southwell

2m Ch (13)	Stay Awake (11 May 1994)	3m51.30s	3m52s
2m Hdl (9)	Merlins Wish (2 May 1994)	3m36.60s	3m40s
2m1f Ch (14)	Master Nimbus (16 Aug 2009)	4m00.90s	4m06s
2m1f Hdl (10)	Truly Fruitful (16 Aug 2009)	3m50.30s	3m54s
2m2f Hdl (10)	Here's The Deal (8 May 1995)	4m19.60s	4m12s
2m4f110yds Ch (16)	Bally Parson (8 May 1995)	5m02.90s	5m04s
2m4f110yds Hdl (11)	Man of The Grange (2 May 1994)	4m47.90s	4m49s
2m5f110yds Ch (17)	Killard Point (3 Jun 2007)	5m15.40s	5m18s
2m5f110yds Hdl (12)	Willies Way (16 Aug 2000)	5m01.10s	5m03s
3m110yds Ch (19)	Soloman Springs (6 May 1999)	6m01.90s	6m06s
3m110yds Hdl (13)	Soloman Springs (8 May 1995)	5m47.10s	5m48s
3m2f Ch (21)	Son Of Light (12 Aug 2002)	6m25.90s	6m28s
3m2f Hdl (15)	Super Ross (16 Au 2009)	6m10.20s	6m10s

Stratford

2m110yds Hdl (9)	Chusan (7 May 1956)	3m40.40s	3m44s
2m1f110yds Ch (13)	Enlightenment (9 Sep 2007)	3m58.10s	4m02s
2m3f Hdl (10)	Mister Ermyn (29 Jul 2000)	4m19.70s	4m20s
2m4f Ch (15)	Majy D'Auteuil (28 Jul 2011)	4m39.20s	4m42s
2m5f110yds Ch (16)	Spare Change (16 Sep 2007)	4m56.60s	5m03s
2m6f110yds Hdl (12)	Broken Wing (31 May 1986)	5m06.80s	5m11s
2m7f Ch (17)	Fieldsofclover (15 Jun 2008)	5m24.90s	5m28s
3m Ch (18)	Keltic Lord (17 Jul 2005)	5m41.80s	5m44s
3m3f Hdl (14)	Burren Moonshine (11 Jun 2006)	6m13.10s	6m19s
3m4f Ch (21)	Dusty Dane (28 May 2010)	6m44.20s	6m47s
4m Ch (24)	Stewarts Pride (1 Jul 2001)	7m53.90s	7m50s

Taunton

2m110yds Ch (12)	I Have Him (28 Apr 1995)	3m49.50s	3m51s
2m1f Hdl (9)	Indian Jockey (3 Oct 1996)	3m39.40s	3m44s
2m3f Ch (14)	Harik (24 Mar 2003)	4m30.70s	4m31s
2m3f110yds Hdl (10)	Nova Run (14 Nov 1996)	4m21.70s	4m23s
2m7f110yds Ch (17)	Glacial Delight (24 Apr 2006)	5m39.80s	5m35s
3m110yds Hdl (12)	On My Toes (15 Oct 1998)	5m30.20s	5m33s
3m3f Ch (19)	Even More (25 Nov 2004)	6m52.90s	6m30s
3m6f Ch (21)	Torside (26 Mar 1987)	7m50.50s	7m20s
4m2f110yds Ch (24)	Cold Mountain (29 Mar 2011)	8m59.00s	8m33s

Towcester

2m Hdl (8)	Nascracker (22 May 1987)	3m39.50s	3m45s
2m110yds Ch (12)	Commemoration Day (19 Jun 2008)	3m55.80s	4m01s
2m3f110yds Ch (13)	Home (20 May 2011)	4m53.50s	4m47s
2m3f110yds Hdl (10)	Banningham Blaze (5 Oct 2005)	4m45.10s	4m37s
2m5f Hdl (11)	Mailcom (3 May 1993)	5m00.90s	5m01s
2m6f Ch (16)	Paint The Clouds (17 May 2011)	5m21.00s	5m24s
3m Hdl (12)	Dropshot (25 May 1984)	5m44.00s	5m46s
3m110yds Ch (18)	Keepitsecret (19 Jun 2008)	6m00.70s	6m08s

Uttoxeter

2m Ch (12)	Tapageur (8 Aug 1991)	3m41.50s	3m49s
2m Hdl (10)	Mill De Lease (21 Sep 1989)	3m28.20s	3m38s
2m4f Ch (15)	Bertone (5 Oct 1996)	4m42.60s	4m47s
2m4f110yds Hdl (12)	Chicago's Best (11 Jun 1995)	4m39.10s	4m43s
2m5f Ch (16)	McKenzie (27 Apr 1974)	4m54.20s	5m02s

2m6f110yds Ch (16)	Coq Hardi (10 May 2009)	5m39.50s	5m27s
2m6f110yds Hdl (12)	Fealing Real (27 Jun 2010)	5m06.80s	5m12s
3m Ch (18)	Terramarique (31 Jul 2006)	5m49.80s	5m49s
3m Hdl (14)	Fourty Acers (11 May 2008)	5m43.40s	5m37s
3m2f Ch (20)	McGregor The Third (5 Oct 1996)	6m23.60s	6m20s
3m4f Ch (21)	Ottowa (7 Feb 1998)	7m33.90s	6m52s
4m1f110yds Ch (24)	Russian Trigger (14 Mar 2009)	8m52.50s	8m27s

Warwick

2m Ch (12)	Lake Imperial (5 Nov 2007)	3m48.90s	3m44s
2m Hdl (8)	High Knowl (17 Sep 1988)	3m30.80s	3m37s
2m110yds Ch (12)	Bambi De L'Orme (7 May 2005)	3m46.30s	3m51s
2m3f Hdl (10)	Runaway Pete (2 Nov 1996)	4m15.00s	4m20s
2m4f110yds Ch (17)	Dudie (16 May 1987)	4m53.30s	4m56s
2m5f Hdl (11)	Three Eagles (11 May 2002)	4m43.60s	4m48s
3m110yds Ch (18)	Shephards Rest (2 Apr 2002)	6m03.90s	6m02s
3m1f Hdl (11)	City Poser (2 Apr 2002)	5m53.50s	5m50s
3m2f Ch (20)	Castle Warden (6 May 1989)	6m16.10s	6m26s
3m5f Ch (22)	Arnold Layne (23 Mar 2011)	7m12.09s	7m14s
4m1f110yds Ch (27)	Jolly's Clump (24 Jan 1976)	8m36.40s	8m20s

Wetherby

2m Ch (13)	Mutual Friend (20 May 2010)	3m44.90s	3m48s
2m Hdl (9)	Annie's Answer (3 Nov 2007)	3m44.80s	3m41s
2m110yds Hdl (9)	Olivino (26 Apr 2009)	3m43.90s	3m48s
2m3f110yds Hdl (10)	Lothian Falcon (3 Nov 2007)	4m44.60s	4m32s
2m4f Hdl (11)	Lady Wright (26 Apr 2009)	4m42.00s	4m39s
2m4f110yds Ch (15)	Drever Route (13 Oct 2010)	4m47.80s	4m55s
2m6f Hdl (12)	San Deng (26 Apr 2009)	5m05.70s	5m10s
	Oscar Barton (17 Apr 2011)		
2m6f110yds Ch (17)	Pistol Basc (13 Oct 2010)	5m24.90s	5m25s
2m7f Hdl (12)	Doris's Gift (8 May 2008)	5m38.40s	5m24s
3m110yds Hdl (13)	Ballyhale (17 Nov 2007)	6m19.50s	5m46s
3m1f Ch (18)	Nacarat (30 Oct 2010)	5m52.10s	6m05s
3m1f Hdl (13)	Fair Along (31 Oct 2009)	6m01.90s	5m53s
3m4f110yds Ch (22)	Super Road Train (17 Nov 2007)	7m32.00s	/

Wincanton

2m Ch (13)	Sou'wester (18 Apr 2010)	3m44.30s	3m46s
2m Hdl (8)	Nearby (6 Nov 2010)	3m25.80s	3m34s
2m4f Hdl (10)	Uffa Fox (14 Oct 2010)	4m29.46s	4m33s
2m5f Ch (17)	Edredon Bleu (26 Oct 2003)	4m59.20s	5m02s
2m6f Hdl (11)	Santera (6 Nov 2010)	4m57.00s	5m04s
3m1f110yds Ch (21)	Swansea Bay (8 Nov 2003)	6m09.70s	6m17s
3m3f110yds Ch (22)	Gullible Gordon (24 Oct 2010)	6m37.20s	6m40s

Worcester

2m Ch (12)	Fit To Drive (25 Sep 2009)	3m41.50s	3m49s
2m Hdl (8)	Santopadre (11 May 1988)	3m35.30s	3m40s
2m2f Hdl (9)	Lady For Life (5 Aug 2000)	4m02.50s	4m06s
2m4f Hdl (10)	Son Of Flicka (5 Jun 2010)	4m31.50s	4m35s
2m4f110yds Ch (15)	Sir Ian (24 Sep 2010)	4m50.38s	4m57s
2m5f110yds Hdl (10)	Elite Reg (19 May 1993)	4m48.50s	4m56s
2m7f Ch (18)	Liberate (22 Jun 2011)	5m31.90	5m36s
2m7f110yds Ch (18)	Beauchamp Prince (15 Apr 2007)	5m42.70s	5m43s
3m Hdl (12)	Polar Champ (5 Aug 2000)	5m29.80s	5m32s

Outlook

Top point recruits with Cathal Gahan

Italian Master is a name to remember

THE world of point-to-points offers trainers an opportunity to educate younger horses in a controlled environment without having to deal with the hustle and bustle of a racecourse. It's also a chance to showcase a top youngster's talents in the hope of attracting big money from those operating under rules.

Therefore, the point-to-point arena continues to provide a fine stamping ground for future stars, with Best Mate, Imperial Commander, Denman and Peddlers Cross among those who plied their trade in this sphere before going on to greater things.

With this in mind it makes sense to note any major young eye-catchers, and the following horses strike me as those who could make headlines this season and beyond.

Barrakilla 4yo bay gelding
1- *Milan - Kigali (Torus)*

He always took the eye on breeding as a half-brother to the talented China Rock and fulfiled that promise with an eased-down win in a Tallow maiden back in February. This four-year-old, is a big raw type and there is little doubt that jumping fences is where his future lies.

Dannanceys Hill 4yo bay gelding
1- *Revoque - Some Orchestra (Orchestra)*

He was a 10l winner of a Kirkstown maiden in April and has since moved on to Donald McCain. Although he beat a below-average field, he did everything very easily. He would have no problems winning a bumper and should take well to hurdles.

Dramatic Duke 5yo bay gelding
1- *Old Vic - Dramatic Dame (Buckskin)*

He produced a jaw-dropping performance at Lisronagh in December where he travelled powerfully and winged his fences. He also possesses an excellent National Hunt pedigree as a half-brother to the point-to-point and multiple bumper winner Mount Benbulben from the family of smart jumpers In Compliance and One Cool Cookie. He is now in training with Jonjo O'Neill and is potentially very good.

Italian Master 5yo bay/brown gelding
1- *Milan - Augusta Brook (Over The River)*

He was another winner of a Dromahane point in March. The winning margin of half a length was slightly flattering to the runner-up as this son of Milan was only building up a head of steam near the finish. In the care of Paul Nicholls, he is a top prospect and is sure to be aimed at all the best novice races this year. He should make a fine chaser.

Make Your Mark 4yo bay gelding
1- Beneficial - Bell Star (Roselier)

He was another debut winner who showed a real engine but, unlike others on this list, his jumping was very slow and deliberate at Lisronagh in April. Physically, though, he's one of the most imposing four-year-olds I have seen on the circuit. He has plenty of filling out to do so whatever he does this season expect him to improve, but he's a sure-fire bumper winner and a top staying chaser in the making.

Minella For Steak 4yo bay gelding
1- King's Theatre - Preview Days (Supreme Leader)

He came across as being green on debut at Durrow in February but still beat a nice prospect in Folsom Blue by 4l. There was much to like about the way he jumped and travelled, and he should make a stayer in time. New connections paid £230,000 for him at the Cheltenham April sales. He is also nicely bred, being closely related to the staying chase winner Professor Hegarty.

Mythical Warrior 4yo b/br gelding
F- Brian Boru - Divining (Dowsing)

He ran at the Horse and Jockey meeting in March where he fell at the last when about 6l clear. He looked to be cruising to victory and but for that fall would have done so. The form reads well with the second and third having both won since. He looked a typical good-ground horse and liked to get in low when jumping his fences, so expect him to make a nice novice hurdler.

Prince Ludovic 4yo bay gelding
B1- Luso - Beaver Run (Be My Native)

He put in a truly superb round of jumping when winning at the second time of asking at Loughbrickland last March. He was unlucky to be brought down first time up in a Lemonfield point won by another nice type in Formidableopponent a few weeks earlier. That experience seemed to do him no harm and, when a horse wins with his ears pricked like he did, you know they are a good one.

Rock Of Allen 4yo bay gelding
1- Chevalier - Umlaut (Zafonic)

He's a physically imposing sort who did everything with considerable ease at Dromahane in March when winning by 2l. He has it all – he can jump, travel and has plenty of scope for improvement. His action suggests he's a soft-ground horse and he's now in training with Henrietta Knight.

Saint Roque 5yo bay gelding
1- Lavirco - Moody Cloud (Cyborg)

A half-brother to the smart Kazal and the very smart Quito De La Roque, he winged every fence at Dromahane in March. He came there with his head in his chest two out and quickened up well to win by 8l. That race has worked out well with the second, third and fourth all winning since. He has joined Paul Nicholls and could be very smart.

Slightly Tanned 5yo bay gelding
1- Brian Boru - Connells Cross (Be My Native)

He made all to win at Askeaton on his debut when given an uncomplicated by Liz Lalor. He's not the biggest horse in the world but possesses a high cruising speed and stays well, which will stand him in good stead under rules. He's also with Paul Nicholls.

Tarlan 5yo bay gelding
F1- Milan - Nethertara (Netherkelly)

A faller at the third fence on debut at Knockanard last February, he couldn't have done it much better next time up at Lemonfield. Held up 8l off the pace, his rider only had to press the button and he quickened up well to lead jumping the second-last. He put in a smart round of jumping and is another to join Donald McCain.

Tobeluckyenough 6yo bay gelding
1/ Kayf Tara - Singing Citystreet (Rock City)

Connections forked out 75,000gns at the Doncaster August sales for this Inch maiden winner. He won in very good style, clocking the quickest time on the card. Now with Kim Bailey, he is sure to make a good impression under rules.

WIN!

Free subscription to **The Jumps Form Book!**

We are offering a free subscription to **THE JUMPS FORM BOOK 2011-2012**, the BHA's official form book – every week from December to April, you could be getting the previous week's results in full, with Notebook comments highlighting future winners, adjusted Official Ratings and Racing Post ratings.

All you have to do is identify the *two horses* on the following pages. They both finished second at the Cheltenham Festival last season but went one better at Punchestown. That's enough clues for now, so get your thinking caps on!

Send your answers along with your details on the entry form below, to:

Jumps Annual Competition, Racing & Football Outlook,
Floor 23, 1 Canada Square, London, E14 5AP.

Entries must reach us no later than first post on Saturday 3 December. The winner and the right answers will be printed in the *RFO*'s December 6 edition. Six runners-up will receive a copy of last year's complete form book.

1

2

Name

Address

Town

Postcode

In the event of more than one correct entry, the winner will be drawn at random from the correct entries. The Editor's decision is final and no correspondence will be entered into.

Horse index

All horses discussed, with page numbers, except for references in the 'Big Race Results' section, for which there is a seperate index following that section

Aghill...9
Aikman 17, 63
Airmen's Friend 56
Aiteon Thirtythree 40
Akula..74
Al Ferof....................28, 43, 57, 81, 86
Alarazi...73
Alderluck...65
Allow Me 17
Amirico 9
Araldur..55
Arctic Actress.................................55
Arvika Ligeonniere 32, 52
Aurorian 9
Baan..74
Baby Shine......................................73
Ballabriggs......................................61
Ballybach 65
Ballyclough......................................60
Ballyvoneen 74
Barrakilla.......................................232
Benny Be Good 64
Best Lover 17
Betavix..9
Big Buck's 48, 87
Big Zeb 46, 85
Binocular 48, 53, 86
Bishops Heir...................................17
Black Noddy....................................67
Blenheim Brook 62
Bobs Worth.....................................54
Bold Sir Brian 62
Bostons Angel 39
Boxer Georg....................................77
Burton Port 40, 53
Bygones Of Brid.............................28
Camas Bridge 67
Captain Americo..............................17
Captain Chris 28, 39, 46, 59
Captain Conan 78
Chapolimoss 9
Chicago Grey...................................32
Chorizo 24
Classic Cut 17
Cocacobana.....................................24

Conceptual Art 18
Constant Cupid 24
Cristal Bonuo 29
Cue Card 43
Dancing Emily 24
Dannanceys Hill 232
Dare Me 29
Darlan 55
Daymar Bay 67
Dee Ee Williams 65
Destroyer Deployed 60
Dhaafer..56
Diamond Harry 40
Divers 62
Divine Folly......................................10
Dramatic Duke 232
Dualla Lord 59
Dynaste..59
Easter Meteor 67
El Dancer 73
Ericht 55
Fair Bramble 56
Fairview Sue 24
Fashionable Girl 74
Final Gift 59
Fine Parchment 56
Finian's Rainbow 46, 53
First Lieutenant...........................32, 43
Flat Out..46
Font..10
Fourth Estate 55
Frontier Dancer 11
General Kutuzov...............................66
Genuine Pearl...................................11
Ghizao 46
Gibb River..54
Glenwood Knight 61
Go Set Go...74
Gods My Judge 56
Golden Firebird 56
Golden Silver 85
Grandads Horse...............................69
Grandioso...58
Grandouet 48, 55
Grands Crus 41, 59

Great Endeavour 59
Gypsy George 24
Haarth Sovereign 11
Habbie Simpson.................................56
Harry Hunt 24
Hazy Tom 70, 79
Head-Hunted 56
Hell's Bay 29
Heron's Well 77
Hidden Cyclone 33
Hidden Keel 70
Hildisvini 69
Himayna 24
Hit The Headlines..............................55
Hold On Julio 56
Hurricane Fly 48, 50, 79, 86
Imperial Commander 84
Invictus 56
Iolith 56
Iron Condor 74
Italian Master 232
I've Been Framed 74
Jessies Dream 39
Jetnova..56
Joan D'Arc 74
Kadouchski......................................75
Kalahari King 63
Kauto Star......................................84
Kauto Stone 29, 38, 59, 85
King Ozzy 11
Kings Grey 64
Knockalongi 56
Kumbeshwar 56
Lady Myfanwy 77
Lets Get Serious...............................55
Long Run 36, 53, 78, 84
Lovethehigherlaw 33, 51
Low Gale 56
Majorica King 56
Make Your Mark 233
Marengo Bay 56
Master Fiddle 42, 54
Master Minded 38, 46, 85
Master Of The Hall 53
Medermit 55
Medinas 56
....68
....43
....30, 40
....11
....41

Milgen Bay 56
Mille Chief......................................55
Minella Class 54
Minella For Steak 233
Minella Theatre................................12
Miss Browne's Fancy 25
Mon Parrain 36, 46
Mono Man 55
Montbazon 56
Morning Moment 71
Morning Royalty 33
Mr Gardner 53
My Flora 76
My Matilda 12
Mythical Warrior 233
Neil Harvey 65
Next Hight......................................56
Noble Prince..............................41, 46
Nomecheki 65
Ogee..72
Omaruru 72
On The Fringe 77
On Trend 66
Ontheslate 74
Oscar Papa.....................................66
Oscars Well 48, 51
Oscar Whisky 48, 54, 87
Our Island 81
Owen Glendower 54
Paintball 70
Pandorama.................................38, 84
Pascha Bere 66
Peddlers Cross.................30, 43, 61, 86
Pere Blanc 85
Plus Jamais 18
Poker De Sivola 62
Poquelin 41
Porta Vogie 25
Poungach.......................................82
Premier Grand Cru.......................18, 63
Presented 25
Pride In Battle 56
Prince Ludovic 233
Prince Of Pirates 54
Qhilimar 70
Quanah Parker 74
Quantitativeeasing 53
Quel Bruere 25
Quel Esprit 41
Quevega..79
Quicuyo 18

Quito De La Roque 33, 39, 51
Quizwork.................................25
Quotica De Poyans 56
Quwetwo 58
Ravethebrave 12
Realt Dubh 34, 46, 50
Rebel Du Maquis 58
Remember Now 30
Rising Time.......................................34
Riverside Theatre 41, 53
Rock Of Allen 233
Rory Boy..26
Royal Wedding 65
Rubi Light 41
Russian Flag....................................74
Sa Suffit 18
Safe Investment 12
Saint Are..............................30, 60
Saint Roque 233
Salden Licht 56, 78
Salsify 77
Salut Flo 31
Samain 34
Sanctuaire 58
Shakalakaboomboom 53
Shammy Buskins 12
Shocking Times 56
Siberian Tiger 60
Signalman 19
Silk Affair...74
Silver By Nature 62
Silviniaco Conti....................58, 85
Simonsig..78
Sir Des Champs 34, 52
Sire De Grugy..................................68
Sizing Europe....................41, 46, 84
Slightly Tanned 233
Smad Place 56
Smart Freddy 13
Society Shares 26
Somersby 41
Son Amix 35
Specialagent Alfie...........................66
Spirit Of Adjisa 60
Spirit Son 31, 48, 53, 78, 86
Sprinter Sacre 31, 43, 54, 78
Steps To Freedom 35
Stoney's Treasure...........................55
Sum Laff 56
Sunley Peace 68
Super Villan 13

Surenaga 77
Swallow 19
Swift Lord 68
Swing Bowler 59
Tail Of The Bank 82
Tante Sissi 56
Tarlan 233
Tazbar.....................................64, 85
The Black Baron...............................74
Thoriak 19
Thousand Stars 87
Three Chords 71
Tickatack 26
Time For Rupert 39, 71
Titeuf De Tierce 56
Tobeluckyenough...........................233
Tocca Ferro.....................................67
Tornado Bob....................................61
Torphichen 55
Traditional Bob 27
Trenchant 56
Tullamore Dew 65, 82
Turtlethomas....................................13
Tweedledrum 78
Ueueteotl...20
Universal Soldier 13
Valdez..56
Verde Goodwood 27
Vision Of Lights 27
Volcan Surprise 56
Vosges 20, 63
Waaheb 35
Walkon 56
Wayward Prince 71
Weapon's Amnesty 35, 40
Weird Al 72
West End Rocker 55
What A Friend...........................41, 58
Whoops A Daisy...............................55
Wiesentraum 73
Willies Yard 27
Wily Fox 74
Wishfull Thinking 31, 41, 46, 60
Wychwoods Mist ....
Young Jim..
Zarkandar............................
Zarrafakt ....
Zaru ....
Zemsky.